The Actors in Europe's Foreign Policy

Edited by
Christopher Hill

London and New York

First published 1996
by Routledge
11 New Fetter Lane, London EC4P 4EE

Simultaneously published in the USA and Canada
by Routledge
29 West 35th Street, New York, NY 10001

Routledge is an International Thomson Publishing company

Typeset in Baskerville by
Ponting–Green Publishing Services, Chesham, Bucks
Printed and bound in Great Britain by
Mackays of Chatham PLC, Chatham, Kent

British Library Cataloguing in Publication Data
A catalogue record for this book is available from the
British Library

Library of Congress Cataloguing in Publication Data
The Actors in Europe's foreign policy / edited by
Christopher Hill.
          p.   cm.
    Includes bibliographical references and index.
    1. Europe–Foreign relations–1989– 2. European Union.
    I. Hill, Christopher, 1948– .
    D2009.A37   1996
    327.4–dc20   96–11315
                                                          CIP

ISBN   0–415–12222–8 (hbk)
ISBN   0–415–12223–6 (pbk)

The Actors in Europe's Foreign Policy

The question of whether Europe has a collective foreign policy is an issue that has surfaced with prominence during many recent crises, most notably when Iraq invaded Kuwait and over the recent war in the Balkans. The contributors in this book argue that the European Union has certainly made strides towards acting as a single bloc, but that expectations have raced ahead of achievements.

The aim of the book's multinational authorship is to look at the reality of European foreign policy-making rather than the hopes held out for it. They do so by examining the policy of the member states and their experience in trying to make their national concerns converge with the collective view. The Commission, the main supranational institution to be active in external relations, is discussed in a separate chapter. The authors seek to go beyond generalities about Europe to portray the actual positions of member states and to what extent they are moving towards a collective voice.

The book shows how the foreign policies of the individual states now work within a broad common framework and that the key to an understanding of the international politics of Western Europe is the interplay between the national and the collective.

Christopher Hill is Montague Burton Professor of International Relations at the London School of Economics. He has written widely on issues of foreign policy analysis, particularly British foreign policy and the external relations of the European Community.

Contents

Contributors

David Allen   Senior Lecturer in European Studies, University of Loughborough, UK.

Esther Barbé   Professor of International Relations, Facultat de Ciències Politiques i de Sociologia, Universitat Autònoma de Barcelona, Spain.

Gianni Bonvicini   Director, Istituto Affari Internazionali, Rome, Italy.

Christian Franck   Professor at the Institut d'Etudes Européennes, Université Catholique Louvain-la-Neuve, Louvain-la-Neuve, Belgium.

Bertel Heurlin   Research Director, Danish Institute of International Affairs and Jean Monnet Professor, University of Copenhagen, Denmark.

Christopher Hill   Montague Burton Professor of International Relations, London School of Economics and Political Science, UK.

Patrick Keatinge   Jean Monnet Professor of European Integration, Trinity College, Dublin, Ireland.

Françoise de La Serre   Directeur de Recherches, Centre d'Etudes et de Recherches internationales (CERI), Fondation nationale des Sciences politiques, Paris, France.

Pierre-Louis Lorenz   Member of the Diplomatic Service of Luxembourg, presently Luxembourg Ambassador in Beijing, China.

Simon Nuttall   Visiting Fellow, Centre for International Studies, London School of Economics and Political Science, UK, and Visiting Professor, College of Europe, Bruges, Belgium.

Alfred Pijpers   Senior Staff Member, Europa Institute, University of Amsterdam, and Department of Political Science, University of Leiden, the Netherlands.

Reinhardt Rummel   Senior researcher, Stiftung Wissenschaft und Politik, Ebenhausen, Germany.

Panos Tsakaloyannis Visiting Professor, Athens University of Economics and Business, Department of International and European Economic Studies, Athens, Greece.

Álvaro de Vasconcelos Director, Istituto de Estudos Estratégicos e Internacionais, Lisbon, Portugal.

William Wallace Reader in the Department of International Relations, London School of Economics and Political Science, UK, and Professor at the Central European University, Budapest, Hungary.

Preface

This book is the successor to *National Foreign Policies and European Political Cooperation*, published by George Allen and Unwin for the Royal Institute of International Affairs in 1983. The present volume advances the themes explored in the first in a number of significant respects. Unusually, it also draws on a high proportion of the same participants as in 1983, thus making possible a high degree of continuity and comparability.

National Foreign Policies met a clear need, being the first comparative study of European foreign policies which was also the product of a multinational group of scholars from all the EC states. It sold out its print run and was thereafter in persistent demand from students and observers of European affairs. It represented a particular perspective on European foreign policy which was otherwise barely represented in the literature – and is still thin on the ground. This is far from being an ideological position – the contributors disagree widely amongst themselves on, for example, the desired future path for the European Union. It is, rather, a corrective to the general tendency to discuss European Political Cooperation (EPC), and from 1993 the Common Foreign and Security Policy (CFSP) largely in terms of the common positions and joint actions which they are supposed to have produced, with the states left on the margins of the analysis. This tendency is more common these days than the opposite, crassly realist mistake of assuming that Europe's international presence amounts to little more than the sum of the national interests of the EU's two or three major states. Rather, the premise of both this volume and that of 1983 was that this important and fascinating new development in international diplomacy can only be understood properly in terms of the interplay between the attempts at collective action on the one hand and the national foreign policies which continue vigorously, on the other.

Accordingly, from the early 1990s I have had it in mind to produce a sequel to *National Foreign Policies* which would do more than simply change dates and add a page or two of contemporary history to each chapter. That I was able to do was thanks to the hospitality and resources of the European University Institute at San Domenico di Fiesole near Florence, where I was privileged to spend a sabbatical year. At the end of that time, in July 1993, the European Policy Unit of the Institute hosted an expert conference on the theme of 'The Community, the Member States and Foreign Policy: Coming Together or Drifting Apart?'. The twin aims of the conference were (i) to examine whether or not EPC had fundamentally changed in character over the previous decade, in particular as a result of the upheavals of 1989–93; and (ii) to analyse the interaction between the various participants in EPC, both states and Community institutions.

These two aims were designed to produce two complementary volumes, of which this is the first, and the second, *The Changing Context of European Foreign Policy*, concentrates on issues and structures. Short papers were commissioned for both which were discussed extensively at the conference. These were used, together with the tapes of the proceedings, as the basis of full-length chapter drafts, and it is these which, duly revised in their turn, make up what follows. All the chapters in this book are wholly new. The only addition to the conference cast list is William Wallace, who had in any case shown enthusiastic support for the project from the start and who was simply unable to be present in Florence. Moreover, the only chapter from the 1983 book which does not have at least one of its authors present in the 1996 equivalent is that on Denmark, where Bertel Heurlin has taken over from Christian Thune and his deceased colleague Niels Jorgen Haagerup.

Three chapters have been added to the 1983 base. Portugal and Spain, which joined the EC in 1986, clearly needed representing, while it was thought important, particularly in the contemporary context of the creation of the CFSP and its formalization of a joint right of initiative for the European Commission in foreign policy that the latter's steadily more distinctive role should be dissected. On the other hand, I have not included the three states which have joined the EU on 1 January 1995, on the grounds that their experience of the practice of the CFSP is not yet sufficient for us to be able to say anything meaningful. Of course, there are important issues arising out of the accession of such states with different foreign policy traditions, and these will be dealt with by Elfriede Regelsberger in the *Changing Context* volume which follows.

Some theorists in international relations will certainly consider that a book which takes an avowedly 'national' approach to the study of the subject, indeed even one which focuses on 'foreign policy', is inherently anachronistic, given – as they see it – the decreasing ability of the state to affect outcomes. One answer to this is simply to point to the current gloom in policy circles about what 'Europe' can achieve in Bosnia, and to the central role of the two traditional powers, Britain and France. This would be superficial. The pendulum of events will swing and it will not be long before there is a renewed emphasis on interdependence and on collective action. A more profound response is to take the longer view and to expect a dialectical relationship between the actors and the system, between the nation-states and the EU institutional collectivity, to endure for some time. This dialectic is continually being played out, even if at times – such as that of the Intergovernmental Conference due to take place in 1996 – the issues come to a particular head. The hope here is that the analysis presented of the ways in which national foreign policies do or do not fit together will help all students of Europe's foreign relations, insiders or outsiders, academics or practitioners, to acquire a better sense of the multiple levels of what we call for the sake of brevity 'European foreign policy', and in particular of the importance of seeing a problem from a variety of different national perspectives. The choice as title for the book of the term 'actors' rather than 'states' or 'national foreign policies' is not intended to denote any fundamental downgrading of the state as actor. Its use simply makes it possible to include the Commission alongside the member states (after all, it might on a priori grounds be thought to be at least as influential as the smaller states) and it draws attention to the fact that within each national system there are different bureaucracies and political groupings which have the potential to act transnationally in the wider system – as, for example, defence ministries have now become drawn into the CFSP and therefore to some extent compete with the foreign ministries which traditionally dominated EPC. That is, if 'Europe' is a notion to be decomposed in external relations, then it should be decomposed first into states and then if necessary also into the domestic constituents of states, which are beginning to get more directly involved in foreign relations.[1]

If coherence is the problem in European foreign policy then it is no less a bugbear of collective publications. The editor took the view, as in 1983, that too strict an attempt to homogenize the chapters would either be counter-productive or produce dull results. On the other hand it was important to ensure that the central themes were addressed by all. To this end the contributors were asked to bear in mind certain questions, both general and particular. These addressed the following issues:

- the distinctive elements of their country's attitudes towards EPC/CFSP, and the impact of the 'socialization effect' of EPC;
- the extent to which changes in the attitudes of governments and opinion élites had taken place since 1982;
- the extent to which the country's orientation towards other states and institutions than the EC had made participation in EPC difficult;
- the impact of convergence between the external economic relations of the EC and EPC on the country;
- the extent to which domestic political and administrative factors had complicated the reaching of agreement with EPC partners;
- the ways in which the country had responded to the growing salience of security and defence issues in the EPC context;
- the views taken in the country of the various legal–institutional changes in EPC over the years since 1982, both in prospect and retrospect;

- the way in which the country had handled its responsibilities in relation to EPC, particularly those deriving from the Presidency.

These questions are not all answered in every chapter, at least not directly. For each country some will be far more relevant than others. But in each contribution the reader will find a wealth of material relevant both to the second-order issue and to the overall central question, namely, in the context of a developing 'European' diplomacy, to what extent does the idea of a 'national foreign policy' still make sense?

In the editing of this work I have incurred a number of debts of gratitude which it is a pleasure now to discharge. My thanks first go to the other contributors to this volume, and to the many participants in the original meeting whose thoughts are not directly recorded here. Without the hard work and good humour of them all, despite their many other commitments, nothing could have happened. More specifically I am most grateful to the European University Institute, and in particular to its then Principal, M Emile Noel, for having elected me a Jean Monnet Fellow for 1992–3 and then for having made it possible to hold the conference which has spawned this book. I am also grateful to the Commission of the European Communities for providing supplementary funds which enabled us to expand the range of participants in the conference. Professor Roger Morgan of the Department of Social and Political Sciences (and in 1993 Director of the European Policy Unit) has provided enthusiastic and knowledgeable support throughout which I very much appreciate. Also at the EUI, Margriet Wassing did a first-class job in organizing the conference and making it possible for me to concentrate on the academic aspects.

As always, I am grateful to my colleagues in the Department of International Relations at the London School of Economics and Political Science who have both covered for me during absence and provided a stimulating environment to which to return. Margot Light and James Mayall have been particularly helpful, while Elaine Childs and Judy Weedon have been patient and efficient when I have sought help with keyboarding, formatting and communications between London and Florence. Martine Lignon and Lisa Burdett provided invaluable help with translations. It has been a pleasure to work with them, as with all the others involved in this collective book.

Christopher Hill
London School of Economics and Political Science
1995

NOTES

1 For recent works on this theme see Hans J. Michelmann and Panayotis Soldatos (eds), *Federalism and International Relations. The Role of Subnational Units*, Oxford, Clarendon Press, 1990 and Brian Hocking (ed.), *Foreign Relations and Federal States*, London, Leicester University Press, 1993.

Introduction

Actors and actions

Christopher Hill and William Wallace

It is, in principle, relatively easy to describe the assumptions and mechanisms through which established sovereign nation-states conduct foreign policy. The conduct of foreign policy by federal states – the pursuit of common foreign and defence policy by entities which share aspects of domestic sovereignty, but which unite their competencies in dealing with the outside world – is more complex, but can nevertheless be contained within the conventional concepts of international relations.[1] The evolution of European Political Cooperation (EPC), however, presents a challenge of a different order. Is this a new form of collective diplomacy which has left the sovereignty of the participating member states fundamentally unaffected, to be understood within the framework of realist theory? Has it led to the emergence of patterns of group behaviour, implicit and explicit rules, which are best understood within the framework of regime theory and liberal institutionalism? Or are we witnessing a process of *engrenage*, in which habits of working together have gradually upgraded perceptions of common interest, to be understood better through the insights of neo-functionalist theory? Western Europe as a collective entity may well have established a 'presence' in the international arena; but it is not at all clear that it has become an effective or authoritative international actor.[2] 'The failure ... of the academic community ... either to relate EPC into any meaningful systems theory, integration theory or international relations theory, let alone create a new EPC general theory' stems from the elusive character of the phenomenon.[3]

Since these last words were written a new generation of theorists has begun to take a serious interest in the unique phenomenon of EPC, prompted partly by its promised transformation into the Common Foreign and Security Policy (CFSP) and partly by the logic of scholarship in International Relations. The renewed interest in the USA in the nature of European integration has meant that the largest academic-industrial complex in the world has ended its twenty years' silence on the European Community. The preoccupation with interstate cooperation in general means that an advanced form of structured cooperation, such as EPC is, must attract attention from liberal institutionalists, such as Robert Keohane, or Wolfgang Wessels and Joseph Weiler. Their preferred concepts, such as regime and consociationalism, have an obvious application to an issue area like EPC in which governments are still the basic unit of analysis.[4] This is, of course, even more true of those one might term the 'realist institutionalists', such as Stanley Hoffman and Andrew Moravcsik (and Keohane in some of his guises). Their emphasis on interstate bargains, whatever its tautologies, is easy to apply to EPC.[5]

On the other side of the intellectual Potomac, the post-modernists have also realized that the EC experience provides a fruitful area of enquiry, that is how a European identity might be emerging over and above the existing national, regional and indeed personal identities which are the legacy of history. The notions of multiple levels of identity and of competing national discourses find a ready home in the Tower of Babel which EPC often resembles.[6]

These new well-springs of interest, however, have only just begun to affect thinking about European foreign policy. Hoffman, Keohane and Moravscik concentrate on the overall institutional evolution of the EU, and refer only in passing to foreign policy. Weiler and Wessels are, of course, among the foremost experts on EPC, but theory has not been their principal concern. For their part those interested in the 'discourses' of European politics, such as Walter Carlsnaes and Ole Waever, have focused directly on foreign policy, but so far they have inevitably sketched only the outlines of a way forward rather than developed an operational analysis of the multiple complexities of 'Europe's' external role.

THE HYDRA OF EUROPEAN FOREIGN POLICY

Even before the transformation of the European international order which began with the disintegration of the East German regime in 1989 and is still under way in 1995, institutional patterns for cooperation among the member states of the European Community in relations with third countries presented a tangled picture, in which the external observer could discern only with difficulty the distinction between actors and collaborative actions. During the 1980s the EC itself had expanded its network of external representations from the Mediterranean and Lomé-associated states across Asia and Latin America. The collapse first of the Warsaw Pact and then of the Soviet Union led to a further expansion, providing the EC Commission with direct representation in more third countries than the majority of member states maintained themselves; with newly independent governments struggling to understand the subtle distinctions between Community competence and political cooperation, when to deal with national embassies, when with the embassy holding the rotating presidency, and when with the EC Delegation itself. The development within the EC Commission

Secretariat of a unit responsible for liaison with EPC, paralleled after the Single European Act by an independent secretariat servicing the presidency's responsibilities for EPC, increased the complexity of the European Community's international relations.[7] The revival of the Western European Union (WEU) in the early 1980s as a forum for consultation on security among EC member states (within the framework of the Atlantic Alliance, and closely linked to it) added to the proliferation of meetings, declarations and joint actions, revolving in an ever-tightening spiral around a common set of preoccupations.[8] The mixed quality of actions emerging from this complex process was exemplified in the interlinking of different institutional networks and capabilities in the shared actions of EC member states. EC competences were used to implement EPC decisions – for example to impose economic sanctions on Argentina after the invasion of the Falklands. The WEU in the 1980s provided an institutional framework for West European navies to cooperate in joint minesweeping activities and maritime patrols in Middle East waters, responding to American pressure for political and military support from its West European allies. National governments retained the right of decision over involvement or non-involvement in such common actions; but the availability of these institutional mechanisms both increased their ability to operate jointly when they wished to do so and increased the expectation from other governments (above all the USA) that they would do so.

Developments since 1989 have sharpened the paradoxes of this mixed system of common actions, shared competences, joint declarations and transgovernmental cooperation. The removal of the Soviet threat has loosened the American commitment to Western Europe; leaving EC member states without American politico-military leadership to define the choices to which they could respond, forcing them to confront hard choices over political engagement and military commitment in a disintegrating Yugoslavia. The intergovernmental conferences of 1991, launched as German unification was becoming a reality and completed as the Soviet Union fell apart, committed EC members to 'define and implement a common foreign and security policy . . . covering all areas of foreign and security policy'; 'including the eventual framing of a common defence policy, which might in time lead to a common defence.'[9] Replacement of a hostile socialist coalition to the EC's east by a crowd of democratizing states, jostling each other in their efforts to come closer to the EC and NATO and to gain political and economic links with West European states, raised expectations which EC member governments struggled collectively and individually to meet. Four years on, in the midst of the despair over Bosnia, the language of the coming CFSP seems almost a period piece.

The Iraqi invasion of Kuwait in 1990 was followed by coordinated West European operations in enforcing a 'safe haven' in northern Iraq, and by the participation of several member states in the US-led UN intervention in Somalia – for which the European Community Council of Ministers agreed to support the costs of the Belgian 'Blue Berets' battalion out of the European Development Fund budget, taking the intermingling of different institutional frameworks and competences towards the common funding of military operations.[10] Rapid expansion of UN peacekeeping activities in the early 1990s, with contingents from different EC states committed to almost all peacekeeping forces, raised the importance of coordinated decisions within the UN – as it also raised the importance of coordinating the votes of the two permanent members of the UN Security Council within the EU with those of the other member states. Here again the uncertainties of American leadership in a post-Cold War world left West European govern-ments uncomfortably exposed in agreeing joint decisions which committed them to shouldering a major part of the burden of their implementation, before they were politically or institutionally ready for it. This was most uncomfortably evident over Bosnia, where the cycle of decision-making (and decision avoidance) went from EPC/CFSP to NATO to the UN and back, leaving EU members to supply the largest proportion of troops on the ground. This new overlap between foreign policy cooperation, core Com-munity activities and military operations had been apparent in the UN Iraq–Kuwait operation, for which several former socialist states from East-central and Eastern Europe had volunteered small contingents to demonstrate their new commitment to 'the West' and their eligibility for NATO and EC membership. In Bosnia the reinforcement of the Nordic contingent to a full battalion, in 1993, was underlined to EC/EU governments by Swedish negotiators and diplomats as a clear signal that Sweden was prepared to shoulder its full responsibilities in the development of CFSP (just as Hungary had tried to indicate its fitness for membership of the EU by offering its MIG aircraft for patrols over the Balkans).

The Maastricht Treaty on European Union at last came into effect in November 1993. Opposition to ratification within several member states had focused on monetary union and on general issues of the loss of sovereignty, rather than on the obscurely drafted provisions of the 'Second Pillar' on common foreign and security policy, even if questions over the latter had been raised, predictably enough, in the Danish and Irish referenda.[11] Ahead of ratification the EC Commission had already moved to expand its staff and resources in the sphere of 'classic' foreign policy, by dividing its Directorate-General for External Affairs (DG1) into two, with a new DG1A consolidating responsibility for Commission inputs into the formally intergovernmental processes of CFSP. Implementation of the 'Declaration on Western European Union' which had been attached to the Treaty had also moved ahead without waiting for ratification, with the WEU Secretariat moving from Paris and London to Brussels by the end of 1992 and with the establishment of a small military 'planning cell'. US military withdrawal and national defence adjustments were also carrying EC members towards closer cooperation, even integration; the Franco-German Eurocorps alongside the (British-led) NATO Rapid Reaction Corps, with smaller states committing forces to these new integrated bodies to provide them with new rationales – and to protect them from finance ministry cuts.[12]

With ratification the integration of the EPC Secretariat into the Council Secretariat, already far advanced, was completed; a senior (British) diplomat was now seconded to head this upgraded support structure for the new-built second pillar. The question of whether the funding of this section of the Council Secretariat should now fall under the Community budget, and thus be subject to the scrutiny of the European Parliament, exercised many minds and much time among foreign ministries in the winter of 1993–4, with the British government fighting a rearguard action against any further slippage of foreign policy cooperation towards the tighter Community framework.

The difficulty the analyst faces in describing such a hybrid had thus been sharply increased in the early 1990s by rapid changes in the international environment and by changes in its institutional structures which followed from the 1991 IGC. Expectations of West European governments, as a group, had risen: from the former socialist states, from a deliberately less committed American administration, from less-developed countries operating through the UN, even from active groups within their domestic publics. Capabilities had been adjusted, but – as in previous negotiations over strengthening the institutions and decision-making procedures of EPC – only modestly and reluctantly. There remained 'a dangerous tension' at the heart of CFSP: a 'capability–expectations gap' which reflected the contradiction between the ambitions of EU member governments to play a larger international role and their reluctance to move beyond an intergovernmental framework in doing so.[13]

This is unlikely to prove an efficient framework for foreign policy cooperation among EU member states, in an unstable international environment, with the prospect of further (and continuing) enlargement of the EU and the commitment to another intergovernmental conference for 1996. What is however evident is both the embedded character of the structures of cooperation so far established, and the substantial obstacles to any radical moves either towards an explicitly federal foreign policy or to a reassertion of national autonomy. European foreign policy is 'a system of external relations', a collective enterprise through which national actors conduct partly common, and partly separate, international actions.[14] To explore the nature and limits of that system, the inertial forces which both maintain its momentum and inhibit changes of direction, requires not only examination of the system itself but also of the nation-states on which it rests and the domestic contexts within which they make foreign policy. Only then we will be able to get a close-textured sense of whether the system is 'stuck', or whether it retains a forwards, homogenizing, momentum.

THE DOMESTIC DEFICIT: OR, DON'T TELL THE CHILDREN

Two decades of European Political Cooperation have transformed the working practices of West European foreign ministers and ministries. They have assembled volumes of declarations, have struggled to build patterns of convergent voting in international organizations, and have occupied the energies of national diplomats in West European capitals and in third countries across the world. From the perspective of a diplomat in the foreign ministry of a member state, styles of operating and communication have been transformed. The COREU telex network, EPC working groups, joint declarations, joint reporting, even the beginnings of staff exchanges among foreign ministries and shared embassies: all these have moved the conduct of national foreign policy away from the old nation-state national sovereignty model towards a collective endeavour, a form of high-level networking with transformationalist effects and even more potential.

From the perspective of national domestic politics the changes have been more subtle, and much more limited. Governments still report to parliaments on national positions, emphasizing (and often overemphasizing) the distinctiveness of their input into European consultations, and downplaying the extent to which they have compromised national priorities in struggling to reach common policies. Such understatement is motivated by the desire for a quiet life, but also by the need to disguise foreign policy integration when it occurs – few decision-makers wish to stir the questions of principle contained in the issue of the democratic control of collective foreign policy.

Parliamentary oversight of Community business is only limited and intermittent; scrutiny committees wading through detailed Commission proposals, and backbenchers and opposition spokesmen responding to ministerial statements. The elusive character of foreign policy cooperation makes for greater difficulties in attempting to monitor the actions of national governments and the progress of common policies.

National parliaments in almost all West European states had long found foreign policy a more difficult area in which to hold their governments to account than most aspects of domestic policy. Foreign policy and defence were traditionally considered matters outside and above the partisan domestic debate: directly linked to the preservation of sovereignty, and therefore to be entrusted to the executive. The British House of Commons only acquired a committee on foreign affairs in 1979, while in France the constitution of the Fifth Republic reserved to the President, rather than the Prime Minister, primacy in defence and foreign policy. The evolution of European Political Cooperation thus went largely unnoticed and un-reported in national parliaments, hence also in national media. The prominent role which prime ministers and foreign ministers played in international diplomacy when they took their turn in the Presidency was noted, and applauded; but without understanding that this rested upon an intricate substructure of committees and working groups, of telegrams jointly drafted and reports jointly agreed, to create the consensus on which the effectiveness of the Presidency depended.

There thus developed in the 1970s and 1980s a chasm between the practice of foreign policy cooperation and popular perceptions of continuing national autonomy in foreign policy, parallel to the general chasm between technocratic and popular Europe which produced such unforeseen difficulties over the ratification of the Maastricht Treaty. After ten years and more of EPC foreign ministers were operating between two levels: one largely hidden from public view, the other played out before their national parties, press and public. 'Gymnich' meetings in private in country houses were the epitome of this dual activity: ministers getting to know each other without the controlling presence of more than a handful of officials and with the press excluded from all but a valedictory briefing. But the accumulation of meetings, within EPC itself, within the framework of the EC Council of Ministers, the WEU, NATO, the UN General Assembly, which brought the foreign ministers of EC member states together as a group more frequently than most of them met their national Cabinet colleagues, was not immediately apparent to outside observers.[15] The political public focused intermittently on the outputs of this activity, particularly where ambitions were high, as over the Middle East or South Africa, but the fact that there was little basic understanding of how the process worked, and what were its limits, only heightened misunderstandings and disillusion when things went wrong.

The 'two-audience' problem which some have now highlighted as a problem for governments caught up in multilateral diplomacy had been a familiar problem to Community member governments since the formation of the EC: mediated by the cultivation of special briefings with national press correspondents in Brussels, with each minister emerging from the hard bargaining of a Council session to proclaim to 'his' press that he had won a splendid victory for national interests.[16] The multilateral diplomacy of which Putnam developed this insight was the highly visible process of G-7 summitry, attended each year by thousands of national journalists each asking to be fed a 'national angle' on the story of multilateral compromise.[17]

EPC however is a much more discreet process, involving few concrete decisions and little expenditure – until it reaches the point of utilizing Community competences, or more drastically (as in the Yugoslav crisis in 1991) of debating the commitment of troops by member governments. Its appeal for foreign ministers and for their officials has partly derived from this self-contained characteristic: the secrecy of discussions, in sharp contrast to the leakiness of Community negotiations, the absence of domestic lobbies and entrenched interest groups. The opposite side of this coin is its distance from domestic debate, even domestic awareness. When disagreements break out of the confidential world into the broader political

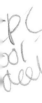

arena, there has therefore been little understanding in the national press, let alone within the wider public, of the constraints and group pressures under which participating foreign ministries have been operating, nor of the compromises struck to national advantage as well as disadvantage in the ongoing processes of consultation. In this respect there has been a subtle difference from the foreign economic policy dimension, where – as in the GATT negotiations for example – the very public discussion of competing national and sectional interests has enabled Commission negotiators to obtain leverage by pleading 'domestic' constraints in a similar manner to that in which American representatives play the Congressional card.

IDENTITY

Effective foreign policy rests upon a shared sense of national identity, of a nation-state's 'place in the world', its friends and enemies, its interests and aspirations. These underlying assumptions are embedded in national history and myth, changing slowly over time as political leaders reinterpret them and external and internal developments reshape them.[18] Debates on foreign policy take place within the constraints this conventional wisdom about national interests sets upon acceptable choices; the symbols and reference points they provide enabling ministers to relate current decisions to familiar ideas. By extension it is exceptionally difficult for both decision-makers and publics when this very sense of national identity is in the process of changing, or becomes contested, not least because of the European foreign policy arrangements which have opened up new avenues for action but only the prospect of a new identity.

The European Community rests upon a relatively weak sense of shared history and identity; partly because of the diverse historical experiences of its members, partly because its institutions have lacked the influence over education or the ability to create and manipulate symbols which national governments had themselves used to strengthen communal identities,[19] and partly because the forging of identity takes time, and comes through hard-won experience, including shared failures; it cannot be bought off the shelf.

This in itself is a substantial obstacle to the development of common foreign policy, which is made more acute by the absence of any popular resonance for European Political Cooperation, or awareness of the accumulated decisions its participants have agreed. Convergent governments, without informed oppositions or electorates, do not lead to convergent domestic debates on foreign policy. Changes of government, or the eruption of issues which strike chords (or can be exploited to strike chords) in the national psyche – like Macedonia for the Greek public in 1993, or Croatia for significant parts of the German public in 1991 – thus uproot this shallow transgovernmental consensus, reimposing the assumptions of separate and special national interests which the development of EPC over two decades, and its evolution into CFSP, has done little to alter.

The loss of the unifying threat of Soviet expansion has exposed this weakness of shared identity fully. It was disguised by the presence of two 'others' during the Cold War – the official Soviet enemy, and the overweening American ally, against both of whom it was natural for the Europeans to caucus. Now the Europeans are forced to consider more directly who they are or might become – and it is proving difficult. The geography as well as the history of the Twelve makes for divergent responses to external crises, for different priorities in pursuing external policy. The stability of Poland and the Czech Republic are evidently of much more direct concern to Germany than to Spain; the stability of Morocco and Algeria much more urgent matters for Spain and France than for Germany and the Netherlands. Italian engagement in Baltic security issues would require a rationale which is not self-evident to the Italian public; Danish engagement in Mediterranean security would require the same (paradoxically, of course, Danish troops are currently part of UNPROFOR while Italians remain excluded). Further enlargement – now more likely than not – would only widen the diversity of national assumptions and interests to be reconciled, within a process which has not yet learned how to begin to redefine the interests and assumptions of its present members.

On the other hand one should not dismiss the possibility that participation in EPC itself helps to foster a sense of shared identity. This outside–in process modifies the perpetual operation of domestic differences, and it comes from the way in which the attempts to create particular common foreign policies – however intermittently successful – are 'part of the process of creating a collective memory, based on shared myths', out of which whatever principles come to be important to EPC can be read back.[20] They stimulate a consciousness of and a debate about what Europe ought to be doing in the world. In fact where EPC is weak on leverage it is strong on values, and European diplomacy has steadily become associated in the public mind with a distinctive set of principles. Christopher Hill defined these in 1983 as:

> emphasising diplomatic rather than coercive instruments, the centrality of mediation in conflict resolution, the importance of long-term economic solutions to political problems, and the need for indigenous peoples to determine their own fate – all of these in contradistinction to the norms of superpower politics.[21]

In the last ten years the need for Europe to distinguish itself from superpower bigemony has disappeared, and the complications of supporting 'indigenous' political movements have become ever more apparent with the explosion of new nationalisms. Otherwise, the analysis holds, and indeed one might add that despite an emerging capacity in the security field, the Europeans as yet show no desire to use force other than for defence, while they have become more confident about pressing their demands for human rights improvements inside third states, both by countless EPC declarations and by attaching conditions to the provision of economic aid.

Accordingly, even if there is still a chronic democratic deficit in EPC, at national and European Parliament levels, so that governments do not feel themselves restricted in very concrete ways, paradoxically their very actions have stimulated a wider public awareness of foreign policy and perhaps of what they wish Europe to stand for. In terms of its statements, actions and moral claims EPC has highlighted values which it is now difficult to eschew, whatever the practical problems. That is why the EU cannot simply take an isolationist, hard-headed line on Bosnia, standing back until events resolve themselves. They are caught in the web of their own pronouncements and the values they represent – even if the other weaknesses of the system also seem to make effective action impossible. This is the true meaning of the 'acquis politique'.

STANDS THE STATE STILL WHERE IT DID?

How has the state been affected by its involvement in this inchoate system of multiple institutions and uncertain identities? The realist imagery of solid nation-states pursuing coherent national interests through efficient foreign policy-making processes, unchallenged by divisions within their governments or by domestic dissent, was always a simplification of the complexities of international relations. Bismarck's foreign policy came close to this ideal type; but, except in wartime, no Western democracy has been free of domestic divisions or of transnational linkages between domestic groups and their counterparts within other states. The nation-states of continental Western Europe rebuilt their sovereignties and foreign policies in the years of reconstruction after 1945 on the basis of a compromise between sovereignty and integration, under the determined if benevolent hegemony of the USA.[22]

West European states struck two bargains over the reestablishment of their legitimacy and international autonomy: one external, accepting American protection and leadership for their defence, the other among themselves, providing their populations with steadily rising levels of income and welfare through economic growth of which the price was economic integration.[23] Britain retained the illusion of greater autonomy, at the cost both of accepting a greater degree of dependence on the USA and of gaining less benefit from the surge of economic growth which the creation of the EEC promoted. France recreated the icon of national sovereignty and great power status, while attempting to utilize West German support and economic cooperation to supply the resources it could no longer generate on its own. Political Cooperation, after all, had its origins in the Fouchet Plan, President de Gaulle's first attempt to harness the combined weight of the EEC to French perceptions of West European interests.

Federal Germany was, until the unification of 1990, a semi-sovereign state, dependent on its allies for protection against the Soviet threat and inhibited by the history of the Second World War from defining or explicitly pursuing its own national interests. The WEU, and later EPC, both served to contain a revived and rearmed Germany within multilateral frameworks devised by their neighbours. That EPC then 'provided a useful cover for the Federal Republic's East European aspirations', through joint diplomacy in the Conference on Security and Cooperation in Europe and through joint West European pressures on US administrations to moderate their policies towards Eastern Europe, only reinforces the observation that EPC represented in itself a compromise: between the independent pursuit of national interests and their redefinition as shared interests to be pursued through common foreign policy.[24] Each of the participating member states interpreted the compromise they made in terms of their distinctive national needs and traditions. Some emphasized national traditions, others more redefinition. But each, without question, was compromising its claims to sovereign autonomy – already limited by their acceptance of NATO, of American-led structures for international economic cooperation and of the tighter constraints of the EEC – in return for a hoped for accretion of international influence through membership of this group. Intergovernmentalism in theory does not erode sovereignty; in practice, over time, it too has ties that bind.

The states of Western Europe which conducted their foreign policies through European Political Cooperation should thus be seen, even in the early 1970s, as partially sovereign and partially constrained, not as the classical sovereign states of realist theory. The rising intensity of interaction of their ministers and officials in the 1980s, not only among foreign ministries but also among more and more domestic ministries, not excluding ministries of defence, intelligence services and interior ministries, further disaggregated the external solidarity of the state.[25] A certain socialization within these transgovernmental groups, working with each other on specific issues on which they share professional expertise and professional pride, has led 'national interests' to be subtly redefined, and more vigorously contested among different ministries. The result is that there is now more confusion than ever about whose interest is being served in any given situation, not least because the idea of the collective interest has been no more successfully elevated to the Europe level than has the concept of identity.

Joint reporting, and joint preparation of declarations and actions for

foreign ministers (and their colleagues) to consider, has taken the inter-
penetration of governments further, with the preparatory stages of national
policy-making already infused with shared information and consensus
building. Officials with less than twenty years' experience of national
diplomatic services have grown up entirely within the context of European
Political Cooperation, taking as given the exchange of confidential information not only about third countries but about their own governments'
intentions and domestic constraints, the sharing of tasks (and sometimes of
facilities) in third countries, the acceptance of officials on secondment to
their home ministry as no longer 'foreign' but as colleagues. The liberal
institutionalists' image of rational policy-makers bargaining with each other
within established regimes leaves too little room for this *engrenage* effect.
'Where you stand depends upon where you sit', as Don K. Price used to tell
his Harvard students (in retrospect perhaps the first post-modern observation to hit the study of foreign policy). Officials and ministers who sit
together on planes and round tables in Brussels or in each other's capitals
begin to judge 'rationality' from within a different framework from that they
began with.

As with so many other areas of West European integration, we have thus
observed a progressive shift away from accepted models of state-to-state
international relations, without moving too far towards the alternative
accepted model of a federal state. British and French insistence on a three-
pillar structure for the Maastricht Treaty has kept joint actions in foreign
policy, justice and home affairs as far under national control as seemed
practical; carefully excluding the European Court of Justice and (as far as
possible) the European Parliament from overseeing their activities, and
limiting Commission involvement to an advisory but not a policy-initiating
role. Yet habits of cooperation, accepted advantages of shared information,
responses to common threats, cost saving through increased collaboration,
have all significantly altered patterns of national policy-making. This is an
intensive system of external relations, in which the cooperating actors which
constitute the system intertwine.[26]

Furthermore, some member states are particularly keen on being intertwined in the system. It should not be forgotten that the analysis of EPC
depends fundamentally on a comparative politics capacity to delineate the
common features of a given group of states but also their differences. When
we think therefore of the propensity of EPC to get stuck through the
defections of its bigger players, we should remember that the majority of
the states involved is interested in keeping forward momentum going. States
as varied as Italy, Belgium and Ireland all want to see the CFSP develop, first
as a means of maximizing the protection which a powerful group can
provide, and second, and paradoxically, to increase the possibility of their
own national influence over their larger partners.

PRESENCE AND ACTORNESS

The member states of the European Union have established a collective 'presence' in the international arena, without achieving the ability to act collectively except through cumbersome consultative procedures and partially effective diplomatic, economic and military instruments. Even then they depend on favourable conjunctions of external circumstances and operate largely in the longer term. True actorness requires not only a clear identity and a self-contained decision-making system, but also the practical capabilities to effect policy.[27] In all of these dimensions the EU falls some way short. Its presence in the world is therefore real but incoherent, leaving third countries (which nonetheless seem to welcome it as a new 'pole' in the international system) to cope with relations with the European Community (through the Commission) alongside bilateral relations with the member states to puzzle over the role and functions of WEU and over the duplication of national embassies by Community representations which see themselves as playing an increasingly political role. The reservation of powers of initiative and implementation to the participating member states has historically held the line closer to the principles of national sovereignty than that drawn within the Community, where the Commission plays a more active role – although the concession of a joint right of initiative to the latter in the CFSP may open up new possibilities. But the cost of such a limited transfer of authority was to be seen in the confusions of West European reactions to the Yugoslav crisis, as to the Afghanistan crisis of a dozen years before: of confusion and incoherence, of failures to prepare against predicted contingencies, of responsibilities passed from one government to another without collective acceptance by the group as a whole.

Twenty years of cooperation on foreign policy have transformed the making of national foreign policies within all of the member states of the EU. A certain 'ratchet effect' is observable in hindsight; each crisis, each humbling failure leading to modest but cumulative improvements in commitment and procedure.[28] This has counterbalanced the 'historical drag' imposed by the continued existence of national foreign policies. Yet the strains which a rapidly changing external environment have imposed upon the still limited capabilities of the system between 1990 and 1994 have been intense; and the further strains which a continuing process of enlargement would impose may have to be faced before the next Intergovernmental Conference. This is an established system of external relations, of shared actions among national and international institutional actors. But it is a system which is not too firmly established, and with moving foundations. The impact of external challenges and internal constraints is unlikely to leave it unchanged over the next few years. Whether the response of the participating member states, now deeply embedded in the practices and procedures of the system, will be to increase its capabilities or to seek to reduce expectations – outside the EU above all – about what it can achieve is a matter for political decisions, not academic prediction.

The parameters of choice can, however, be seen clearly enough. The full 'renationalization' of foreign policy, despite realist scepticism and popular disillusion such as that over Bosnia, seems unlikely given the vested interest of member states in continuing the system at which they have worked so hard over twenty-five years. But there are also forces from the 'structure' of the international system which are working to keep a CFSP in place. The geopolitics of the post-Cold War world have created a great vacuum in central Europe, which neither Russia nor the USA are any longer suitable to fill. The Central Europeans themselves are desperate to join the EU and therefore effectively to abolish the distinctions between West, Central and Eastern Europe. If they succeed there can be little doubt that the consequent division between 'Europe' and Russia will force the EU into further foreign policy development. The current condition, of a hydra-headed 'agency', has been made possible first by the USA taking responsibility for European security and then by the current fluidity of structures in international politics. This may endure indefinitely. It is more likely, however, that events will relentlessly expose the EU's indecision and force a resolution, either in the direction of an assertive, coordinated leadership by the 'major actors' that occupy the first half of this book, or in that of a truly consolidated federal foreign policy. The choice is there to be made.

NOTES

1 Brian Hocking (ed.), *Foreign Relations and Federal States*, London, Leicester University Press, 1993.
2 The idea of a 'presence', short of the full actorness aspired to, was invented by David Allen and Michael Smith. See their 'Western Europe's presence in the contemporary international arena', *Review of International Studies*, vol.16, no.1, January 1990, pp.19–38, reprinted in Martin Holland (ed.), *The Future of European Political Cooperation: Essays in Theory and Practice*, London, Macmillan, 1991.
3 Joseph Weiler and Wolfgang Wessels, 'EPC and the challenge of theory', in Alfred Pijpers, Elfriede Regelsberger and Wolfgang Wessels (eds), *European Political Cooperation in the 1980s*, Dordrecht, Martinus Nijhoff, 1988, pp.229–58.
4 See Robert Keohane, 'Multilateralism: an agenda for research', *International Journal*, vol. XLV, no. 4, Autumn 1990; Stanley Hoffmann and Robert Keohane (eds), *The New European Community: Decisionmaking and Institutional Change*, Boulder, Westview Press, 1991. They argue (p.15) that 'the most appropriate label for the political process of the European Community is Haas's notion of "supranationality"', and that although the analysis must begin with states it should not also finish with them. See also Weiler and Wessels, op.cit.
5 See Andrew Moravcsik, 'Negotiating the Single European Act: national interests and conventional statecraft in the European Community', *International Organization*, vol. 45, no. 1, 1991, pp.651–88 (reprinted in Hoffmann and Keohane, op.cit.). To differentiate Hoffmann and Keohane, let alone the different guises

of Keohane, might be to make a distinction without a difference. But Hoffmann has always taken a broadly realist (albeit an historically sensitive) view of international relations, whereas Keohane certainly began by writing extensively on transnationalism, and his understanding of international cooperation has not always been interest based.

6 See Walter Carlsnaes and Steve Smith (eds), *European Foreign Policy: The EC and Changing Perspectives in Europe*, London, Sage/ECPR, 1994, and in particular the last two chapters, 'Resisting the temptation of post foreign policy analysis', and 'In lieu of a conclusion: compatibility and the agency-structure issue in foreign policy analysis', by Ole Waever and Walter Carlsnaes respectively.

7 Simon J. Nuttall, *European Political Cooperation*, Oxford, Clarendon Press, 1992, Chapter 7.

8 William Wallace, 'Relaunching the WEU: variable geometry, institutional duplication or policy drift?', in Panos Tsakaloyannis (ed.), *The Reactivation of the WEU: The Effects on the EC and its Institutions*, Maastricht, EIPA, 1985.

9 Treaty on European Union, Articles J.1.1, J.4.1.

10 The 'exceptional' circumstances which justified this remarkable decision were that the EC had been unable to spend its financial commitment for Somali aid, due to civil conflicts there; so that it could be argued that expenditure on 'military assistance to the civil power' was a proper charge on the EC aid budget. See *Agence Europe, Daily Bulletin*, 4 September 1992, p.7.

11 It will be remembered that protests over the presumed loss of sovereignty in the area of foreign policy had delayed the Irish ratification of the Single European Act in 1986–7. See Chapter 10 of this book by Patrick Keatinge, pp.211–12.

12 Anand Menon, Anthony Forster and William Wallace, 'A common European defence?', *Survival*, vol. 34, no. 3, Autumn 1992, pp.98–118.

13 Christopher Hill, 'The capability–expectations gap, or conceptualizing Europe's international role', *Journal of Common Market Studies*, vol. 31, no. 3, September 1993, pp.305–28, reprinted in Simon Bulmer and Andrew Scott (eds), *Economic and Political Integration in Europe: Internal Dynamics and Global Context*, Oxford, Blackwell, 1994.

14 Hill, 'The capability–expectations gap', p.322.

15 Exact figures on frequency of meetings have not to our knowledge been collected. Douglas Hurd however remarked in a lecture at the Institut d'Etudes Politiques in Paris, in September 1990, which was chaired by his French counterpart, that this was the tenth time the two foreign ministers had met in two weeks, in five different countries.

16 Robert Putnam, 'Diplomacy and domestic politics: the logic of two level games', *International Organization*, vol. 42, no. 3, 1988, pp.427–60.

17 Robert Putnam and Nicholas Bayne, *Hanging Together: Cooperation and Conflict in the Seven-Power Summits*, 2nd edn, London, Sage, 1987.

18 Richard Little and Steve Smith (eds), *Belief Systems and International Relations*, Oxford, Blackwell, 1988; William Wallace, 'Foreign policy and national identity in the United Kingdom', *International Affairs*, vol. 67, no. 1, January 1991, pp.65–80.

19 Anthony D. Smith, 'National identity and the idea of European unity', *International Affairs*, vol. 68, no. 1, January 1992, pp.55–76.

20 See Christopher Hill, 'Introduction: the Falklands War and European foreign policy', in Stelios Stavridis and Christopher Hill, *The Domestic Sources of Foreign Policy: West European Reactions to the Falklands Conflict*, Oxford, Berg, 1996.

21 Christopher Hill, 'National interests – the insuperable obstacles?' in *National Foreign Policies*, op.cit, p.200.

22 David W. Ellwood, *Rebuilding Europe: Western Europe, America and Postwar*

Reconstruction, London, Longman, 1992; Michael J. Hogan, *The Marshall Plan: America, Britain and the Reconstruction of Western Europe 1947–52*, Cambridge, Cambridge University Press, 1987.

23 Alan Milward, *The European Rescue of the Nation State*, London, Routledge, 1992, provides a persuasive and well-documented argument about the striking of this second bargain.

24 Alfred E. Pijpers, 'European political cooperation and the realist paradigm', in Martin Holland (ed.), *The Future of European Political Cooperation*, op.cit., p.26.

25 Wolfgang Wessels, 'Administrative interaction', in William Wallace (ed.), *The Dynamics of European Integration*, London, Pinter, 1990, Chapter 13, pp.229–41.

26 On the wider issue of the evolution of the state in Western Europe, see William Wallace, 'Rescue or retreat? The nation-state in Western Europe, 1945–1993', *Political Studies*, vol. 42, special issue, 1994.

27 For the definition of actorness see Gunnar Sjostedt, *The External Role of the European Community*, Farnborough, Saxon House, 1977; and Hill, 'The capability–expectations gap', *Journal of Common Market Studies*, vol. 31, no. 3, September 1993. The summarized definition given here has been adapted to take the discussion of identity into account.

28 Christopher Hill, 'Shaping a federal foreign policy for Europe', in Brian Hocking (ed.), *Foreign Relations and Federal States*, London, Leicester University Press, 1993, Chapter 15, p.275.

Part I

The major actors

Chapter 1

France

The impact of François Mitterrand

Françoise de La Serre

The gradual development of European Political Cooperation (EPC) during the 1970s had at the same time sanctioned French preferences with regard to European foreign policy and testified to a significant erosion of the ambitions once displayed by General de Gaulle during the successive Fouchet plans.

By the end of Valéry Giscard d'Estaing's period in office, the experience of harmonization of national foreign policies on the basis of the reports which had shaped European cooperation had somehow presented France with the best of both worlds: it had enhanced the power of French diplomacy while removing any constraints on what was left of international ambitions and will to independence. The start of a European foreign policy proper did not question any of those attributes of power which allowed France, among the middle-ranking powers, to remain 'great': namely, an independent nuclear force and the status conferred by permanent membership of the Security Council.[1]

Ten years later the treaty on European Union, following joint initiatives by France and Germany, includes the setting up of a Common Foreign and Security Policy (CFSP) the scope of which does not in the long term exclude a common defence policy. In comparison with the situation which previously prevailed, this surely suggests a qualitative leap.

It is therefore legitimate to raise the question of the role played during the 1980s by successive French governments in the genesis of the CFSP without however losing sight of the fact that the 1958 Constitution – and above all the practices adhered to throughout the Fifth Republic – have firmly established foreign policy as the exclusive preserve of the President. Thus François Mitterrand, even during the 'cohabitation' period of 1986–8, has been the decisive actor in the conduct of European policy. Indeed he has claimed responsibility for this function on more than one occasion. Be it in the selection of actors (Foreign Affairs Ministers, senior civil servants, personal representatives, envoys) or the setting out of positions, the grip of the Elysée on European affairs intensified as the construction of Europe became the defining issue of the seven-year presidential term.[2] Foreign

Affairs and European Affairs Ministers have remained under close surveillance from the Elysée. The contribution of the Socialist Party to the definition of European foreign policy has been insignificant. Parliamentary and public debate has remained virtually non-existent. In so far as it characterizes the decision-making process in the field of foreign policy this situation has been analysed in a work eloquently entitled *La monarchie nucléaire*.[3] It also justifies the title of this chapter.

However it is not always easy within this evolution to distinguish what part is played by convictions and what by circumstances; what derives from a philosophy and a vision of European construction and what has been imposed by the end of the Cold War and German reunification. Should the observed evolution be analysed within the framework of continuity, under the dead hand of traditions which affect French foreign policy, or does it signal a genuine will to change? Are we being presented with an old politics dressed up in new clothes or are we witnessing a true conversion to the idea of a common foreign and security policy?

THE GAULLO-SOCIALIST INTERLUDE

'Foreign policy revolves around some simple ideas: national independence, balance of the great military powers, construction of Europe, the right to self-determination, the development of poor countries.' Thus François Mitterrand expresses himself in the introduction to the various speeches on foreign policy published in 1986.[4] This suggests that the necessity of a great European policy had imposed itself from the very beginning of the first seven-year term. However, such a necessity does not seem to have constituted the priority of priorities which in the beginning appeared to be located elsewhere: a new economic world order, East–West relations, the strategic balance and the problems of Euro-missiles, the Middle East and Latin America.

To be sure, from their accession to power, both the President of the Republic and the Prime Minister, Pierre Mauroy, insisted on underlining their commitment to Europe, a commitment to which – for the sake of the 1979 European election – the Socialist Party, once profoundly divided on the subject, had finally rallied. But this European commitment has to be seen within the terms of the general philosophy that inspired the new foreign policy defined by the Foreign Affairs Minister, Claude Cheysson: 'There is no foreign policy for a country like France, but a translation to the exterior of its interior politics, an integration of internal demands and priorities into international politics.'[5]

From the outset therefore the problem arose of the consequences for French European policy of the radical changes announced in economic policy, and of the priorities declared in foreign policy. The impact on the way the French government deals with Community business was immediate. The subordination of the external to the internal produced a policy which tended, by endowing the EEC with adequate policies in the social, regional and industrial fields, to correct or to fill the lacunae of a European construction perceived as excessively liberal in economic terms. Thus as early as the European Council meeting of 29–30 June 1981, François Mitterrand proposed to his partners an ambitious programme for economic recovery through consumption, the issuing of bonds aimed at supporting investment and above all, the creation of a 'European social space'. Inspired by 'the idea that Europe will be socialist or nothing', these proposals were developed in the Memorandum presented by the Minister for European Affairs, André Chandernagor, in October 1981. They aimed to have France's choices endorsed by her European partners and to make the Community the support and extension of national policies. The point, under the guise of boosting European construction, was to give the Mauroy government the means to pursue its national economic and social agenda without at the same time positioning itself outside the Common Market.

Was this logic extended to foreign policy? Now that the Left had come to power, what significance would the advent of what some had foreseen as 'Gaullo-socialism'[6] have for European Political Cooperation? Rather than an effective conduit for national ambitions and objectives, could it constitute an obstacle to new French ambitions in the field of international policy?

Objectives and procedures: an acceptance in principle

In formal terms Paris has never had any objection in principle to the Cooperation of the Ten in the field of foreign policy. By her unreserved adoption of the Third Report on EPC – the so-called London Report – in October 1981, France subscribed to the various innovations meant to improve the harmonization of the foreign policies of the various member states: a mechanism allowing for a crisis meeting to be called at the request of only three member states, the association of the Commission with all the groups and mechanisms of EPC. The first point would more than likely have been approved by the previous government, though hardly the second. A continuity of policy is evidenced however, both in the refusal to accede to the proposal by London that a Political Secretariat be set up and the acceptance only of a reinforcement of the EC Presidency.

Behind the formal position however, the spirit in which EPC had to take place indicated a return to a more orthodox position. Indeed all approaches which might privilege the conduct of Europe's external actions, including the concepts of 'principal nation' and 'Directoire' (both notions entertained by Valéry Giscard d'Estaing towards the end of his mandate) were rejected.[7] As André Chandernagor states, 'France has no "small partners", it just has "partners"', sentiments echoed by Claude Cheysson: 'There will be no Paris–Bonn axis; there will be a privileged relationship between France and West Germany, but it will not exclude bilateral relations with other states whether on Community or non-Community problems.[8]

The procedures shaped by the London Report however, represented the most to which France was prepared to consent. Indeed the Mitterrand government was not at all receptive to the concerns voiced throughout 1981 by Hans-Dietrich Genscher, the German Foreign Affairs Minister, about a European foreign policy capable of lending its weight to the East–West dialogue and of playing a part in the field of security. The draft European Act, jointly presented by Germany and Italy in November 1981 (the 'Genscher–Colombo Plan') did not provoke any official comment and was met with an obvious lack of enthusiasm. Messrs Colombo's and Genschers's ambition was to resuscitate the objective of Political Union, particularly through the setting up of a common foreign policy which would allow member states to act together in world affairs. They also expressed the wish for 'the coordination of security policy and the adoption of common European positions in this sphere'.[9] To this statement of political objectives was added a more properly institutional section considering the possible participation of Defence Ministers in the work of EPC and the setting up of a Secretariat for Political Cooperation.

The discussions which took place among the partners in 1982 and which, within the framework of the solemn Statement on European Union, led to a significant reduction of the initial ambitions, confirm the lack of any French interest in a relaunching of Political Union that would imply the development of a common foreign and security policy. In fact rather than putting questions of security on the EPC agenda, since the very beginning of Mitterrand's term of office, Paris had favoured a revival of the WEU.

The speech made at the WEU Assembly on 1 December 1981 by the Secretary of State, M Lemoine, testifies to this, as do comments made by Cheysson on the following day to the effect that, 'the WEU must be revived'.[10] In 1982 the solicitude of the French government towards this organization was successively to lead the Foreign Minister, Claude Cheysson, the Prime Minister, Pierre Mauroy and the Defence Minister, Charles Hernu, to address the WEU Assembly. From these interventions a very clear message emerges: given that the European Community has no competence with regard to defence it is necessary, despite the diversity of national situations, to resort to the WEU to debate, solely among Europeans, the European dimension of security and to promote cooperation with respect to armaments. 'All this must be done most delicately since nothing should be attempted which would threaten to uncouple the defence of Europe from that of the [North Atlantic] Alliance in general',[11] and in the recognition that such an endeavour should not be rushed into.

A selective approach to the 'acquis politique'[12]

Thus, locked into a specific framework and well-defined procedures and, despite the theoretical support it enjoys, EPC varied in the weight it carried in the formulation of French external policy during the first years of Mitterrand's term of office.

It is obvious that in the crisis between Argentina and the UK over the Falkland Islands, membership of the Community provoked an immediate reaction of solidarity with the UK. This recalls the attitude once taken by De Gaulle in similar circumstances towards the USA and Cuba in 1962. Convinced that the Community 'has its positive and negative aspects and that one should help our partners when they are in difficulties', within the framework of the EPC the French government demonstrated unfailing support for the UK, regardless of whatever second thoughts François Mitterrand might have had on the substance of the respective claims and on the cost of such a policy in terms of the image of France in Latin America[13]

But such feelings of constraint, born out of an obligation of solidarity and respect for international law, constitute an exception in relation to EPC. In general the obligation to consult one's partners before any important initiative of national diplomacy does not seem to have been of major concern for the French government. Indeed France's partners have often voiced their astonishment at not having been informed – let alone consulted – before the launching of a number of such initiatives. Examples are the Franco-Mexican statement of 28 August 1981 on El Salvador, in which the representative status of the Democratic Revolutionary Front was recognized, or the decision – announced in January 1982 – to sell arms to the Sandinista regime in Nicaragua. Similarly, the challenge issued by Paris to some aspects of the 'acquis politique', particularly in the Middle East, resembled the politics of the 'fait accompli'.

Indeed it was in regard to the Arab–Israeli conflict that France insisted most strongly on differentiating her position. As early as the Luxembourg meeting of the European Council, and even more explicitly during the subsequent press conference, Mitterrand challenged the Venice Declaration issued after the European Council of 13 June 1980, acceding only to those principles within the text which he considered would serve as a basis for a settlement of the conflict. The document in question, with its insistence on a 'global settlement', was considered too favourable to the Arab position, too critical of Camp David and, in envisaging a 'European initiative' which had been impugned in advance by one of the parties to the conflict, too presumptuous. French policy was henceforth defined in the following way: a reminder of the principles which were to serve as the basis for the settlement, such as appeared in the Venice text and in the statement of the Ten on 23 November on the participation of four European countries, including France, in the observation force based in the Sinai;

acceptance of a Palestinian state; concern for balanced relations with both conflicting parties; preference for a policy of small incremental gains which would take into account the insufficient but on the whole positive contribution of the Camp David agreement.

On 7 December, during his visit to Israel, the French Minister for External Relations, Claude Cheysson, having confirmed the outmoded character of the Venice text, added to these various points France's refusal to join any initiative which was not expressly undertaken at the request of the conflicting parties. Thus contrasting the 'initiative' planned in Venice to the responses produced by the Egyptian requests over the Sinai force and to the interest expressed in the Fahd plan, he said: 'Not being a country of the region we have, in ourselves, neither project nor initiatives to offer. There will be no French project, there will be no French initiative, there will be, as long as we are in Government, no European project, no European initiative.'[14]

Whatever the relative impasse in which the Venice-planned initiative found itself after the subsequent developments in the region, the statement by France, without consultation of or warning to her partners, that there would be no more European initiatives, caused surprise by its abrupt and uncompromising tone. Not only did it mark a change from official French policy as defined by President Mitterrand in his September press conference (far from contrasting Camp David and Venice, he had declared on that occasion, 'I will take both'). But it also contradicted the 23 November statement in which the Ten had made explicit reference to the June 1980 text. Above all it questioned both the spirit and the results of Political Cooperation by undermining a process initiated ten years earlier, which had allowed for a harmonization of European foreign policies on an issue over which they had hitherto been profoundly divided.

In terms of East–West relations, by contrast, French diplomacy had accommodated previous European stances even if this meant inflecting them with a sense of greater intransigence toward Moscow. Thus during the Luxembourg meeting of the European Council held in June 1981, Paris subscribed to the plan suggested for Afghanistan and during the Madrid Conference on the aftermath of the CSCE took a very firm line. The range of attitudes within the Community concerning events in Poland allowed French policy to situate itself within the European framework without too much difficulty. After the 'of course we will do nothing', uttered by Claude Cheysson at the onset of the crisis, the compromise adopted by the Ten on 4 January 1982 suited the French demand for firmness on principles and for a low profile on possible sanctions. The conclusion a few days later of an agreement providing for the delivery to France by the USSR of important quantities of gas confirms the minimalist approach adopted by France to the proposed imposition of sanctions on the Soviet Union.

The convergence among Europeans on the subject of East–West relations indicated that times had changed and that the once burning issue of Euro-American relations no longer isolated France from the 'ensemble' of her partners. A whole series of factors – crisis in American leadership, crisis of détente, evolution of European attitudes on the problems of defence – created a much more fluid situation. The affirmation of a permanent non-identity of interests with the USA was no longer attributable to France alone. On the contrary it was to a degree increasingly more typical of other European partners. Witness the reactions to events in Poland and the solidarity in resistance to the American embargo on materials and equipment for the Siberian gas pipeline. By comparison with the preceding period the nature of the links to be forged between the Community and the USA had therefore ceased to be the main bone of contention between France and her partners, even if Paris had little hesitation in criticizing the schemes of the 'Imperial Republic' in the Third World.

THE POSTING OF A GREAT EUROPEAN DESIGN

'1984 will be the year of Europe. France, which is European, does not want to miss this chance.' By expressing himself thus on 31 December 1983 on the eve of France's taking over the Presidency of the Community, the President of the Republic announced the launching of a great European project.

Thus were confirmed the precursors, furnished throughout 1983, of an evolution which gradually became a rupture in relation to the beginning of the seven-year term. The break derived from an ensemble of reasons in which the internal and external, the economic and the political were intertwined. After three consecutive devaluations, François Mitterrand and the Prime Minister, Pierre Mauroy, (not without controversy within the government and the Socialist Party) clearly chose the European option: to remain within the EMS and to adopt anti-inflationary policies, thus erasing the difference of France and sounding the death knell of the slogan 'Europe will be Socialist or nothing'.

But the transition between the Socialist vision and a Europeanist definition of the problem cannot be explained solely in terms of the failure of the policy of economic recovery which had been adhered to for two years. It also derives from the renunciation of the utopias which had marked foreign policy at the beginning of Mitterrand's term of office. The hope of a universal diplomacy which would combine national independence and an ambitious Third World policy has been gradually replaced by the recognition that Europe constitutes the appropriate and indeed necessary framework for a major state's foreign policy. From 1983 there was, in a way, an explicit acceptance of the realities which have imposed themselves on French leaders since the Second World War: the necessity of a vigilant containment of Germany and of binding her firmly to the West, of providing

France, through European competition, with the frame and the spur required for her modernization, of using within the international system the enhanced powers bestowed by membership of the Community. For François Mitterrand the evolution of the international context confirms the 'necessary' character of the construction of Europe: 'Western Europe, in military terms dependent, in political terms divided, in technological terms anachronistic, will every day become more vulnerable to the solicitations which sway her: submission to American imperialism or succumbing to neutralism – necessarily the route to Soviet domination.'[15] Thus summarized are the fears induced by the imbalance of forces within Europe and by the possible drift of Germany toward national neutralism. To these must be added the fear that the Strategic Defence Initiative (SDI) launched by the USA in 1983 would exacerbate Europe's technological dependency and give rise to 'the decoupling, or the separation into two unequally protected systems of defence, of America and Europe'.[16]

Hence the return to a global European policy binding Germany to the West, ensuring the recovery of the economy and providing the framework for relative autonomy in the face of the American ally. This is clearly what emerges from the speech delivered at the Bundestag on 20 January 1983, a speech in which these two concerns, for balance in terms of security and for a relaunching of the Community, are explicitly linked.[17]

Political Cooperation: prodigal son of the European Union?

The French Presidency of the European Union from January to July 1984 made concrete the orientation outlined above, first by settling outstanding disagreements (and by unknotting the embroglio of the agro-budget), and then by opening up a new perspective, that of European Union. In this respect France was indeed largely responsible for the exploration of new avenues on which Europe developed. What had been formulated as a question in the Bundestag speech ('how to trace a future perspective for the Community?') had become a proposal by the time the European Parliament met in Strasbourg on 24 May 1984.[18]

Thus were clarified both the object – the elaboration of a Treaty on the Union – and the method: a remake of the Spaak committee which was to lead to a new Messina. But the content as much as the end product of the enterprise remained rather vague. What is the meaning of the statement in which François Mitterrand made claims for the European Parliament's draft Treaty? Was it a rallying call for a more supranational project or the adhesion to a project that could be claimed to reconcile economic integration and political cooperation, the former essentially federal, and the latter confederal in its inspiration?

The prevailing impression in any case is that among the 'new ways' to be explored in order to concretize political union, foreign and security policy were not major priorities. They lay elsewhere: better functioning of institutions and of the decision-making process and – compelled by SDI – the construction of a European space for industry and technology.[19] At this stage France seemed to accept the absence of any Community competence *vis-à-vis* foreign and security policy. Apparently satisfied with the functioning of Political Cooperation ('The European Councils have adopted resolutions appropriate to the acute problems which occupy the world stage'), François Mitterrand considered that, 'it does not pertain to the European Communities to take into account aspirations to common security and defence'.[20] As far as European Political Cooperation is concerned the only thing to emerge was the desire that it be 'improved' and that a standing political secretariat responsible to the European Council be set up. While the ad hoc committee on institutional questions, initiated in Fontainebleau in June 1984, suggested 'the creation of a permanent political secretariat to enable successive Presidencies to ensure continuity and cohesiveness of action', France – up until the European Council of Milan – was only to support the idea of a secretariat as 'an instrument available to the European Council, particularly in its task of ensuring the continuity of EPC'.

This was certainly the idea which was developed in the proposal for 'a Treaty for European Union', unexpectedly floated by France and Germany before the Milan meeting of the European Council in June 1985.[21] Given that up until then European Political Cooperation did not seem to be the approach favoured by Paris as a way of lending content to the European Union, it is paradoxical that the text concentrates only on Political Cooperation. Of course the objective remains: 'to transform without delay the whole of the relations among their states into a European Union, based on the Communities operating in accordance with their own rules and on Political Cooperation operating under the articles set out in the text'. But the means to achieve this Union are limited to a codification of EPC as it exists and functions. The Franco-German text only reiterates, sometimes word for word, the document handed out to her partners a few weeks earlier by the UK, during the Stresa meeting.

Whatever the questions provoked by the apparently improvised Franco-German initiative,[22] the latter revealed French intentions with regard to European Union. It also announced the positions defended during the intergovernmental conference finally called by the Milan summit, for which France voted – albeit without enthusiasm. Charged with elaborating a Treaty on common foreign and security policy on the basis of Franco-German and British documents and the Dooge report, the conference proposed a codification and formalization of EPC, in the form of an international Treaty. Without important advances and in the absence of any serious breakthrough in the field of security – since the Europe of the Twelve was not recognized as the favoured framework for dealing with such problems – foreign and security policy, at least as it appears in the Single Act, accorded with French preferences. However the setting up of a secretariat for EPC constituted a setback for France. Placed under the authority of the Presidency, and situated in Brussels rather than Paris, the secretariat was more a light administrative overlay than the General Secretariat of the European Union proposed in the Franco-German document. It was true that the combined opposition of both the majority of partner-states and of the Commission, to a proposal which sought (already!) to create a second pillar within the Union, left it very little chance of success.

In fact French positions toward EPC are easily explained. On the one hand it is obvious that the recognition of external constraints, the posting of a European project, the reactivation of the special relationship with Germany have put an end to the politics of 'going it alone' adhered to throughout 1981–2. Rather than preferring a national approach, there is now a will to make European Political Cooperation and French foreign policy correspond. This attitude allows France to mould itself in the shape of the EPC by having its point of view heard and using the EPC as a relay and springboard for French positions. But at the same time the absence of constraints on national foreign policy, an absence which springs from the Single Act, allows France, as in the past, to differentiate itself.[23]

In the field of East–West relations, particularly at times of crises in *détente*, France had always situated herself on a median line, advocating both firmness and openness to dialogue. EPC afforded her a relatively comfortable position, avoiding isolation from Washington (during the episode of sanctions against USSR) and allowing her to counterpoint Soviet–American discussions on disarmament by highlighting the specific contribution of the Twelve to the renewal of *détente* and their commitment to the CSCE process. Witness for example these comments by Roland Dumas accompanying the statement on East–West relations of 12 February 1985: 'I insist on the fact that we have reaffirmed the French thesis on East–West relations, particularly as regards arms control, namely that we approve and support the negotiations between the USSR and the US which are genuinely about to start.'[24]

On Middle Eastern affairs in general and on the Arab–Israeli conflict in particular, EPC provided France with the framework which allowed her to soften the positions which she had insisted on in 1981. In effect France has evolved positions closer to those of her partners, combining the principles which were to govern the solution to the Arab–Israeli conflict with the recognition of the limits imposed on the influence of the Twelve. This evolution has, however, been accomplished without renouncing all forms of 'initiative'. As early as the Dublin meeting of the European Council in 1984, France consented to the 'intensification of contacts with all parties involved with a view to finding ways to facilitate moves toward negotiation'.

Similarly in 1987, France contributed to rallying the Twelve's support for the International Peace Conference in the Middle East, held under the aegis of the UN.

On other issues the EPC has been the moving force of policies which French diplomacy actively supported. In Central America for example, the policy initiated by the Twelve in 1983 accords with the French government's analysis that the conflicts of the region derive from insufficient economic development and social inequalities, and must therefore be kept separate from the East–West conflict. The distancing from the USA begun at the San José meeting in Costa Rica and the support given to the peace process initiated by the Contadora countries fitted in perfectly with French expectations and proposals.

The definition by the Twelve of a policy on the situation created in South Africa by the reinforcement of apartheid also provides a good example of what EPC could offer France in relation to what has been presented as a priority of Mitterrand's foreign policy: the defence of human rights. Without precluding more radical initiatives, such as the recall by the Fabius government in July 1985 of its ambassador in Pretoria, and the withholding of investments, EPC (albeit not without procrastination) provided France with a framework for the collective action which led eventually, in 1986, to the imposition of some important restrictive measures. Given the reservations expressed by some key member states – notably Germany and the UK – over various aspects of the 'sanctions', France had some good reasons to congratulate itself about the actions taken within the EPC.

This admittedly incomplete list of examples indicates that, as in the past, Political Cooperation frequently allowed France to dress up its own national interest in European clothes, without imposing any real constraints on what was left of her international ambitions and will to independence. Governed by the rule of consensus and not extending to essential or sensitive areas like defence, EPC does not impinge on spheres which France, like Britain, wishes to see excluded from concerted action by the Twelve on a long-term basis.

The timid breakthrough of the Single Act on security notwithstanding, it was clear that Political Cooperation was not considered the appropriate framework for a discussion on European security. The reason most often invoked (i.e. Ireland's neutrality), is a convenient alibi. 'The extreme difficulty and the necessity' of European defence evoked by Mitterrand in his Strasbourg speech, confirmed that the latter continued – as at the beginning of his first term of office – to be located within the framework of the WEU. This is a WEU whose reactivation has in part been due to French initiatives and in which Germany has recovered (Franco-German cooperation compelled it) full member status as regards conventional weapons. The setting of a European defence as an objective, the opening of the Franco-German dialogue to encompass questions of defence, and the reactivation of the WEU as a political forum were, however, all signs that, with respect to the European process, France was already advanced on a course which was, furthermore, being advocated by the RPR–UDF opposition.[25] The French concept of a defence which is autonomous and centred on the 'national sanctuary' concept has indeed evolved into a wider conception of security establishing an explicit link between the security of France and that of her European neighbours. Witness notably the emphasis placed on solidarity with the European allies on the occasion of the creation of the Rapid Reaction Force (Force d'Action Rapide, FAR) and the fact that the FAR has 'among other missions, that of acting side by side with German forces'.[26] Witness also the fact that, while reaffirming the permanence of the doctrine, 'French officials surround the notion of vital interests with the maximum of uncertainties as to the circumstances in which France might be led to envisage overstepping the nuclear threshold'.[27] To these signs of evolution must be added the French attitude to the WEU and notably the 'platform' adopted in October 1987, regarding interests in the field of security. In spite of the unsettling role played by the SDI, particularly in Franco-German relations, Paris no longer plays the WEU against the Alliance but considers it rather as its 'European pillar'. All that without at this stage having defined the relationship between the WEU and the European Community: are they to be competitive or complementary?

The election in March 1986 of a RPR–UDF majority in the National Assembly and the experience of the first 'cohabitation' between a President and a Prime Minister of opposing parties, had no noticeable consequences on French policy within EPC, in spite of the reduced interest shown by the new Foreign Minister, Jean-Bernard Raimond, in the European dimension of France's foreign policy. Given a context of consensus over the major choices facing France in foreign policy, and given the absolute preeminence of the Elysée in the spheres of defence, Franco-German relations and disarmament,[28] the Chirac government could bring only minor changes to both the broad approach and the particularities of EPC business. During the debate on the ratification of the Single Act, ministerial interventions, following the report presented by Jean de Lipkowski, betrayed neither real interest in nor true anxiety over this dimension of the future European Union. But it is worth noting, as of March 1986, a lessening of French activism on the issue of South Africa and her desire not to differentiate herself from the 'middle ground' defined by the Twelve.

With regard to terrorism and especially in dealings with Libya, a selective approach to the possibilities offered by EPC is also noticeable. By refusing the USA permission to overfly its territory in order to carry out the raid on Tripoli, France asserted its individuality while also demonstrating a certain firmness.[29] Similarly, in the Hindawi affair (October 1986), France opposed the radical measures against Syria proposed by the UK before accepting a watered down version of them fifteen days later. Faced with terrorist actions on French soil and the taking of French hostages in the Lebanon, the government seemed to want to spare Syria's feelings.

Finally, although the new government wanted to have its distinctive voice heard on the problems of defence, it did not question the orientations of the Fabius government. Quite the contrary. In December 1986, at the WEU, Jaques Chirac launched the idea of a European Charter on security, designed to enable Europeans to assert the specificity of their interests in the context of the Soviet–American dialogue and of the prospect of the denuclearization of Europe. In October 1987, after adopting the 'Platform' at The Hague, the Prime Minister's office displayed its satisfaction in the following terms: 'this text constitutes the first collective manifestation by Europeans of the assertion of their identity and it thus adds a new dimension to the construction of Europe'.[30]

THE END OF FRENCH EXCEPTIONALISM?

Thus shaped by the Single Act, EPC might have carried on down the same path to the satisfaction of most of its participants, and particularly France.[31] But two shockwaves, the end of the Cold War and the outbreak of the Gulf War, rocked the diplomatic and strategic situation, and with it French options with respect to European foreign policy.

France, probably more than other European countries, had been directly hit by the collapse of the structures of the Cold War. Until then her foreign policy had developed in the shadow of the order established at Yalta (even if the latter was perpetually denounced), making use of all the margins for manoeuvre afforded by a singularity founded on autonomy in defence policy. Within the European framework, France had secured the containment of Western Germany through the process of integration, while striving to limit constraints which could have affected her own status. Within the Community there was a tacit recognition of French political supremacy balancing German economic power, thus making France into a power less 'equal' than the others. The end of the division of Europe, the collapse of the Soviet Union, the return of Germany to normality, have profoundly shaken the foundations of French foreign policy. Changes in the diplomatic and strategic landscape, the necessary accommodation of the new German power and the Gulf crisis all combined to impose on French foreign policy a form of 'aggiornamento'.[32] This effort of adjustment was hesitant, contradictory and remains unachieved. In these new conditions France is showing an obvious interest in the possible channel of influence offered by the CFSP. But the resistance which the CFSP continues to incite is no less obvious.

CFSP: dilemmas and strategy

The process which led to the introduction of a CFSP in the Treaty on European Union can largely be explained by the French desire to reinforce European integration in order to bind a reunified Germany to it. This desire did not emerge immediately after the fall of the Berlin wall but took some time to materialize. Of course all the governments of the Fifth Republic had proclaimed their commitment to the object of a German reunification founded on the right to self-determination. But the 1950s vision of a united Europe welcoming back to the fold a unified Germany has, after the events of 1989, been replaced by the prospect of a united Germany inserting herself into a yet to be achieved Community. On the French part, this reversal of fortunes precipitated the convergence of two contradictory fears: seeing Germany dominating the Community and/or distancing herself from the EC in order to have a very active policy in Central Europe. After a period of drift and wishful thinking during which the government willed itself to believe in the possible coexistence of two German states, the prospect of an accelerated reunification going hand in hand with Germany's affirmation of her bond with the West, presented France with the following dilemma: confronted with the problems raised by German reunification, should the priority be the reinforcement of a European integration which risked both de facto German domination and the loss of a significant part of French sovereignty? On the other hand, should it be the preservation of a margin of national manoeuvre within a larger, looser entity – for example an enlarged European Confederation – one which would grant Germany a dangerous degree of latitude in its movements?[33]

In mid-1990 the government chose reinforcement of the Community, resulting in the Franco-German proposals for combining Economic and Monetary Union with a Political Union largely founded on a common foreign and security policy. But with what objectives and with what content? And what are the implications for the EPC? If one analyses the various proposals made jointly by France and Germany, the ambitions contained within them are huge. After the proposal on 19 April 1990 to define and implement a CFSP, the letter addressed on 6 December to Giulio Andreotti, the then president of the European Council, goes some way towards clarifying the concept:

> as regards the CFSP, its vocation would be to present the essential interests and the common values of the Union . . . the European Council should define the priority areas of common action. . . . Moreover, political union should include a true common security policy which could, in time lead to a common defence. . . . The conference should review how the WEU and political union might establish a clear organic relationship . . . and how with increased operational capacities the

WEU might in time become part of political union and elaborate on the latter's behalf, a common security policy.

Thus French intentions were outlined. Subsequent contributions were to develop the initial canvas and essentially bring out a dominant concern: that of eventually endowing the European Union with a common defence. This is the tenor of the Dumas–Genscher proposals presented in February 1991 which make WEU the core of the proposed scheme. Defined as 'an integral part of the process of European Unification', the WEU would be assigned a major operational role during the developmental phase of the common defence policy prior to its pure and simple integration within Political Union. These proposals were to be reiterated in the Franco-German text of 15 October as articles in the Treaty.[34]

Compared to the declared ambitions, the positions defended by France during the negotiations obviously revealed a discrepancy between the discourse on the objectives, and the limited scope of the proposed innovations. This is particularly true of foreign policy where the modifications required by Paris scarcely amounted to more than the reinforcement of EPC. In pushing for a CFSP, France wished it to be enclosed within precisely defined limits. First the French government constantly situated itself within the camp which opposed the 'communautarisation' of the CFSP that would have sprung from a unitary approach to external relations and would have resulted in granting the Commission a determining role. The stated preference for maintaining the CFSP within an intergovernmental framework is reflected in the architecture of the Treaty. There is no doubt that the structure of three pillars of different strength, governed by different procedures and united under a common pediment, was proposed and defended by France. The upholding of the CFSP as a system of intergovernmental cooperation, subject to the authority of the European Council, signalled Paris' reservations about the 'communautarisation' of an area so sensitive in terms of national sovereignty. In the same way, as far as decision-making is concerned, there was no real French pressure to go beyond the provisions of the Single Act, since the timid introduction of qualified majority voting with respect to the implementation of common actions, was not really constraining. With regard to the CFSP therefore, France has on the whole defended a reinforced Political Cooperation[35] which in comparison with the preceding situation, constitutes some progress but does not represent the 'saut qualitatif' which the demonstration of Europe's impotence during the Gulf war and the Yugoslavian crisis might otherwise have inspired.

While these French positions fit fairly well with the views expressed by Britain, the particularity of the French approach in the negotiation of the CFSP appears in the desire to charge the European Union with 'the defence of Europe, for Europe, by Europeans'.[36] This step represents the continuity of French positions from two points of view. On the one hand, in accordance with the options always defended by Paris, it pleads for a beginning to a European defence which would be distinct from the integrated organization of NATO, without for all that representing a machine of warfare opposed to the Alliance. On the other hand, it extends the efforts undertaken by France since the beginning of the 1980s to make the WEU the centrepiece of this apparatus. The novelty comes from the proposal that the WEU should be considered as an 'integral part of European unification' and made into the armed wing of the Union. To a large extent these provisions of the Treaty satisfy the objectives set out by France. 'The eventual definition of common defence policy which could, in due time, lead to a common defence' constitutes for Paris a significant progress, in spite of the obvious compromise of the formulation. The provisions relating to the object to be achieved, the framework within which this object is to be achieved, and the organic link established between the Union and the WEU, all actually mark a victory for Germany and France – supported by Spain and Belgium – over the UK, the Netherlands, Portugal and, to a lesser extent, Italy. For these countries, in so far as real responsibility for defence rests with NATO, the WEU could be endowed only with limited responsibilities, perhaps to operations outside the NATO theatre. Its main vocation being the European pillar of the Alliance, the WEU would have no reason to be organically linked to the European Union.

The compromise sanctioned in the Treaty is the formal sign that the Franco-German thesis has prevailed. Yet the statement on the WEU appended to the Treaty tends rather to favour the WEU–NATO link at the expense of the WEU–European Union link, against the wishes of France. When the question of concretely making the WEU the core of European defence arises, do these texts give France any assurance that its point of view will prevail? Furthermore is this not yet another instance of the discrepancy between the declared objective of European defence and the adjustments that France is prepared to make to national policy?

Europeanization versus the concern for rank

Several explanations can be advanced for the positions defended by France in the negotiations on the CFSP. The first relates to the analysis by the French government of European disunity and the constant dissension among partners as much in evidence during the Gulf crisis as over the Yugoslavian conflict. In her resistance to the break up of Yugoslavia, France in the first phase found herself in disagreement successively with Bonn and Rome on the recognition of Slovenia and Croatia and with London on the wisdom of armed intervention. Similarly, during the Gulf War, the difficulty that some of her partners had in going from condemnation to participation in the UN intervention provoked some critical questioning in Paris about the developing CFSP. This led France not to favour such procedures (notably with regard to decision-making) as might result in a minimalist, lowest common denominator foreign policy which then could in some cases obstruct a more assertive French policy. This was explained by the Foreign Minister, Dumas, who declared: 'France is prepared to endow Europe with the means of her ambitions if our partners are in a similar frame of mind and if political aspirations are strong enough to overcome the inertia of multifarious national traditions.'[37]

A second explanation can be offered of the discrepancy between the discourse on objectives and France's actual negotiating position. It stems from the fact that, faithful to his conviction that 'time must be given time', Mitterrand favoured a gradual process which in the name of pragmatism, excluded any radical reform of the CFSP. France's affirmation of this objective – like that of the 'federalist vocation of the Union' – was not accompanied by any pressure to hasten its realization. Britain's hostility provided a convenient alibi for extending the process in time, which perfectly suited the French agenda. There is no shortage of declarations which illustrate this stance. The statement by Elisabeth Guigou, Minister for European Affairs that 'we will not have the CFSP tomorrow morning'[38] is echoed by that of M Dumas on defence: 'The WEU may become the pillar of a common defence policy.... Let us be clear. The point is not to replace current national responsibilities with a collective approach. Security is the concern of all. Defence is everyone's business. Political Union will ensure the juncture between security and defence'.[39]

At a more fundamental level the French attitude towards the CFSP is indicative of the contradictory pressures exerted on foreign policy by the ending of the Cold War. Tensions exist between the declared priority of Europeanizing foreign policy, which binds Germany to the Union but limits France's margins for manoeuvre, and the desire to maintain France's 'ranking' as a world power, a desire asserted all the more stridently as this status has been shaken by changes within Europe.

The Gulf crisis perfectly illustrated the dilemma which French foreign policy faced. In the early days, France naturally played the game of concerted European action, without ever giving up the diplomatic activism founded on her status as permanent member of the Security Council and on the Gaullist legacy of a developed policy towards the Arab world.[40] But in the second stage, after Iraq had challenged the good offices of the Europeans and contrary to the spirit of the developing CFSP, France played a purely national card in presenting a plan for the resolution of the conflict to the Security Council without consulting her partners.

The Gulf War therefore not only revealed the persistence of France's desire to play an autonomous international role[41] but also compounded questions raised by the upheavals in Europe about the whole notion of power. The failure of France's initiative of 14 January, coupled with her limited participation in military operations seems to have hastened the calling into question of the diplomatic and strategic bases of the status quo. For some observers, this could lead to 'the progressive abandonment of an exceptionalism conceived either as an end in itself or as an element effectively contributing to France's ranking in the post-Cold War era. Instead of maintaining her rank by systematically affirming her singularity, France can more easily accomplish this thanks to her influence amongst her partners in the UN, the European Union, the WEU and/or the Franco-German partnership'.[42]

But if, as seems most likely, this quest for influence is to be played out first and foremost within the European Union, the necessary compromise between Europeanization and the concern to preserve the ranking of a great power will be fraught with difficulties. For instance it is inconceivable, at least for the foreseeable future, that France would accept the Italian suggestion that, for the sake of the CFSP, its seat as a permanent member of the Security Council should be Europeanized. Unable, however, to defend wholly the institutional status quo, France has ended up by accepting that the Security Council be enlarged to include Germany and Japan, on the proviso that candidates for a permanent seat should participate in military operations. While the French government declared itself satisfied with the interpretation of the fundamental German Law given in 1994 by the Karlsruhe Constitutional Court, it still has reservations about Japan, whose Constitution forbids military interventions abroad.[43]

On the other hand, there are some signs pointing to the abandonment of singularity. They can for instance be seen in the field which to date has best epitomized French exceptionalism, that is defence. The lessons of the Gulf War and the Yugoslavian conflict, together with the need to reflect upon a European system of defence, have led to a further erosion of the dogma of national independence. The compromise on the role of the WEU brought about by the Maastricht Treaty, and improved relations with NATO, manifested notably in the agreement on Eurocorps in late 1992, are all signs of an evolution which the White Paper on defence of March 1994 confirms. This text reaffirms very clearly indeed the priority given to the European and multinational dimension of defence, the modalities of whose implementation remain to be clarified.

It is difficult therefore in the present situation to differentiate between that which results from clear political choices and that which flows from incremental adjustments. But, as is evident in the following statement by the then Foreign Minister, Alain Juppé, made at a recent Conference of Ambassadors, there is an undeniable shift at least at the level of discourse:

It is necessary that all our embassies in non-EU countries take European policy into account. The external action of the Union is sometimes perceived as offending our national policy or competing with it. . . . This is an erroneous impression, at best a reaction which should be corrected. It is your role, as ambassadors of France, both to assert the identity of European Union and to explain the specific positions defended by France within the institutions thereof. It is without reservations therefore, that you will endeavour, wherever you are, to affirm the political identity of the Union.[44]

NOTES

1 F. de La Serre and P. Moreau-Defarges, 'France, a penchant for leadership', in C. Hill (ed.), *European Political Cooperation and National Foreign Policies*, London, George Allen and Unwin, 1983, pp.56–71.
2 Christian Lequesne, *Paris–Bruxelles, Comment se fait la politique européenne de la France*, Paris, Presses de la FNSP, 1993, pp.134–74.
3 Samy Cohen, *La monarchie nucléaire*, Paris, Hachette, 1986; and 'Diplomatie: le syndrome de la présidence omnisciente', *Esprit*, September 1990, pp.55–64.
4 F. Mitterrand, *Réflexions sur la politique étrangère de la France*, Paris, Fayard, 1987, p.7.
5 Interview on TFI, 16 June 1981, *La politique étrangère de la France, Textes et documents* (juillet–août 1981), Paris, La Documentation Française, p.49.
6 The phrase was coined by J. Huntzinger in 'La politique étrangère du parti Socialiste', *Politique Etrangère*, 2, 1975.
7 'I am convinced that the big European countries – Germany, Great Britain, Italy and France – are desirous of playing a useful role.'
8 Interview in *Le Monde*, 28 May 1981.
9 For further details, see S. Nuttall, *European Political Cooperation*, Oxford, Clarendon Press, 1992, pp.183–91.
10 Interview in *Le Monde*, 2 December 1981.
11 Address by C. Cheysson given at the XVIII session of the WEU Assembly on 15 June 1982, *La politique étrangère de la France*, op.cit., April–June 1982, p.156.
12 'Acquis' might roughly be defined as: that which in any given field has been acquired over time to the point where it constitutes a discernible legacy. In this sense the 'acquis politique' is the set of attitudes and procedures attaching to EPC, which new entrants to the EC/EU are expected to accept.
13 See, among other statements, the interview given on 14 June 1982: 'Argentina has violently attacked and she was wrong. As to the problem of sovereignty proper, it is something which should be discussed ... France, which is in a relation of solidarity with Great Britain, does not want to be drawn into any operation whatsoever which might be seen as a rupture with Latin America, which is dear to us.'
14 *La politique étrangère de la France*, op.cit., November–December 1981.
15 F. Mitterrand, *Réflexions sur la politique étrangère de la France*, op.cit., p.68.
16 Ibid., p.56.
17 Ibid., pp.183–208.
18 Ibid., p.296.
19 See among others, the speech made in The Hague on 7 February 1984. Ibid., pp.267–70 and the *Memorandum* presented by France before the Milan meeting of the European Council: 'France would like to see prospects organised around four themes: a Europe of technology (to be built), a Europe of citizens (to be speeded up), an economic and social Europe (to be improved), a European

Union to be created as the sketch for a political entity which some of us are yearning for.'

20   Speech given to the European Parliament, ibid., p.293.
21   Text of the Franco-German proposal, *Le Monde*, 29 June 1985.
22   See S. Nuttall, op.cit.
23   See comments on EPC made by Roland Dumas, particularly the minutes of the ministerial meeting held on 12 February 1985, in *La politique étrangère de la France*, op.cit., January–February 1985, p.43. See also the interview given to Vorwaerste, *La politique étrangère de la France*, op.cit., May–June 1985, p.147.
24   *La politique étrangère de la France*, op.cit., January–February 1985, p.43.
25   'La défense de la France. Proposition pour un renouveau', RPR, June 1985. 'Défendre l'Europe. Propositions de l'U.D.F.', March 1984. On this debate, see Nicole Gnesotto, 'Les partis politiques français et la coopération franco-allemande', in K. Kaiser and P. Lellouche (eds) *Le couple franco-allemand et la défense de l'Europe*, Travaux et Recherches de l'IFRI, Paris 1986, pp.59–67.
26   F. Mitterrand, *Réflexions sur la politique étrangère de la France*, op.cit., p.98.
27   F. Heisbourg, 'Le changement dans la continuité', *Politique Etrangère*, 2, 1985, p.392. See also the speech given by Chirac, then Prime Minister, to the Institut des Hautes Etudes de Défense Nationale on 12 September 1986: 'Here I would like to stress that while the survival of a nation depends upon her borders, her security depends on the borders of her neighbours.'
28   Only Community business proper belongs to the province managed jointly by the Elysée and Matignon. See S. Cohen, 'La politique étrangère entre l'Elysée et Matignon', *Politique Etrangère*, 3, 1989, pp.487–502.
29   'If Libya was cited in the statement of the Twelve, it is thanks to the initiative of the French delegation', declares the Minister for Foreign Affairs, J.-B. Raimond on 16 April, the day after the US raid on Tripoli. *La politique étrangère de la France*, op.cit., March–April 1986, p.43.
30   *Le Monde*, 29 October 1987.
31   F. de La Serre, 'The scope of national adaption to EPC', in A. Pijpers, E. Regelsberger and W. Wessels (eds), *European Political Cooperation in the 1980s*, Dortrecht, Martinus Nijhoff, 1988, pp.194–210.
32   That is, an updating; Claire Trean, 'La France et le nouvel ordre Européen', *Politique Etrangère*, 3, 1990, pp.132–46.
33   Stanley Hoffman, 'La France et le nouvel ordre Européen', *Politique Etrangère*, 3, 1990, pp.503–13.
34   See the text of the various Franco-German proposals in F. Laursen and S. Van Hoonacker (eds), *The Intergovernmental Conference on Political Union*, Maastricht, European Institute of Public Administration, 1992.
35   Moreover, it is significant that the implementation of Title V of the Maastricht Treaty did not result in any major change in the organization of the various departments of the Quai d'Orsay (Ministry of Foreign Affairs). The reform announced on 2 September 1993 left in place the dichotomy between economic and political affairs. (See F. de La Serre and P. Moreau-Defarges, op.cit., pp.61–3; C. Lequesne, op.cit., pp.83–9.) A deputy general secretary in charge of European and Economic Affairs has authority over the Department of European Cooperation, which enjoys competence over economic cooperation and bilateral relations with the Twelve and with nations applying to join. The CFSP department remains under the authority of the other deputy general secretary in charge of Politics and Security Affairs. The only innovations concern the merging of the former EPC working groups into Council working groups and the presence, within the Permanent Representation in Brussels of a senior counsellor in charge of CFSP.

36 Statement by R. Dumas, *Le Monde*, 31 October 1991.

37 Interview given to *Le Monde*, 12 March 1991.

38 Interview given to *Le Monde*, 23–4 June 1991.

39 Statement to the National Assembly, 10 October 1991. *La politique étrangère de la France*, op.cit., September–October 1991.

40 For example, trips to Baghdad undertaken by M Vauzelle, President of the Commission on Foreign Affairs at the National Assembly in the beginning of January 1991 and by several unofficial envoys with a view to preserving a channel of communication with Iraq.

41 It is significant here that in his first televised speech after the Gulf War, President Mitterrand did not once mention Europe.

42 F. Heisbourg, 'La France et la crise du Golfe', in N. Gnesotto and J. Roper, (eds), *L'Europe occidentale et le Golfe*, Institut d'études de sécurité de l'UEO, Paris, 1991, p.37.

43 On this point see the agreement between statements made by Roland Dumas to *Le Monde*, 12 March 1991, and those of the then Minister for Foreign Affairs, Alain Juppé, *Le Monde*, 25–6 December 1994.

44 Speech to the Conference of Ambassadors given by Alain Juppé, Paris, 1 September 1994, *Bulletin d'Information du Ministère des Affaires Etrangères*.

Chapter 2

Germany's role in the CFSP

'Normalität' or 'Sonderweg'?

Reinhardt Rummel

INTRODUCTION

When in the second half of 1994 Germany held the Presidency of the European Union (EU) the Federal Republic and, in fact, Europe were not the same as on the last occasion that Bonn had routinely taken on the office in the Community, in 1988. Within days of 1 July 1994 President Clinton had offered Bonn a 'unique relationship' with Washington, the German Federal Constitutional Court had accepted armed military peacekeeping missions and President Mitterrand had invited the 294th Panzergrenadier-bataillon to ride down the Champs Elysées on Bastille Day. These unrelated events demonstrated that united Germany now operates from a strategically new position. It also operates in a radically new international context: with Russian troops gone home, Moscow participating in the Group of Seven meeting of leading industrial nations and signing the 'Partnership for Peace' with the North Atlantic Treaty Organization (NATO) as well as concluding the 'Partnership and Cooperation Agreement' with the EU, the European integration process is definitely placed in a new world.

For Germany, as for any other of the member states of the EU, co-operation in foreign and security policy has continued to be both a way to shape Europe's integration and a means to adapt to change in the international arena. For twenty-five years, at first during the times of European Political Cooperation (EPC) and then since the establishment of Common Foreign and Security Policy (CFSP), Bonn has been one of the most active in the dual process of building consensus among an ever larger group of European countries and of rendering the external reach of this group commensurate with its economic potential. Despite the fact that this attempt has not been leading very far (as compared to the external relations of the Community), Bonn was among those profiting most from collective foreign and security policy, because history had pushed the Federal Republic into multilateral internationalism, leaving little room for alternatives.

Since Germany has been united and has recovered its full sovereignty and since it is now surrounded by friendly neighbours on all sides questions have been raised as to whether Bonn will continue or discontinue its traditional adherence to the European integration process. If the largest country of the EU were to shift its orientation and to follow a more unilateralist path, the impact on the other members, on the Union as a whole, and on the political order in Europe could be dramatic. This would also be the case, if Germany, while complying with the economic and monetary provisions of the Maastricht Treaty, decided either to refrain from developing political union further (and specifically its foreign and security policy branch) or to push even harder to communitarize CFSP than it has done so far.

Will the new Federal Republic participate as an ordinary member country ('Normalität') or will it follow a special path ('Sonderweg')? The analysis of this chapter concludes that Germany will continue to regard European integration as its prime objective and the CFSP as a major vehicle for it.[1] At the present stage Bonn regards widening the Union towards the East as CFSP's first priority, and one which can only be achieved successfully via a substantial deepening of the European Union.

THE GERMAN QUESTION AND EPC/CFSP: BEFORE, DURING AND AFTER UNIFICATION

The core function of EPC/CFSP for Bonn has shifted over time and was different before, during and after German unification. Unlike its partners Germany has had to live with particularly burdensome circumstances. It has suffered more than others from the dividing line which split Europe and Germany apart during the Cold War. It has had to reunite the country in the midst of the most unstable international environment, and now again it has to carry the largest burden – most of the costs of instability and transformation in Eastern Europe – since Europe has become 'whole and free'. Germany's position on the European front line has not been the only factor in determining Bonn's relations with EPC and CFSP but it has certainly been the most distinctive one. It has made it difficult for Germany to behave just like a 'normal' member state.

During the 1970s and the 1980s German diplomacy used EPC as an instrument to widen the scope of its foreign policy which, at that time, was relatively timid and parochial.[2] The Federal Republic and in a different way the German Democratic Republic (GDR), too, were constrained by continued allied control and by their position as political–military strongholds of their respective ideological camps. The two Germanys became members of the United Nations (UN) only in 1973. Unlike the GDR the Federal Republic demonstrated a reluctance to assert the full extent of its state interests internationally. Bonn was vulnerable to any pressure related to the German question. 'Ostpolitik' and 'détente' complicated this precarious position as both concepts were meant to alleviate the fate of the people in the East while leaving the structurally antagonistic East–West divide untouched. For reasons of legitimation and credibility Bonn needed Western partners and institutions to protect itself against political pressure and to operate internationally without being suspected – by proponents in the East as well as in the West – of renewed German hegemonial ambitions.

Next to NATO and the Western European Union (WEU) the Community and its diplomatic companion EPC were the most important of the frameworks which not only salved the Federal Republic's psychological problems but assured Bonn's Western orientation ('Westbindung') and helped to keep the German unification question open ('Offenhalte-Politik'). At the same time the contractual and practical integration of Germany in Western networks and alliances guaranteed a certain amount of influence on Bonn's external behaviour. Group discipline within these circles was taken seriously by the Federal Republic. This policy of 'Einbindung' was as much in the interest of the Federal Republic as it was in the interest of its neighbours and allies. The longer this policy lasted the more Bonn became emancipated, shrugging off elements of archaic control as in WEU, and increasingly using the setup for its own purposes. Within EPC, however, German diplomats continued to abide by the spirit of solidarity.

Up to the fall of the Wall Bonn relied mainly on NATO to assure its vital interests. In sensitive questions concerning the legal status of the Federal Republic or German–German relations it would draw on the so-called Berlin Group (the three allied Western powers plus the Federal Republic). In critical situations arising from conflicts with the East Germans or the Soviets it used to trust in the close link with Washington. Questions on the divided German nation did not figure on EPC's agenda. EPC was regarded as the place where foreign policy issues were to be treated. Bonn declared that German–German relations were intra-German relations, just as trade between the FRG and the GDR was rated as intra-German trade. For the Federal Republic EPC, therefore, was more of a diplomatic sideshow, a training ground in collective foreign policy, and a component of the European process of community building, than a central frame of reference for questions of national survival. This was obvious, when to the surprise of many including the Germans themselves unification came about within a few months in 1990.

The dash to German unification started with Chancellor Kohl's ten-point plan of November 1989 for a confederation of the two states. It led to the monetary union of the two states in July 1990, and was completed with the merger of the new Länder into the old Federal Republic in the following October.[3] While the internal marriage of the two states was almost exclusively a bilateral enterprise with Helmut Kohl rejecting Jacques Delors' offer to communitarize part of the unification policy, the external aspects of unification were managed within the so-called Two-plus-Four Group:

Bonn and East Berlin together negotiated with France, the UK, the USA and the Soviet Union the treaty which ends all their rights on the territory of the FRG and the GDR and re-establishes full sovereignty for Germany.[4] Bonn's EPC partners were informed about the procedural formula for unification adopted in February 1990 in Ottawa by the six on the fringes of a meeting of the two alliances, NATO and Warsaw Pact. During their ministerial session in Dublin later that month, the Twelve devoted a large part of their discussions to the German question, welcoming the Ottawa decisions. EPC had no direct role or say in the negotiations. Paradoxically the Community had only minor influence in those questions which affected its existence in a major way. The political deficit of a European construction without a true foreign and security policy could not have been more obvious. Unification was negotiated on the domestic and the international level, not on the European level.

Neither the pressure of some of Germany's EC partners – nor the demands of EC Commissioner Andriessen who claimed that Chapter III of the Single European Act (SEA) justified the participation of EPC – could involve the Community in the negotiations of either the internal and/or external aspects of German unification. There were no legal bases for it. The fact that the German governments had chosen to bring about unification via Article 23 of the Basic Law, and a simple extension of the number of German Länder from eleven to sixteen, denied Brussels the chance to apply Article 237 of the Rome Treaty.[5] For the first time an enlargement of the Community occurred without increasing the number of member states. It was also brought about against the previously declared determination by the Twelve that no enlargement would be considered before the completion of the Single Market at the end of 1992.

Most nations in Europe were rather worried during these weeks of rapid and significant change. Some were undecided as to whether they should reject or welcome German unity while knowing that, in reality, they had no choice but to accept what the people on the streets of Leipzig and Dresden had asked for. Some had the sense of a major upset in the power balance in Europe, the danger of an uncontrolled process of reshuffling of alliances, and saw Germany now as a loose cannon. With these concerns in the background a special session of the European Council was held in April 1990 in order to get assurances that Germany would remain a faithful participant and promoter of the integration process, while resisting the temptation to ask for a special status. At this meeting the twelve Heads of State and Government and the President of the Commission accepted and supported the mode of German unification and the implicit enlargement of the Community.[6]

The concern in Western Europe now shifted to the assumption that Chancellor Kohl's preoccupation with German unity might slow down the process of European integration, including the proposed economic and monetary union and the establishment of a Single Market by the end of 1992. In December 1989 the European Council in Strasbourg had already declared that German unity should be embedded in the perspective of the European integration. When German unification started to quicken in the spring of 1990, most EC leaders felt that the process toward European union should also be accelerated. Bonn was anxious to demonstrate that it was continuing down the path of integration and urged its partners to make an extra effort to this end. With their common initiative in April 1990 to develop the Community into the European Union Chancellor Kohl and President Mitterrand suggested that the already scheduled intergovernmental conference on economic and monetary matters should extend its scope and that a second such conference on political matters should be held at the same time. While the Franco-German push for monetary union had been more or less accepted by EC member countries, there was still a great reluctance to render the Community more democratic and to extend its competences in the fields of foreign and security policy, and home affairs. France itself showed signs of lukewarmness during the process.

To Bonn's surprise its European allies seemed to be satisfied with German assurances that the united country would be prepared to give up the symbol of its strength, the Deutschmark, and remain a faithful member of NATO.[7] The German desire to develop the external and defence component of the Union and to tie Germany and its eleven partners firmly into it was not regarded as essential by some of its EPC partners. In particular, France and the UK were not prepared, as Bonn was, to communitarize external relations and security matters. Successive proposals were watered down by them.[8] The second and third pillars of the Treaty of the EU (TEU) and the envisaged institutional progress turned out to be rather weak. The only concession which Bonn achieved was the inclusion of an evolution clause which may be used effectively in the 1996 revision process.

Since, against all expectations, Germany continued after unification to play the role of the 'Musterknabe' of integration, why still worry? Some expected a united Germany to dominate the unification process and to lift itself above the group of the other big member states (i.e. France, UK, Italy and Spain). However, with the exception of a larger German parliamentary representation Bonn refrained from any claims on its EC/EPC partners which could have been based on the new size of the country. Bonn did not seem to dream of a Community leadership role and it did not enjoy a visibly greater influence among the Twelve either.[9] On the contrary, Bonn was confronted with the assumption of its neighbours that German policy, supported by nationalist and neutralist forces particularly in the East of the country, would turn more inward looking, a fear which has partly materialized, as we shall see later. The opposite assumption was also made: that Germany would conduct a more independent outward-looking foreign policy. In that case it would profit from its new political and economic potential and would, under the cover of pan-European bridge building, forge a partnership with the Soviet Union or even aspire to a nuclear option of its own.[10] Each of these extremist ideas would have meant the end of the concept of a communitarian foreign policy.

This hypothetical debate underestimated the fundamental change which had occurred with German unification.[11] The main reason which had kept (or could have kept) Bonn from intensifying the Community (the Federal Republic did not want to do anything which could endanger German reunification and positive relations with Eastern Europe) was overcome. The breaking of the German blockage enables for the first time in Bonn's view the creation of a real common foreign and security policy. Even those in the political spectrum who traditionally opposed the 'militarization of the Community', like the left in the Social Democrats and the Greens, are now partly for it. Their argument is that a sovereign Germany needs as many multilateral ties as possible in addition to that with a weakened NATO. This may be a double miscalculation. First, in order to bring about a collective foreign and security policy, and to develop the European Union as a whole, more preconditions have to be met: other member states will have to be prepared to share national sovereignty on the same scale as the Germans. So the plan may not materialize. If it does, and this might be the second miscalculation, Germany may have to comply with the military traditions of its neighbours and become more 'defencist' against its will.[12] While the German government practised a policy of non-consultation with EPC during the Two-plus-Four negotiations, it has made up for it by unblocking and advancing the integration process into security matters and potentially into defence. No wonder that CFSP is now at the forefront of Germany's integrationist ambitions.

In the four years since unification Germany has learnt to live with the new situation inside and outside the country. Not only are the costs of unification much higher than expected, but it will take much longer before the economic and mental rift between the East German and the West German population can be overcome. At a time when Germany had to go through the worst economic recession since the inception of the Federal Republic the country had also to cope with the highest rate of unemployment and the largest inflow ever of asylum seekers, refugees and German immigrants. Increased social tension and reduced confidence in the established political parties have been the result of this aggregation of domestic problems which has put the political system of Germany to an unprecedented test. The Federal Republic is still going through a psychologically difficult period where the country is bigger but also weaker, while many of its neighbours and partners display more 'Schadenfreude' than understanding. Can the CFSP be of help in this situation? Can it be the framework where Bonn explains to its partners the interaction of internal and external challenges?

If this has not been the case so far, it will surely have to occur in the future, because in addition to internal strains the Federal Republic has had to adapt to the consequences of the end of the bipolar security system. More than any other West European country a united Germany is exposed to destabilizing centrifugal forces which have been unleashed in the eastern and southeastern part of the continent. Consequently the focus of the German government has shifted from 'Einbindung' to asserting German concerns with the non-Western part of the continent. Virtually all the political forces in Germany support this shift.[13]

But there is an additional reason for Bonn's orientation toward the East. German leaders from Adenauer to Kohl have always followed the line that German unification could only be achieved within a united Europe. Instead, what has come about has been a uniting Germany within an unfinished Union. This situation fuels further concerns as German leaders of all political shades declare the unification of Europe to be their next strategic goal. This time, Germany's vital question is not to be answered by the allied powers of Berlin, nor will it be on the agenda of NATO alone. It will become a topic no less for the EU. Now that the continuation of the German 'Westbindung' is assured, Bonn emphasizes the need for the development of the Union's structural ties with the East. The goal of Eastern enlargement and of multiplied connections with Russia and Ukraine has replaced German unification as Bonn's condition for the EU's further integration. In this context CFSP is regarded as an instrument with some untapped potential, while, so far, and now within the CFSP, the EU's external economic instruments provide most of the substance and focus.

The post-unification situation has helped Germany to avoid a 'Sonderweg' and to remain committed to European integration, but it is not helping Germany to become a normal member of CFSP. While many expect the Federal Republic to take on more responsibility in Europe and beyond (see President Clinton's notion of a unique partnership), Bonn's Finance Minister knows that the huge transfers to the new Länder do not allow Germany in the medium term to support international activities in the expected range, and Bonn's Ministers for Foreign Affairs and for Defence know that it will take time before the Germans will participate in a normal way in international collective security operations. Although the constellation of European forces has changed fundamentally, the Germans remain preoccupied with their specific situation, internally and to the East.

STRUCTURAL PREFERENCE: COMBINING THE FRANCO-GERMAN CORE AND THE TRANSATLANTIC PARTNERSHIP

The institutional and power structures in Western Europe (and Europe as a whole) have changed dramatically in recent years. Germany has been an object of these changes as well as contributing to them. New multilateral organizations have been installed (such as the G-24, the European Bank for Reconstruction and Development and the North Atlantic Cooperation Council) and old ones have been reformed (particularly the UN, NATO and CSCE). Against this background an analysis of the Community's foreign policy-making reveals the situation in just one corner of a much wider area of structural change in the Atlantic–Eurasian setting. Within this context of interlocking institutions where the Twelve are represented as a group and as individual states the development from EPC to CFSP occurred in two main respects: the range of issues to be included in coordinated actions was widened and the institutional mode to achieve efficiency was improved. Germany has been a driving force in both evolutions but its precise impact is hard to determine in detail. One can, however, highlight some of the areas where Bonn has demonstrated engagement.

Traditionally, the German debate on 'Europapolitik' has focused on trade, monetary and financial issues and less on questions of foreign policy, security and defence. This asymmetry was regarded as natural: like the Federal Republic the Community was perceived as an economic giant and a political dwarf. During the 1980s this attitude started to change. Bonn, together with Paris, felt that the West Europeans needed a stronger security and defence identity, at first in order to deal with American initiatives such as the Strategic Defence Initiative, later in order to meet constructively Gorbachev's policy of liberalization and the transformation of Eastern Europe. Like other members Germany therefore supported initiatives to extend West European cooperation and integration into security matters and eventually into defence.

During its presidency in the first half of 1983 Bonn helped to bring about the Stuttgart Declaration which includes the political and economic aspects of security in EPC activities. The SEA three years later did not go beyond this point but by then the WEU had been revitalized (in 1984) and its Platform on European Security Interests of 1987 was intended as a contribution to the broadening of the process of European unification. A further step was made at Maastricht when the Twelve followed the Kohl–Mitterrand suggestions of December 1990, pressing for the first time to include all security questions in EPC, to connect WEU to the Political Union, and to strengthen NATO via a European pillar. The extension of the subject matter from foreign policy via security to defence was obviously more than just widening the Union's agenda. It also meant to connect operationally existing institutions like NATO and WEU with new ones like CFSP, to sort out priorities and commitments among member states, and to combine organizations with different functions, decision-making procedures, and memberships. It also sought to find ways of keeping the transatlantic alliance compatible with European integration.

For Bonn this translated mainly into close relations with Paris as well as with Washington. Since the Federal Republic's membership with NATO and its renunciation of nuclear weapons Germany has been dependent on Washington's extended nuclear protection. Although the circumstances have now faded where Germany might need to draw on such guarantees it still would like to rely on the USA in case of a renewed nuclear threat or a reconstitution of aggressive military power comparable to that formerly posed by the Soviet Union. Germany believes that it needs this last resort as it has reconfirmed its non-nuclear status in the Two-plus-Four treaty and as neither France nor the UK have been able to provide such guarantees. This is one of the prime reasons why Germany continues to keep up the Atlantic Alliance and to support its adaptation to a new security environment in Europe and the world. The German government handles all initiatives (such as a European security and defence identity) which might impact negatively on NATO with great care. In this regard Bonn sides with London rather than with Paris which has been regarding the post-Cold War situation as an opportunity to get rid of the American predominance in European security.

Germany's close relations with France, which date back to the conclusion of the Elysée Treaty in 1963, stem from a different source: to overcome the tragic past and to build together a peacefully united Europe. To this end the two countries have been cooperating closer than with any other one of their partners. This was symbolized by the establishment of joint councils on economic and monetary questions as well as on security and defence matters (1988) in order to coordinate policies and to launch common initiatives. Over time the Franco-German pairing has gradually become the engine of the European integration process, either by proposals such as that on common foreign and security policy or by multilateral enterprises such as the Franco-German Corps, which can be and has been joined by other European partners. For the Federal Republic the special relationship with France has had a similar function to the cooperation within EPC: providing recognition and scope for German diplomacy. But beyond this, the liaison with Paris was a symbol of Bonn's determination to create a peaceful and constructive neighbourhood in Europe. Since German reunification the special relationship with Paris has not been reduced; indeed it has been intensified. German leaders regard cooperation between the two neighbours as a dry run ('Probelauf') or model for the recommended development of the Union.[14] Bonn needs this close ally to keep the European integration process going and to serve the concept of a wider integrated Europe. To this latter end, Bonn and Paris have started to form a trilateral team together with Poland.[15]

Seen from Bonn relations with Paris and relations with Washington have been more important than the consultation in EPC or CFSP. As France preferred a certain distance to NATO and given the strategic position of Germany, Bonn has had a greater say in NATO than in EPC or WEU. This is about to change. Since the end of the Cold War security has become more of a political and economic challenge reducing part of NATO's significance which continues to be heavily based on military policy. WEU and the EU have become important actors in bringing about stability in Eastern Europe. Moreover, France has returned to cooperate more closely with NATO in areas of collective security[16] and the Clinton administration is supporting a European security and defence identity. For all these reasons the tension which used to exist between the American and the French concepts of the new security architecture in Europe has been considerably eased. This also makes it easier for Germany to put more weight on the substance of CFSP and WEU and to regard their development as a contribution to the strengthening of both the European Union and the Atlantic Alliance.

In Bonn (as in Paris) the memory of the events of October 1991 is still vivid. Then German Foreign Minister Genscher almost simultaneously helped to launch two initiatives: one with French Foreign Minister Dumas on the development of a European defence policy based on WEU and the Eurocorps and the other with US Secretary of State Baker on the building of a North Atlantic Cooperation Council designed to connect NATO to the group of former Warsaw Pact members. Paris, trying hard to reduce and, if possible, to replace American leadership was furious about Washington's perpetuated dominance in European security and Germany's compliance with it. Unlike the Germans the French invest a great deal of national pride and prestige in the question of who is in command, politically and militarily. Starting with the revitalization of WEU and the formation of the Franco-German brigade France has been keen to demonstrate to the USA that there was some potential for autonomous European action. Bonn went along with France while trying to lure Paris closer back into the Alliance. But not before the January 1994 NATO summit did the USA come up with two propositions which enabled the French and the Europeans to deal constructively with their continuing dependence on American assets.[17] Washington offered to provide WEU with NATO-assigned (American) infrastructure such as communication facilities, satellite surveillance and airlift capabilities. Second, the USA proposed the establishment of Combined Joint Task Forces, composed in an ad hoc fashion of forces from sources inside and outside NATO for collective security purposes. The command in this case would depend on the circumstances.

With these innovations a first bridge was built between the formerly incompatible positions of Paris and Washington. Bonn, which was partly involved in preparing these initiatives, welcomed the proposals whole-heartedly as they seemed to promise that a way had been invented to get around the perennial dilemma of having to choose between Paris and Washington. Certainly, problems of practical implementation remain and many questions still need to be answered, such as who is providing the political assessment and orientation in a given crisis: NATO, WEU or CFSP? NATO documents describe the alliance as the essential framework for security.[18] At least since the Petersberg Declaration of June 1992 WEU, which has transferred all military structures to NATO, has regarded itself as an independent body with major tasks of its own ranging from collective defence via peacekeeping to emergency missions. On the other hand the EU uses WEU as an instrument to deal with defence implications of the Union's foreign and security policy. Likewise the economic aspects of CFSP are kept separate from the external relations of the Community, at least in terms of decision-making. Bonn and Paris had rejected the Dutch proposal of September 1991 to integrate all three pillars of the EU into one.[19] All this means that no permanent way has yet been found to organize a powerful single authority for Western Europe's external activities.

Germany was among those member states which tried to improve the institutional mode so as to achieve more efficiency in common foreign and security policy. In preparation for the SEA Bonn had supported the idea of a secretariat for EPC based in Brussels in order to strengthen the central authority and to achieve a better coordination of various policy components on the European level. However, the German proposal to appoint a political personality as head of the secretariat was not picked up by the majority of the member states.[20] When in 1990 Germany, this time together with France, once again made the proposition to concentrate more decision-making power in Brussels and raise the influence of the European Council by providing it with a secretariat of its own, this was turned down by the Dutch, the Belgians and others. They had the repeated suspicion that Germany, by following French diplomacy, might willingly or unwillingly weaken the communitarian core of the integration structure.

In fact, the Franco-German propositions seemed to be inspired more by the semi-presidential French system than by German federalism. This was also confirmed by the fact that, as in French foreign policy, the Parliament was not given much of a role in the Mitterrand–Kohl letter of December 1990. Apparently the German side had no other choice than to give up on more ambitious plans to democratize the Union. Once CFSP was constitutionally placed outside the Rome Treaty framework the only way in which parliamentary initiative and control could come in was via those common actions financed by the Community budget. One has to understand the importance of this issue in German 'Europapolitik'. The Germans, in large majority, are happy with the results of economic integration in Europe, but they are convinced that this success will not last unless it is accompanied by political integration. Political integration to them is a question of the political system of the Union; it means first and foremost an improvement in democratic control and in the political participation of the citizens. In sectional terms it means going beyond economic and monetary union and including both foreign and security policy and home affairs in the integration process.

During the ratification debate of the TEU in the Bundestag only two issues were discussed in a controversial way, one was the criteria for entering the monetary union, the other was the democratic deficit of the Union. All the opposition parties blamed Kohl for having surrendered on the strengthening of the European Parliament (EP) despite previous promises.[21] The Chancellor had promised to make sure that there would be a balance between economic and political union in the new treaty. In his remarks during that Bundestag debate, Karsten Voigt, a prominent foreign policy expert of the Social Democrat opposition, referred to the need for the democratization of the Union, particularly in the field of foreign and security policy. In the German interpretation the parliament is a major element in the political acceptance of decisions in economic and monetary policy as well as in foreign and security policy and therefore an important contributor to the efficiency of such a policy.[22] The German Federal Court in its October 1993 ruling on TEU was very clear in determining that the democratic foundations of the Union will have to be expanded in parallel and commensurate with the scope of integration.[23] In other words, a German government can only transfer further sovereignty if the EP is given a more important role in the policy-making process of the Union.

While other member governments had to undergo painful moments during their TEU referenda, leaders in Bonn saw only marginal signs of opposition to Maastricht. The provisions for CFSP, an important issue in Denmark, France and the UK, were hardly mentioned by the German critics. As opinion polls show, Germans are in their large majority in favour of integration in the foreign policy and defence sector.[24] Certainly, it would make not much sense to ask people's opinion specifically on CFSP, because knowledge of the matter is very poor. Except for the question of German military missions abroad there is hardly any public debate of German external interests and how to deal with them.[25] When in the autumn of 1993 the Prime Minister of Bavaria, Edmund Stoiber, squarely confronted the centralism of Brussels and asked for a more rigorous implementation of the principle of subsidiarity he singled out foreign and security policy among the few areas where unified action among the Twelve was justified and needed.

The only other subject of strategic importance for CFSP and the structure of the Union that has produced some public controversy in Germany and beyond was the concept of the 'core group'. In September 1994, one month before the federal elections in Germany, the leadership of the CDU/CSU faction in the Bundestag launched a position paper on the future development of the EU, advocating a group of five states to form a core in the further integration process.[26] This idea was motivated by the need to keep the EU efficient despite enlargement and in order to advance the integration process now even if some member states would only be willing or able to join the process later. The two-tier or three-tier Europe had already been central to academic discussion of the 1970s and 1980s, but never before has there been such a proposal by a group of German politicians. Wolfgang Schäuble, Kohl's closest political companion, was in the lead. Chancellor Kohl as well as Foreign Minister Kinkel made clear during this debate that Bonn's continuous priority was to promote integration of all EU member states and to achieve congruency of memberships in EU, WEU, and – concerning its European pillar – also in NATO. The larger opposition parties in Germany, especially the Social Democrats, rejected the core group idea as well.

While the TEU legitimizes the idea that some countries may enter the third stage of monetary union earlier than others, it is hard to see how a core group concept would be spelled out in CFSP unless individual member states were unilaterally to opt out (e.g. Denmark). It remains highly unlikely in the foreseeable future that a German government will choose such a high profile approach and present a core group proposition to its EU partners. The Germans are very interested in making CFSP more efficient but they will continue to emphasize other ways in this regard: more communitarization, more common actions, more institutional coherence, more parliamentary participation, more central competence. Such a path is both largely shared by a few partners in the EU and dramatically opposed by others. It is therefore fair to conclude that, concerning the development of the structural fabric of CFSP, Bonn is not following a Sonderweg. With its public debate on the most desirable path of further integration, ignited by the Schäuble proposition, Germany does in fact demonstrate considerable normality.

POLICY PRIORITIES: EXTENDING THE ZONE OF EUROPEAN STABILITY

For Germany, the transition from EPC to CFSP was intended to involve more than including security matters and improving the institutional setup. It also marked the ambition of determining more precisely the external profile of the EU. This objective was followed up by fixing the areas of common concern in a somewhat theoretical enterprise in the 'Report on the Likely Development of the Common Foreign and Security Policy with a View to Identifying Areas Open to Joint Action' (June 1992, the Lisbon Report). This document identifies a limited number of geographical regions and functional issues as well as international conflict and crisis management as key fields of the EU's external interest. Given Germany's geopolitical position Bonn is clearly more interested in Central and Eastern Europe than in the Maghreb, the Middle East or any other region in the world. When it comes to the horizontal domains such as strengthening democratic principles, peaceful conflict resolution, the respect of human and minority rights, controlling arms proliferation, terrorism and the traffic in illicit drugs, then Germany is at the forefront of countering all of these challenges. On the other hand, in conflict and crisis management Bonn has been displaying some reticence in all those cases where military force had to be used. In this respect, as in the previous section, it will be hard to specify the German role in specific policies within EPC and CFSP.

Since the inception of the Federal Republic Bonn has pursued a policy of reconciliation with the former foes of Germany and has renounced the use of force to realize national interests, in favour of multilateral diplomacy. Haunted by the militaristic German past all governments in Bonn interpreted the German Basic Law as excluding not only unilateral military intervention, but also multilateral peacekeeping missions.[27] Consequently they refused to deploy the Bundeswehr except for the defence of NATO territory. None of the violations of the UN Charter and the CSCE Charter principles, as they occurred from Iraq to Bosnia, were able to change German politicians' minds. In its July 1994 ruling, however, the Federal Constitutional Court made it plain that there are no legal obstacles to sending German forces on UN mandated combat missions.[28] This came as a relief at the operational level of German foreign and security policy. Bonn could now enter into military planning, force restructuring, and training to prepare for peacekeeping missions and, more importantly, German diplomats and military experts could now join in with their partners in WEU, NATO, CSCE and the UN. Given the plans for WEU to become the EU's military arm and to engage primarily in peacekeeping operations Germany had finally fulfilled the preconditions for ending its opting out status and for participating fully in defence cooperation. Bonn had become 'europafähig' (Euro-fit) in this dynamic field of integration.

On the political level it remains to be seen whether leaders in Germany will be more inclined than in the past to engage the Bundeswehr in collective security tasks. To many among the Free Democrats, the Social Democrats and the Greens who used to hide comfortably behind legal arguments in order to avoid a political decision, the Court ruling came as a disappointment. They at least have the consolation that the Court demands a consultation with the Bundestag before a German government can send troops to the peace front ('Parlamentsheer').[29] For historical reasons many countries in Europe will not like to see German soldiers on their soil in a crisis management operation. In this regard all German governments act within the tradition of sensitivity known as the 'Kohl Doctrine'.[30] On the other hand the German population knows that the country can no longer abstain from displaying solidarity in international efforts at collective security. Yet, so far, it is proving hard for Germans (particularly East Germans) to understand and accept the reasons for and obligations of international intervention.

For the time being it is hardly conceivable that any government in Bonn would lead or even suggest a military action abroad as the USA has done many times over and Paris has done recently in Rwanda. Germany will rather be active in all those areas where it has a long tradition of international participation, such as humanitarian help, mediation, or political, technical and financial assistance. A typical initiative in this regard was the British–German proposal to strengthen the instruments of world-wide coordination of assistance during emergencies. The plan was discussed in EPC and then presented to the UN General Assembly, which in its 1991 session adopted the concept. Another example is the Franco-German proposal to the Council in November of 1993 starting an EU action plan which subsequently was presented to the conflicting parties in former Yugoslavia. Its elements were: assuring humanitarian aid, the solution of the conflict in Bosnia-Herzegovina on the basis of proposals elaborated by the International Conference on the Former Yugoslavia, and a modus vivendi for Croatian territory under the UNPROFOR mandate. The outcome of this initiative within CFSP was a Joint Action named 'Humanitarian Help for Bosnia' of some ECU 48m of which the European Commission agreed to contribute half while the rest had to be contributed by member states. In its biannual report on European integration to the Bundestag the Federal Government puts more stress on listing such German financial and human-itarian contributions than on reporting on the diplomatic achievements or peacekeeping activities of the EU and the WEU.[31]

Nevertheless Bonn has not been absent from the diplomatic scene in former Yugoslavia. From the German participation in the very first EC observer mission to Yugoslavia[32] and the push for early recognition of the newly independent states of Slovenia and Croatia at the beginning of 1992 to the participation in the Contact Group and the demand for a lifting of the weapons embargo on Bosnia-Herzegovina, the German government has tried to exert influence. The motivation for this engagement is that Bonn wants to help to reduce violent conflict and its regional spillover in order to avoid the tremendous human and economic costs of continued fighting. In many ways, especially concerning the large inflow of war refugees, the food and technical help supplied, and the financial support for reconstruction, Germany is directly burdened. The most important stimulus for German engagement in former Yugoslavia is, however, that the principle of non-violent conflict resolution is being violated, when it needs to be defended as a major norm, so as to promote the peaceful cohabitation of nations and ethnic groups in Europe. Here again the objective of creating a peaceful and stable environment to the East of the Federal Republic is the driving force.

The Germans have been criticized for some of their initiatives in this context. With their plea for a lifting of the arms embargo for Bosnia-Herzegovina, they seem to disregard the consequences for some of their partner countries, specifically their peacekeeping forces on the ground, of which Germany has none and thus far has claimed that it is unable to deploy. The central reproach to the Germans in the recognition case was that they used a lot of pressure within the Twelve to bring about a decision the consequences of which (security guarantees) they themselves were not prepared to accept. Foreign Minister Genscher's calculation in December 1991 was that he could end the Yugoslav war by putting an effective end to the Balkan federation while others perceived that 'Germany's naïve foreign policy is fuelling a war'.[33] In the meantime, Germany has learnt that the authority which it can bring to bear depends largely on the extent to which it participates in security actions. Ironically, the blame can be extended from Germany to the Community as a whole. At least at the beginning of the Yugoslav conflict the Community had conveyed the impression that this challenge was to be regarded as its own business, but it subsequently shied away from going the extra mile.

The respect for and the implementation of human rights is one of the fields where Germany tries to strengthen its international profile. One occasion in this regard was the World Conference on Human Rights held in Vienna in June 1993. In preparation for this event Bonn had tried to convince its partners in the Community to promote two main goals: to establish the position of a high commissioner for human rights at the UN and to raise the UN budget for the protection of human rights. The first goal, at least, was achieved, and a commissioner was appointed later in 1993. An adequate increase in funds for the implementation of the proposals of the Vienna conference on human rights did not materialize but the human rights centre in Geneva received increased support.

While in the Bosnian case the public has regarded CFSP as a failure, the record of the Community's external economic policy in relations with Eastern Europe has been, in comparison, relatively successful. It managed to combine trade liberalizations, the PHARE and TACIS programmes, and the Europe and Partnership Agreements to deal with the needs which have arisen from the 1989–90 upheaval in Central and Eastern Europe. For Bonn the transition in Eastern Europe has replaced reunification at the top of the list of national priorities. The transformation of the East European countries, their political systems and societies into democratic, social, and ecological market economies is as important to Germany as the incorporation of Russia and Ukraine into the solidaristic network of both European and international institutions. This is why the German government has either initiated or supported EU commitments on enlargement, on consultative relations between CFSP and Central and Eastern European countries, and on intensifying the dialogue on foreign and security policy with both Kiev and Moscow. Among German experts the term 'Anbindung' is now used for the nature of the link with these latter two countries, without however regarding them as EU accession candidates.

France, in an attempt to learn from the mistakes made in former Yugoslavia and to avoid leaving Eastern Europe to the influence of German diplomacy and economy, launched in 1993 the Balladur Plan for a Pact of Stability and managed to have it adopted by the Twelve as a Joint Action of

CFSP. At the beginning Bonn was not happy with this proposal, because the Germans were taken by surprise and they felt that the plan would make EU enlargement more rather than less difficult. Grudgingly they now admit that French diplomacy has (again) shown how to handle diplomatic grand designs. The German Presidency in the second half of 1994 made sure it advanced work toward the planned conclusion of the Stability Pact during the French Presidency in 1995. Bonn's idea was to complement the regional discussions by a support programme which would assist local minorities and transborder cooperation in regions of potential conflict. Such projects would range from language training to the build-up of local infrastructure. These diplomatic and practical efforts of conflict prevention are based on the CSCE principles, CSCE instruments will be used, and the organization will thus be strengthened. In a joint newspaper article French Premier Balladur and Chancellor Kohl expressed their conviction that the initiative would help definitively to overcome the partition of Europe.[34]

In order to develop the all-European peace order Bonn has been pushing since the end of the 1980s for an institutionalization of CSCE and an expansion of its functions. The proposition for a small secretariat and regular meetings of the heads of state and government as well as the foreign ministers of CSCE countries was introduced by the European Council at the November 1990 CSCE summit meeting in Paris.[35] At the same occasion a German initiative, supported by the Twelve, to establish a centre for conflict prevention and for verification was endorsed, while the development of direct relations between the Council of Europe and CSCE were also discussed. Bonn has a tradition of regarding the Council of Europe as an important framework for the improvement and expansion of democratic and social standards in Europe. In a more general vein, the German government shares the analysis that today none of the security related institutions alone is capable of handling the containment of violent conflict. That is why in 1993 German diplomats introduced ideas in CFSP on 'mutually reinforcing institutions', a concept which proposes various criteria for a better coordination of the UN, CSCE, WEU, NATO and the Council of Europe concerning conflict prevention and crisis management.[36]

Stability in Europe and in other parts of the world can also be enhanced by intensified regional cooperation. Bonn, together with its EU partners, has been advocating integration among groups of countries in several parts of Europe, particularly the Visegrad Four, the Baltic Three, and the Black Sea Cooperation Council. Just as Rome invented the Pentagonale in its own neighbourhood, so Bonn was a key to the Baltic Sea cooperation. On the subnational level almost all Bundesländer are engaged in cooperative projects with either their immediate neighbours or with provinces of other countries. Outside of Europe Bonn was among the most active in fostering dialogues with other groups of countries in the world. The tradition of

Foreign Minister Hans-Dietrich Genscher, who started the first such dialogues with the ASEAN countries back in the 1970s has been continued by his successor. During the German Presidency, Klaus Kinkel was keen to initiate and to host the first meeting of the EU with SADC, now enlarged by the Republic of South Africa, and to adopt the 'Berlin Declaration' which contains among other provisions a support programme for regional integration in Southern Africa.[37]

Another field of peculiarly German involvement is regime building in the area of arms control, weapons exports, and nuclear non-proliferation. The new CSCE principles on the transfer of conventional arms are based on a CFSP plan which in turn had been initiated by Britain and Germany in 1993. The relevance of this instrument for the reduction of arms exports is obvious from the fact that CSCE (OSCE) countries hold a share of 90 per cent of global trade in weapons. According to the agreement all CSCE states are committed to transparency and caution concerning arms transfers. This is a thorny area as the CFSP countries themselves have some difficulty in complying with such principles. However, as the start of the Single Market in 1993 obliged the Twelve to begin harmonizing their arms export policies they had to find a common way of dealing with embargos and other measures of restraint (see the eight criteria for arms exports as established by the Lisbon European Council). The harmonization efforts in this area are particularly difficult given that arms export policy is closely related to the traditional understandings of sovereignty and foreign policy among member countries. Germany is in a specific dilemma here as its unilateral adherence to a more restrictive arms export control policy today renders German participation in European arms cooperation much more difficult and hampers its defence industry in taking part in the European defence industrial restructuring efforts. It thereby threatens the survival of German companies and undermines its own future leverage on the development of a harmonized but still restrictive conventional arms export control regime within the European Union.

Although (or perhaps because) Germany does not possess nuclear weapons it regards the control of such arms, their production and their export as an important area of international policy. The Nuclear Non-proliferation Treaty (NPT) expired in 1995 and it was renewed in a conference in New York early in that year – the CFSP countries campaigned for it. In October 1993 Germany introduced a proposal in CFSP to run the entire process of preparation for the NPT conference as a Joint Action. At the centre of the German plan was the proposition to stage a diplomatic offensive among the key states which had not signed the Treaty and among those NPT member states which had not yet opted for prolongation. As the CFSP countries could not agree on a common position initially Bonn decided to reintroduce its proposal in the spring of 1994 and reached approval on that occasion. The other aspects of German nuclear non-proliferation policy, as far as they are related to the International Atomic Energy Agency (IAEA), the Nuclear Suppliers' Group and the Missile Technology Control Regime (MTCR), also involve consultation within CFSP.[38] While the cooperation among the Twelve is relatively intense in these matters, the EU does not appear as an influential actor in such critical cases as North Korea, which refused in 1993 to allow IAEA special inspections. There is a determination in the German government and among experts to enhance the EU's influence in preventing proliferation.[39]

A related field to both nuclear non-proliferation and conventional arms export regulations is the control of trade in goods with a dual-use character. The German government has supported a harmonized trade policy as the corollary of a liberalized trade within the Single Market. The goal of promoting the restrictive German export control regime among the Twelve was hard to achieve. Some of the member states do not regard the potential consequences of dual-use exports as being as dangerous as others do. Their position certainly reflects the still quite different weapons export traditions among the member states. The compromise regulation which was up for decision at the Council in the autumn of 1994 only partly meets German concerns.[40] As in many other instances Bonn tries to set advanced standards which are not acceptable to some of its partners. In these cases it mostly achieves the permission to keep up its standards unilaterally – which may serve German interests but does not shape the external profile of the EU.

CFSP, like EPC before it, depends on an ever larger area of common views and policies, not on the exceptions and 'domaines reservés' of individual member states. Germany, as the largest country among the Twelve, has certainly had an influence on the major areas of CFSP's involvement in world affairs, but apart from isolated cases its ambitions, interests and values have not dominated the EU's external agenda. Certainly, a vivid personality like Genscher, who served as the head of the Auswärtiges Amt for seventeen years, left an imprint on the record of EPC/CFSP activity. Yet, in most areas Bonn was a loyal contributor and supporter rather than an initiator or front runner. Its prime geographical area was Eastern Europe; it did not show as much interest in the Mediterranean, the Middle East, or Latin America. Bonn's functional subjects were all normative non-military issues; its engagement in the military sphere was concentrated more on arms control than on armed intervention. This collection of interests in CFSP resembles more those of the smaller states, and, in this sense, Germany has displayed both 'Normalität' and 'Sonderweg'.

PERSPECTIVES: 'NORMALITÄT' AND 'SONDERWEG'

Whether Bonn will be a normal member state of the future CFSP or whether it will follow a special path is not yet clear. It will be determined by at least three factors: the political trends in Germany; the positions of other EU

member states, particularly France; and the developments in the wider
Euro-Atlantic space, especially in the USA and in Russia. Many political
analysts have stated that Germany (and Japan) have new foreign policy
options in the structure emerging after the end of the Cold War. Theor-
etically and from the perspective of traditional nation-states this may be so,
but in reality the room for choices is very narrow.[41] This does not necessarily
mean that Germany will automatically adapt to other powers' wishes; others
might converge around German concepts and priorities.

The German electorate continues to favour further European integration
by a large majority. In the June 1994 EP elections those parties which most
explicitly opposed Maastricht, the right-wing extremists Die Republikaner
and the newly established anti-Maastricht party of Manfred Brunner, a
former Chef de Cabinet of Commissioner Martin Bangemann, collected
very little support and are not to be represented at Strasbourg. Yet, there is
widespread scepticism among the pro-voters, in two main respects. Many
are disappointed with the lack of enthusiasm for integration in other
countries and, as a consequence, the absence of solidarity in the Union
when it comes to sharing the burden for some of the major challenges
facing the Twelve, such as the stabilization and transformation of Eastern
Europe. The second concern is that integration is not differentiated
enough, that the principle of subsidiarity should be applied more vigorously,
and that the degree of political control and participation should be
substantially higher.

Subsidiarity in connection with the handling of foreign and security policy
is quite a practical concept in Germany. One has to take into account the fact
that the Länder are increasingly involved in external relations. It is not only
that all of Bonn's international obligations have to be accepted by the
Bundesrat if they have direct implications for the Länder, but the Länder
themselves are represented in Brussels (in order to lobby for their interests)
and they in many ways conduct their own 'foreign policies' with neighbouring
countries, likeminded provinces and states either within the EU or outside.

Subnational foreign policy ('Neben-Aussenpolitik') is a growth industry
in Germany, (even if not yet a well-analysed field of international relations)
and it may be that against the background of increasing international
interdependence and in the confederal context of the EU German federal
foreign policy is undergoing a gradual structural change.[42]

The debate on the core group concept notwithstanding, Germany is likely
to be one of those member states which pushes most for substantial
deepening of the EU in the 1996 revision process. The key aims are to
communitarize the second and third pillars of the TEU and to enhance
democracy in the Union. The major interest is to prepare for a much larger
EU and to develop an efficient European entity, not to play the game of
power politics but to be able to cope with some of the larger challenges on
the international agenda ranging from overpopulation to pollution, from

worldwide conflict management to the control of weapons of mass destruction, and from the tasks of transformation in Eastern Europe to the avoidance of the clash of civilizations.

Bonn will follow a double strategy more visibly than in the past. It will try first to launch activity via the EU, but if this leads to no tangible success in a decent timespan, it will cooperate with a smaller group or with partners from outside the Union.[43] France and the USA are the favoured partners in such circumstances. This strategy of 'changing partners in the diplomatic dance' is more likely to be forced on Germany from outside than it would be an expression of German national strife.[44] After the phasing out of historical business with the four powers, especially with Russia, there will be few cases where Germany goes it alone. The art of coopting partners will be at a premium.

As Foreign Minister Kinkel puts it: There is no future any more in unilateral activity.[45] And Defence Minister Rühe adds that one must avoid outdated political and strategic patterns of thought: 'Within the European Union, no country can go its own way. . . . Thinking exclusively in terms of balance of power is thinking of the past – at least when we look at the process of European integration.'[46] These phrases contrast well with those of leading French politicians. In a recent interview Prime Minister Balladur was asked for his philosophy on international action, and of the four principles he mentioned the first was: 'Réserver la plus grande liberté de décision et d'action à la France.'[47] Balladur is convinced that France can continue to conduct an independent policy in world affairs. A German politician would never use the notion of 'independence' in connection with the Federal Republic's foreign policy.

CFSP will continue to be just one, if the most important, framework for German foreign and security policy. Regional and international organizations, from the Council of Europe to the UN will remain significant frameworks of German policy-making, even though the EU is also represented there. Equally important is the multitude of bilateral dialogues and cooperations with third countries, most recently those developed with all states in Eastern Europe. Bonn intensifies these contractual links because they address mutual needs for representation, consultation and the regulation of bilateral problems. This grid is mainly a piece of traditional diplomacy but it may also be regarded as a fallback in case CFSP reduces its dynamics or gets paralyzed. Foreign Minister Kinkel profits from all of these levels of operation. When in the summer of 1994 smugglers of enriched uranium chose Germany as their prime marketplace, Kinkel proposed the establishment of an international plutonium regime. He made the proposal within CFSP but introduced it at Euratom and Europol in parallel and he wrote letters to his colleagues in Russia, Belarus, Ukraine and Kazakstan.

There are four areas of the future development of the EU where Franco-

German cooperation will be crucial: monetary stability, security, democratic legitimation and enlargement. On monetary union and security cooperation Bonn and Paris agree in principle, on democratization and enlargement they hold largely different views. The progress of integration will depend a great deal on a Franco-German understanding in these controversial matters. In the preparation for the 1996 review conference Bonn stressed its interest in raising the popular acceptance of the institutional structure and the scope of CFSP by including representatives of the EP in the 'group of advisers', established during the Corfu European Council meeting in June 1994. Bonn will not simply repeat its initiative of the beginning of the decade when the Treaty of European Union was negotiated in part to strengthen the rights of the EP: this time it will reinforce its efforts. Whether it will win over France to this goal remains as doubtful as it has been in the past. For Paris the deepening of the EU refers mainly to EMU, and second to CFSP. The German government, however, regards the general unification of Europe as a vital question for Germany and for Europe.

The German push for an early admission to the EU of the Visegrad Four has led to opposition from many partner countries, including Spain and France, which fear a neglect of their Mediterranean, Middle East, and African interests. There are obviously 'Germanic' and 'Latin' caucuses in the future EU in the making here. The eastern and the southern regions in Europe are competing for the centre's attention. Bonn, and even more so, Berlin are determined to replace their old and renewed frontline status with a place in the centre of Europe. All relevant political forces in Germany have adopted a broad notion of security comprehending socio-economic developments as the centre piece of stabilization.[48] Equally it is accepted that the transformation process in Eastern Europe will take longer than envisioned. Stability therefore has to be enhanced to a large extent via stronger East–West bonds in the foreign and security area. Hence the German urge to go beyond NATO's Partnership for Peace and to develop a closer link between the East European countries and CFSP.[49] Models of sectoral membership in CFSP as well as an associate status with CFSP for membership candidates have been proposed for this purpose.[50]

Bonn finds partners among EU member states relatively easily for developing West European integration and the transatlantic dialogue but it has little support for its East European concerns. Yet in Eastern Europe institutionalization, stability structures and security networks are the weakest to date. The Germans are more exposed than others to the consequences of this deficit but they have also a larger responsibility to take the lead in focusing the EU on this prime challenge. Bonn needs to play a role which it has not been prepared for, whether psychologically or intellectually. The task is at least as fundamental as conflict management in former Yugoslavia.

The way in which the recognition of Croatia and Slovenia was decided upon among the Twelve seemed to show 'that a more assertive Germany is starting to shape EC foreign policy – even at the risk of fanning the flames of civil war in Yugoslavia'.[51] Bonn's diplomats may need a certain period to adjust to the kind of complex conflict situations which – from now on – may include the risk of German casualties in peacekeeping and peace enforcement actions. Yet even in retrospect German diplomats defend their behaviour in the December days after the 1991 Intergovernmental Conferences.[52] At that time a 'Sonderweg' approach was certainly looming over the horizon.

Today's and tomorrow's task of uniting Europe will be even more demanding. Bonn has given signals that it understands the strategic nature of the challenge. To live up to it, the Federal Republic will need the courage to show more assertiveness. The CDU/CSU paper argues for a combination in the EU of variable geometry and hard core. In an enlarged Union, some countries must be allowed to integrate more slowly. Conversely, others must be allowed to integrate more quickly. German political parties propose an EU hard core expressly to guard against German hegemony. Variable geometry without the magnet of a hard core would lead to European disintegration. The solution is to ensure that other countries join France, Germany and the Benelux in the hard core.

The CDU/CSU paper underlines the necessity of strengthening the EU's capacity to act.[53] Among other things, it proposes an effective federal division of powers between different levels of decision-making. It also suggests defining the EU's fundamental values in a quasi-constitutional document. These ideas are hard to stomach for several member governments. And yet the desire of the Germans and other Europeans to drive on with this agenda must not be underestimated.[54]

NOTES

1   Klaus Kinkel, 'Deutschland in Europa. Zu den Zielen der deutschen Präsidentschaft in der Europäischen Union', *Europa-Archiv*, vol. 49, no. 12, 25 June 1994, pp.335–42.
2   Concerning other functions of EPC for the Federal Republic see Reinhardt Rummel and Wolfgang Wessels, 'Federal Republic of Germany: new responsibilities, old constraints', in Christopher Hill (ed.), *National Foreign Policies and European Political Cooperation*, London, George Allen and Unwin for RIIA, 1983, pp.34–55.
3   The best insider book on the German unification is by Chancellor Kohl's then chief foreign policy adviser, Horst Teltschik, *329 Tage. Innenansichten der Einigung*, Berlin, Siedler, 1991.
4   For the key role played by the USA in bringing about German unification, see Robert D. Blackwill, 'Deutsche Vereinigung und amerikanische Diplomatie', *Aussenpolitik*, vol. 45, no. 3, 1994, pp.211–25. For an overview of the different

positions of the four allied powers towards German reunification, see the special issue of *Europa-Archiv*, vol. 45, no. 4, 25 February 1990.

5 There were two options for the mode of unification: (1) Art. 23 or (2) Art. 146, which would have meant working out a new constitution (instead of the provisional 'Grundgesetz') and an all-German referendum. The decision for route (1) seemed to be, for internal German reasons at least, by far the smoothest.

6 Christian Deubner, 'Die Wiedervereinigung der Deutschen und die Europäische Gemeinschaft', in Cord Jakobeit and Alparslan Yenal (eds), *Gesamteuropa. Analysen, Probleme, Entwicklungsperspektiven*, Bonn, Bundeszentrale für Politische Bildung, 1993, pp.393–413. Gerd Langguth, 'Die deutsche Frage und die Europäische Gemeinschaft', *Aus Politik und Zeitgeschichte*, Beilage zur Wochenzeitung *Das Parlament*, B 29/90, 13 July 1990, pp.13–23.

7 Reunification seemed to correspond better with long-established American goals than with those of France or the UK. See Peter H. Merkl, *German Unification in the European Context*, University Park, Penn., Pennsylvania State University Press, 1994. Merkl particularly refers to the dilemmas of London and Paris:

> France and Britain, in particular, faced the prospect of a considerable shift in their respective weight in the European Community and Western alliance and, worst yet, little leverage in influencing the specific course which developments might take. For France, in particular, the option of exercising leverage through NATO – a crucial lever that was used particularly by the United States – was not available since France had left NATO ... France was reduced to emphasizing the leverage through the European Community which, at this point, was still mostly an economic and not a political union. Britain, by the same logic, could not use its EC leverage because the Thatcher administration was in the middle of a major rearguard battle against the EC programme of 'deepening' European integration after 1992, a battle in which the fear of losing British sovereignty to a European political union, currency, and central bank were joined with age-old prejudices against the French – 'the poodles of the Germans' (Nicholas Ridley) – and the World War I and II animosity against the Germans.
>
> (Merkl 1994: 318)

8 See Barbara Lippert and Rosalind Stevens-Ströhmann, *German Unification and EC Integration: German and British Perspectives*, London, Pinter for RIIA, 1993, pp.115–19. The Head of the Planning Staff of the Auswärtiges Amt regards the provisions for CFSP in TEU as a Franco-German 'compromise'. See Wolfgang Ischinger, 'Gemeinsame Außen- und Sicherheitspolitik – Thesen zur deutsch-französischen Vorreiterrolle', in Ingo Kolboom and Ernst Weisenfeld (eds), *Frankreich in Europa. Ein deutsch-französischer Rundblick*, Bonn, Europa Union Verlag, 1993, p.122.

9 For the effects of reunification on the Community, see Christian Deubner, 'Die Wiedervereinigung der Deutschen und die Europäische Gemeinschaft', in Cord Jakobeit and Alparslan Yenal (eds), *Gesamteuropa. Analysen, Probleme, Entwicklungsperspektiven*, Bonn, Bundeszentrale für Politische Bildung, 1993, pp.393–413.

10 See John Mearsheimer, 'Back to the future: instability in Europe after the Cold War', *International Security*, vol. 15, no. 1, Summer 1990, pp.5–56.

11 See Françoise de La Serre, 'Hat die Europäische Gemeinschaft eine Ostpolitik?', in Christian Deubner (ed.), *Die Europäische Gemeinschaft in einem neuen Europa: Herausforderungen und Strategien*, Baden-Baden, Nomos, 1991, pp.193–207.

12 'Defencism' refers to a realist acceptance of the role of military force in foreign policy, but with a restriction to the defence and deterrence end of the spectrum (militarism and the projection of force abroad). See Martin Ceadel, *Thinking About Peace and War*, Oxford, Oxford University Press, 1987.

13 Some regard the new endeavour toward Eastern Europe as the second half of the game called European unification ('zweite Halbzeit für Europa'). See Wolfgang Ischinger, 'Die Gemeinsame Außen- und Sicherheitspolitik. Zentrale Fragen der Gemeinsamen Außen- und Sicherheitspolitik für die Bundesrepublik', in Karl Kaiser and Hanns W. Maull (eds), *Die Zukunft der europäischen Integration: Folgerungen für die deutsche Politik*, Bonn, Forschungsinstitut der Deutschen Gesellschaft für Auswärtige Politik (DGAP), Arbeitspapiere zur Internationalen Politik No. 78, October 1993, p.58.

14 See Wolfgang Ischinger, 'Gemeinsame Außen- und Sicherheitspolitik – Thesen zur deutsch-französischen Vorreiterrolle', in Ingo Kolboom and Ernst Weisenfeld (eds), *Frankreich in Europa. Ein deutsch-französischer Rundblick*, Bonn, Europa Union Verlag, 1993, p.123.

15 See Valérie Guérin-Sendelbach and Jacek Rulkowski, '"Euro-Trio" Frankreich-Deutschland-Polen', *Aussenpolitik*, vol. 45, no. 3, 1994, pp.246–53.

16 In September 1994 for the first time since 1966 a French Defence Minister participated in a meeting of NATO Defence Ministers (in Seville).

17 See Declaration of the Heads of State and Government in the Meeting of the North Atlantic Council, held at NATO Headquarters, Brussels, 10–11 January 1994, *Europe Documents*, no. 1867, Agence Europe, 12 January 1994, pp.1–7.

18 Ibid., p.1, no. 3: 'We reaffirm that the Alliance is the essential forum for consultations among its members and the venue for agreement on policies bearing on the security and defence commitments of Allies under the Washington Treaty.'

19 The problems which the Netherlands have with united Germany are well addressed by Maarten van Traa, 'Wohlbekannt aber ungeliebt? Der deutsche Nachbar aus niederländischer Sicht', *Europa-Archiv*, vol. 49, no. 17, 10 September 1994, pp.491–8.

20 The now Secretary General of the Council, Jürgen Trumpf, had suggested as early as 1987 to strengthen the European Council and the General Affairs Council by electing their presidents. See Jürgen Trumpf, 'Reflections from three German presidencies – high marks for the German coordination model, low marks for the presidency system', in Wolfgang Wessels and Elfriede Regelsberger (eds), *The Federal Republic of Germany and the European Community: The Presidency and Beyond*, Bonn, Europa Union Verlag, 1988, pp.266–75.

21 The ratification debate of Maastricht in the Bundestag is partly reprinted in the German weekly *Das Parlament*, no. 1, 1 January 1993, pp.21–6. The German parliament ratified the Treaty on European Union with a high majority of 543 votes against 8 (17 abstentions). The Bundesrat, the second chamber representing the 16 Bundesländer, voted unanimously for Maastricht.

22 In contrast to more traditional views, which see accountability and efficiency as in tension.

23 Excerpts from the Federal Constitutional Court ruling are reprinted in: *Europa-Archiv*, vol. 48, no. 22 (1993), pp.D460–476.

24 76 per cent of the Germans are in favour of a common European security and defence policy, slightly more than the average value (73 per cent) in the member states of the European Union. Only Ireland (46 per cent), Denmark (52 per cent), the UK (58 per cent) and Portugal (66 per cent) are below. See *Eurobarometer*, no. 38, Spring 1993.

25 For a record of the security-related discussions in Germany, see Reinhardt

Rummel, 'The German debate on security institutions in Europe', in Marco Carnovale (ed.), *European Security and International Institutions After the Cold War*, London and Basingstoke, Macmillan, 1995.

26 CDU/CSU-Fraktion des Deutschen Bundestages, *Überlegungen zur europäischen Politik*, 1 September 1994, unpublished. Excerpts from the paper are reprinted in the *Frankfurter Allgemeine Zeitung*, 8 September 1994, p.7.

27 See Karl-Heinz Kamp, 'The German Bundeswehr in out-of-area operations: to engage or not to engage?', *The World Today*, vol. 49, no. 8/9, August–September 1993.

28 Excerpts of the ruling are reprinted in *Frankfurter Rundschau*, 22 July 1994, p.16.

29 As each military mission will have to be approved by the Bundestag, the Bundeswehr has now been dubbed a parliamentary army (Parlamentsheer).

30 Right after the ruling of the Constitutional Court, the Bundestag was called back from summer recession for a special meeting politically to endorse and extend those missions which the Bundeswehr was already performing in former Yugoslavia. The Liberals and the Social Democrats who had appealed to the Court on the question now voted for the full participation of German forces in surveillance and embargo enforcement missions. Nevertheless, Defence Minister Volker Rühe confirmed that no German soldiers would be sent to peacekeeping operations on the ground in former Yugoslavia. A well-known journalist has called this policy of non-intervention in historically sensitive regions the 'Kohl Doctrine'. See Josef Joffe, 'The future of European security: an Atlanticist perspective', in Charles L. Barry, *The Search for Peace in Europe. Perspectives from NATO and Eastern Europe*, Washington DC, National Defense University Press, 1993, p.53, note 4.

31 As an example see the report on the second half of the 1993 period, where the statement is made that taking all aid to former Yugoslavia together the EU has provided DM1371m, of which the Federal Republic has contributed DM384m (28 per cent). Deutscher Bundestag, 53, *Bericht der Bundesregierung über die Integration der Bundesrepublik Deutschland in die Europäische Union*, [Berichtszeitraum 1 July to 31 December 1993], no. 12/7132, 23 March 1994, p.79.

32 For an insider's report on the EC monitor mission, see Johannes Preisinger, *Die EG-Beobachtermission im ehemaligen Jugoslawien. Bilanz und Perspektiven*, Frankfurt a. M., Hessische Stiftung Friedens- und Konfliktforschung, HSFK-Report no. 3, 1994.

33 See Anne McEloy, 'Blundering in the Balkans', *The Times*, 19 December 1991, p.1. For a more positive assessment of the German move, see Joseph Fitchett, 'Bonn claims recognition will help end Yugoslav war', *The International Herald Tribune*, 16 January 1991, p.1.

34 Helmut Kohl and Edouard Balladur, 'Ein wesentlicher Schritt auf dem Weg zu einem dauerhaften Frieden auf unserem Kontinent', *Frankfurter Allgemeine Zeitung*, 27 May 1994, p.3. The same article appeared in *Le Monde*.

35 When the position of a CSCE Secretary General was established in 1993, it was filled by a high-ranking German diplomat, Wilhelm Höynck.

36 The concept was adopted by CFSP bodies and is now guiding the division of labour among its institutions.

37 For the Berlin Declaration see *Agence Europe*, no. 6309, 7 September 1994, p.7.

38 For more details on the German nuclear non-proliferation policy in the context of EPC and CFSP see Harald Müller, 'West European cooperation on nuclear proliferation', in Reinhardt Rummel (ed.), *Toward Political Union. Planning a Common Foreign and Security Policy in the European Community*, Boulder, Westview Press, 1992, pp.187–207; and Harald Müller, *Nuclear Nonproliferation Policy as Part*

of the European Union's Common Foreign and Security Policy, Brussels, Centre for European Policy Studies, CEPS Working Document no. 86, May 1994.

39 See the ten-point plan presented by Foreign Minister Kinkel in December of 1993 designed to limit the proliferation of weapons of mass destruction in the world, *Atlantic News,* no. 2581, 17 December 1993. For a thorough analysis of NATO's efforts concerning non-proliferation, see Matthias Dembinski, Alexander Kelle and Harald Müller, *NATO and Nonproliferation: A Critical Appraisal,* Frankfurt a.M., Peace Research Institute Frankfurt, PRIF reports no. 33, April 1994.

40 Bonn aimed at a tight harmonization of control among the Twelve based on Article 113 (qualified majority). The actual proposition, instead, included both article 113 for general trade regulations on dual-use goods and a CFSP Joint Action to decide on the lists of respective goods and countries. See, Deutscher Bundestag, *Bericht der Bundesregierung zum Stand der EG-Harmonisierung des Exportkontrollrechts für Güter und Technologien mit doppeltem Verwendungszweck (Dual-use-Waren),* no. 12/8368, 11 August 1994. The Joint Action was adopted in December 1994.

41 For a classical example of such a misguided view, see Timothy Garton Ash, 'Germany's choice', *Foreign Affairs,* vol. 73, no. 4, Summer 1994, pp.65–81.

42 For one of the most advanced studies in this field, see Hans J. Michelmann and Panayotis Soldatos (eds), *Federalism and International Relations. The Role of Subnational Units,* Oxford, Clarendon Press, 1990. The book includes a case study on Germany. Also, Brian Hocking (ed.), *Managing Foreign Relations in Federal States,* London, Leicester University Press, 1993.

43 'Unser Ziel ist ein möglichst starkes Kerneuropa, aber unsere Präferenz bleibt eindeutig, alle 12 – oder ab 1995 – hoffentlich alle 16 mit an Bord zu haben.' Klaus Kinkel, 'Deutsche Aussenpolitik in einer neuen Weltlage', *Bulletin der Bundesregierung,* no. 76, 29 August 1994, p.714.

44 Mark Frankland, 'Changing partners in the diplomatic dance', *The Observer,* 17 July 1994, p.24. Frankland admits that Germany is the obvious choice as Washington's ally, but he adds sarcastically that a cynical survivor of the Cold War crises might say Germany is the perfect partner for Clinton's hesitant America.

45 'Im Handeln auf eigene Faust liegt keine Zukunft mehr.' Klaus Kinkel, 'Erklärung der Bundesregierung zur deutschen Präsidentschaft im Rat der Europäischen Union', *Bulletin der Bundesregierung,* no. 63, 30 June 1994, p.596.

46 Volker Rühe, *Germany's Responsibility in and for Europe,* Oxford, St. Antony's College, The Konrad Adenauer Memorial Lecture 1994, p.5.

47 Interview with Edouard Balladur, 'Notre politique étrangère', *Le Figaro,* 30 August 1994, p.6.

48 Christian Deubner, 'Deutschland, Frankreich und das Europa der neunziger Jahre im Konflikt von Interessen und Wahrnehmungen', Stiftung Wissenschaft und Politik, Ebenhauser, June 1994, unpublished.

49 Following a German initiative the meeting of the EU foreign ministers at Usedom in September 1994 discussed various models of improving the East–West connections and the early participation of accession candidates in CFSP bodies.

50 See the ideas of the new President of the European Parliament, a German Social Democrat, Klaus Hänsch, *EU-Nachrichten,* no. 37, 19 September 1994, p.3.

51 Martin du Bois, 'Germany's impact on EC policy is evident', *The Wall Street Journal,* 18 December 1991, p.1.

52 According to an assessment from the Auswärtiges Amt developments after the

early recognition of Croatia and Slovenia have confirmed the success of the German strategy. See Peter von Jagow, 'Das Krisenmanagement der EG/EPZ im Jugoslawienkrieg – eine gemischte Bilanz', in Elfriede Regelsberger (ed.), *Die Gemeinsame Außen- und Sicherheitspolitik der Europäischen Union. Profilsuche mit Hindernissen*, Bonn, Europa Union Verlag, 1993, p.87.

53 Brian Breedham, 'The folly of uniting Europe while slicing it in two', *International Herald Tribune*, 14 September 1994, p.4.

54 Jan G. van der Tas, 'A German message Europe must heed', *The Financial Times*, 16 September 1994, p.13.

Chapter 3

United Kingdom

Sharpening contradictions

Christopher Hill

The context of British foreign policy has changed drastically over the last two decades, both at home and abroad. At home, Thatcherism has come and gone, leaving behind it the legacy of earthquakes in the civil service and the political parties, as well as in society at large. The economic base of diplomatic influence has continued to erode in relative terms, with Britain falling behind Italy in the GDP per capita league table in the mid-1980s,[1] while continued high levels of unemployment and the erosion of manufacturing industry have offset the increases in competitiveness achieved under Mrs Thatcher's premiership. What is more, the priorities and modalities of British foreign policy have come under steadily increasing fire in this last quarter of the twentieth century, as the Conservative Party has fallen out of love with the old Establishment and has become more suspicious of diplomacy and diplomats. Although to a degree this has been counterbalanced by a new degree of sympathy for the Foreign and Commonwealth Office (FCO) in left-wing circles, the general awakening of public interest in foreign policy has meant that those responsible for Britain's external relations have not been left in peace on the home front, as they had come to expect in the past. The cost, the scope, the orientation, and particularly the morality of British foreign policy have come under domestic scrutiny as never before, often with embarrassing consequences for those in office. The reassertion of the Labour Party, expressed partly in its repositioning on the pro-EU side of the arguments which still rack the Conservatives has also tended to undermine interparty front-bench consensus on European issues; the EU is now a convenient stick with which the Opposition can belabour the Government.

Abroad, the rupture has been much more dramatic. The central organizing concept of post-Second World War British foreign policy, the Soviet threat, has been removed, while the Federal Republic of Germany has moved from being one of Britain's 'analogue' states (in the term used by the Berrill Report of 1977) to the status, in its unified form, of by far the biggest and most powerful player in the European Union, itself boosted into a higher orbit by the completion of the Single Market, by the new structures of the Maastricht Treaty, and by a series of enlargements which have taken it from nine members in 1975 to fifteen in 1995. In the particular area of European foreign policy cooperation, EPC has made steady procedural and substantive progress over two decades, to the point where it has converged with systemic change to produce the sudden possibility – after forty years of silence on the matter – of a European Defence Community emerging, built on the growing identification between the EU and the Western European Union.

But if the continuity and bipartisan basis of British foreign policy in the first four post-war decades have become more vulnerable to disturbance, they have not disintegrated. On the other side of the ledger, it must be stressed that foreign policy is inherently an exercise in continuity amidst turbulence, and British foreign policy-makers have considerable experience in performing the required balancing acts. In these recent years they have maintained the gradualist tradition by arranging, thirteen years in advance of the deadline, for the handover of Hong Kong to China, by ensuring that the Commonwealth and the 'special relationship' with the USA are not suddenly uprooted but rather wither slowly away, and by continuing with a globalist role as a permanent member of the UN Security Council, as major supplier of arms sales and military training to the Third World and as occasional intervener in dramatic conflicts like the Falklands War and the second Gulf War. Of course, from the normative point of view these activities may be variously interpreted: as evidence of pragmatic adaption to change, as the remnants of a fossilized imperialist preoccupation, as the courageous upholding of the values of democracy and order, or as a hypocritical and morally bankrupt form of posturing. These debates are regularly and animatedly conducted in other places.[2] The purpose here is to analyse the impact which membership of EPC/CFSP has had on British foreign policy, and the extent to which Britain has moulded – as it has undoubtedly sought to do from the beginning – the evolution of 'European foreign policy'.

One hypothesis would be that Britain, pursuing as ever in its foreign policy predictability without final commitments, has managed successfully to slow down the pace of change in European foreign policy cooperation and to preserve its essentially cooperative rather than integrative base, despite the best efforts of states like Germany and Belgium to engage in transformationalist politics. This would be disputed by some of the Conservative politicians of the period (notably Sir Geoffrey Howe and Douglas Hurd, the two principal figures to hold the office of Foreign Secretary since 1982)[3] on the grounds that Britain has sought, constructively, to promote the harmonization of national foreign policies so long as that does not call into question the sovereign right to go it alone where that might be deemed necessary. Nevertheless the perception from the other side of the Channel would certainly be that Britain, despite being more interested in and effective in the area of EPC, has always ensured – as in preventing the Stuttgart Solemn Declaration of 1983 being called an 'Act', and in pushing for the pillared structure of Maastricht – that foreign policy cooperation is only communitarized at the margin.[4]

One of the reasons for this broadly accurate perception is not, however, as relevant as it might seem, namely that the most significant challenges for British foreign policy in recent years have actually reinforced old attitudes and patterns of behaviour. Certainly this is true of the perceived successes: the Falklands War victory of 1982; the talent-spotting and successful courtship of Mikhail Gorbachev; the eventual collapse of Soviet communism; the revival of the UN Security Council in the form of the (intermittently) collective diplomacy of the permanent members (the 'P5'); the expulsion of Iraq from Kuwaiti territory in 1991.[5] These have involved Britain in two major wars and much detailed bilateral negotiation. They have all served to maintain a global outlook and the self-perception of Britain as an important state with interests and responsibilities beyond those of the average middle-range power. They have made it virtually impossible to reduce defence spendings to WEU average levels,[6] and they have sustained in some significant sections of the élite the belief in a special relationship with the USA. But it is not globalism or nostalgia which leads Britain still to insist on retaining ultimate control over its own foreign policy.[7] That has far more to do with the identification of parliamentary democracy with national sovereignty – both are rooted in the powers of the House of Commons – and an historical scepticism towards the chances of order persisting in continental Europe, so often a source of danger for Britain and so seldom a source of strength.

Against this some events, particularly such 'failures' as the relinquishing of Hong Kong and the long drawn out and humiliatingly one-sided negotiations with China over the future of the colony,[8] have led the more self-consciously forward-thinking members of the policy class to focus on the need for European collective action in the world and to argue that Britain can now realistically achieve very little through its own resources, thus taking one stage further the process which began with the Anglo-Japanese alliance of 1902, progressed through Lend-Lease in 1941 and the commitment to NATO in 1949, and was dramatically expressed in 1967–8 through the devaluation of the Pound and the announcement of an end to the military presence east of Suez. This view favours a full-hearted 'continental commitment', so that Britain can be relied upon by its partners, but essentially in the form of an alliance of cooperative states à la NATO, and certainly not on the model of a superseding single European state.

On the basis of the above outline of the changes in the context of British foreign policy, and the contrasting responses it has evoked, the argument will be made in this chapter that the ideology of the Thatcherite (and Majorite) years, together with their accompanying events, have sharpened the contradictions in British foreign policy to the point where something will soon have to give, and where the traditional ability of the British elite to manage change from above will come under even greater pressure than has been evident since 1945.

THATCHERISM AND EPC: PARENTHESIS OR PARADIGM?

It is natural to assume that Mrs Thatcher's formidable personality left its stamp on all the major areas of British public policy during the years 1979–90. In foreign policy and matters European it might therefore seem self-evident that her ardent nationalism and preference for *têtes-à-têtes* at the White House to the horse-trading of European Council meetings, must have set narrow limits to how far the Foreign Office could go in joint harness with its EPC partners. This is, however, by no means a wholly correct picture. There are important qualifications to be made.

The first simply erodes the period in question. From the time she took office until the invasion of the Falkland Islands on 2 April 1982, Margaret Thatcher was heavily reliant on her first Foreign Secretary, Lord Carrington. Carrington had almost a free hand in working towards the procedural reforms of the London Report of October 1981, and in the time-consuming initiatives over Afghanistan (the neutralization proposal) and over the Arab–Israeli dispute. Only after Carrington's unforeseeable resignation on 5 April 1982 and her subsequent three months of total immersion in the war, did the Prime Minister herself take over foreign policy – a task she soon acquired a taste for.

If we also posit that once Thatcher had been removed from power the Major government immediately returned to a more pragmatic approach to European cooperation in general (staking their reputations on the Maastricht Treaty and starting from the more positive assumption that Britain 'is irrevocably part of Europe')[9] then the period of Thatcherite foreign policy is reduced even further, to the years 1982–90. We might then, rather in the way that Paul Kennedy sees the period of global imperialism from c1600–1960 as a hiatus in a more natural involvement with Europe,[10] see the 1980s as little more than the dramatic interruption of a longer trend towards the Europeanization of British foreign policy.

This treatment of Mrs Thatcher's assertive foreign policy style as essentially epiphenomenal, style more than substance, implies a sharp dividing line between EPC and classical foreign policy on the one hand, and EC institutional development on the other, given that the British Prime Minister dominated general EC affairs during her time in office – first through the budget rebate rows of 1979–84, then through the Single Market initiative (1985–90) and finally through her opposition to Monetary Union and the boost to political integration which that implied (1988–90). And yet these were years in which the dividing line between 'Community' external relations and EPC was becoming ever more blurred, and foreign policy was increasingly being seen as a leading sector in the debate over political union. To what extent then, did Margaret Thatcher in fact rock the boat of European foreign policy cooperation?

She certainly made it clear that British foreign policy was not wholly dependent on the European sphere for survival. For much of the time the EPC mechanisms were generally treated as of secondary importance, and indeed, the Thatcher memoirs have no reference to EPC in their otherwise extensive index.[11] The rhetoric of Thatcherite foreign policy was almost wholly to do with the importance of the Atlantic alliance, with the closeness of personal and historic ties between Britain and the USA, and with the need to master the threat of Soviet communism. It was a coincidence, but still a striking one, that Mrs Thatcher disappeared from power just as the Cold War started to crumble. It was as if, like her hero Churchill, she was a figure of a particular time, who could not survive without the oxygen of international conflict to boost her.

In the 1980s British foreign policy was dominated either by East–West relations – arms control, proxy wars in the Third World, then the fostering of Gorbachev and the return to *détente* on Western terms – or by wrangles arising out of old imperial commitments, over the Falklands, South Africa and Hong Kong. On most of these, EPC had little to say, barred as it was from involvement in military questions, and sensitive as it had to be over any trespass on the ground of either NATO or the *chasses gardées* of a large member state. European foreign policy always had a gaping hole in it arising out of the lack of an explicit policy towards either superpower, and Mrs Thatcher's extensive efforts to influence both Washington and Moscow were relatively uncomplicated by EPC.

During the Falklands War Britain's initially desperate situation meant that help had to be taken where it could be found, and Thatcher welcomed the support from the other nine members of the EC. On the other hand, she did not draw the conclusion that a certain give and take might be necessary on other aspects of diplomacy within the Community, with the result that an attempted veto on farm price increases under the CAP was simply ignored by the other Nine, and after only a month Ireland and Italy had slipped the moorings of solidarity and opted out of joint sanctions against Argentina. The years which followed made it seem that the British Prime Minister had remembered more of these latter events than of the initial phase of support for Britain.[12]

Certainly on the African dimension of British foreign policy, the Thatcher government either simply bypassed EPC or actively opposed the majority which tended to form there in favour of sanctions against South Africa. On Namibia it was content to work in the framework of the Contact Group of five states (i.e. with the USA, France, Germany and Canada); on Mozambique it coordinated with EC assistance to that and the other 'front line' states, but essentially pursued a unilateral path of providing military training; on Angola Jonas Savimbi and UNITA got more of a hearing in London than in most other European capitals; aid to Somalia was suspended in 1988 after concerns over human rights and chemical weapons, but in conjunction with the USA and Germany rather than as a common European stance;[13] and over South Africa, of course, Britain fought a dogged rear-guard action in the first half of the 1980s against sanctions, acceding to the eventual decision to go ahead with little enthusiasm, and then jumping ship in February 1990 the moment it seemed that reform was at hand, six months before a collective European decision to bring sanctions to an end.[14]

Hong Kong, by contrast, was *ultra vires* so far as Britain's partners were concerned, being a Crown Colony and therefore part of 'internal' affairs. In this it was like Gibraltar and Northern Ireland, however much Spain on the former and various states on the latter might have liked to Europeanize the issue. Questions could be asked on such issues in the European Parliament, but the Presidency was never empowered to answer. So far as Hong Kong was concerned this was doubtless a great relief for the other Eleven, anxious not to be associated with Britain's dilemmas over which to antagonize the most, the population of the Colony or the government in Beijing (to say nothing of international opinion over the Vietnamese Boat People, held in detention camps in Hong Kong and quietly but forcibly repatriated). Here Thatcher might have welcomed a spreading of responsibility, the provision of European 'cover', but for once was hoist with her own petard.

The public picture then, seems to suggest that the Thatcher years saw a downgrading of EPC from the days of Carrington, in line with the general hostility of the Prime Minister to the Community and all its works, and indeed with her increasing feelings of antagonism towards the Foreign and Commonwealth Office, which at its highest levels had soon become enthusiastic about the opportunities presented by participation in EPC. Yet despite all this, and the undoubted distinctiveness of her style, there are good grounds for arguing that the Thatcher years are still part of the broad continuity which British foreign policy has displayed over twenty-five years of central involvement in EPC.[15] On this view, both Thatcher and her successor Major (more emollient in tone on questions of cooperation with Europe) conformed to the basic paradigm of a Britain which accepts an increasing enmeshment in the European foreign policy network, while (like the other major players) never being wholly trapped or having to surrender its national freedom of manoeuvre. If a British or French (or indeed, a Greek or Danish) government wishes to do so, it is still possible to fly in the face of what the Maastricht Treaty calls 'common positions', or simply to prevent their emergence by ploughing its own furrow from the outset. The extent to which a government will wish to act unilaterally, of course, is a

function of circumstances, both domestic and external, and of the tempera-
ment and beliefs of key decision-makers. A pro-EPC Foreign Secretary like
Douglas Hurd still had little difficulty in pointing out the limits of the
process, over such issues as the Gulf crisis of 1990–91, or the innumerable
failures over Bosnia. No doubt a Labour administration under Tony Blair,
notwithstanding its public enthusiasm for joint European policies, would
be equally quick to act alone, or not at all, where they judged the alternative
as damaging to British vital interests, and/or likely to whip up a storm
at home.

For her part, beneath the surface of the anti-European and anti-FCO
discourse Mrs Thatcher was not as uncooperative in EPC as she seemed.
This was partly because from 1983–9 she was working with a Foreign
Secretary in Sir Geoffrey Howe who increasingly saw it as his task to tone
down her stridency and to secure enough clear space for himself and his
officials to get on with the business of European diplomacy with as little
disruption from Number 10 Downing Street as he could. In the end, as we
know, this proved impossible, and Howe had to resort to subterfuges with
Cabinet colleagues, not least before the Madrid Summit of 1989, to
manoeuvre his Prime Minister into accepting that Britain might enter the
Exchange Rate Mechanism of the European Monetary System. This was to
lead to his own angry departure from the FCO later that same year, and
finally to his dramatic speech in the Commons of November 1990 which
effectively brought Mrs Thatcher down.

But all this was not EPC, and even on a looser definition, not really foreign
policy. Quite a lot of the latter continued in a less troubled and dramatic
vein. What is more, it cannot be argued that this only happened because
Howe was in charge and the PM unable to interfere. There has rarely been
an occupant of Number 10 so willing and able to interfere with the Foreign
Office as Margaret Thatcher. After the demise of Carrington and the victory
over Argentina, foreign policy increasingly became her first priority (particularly after the successful battle with the National Union of Miners in
1984), and her 'kitchen cabinet' of advisers, which had Charles Powell
and Bernard Ingham at its heart, but also included such figures as the
historians Hugh Thomas and Norman Stone) gave her the backup which
enabled someone with her enormous personal energy to master daily detail
as well as grand strategy.

Margaret Thatcher may have been frustrated by the FCO and its predi-
lection for European cooperation (few in the FCO itself favoured the kind
of integration Mitterrand and Kohl seemed to want), but she still knew that
she could not dispense with its professionalism or with the diplomatic
networks in which it was embedded. After their retirement, she appointed
successively as her personal Foreign Policy Advisers the ex-Ambassadors Sir
Anthony Parsons and Sir Percy Cradock, and she admired the expertise of
some on the European circuit like Sir Michael Butler and Sir Nicholas

Henderson. She criticized the FCO in general for 'its insatiable appetite for nuances and conditions which can blur the clearest vision',[16] but she also realized that used properly, the top officials in the Diplomatic Service were recognized throughout the Community as having the talents to make the EPC/EC system work in Britain's interests – most continental diplomats would deeply regret Britain withdrawing from the EU, less for the power or resources which Britain brings than for the skill with which its envoys help EPC to function, internally and in relations with third countries.

Because EPC was an intergovernmental system it did not pose the same threat to Thatcher's broadly realist view of international relations[17] as did the idea of a single currency replacing the Pound. The Prime Minister was hardheaded enough, after all, about the need to work with allies in NATO and to avoid romantic illusions about Britannia ruling the waves. What she did not want was to see either the foundations or the symbols of national foreign policy eroded. Short of the introduction of majority voting (which did not come until after her demise, in the Treaty on European Union), EPC did not threaten to do this.

In fact, the Thatcher government, like its predecessors since 1973, discovered that EPC could be turned to advantage, and on occasions like that of the Falklands War, could prove indispensable. Despite the desire to be close to the USA, there were even cases when it proved politic to distance British policy from that of Washington, and then the cover provided by a collective mechanism was invaluable. This was true, for example, over policy towards Central America in the early and mid-1980s, where Britain was less persuaded by American arguments about a renewed outbreak of falling dominoes than by those who feared an unnecessary heightening of tension in East–West relations which would inevitably reverberate in Europe. In consequence, Britain maintained solidarity over the meeting of all ten European Foreign Ministers with the central Americans and the Contadora group in San José, Costa Rica, in September 1984, and played host to Nicaraguan Vice President Ramirez in London the next year, both over evident US hostility.

The area of counter-terrorism, no less than central America, found the Thatcher government anxious for support from its European partners, and not unaware that the confrontationalist US line could sometimes be counter-productive. It is true that in the most spectacular cases, that of the US attack on Libya in 1986, and the attempt to impose sanctions on Syria after the Hindawi bomb attempt on an El-Al jumbo jet at London Heathrow the same year, Mrs Thatcher first deceived her fellow Europeans, and then signally failed to get their sympathetic support. Beneath the surface, however, the quiet work by Ministries of the Interior (i.e. the 'Home Office' in Britain) which had been continuing on counter-terrorism since the mid-1970s was consolidated, and from 1986 a permanent Working Group on the political aspects of the problem was set up within EPC. British officials and politicians knew that this kind of detailed liaison was worth a thousand hot air balloons rhetoric, and they were not so displeased with either the practical progress in gradually improving security at airports and the like, or the delicate balancing act in which EPC was engaged between condemning terrorism and maintaining better relations with the Arab Middle East than the USA was able to enjoy.[18] Moreover Britain had little option but to turn to its European partners for solidarity over the Rushdie affair, or for cover in keeping channels open to China after the shootings in Tienanmen Square.

Beyond terrorism and the Cold War there are, of course, myriad middle-range items of diplomacy handled in EPC, and the Thatcher government showed no sign of wishing to relinquish the advantages of coordinated *démarches* (for example on human rights questions), of EC sanctions or of the increasing moves towards the political conditionality of European development aid. What they did not seem to be able to understand was that the more such instruments of policy were employed at the European level, the more the snowball effect took hold with demands for a truly (i.e. an integrated) 'European foreign policy' becoming ever more insistent. This sort of trend was bound to lead to pressure for more 'consistency', as the Single European Act called it, between EPC and Community external relations, and for the 'communitarization' of classical foreign policy, by which is meant a central role for the Commission, the European Parliament and the European Court, and the acceptance of majority voting. All these things were anathema to a Thatcher administration, but they should not have been surprised that their selective approach to European diplomacy, supporting many joint endeavours, ignoring others, and at times complaining loudly about 'European' spinelessness, was almost bound to lead their partners to propose a qualitative leap forward, thereby sharpening the contradictions for Britain.

This inability to see the limits to the 'having your cake and eating it' approach was also a characteristic of the (few) other British governments with experience of EPC. Only Edward Heath accepted that there might be a progressive logic involved in accepting the apparently piecemeal institutional and policy advances in EPC. As for the others, whether the Labour Cabinets of Wilson and Callaghan, or the Conservative government of John Major, they have shared the Thatcher tendency to assume that intergovernmentalism was forever, whatever enthusiasm there might be for extending the policy scope of EPC or for tinkering with its procedures. This is why the argument is made here that despite the distinctive, even melodramatic nature of the Thatcher foreign policy style, in the end her period in office must be judged as not having seriously interrupted the gradual evolution of Britain's working diplomatic relationship with its European partners. Margaret Thatcher could never be reduced to a mere parenthesis in any story. And if her views were not quite paradigmatic, then she certainly did not turn upside down, or even seriously disrupt the history of EPC. That is why, on foreign policy questions, Douglas Hurd was able to serve both her and John Major with barely a ripple of discontinuity, and why both men fought just as tenacious a rearguard action to keep the CFSP inter-governmental as Thatcher had done over the Single Act. The British position on the CFSP was wholly consistent with the previous line taken on EPC. Major and Hurd may have preferred reason to ranting, but they had no intention of going down in history as having presided over the dis-solution of Britain's national foreign policy.

BRITISH OBJECTIVES IN EPC/CFSP

The question which now naturally arises is what is the British position, the 'line' taken so consistently through EPC? It is easy enough to identify the general orientation, relating to underlying values on sovereignty and the federal project, but when it comes to the more specific objectives which might be thought to attach to the idea of European foreign policy cooperation, the task becomes more difficult. In 1983 I identified a twofold British preoccupation, the desire to lead EPC on the one hand, and an instrumental (that is, taking what is useful from the process without making a commitment to carrying it substantially forward) approach on the other. Neither of these tendencies has disappeared in the last decade or so, although both have become attenuated as Britain's sense of isolation in relation to Europe has increased. However changes in the external en-vironment have led to certain important changes of emphasis.

The first is that Britain has been forced to scale down its expectations regarding the leadership of European foreign policy. Britain had been present at the creation of EPC in the early 1970s, and accordingly found it much easier to shape both policies and procedures than in the EEC. It is probably also true that the other eight member states were willing to allow Britain some scope in this area in an attempt to make acclimatization to the idea of 'Europe' easier. Most observers would agree that in the system's first decade Britain was the major force in determining both outputs and institutional developments (e.g. the London Report).

The same judgement cannot be made for the last ten years. France under Mitterrand has not always behaved in accordance with the collective prin-ciple, but it soon became far more positive towards the idea of a common foreign policy, as indicated by the switch of policy which made possible the setting up of the EPC Secretariat in Brussels. For its part, even before unification, Germany had begun to take a more assertive line on policy issues within EPC, as evidenced by the Central American initiative in 1983, and by the long-awaited (if tentative) start to a collective dialogue with the USSR. The ceaseless activity of Hans-Dietrich Genscher was beginning to bear fruit, often in conjunction with an increasingly active Italian foreign ministry.

The consequence of this for Britain has been that whatever the aspirations of Her Majesty's Government, it has proved more and more difficult to set the pace and direction of EPC.[19] British influence is without doubt still considerable, even disproportionate, as its quasi-veto power over military operations in Bosnia has demonstrated. But it does not possess the key characteristic of a leader, of exerting decisive influence across the whole range of issues. During its four terms of office as President of the Community the British have more often than not been so domestically preoccupied as to be unable to take initiatives on the external front.[20]

Instead of assuming that the quality of the diplomatic service, the number of missions worldwide and the status of Britain in the UN entitled the country to play a dominant role in Europe's collective diplomacy, decision-makers have thus been forced to recognize that the best Britain can aspire to is to be a 'partner in leadership', to adapt George Bush's view of the USA–EU relationship. Twenty years ago the only possible rival to Britain as the dominant force in EPC was France, and the French were hampered by the nature of their foreign policy-making process, in which the structure of the Quai d'Orsay and its relationship to the Elysée were not well suited for a system like EPC which puts a premium on political coordination.[21] Now Britain is only one of three important states in EPC, with Spain and Italy active in the wings. French institutional deficiencies have been counterbalanced partly through the impact of the long Mitterrand period in office, which from 1981–95 provided great continuity in foreign policy, and was reinforced at the European level when Jacques Delors (a fellow French Socialist and friend of Mitterrand) held the office of President of the European Commission (1984–94).

Also of vital importance to France here as in most other aspects of its European policy, has been the ever closer relationship with Germany. Whereas in the late 1970s and early 1980s it was likely to be Britain which took most of the initiatives in EPC, from the mid-1980s (we may date it from the Milan Summit of June 1985 at which Paris and Bonn stole London's thunder with their draft treaty, seeking to tie EPC in to the wider process of political union)[22] Britain has been caught persistently flat-footed by a series of carefully prepared joint Franco-German proposals which have made it all too plain who is setting the pace in political cooperation. British policy, by contrast, has become largely reactive and concerned with damage limitation.

This is primarily because Britain was a satisfied power in the context of the condition EPC had attained by 1981. It did not want change, particularly that which seemed to have as much to do with accelerating the general institutional momentum of the Community as with the merits of foreign policy. But this also meant that it became more difficult to use EPC as a means of papering over the cracks in Britain's wider position in the world. With other member states clearly setting the terms of the debate about a common foreign policy it was no longer very plausible for Britain to present EPC as a 'convenient extension of (its own) national policy'.[23] With a more sophisticated understanding of what EPC amounted to evident in Washington, Moscow and Beijing, and the development of the travelling troika, it became less necessary for outsiders to communicate with the Europeans through the extensive diplomatic networks of Britain and France. It was also the case that Mrs Thatcher's spoiling tactics clearly made the other major states less inclined to take a lead from Britain – a fact not lost on outsiders.

This trend is why the Major/Hurd government made so much of the 'Anglo-Italian initiative' of late 1993 to allow the countries of Central and Eastern Europe into a 'political dialogue' with the EU and its member states. Italy's Berlusconi government of 1994–5, with its apparent sympathy for the British outlook, had been welcomed with open arms in London as the long-awaited ally and counter weight to the Franco-German locomotive. It was a symptom of the degree to which, by the early 1990s, the FCO had become thoroughly alarmed at the extent to which Britain was becoming isolated inside the EU. Under Mrs Thatcher Britain had chosen to be isolated on South Africa and occasionally on anti-terrorism policy; it had shared some of the early US concerns about the revival of the WEU and had taken the initiative of 1983–4 to rebuild relations with eastern Europe largely as a bilateral matter. Thatcher's personal relations with Reagan and Gorbachev did not translate easily into benefits for the other European leaders. But by 1993 it had become clear that a certain preference for unilateralism had now become translated into a compelled isolation, within the big three and to a lesser extent within the EU as a whole.

It was the return to normalcy of Germany and its renewed diplomatic confidence which is the other main reason why Britain is now not even *primus inter pares* within the new CFSP. German assertiveness should not be exaggerated. After Genscher's excitability over the recognitions of Slovenia and Croatia in December 1991, which made it seem as if Bonn was now prepared to flex political as well as economic muscle, Germany has retreated into its more usual quietism, happy to have achieved unification and still inhibited by domestic and external constraints from doing more than supporting UN activities at the margin and using civilian diplomacy to stabilize its neighbours to the east. On the Gulf War and on Bosnia, German foreign policy has been inconsequential.

Nonetheless, from the British viewpoint there can be little doubt that German economic strength has become ever more relevant to classical foreign policy issues, while conversely Britain's relative economic weakness has come to bear more sharply and irresistibly on its status in the world. Mrs Thatcher claimed to have restored Britain's fading image and self-confidence, but insofar as this was true it acted at only a general psychological level and hardly affected the substance of policy. In Eastern Europe it was Britain that made the running in the mid-1980s with Sir Geoffrey Howe's tour of Warsaw Pact capitals, which showed that the second Cold War need not inhibit contacts with Moscow's satellites. But after the revolution burst on the scene in 1989, it was Germany which gave three-quarters of all aid to the newly independent countries of the region, and whose companies were most visible in taking up the new commercial opportunities. The situation is similar with every other diplomatic initiative that requires money as its principal instrument. Britain continues as a major contributor to Lomé, to the EU support of both the Middle East peace process, and to the democratization of South Africa. But it is plain to see that if, as envisaged in the Maastricht Treaty, the CFSP comes to require significant levels of financial expenditure, whether disbursed by nation-states or through an enlarged EU budget, then nothing can happen without the willingness of Germany to commit its resources. Already the most powerful economy in the EU, Germany is now more than a third as big again as Britain in terms of population, and approaching twice its size in terms of GDP.

Even though political power is not simply superstructural to economic, there is a limit to which one can continue, in Douglas Hurd's famous (if embarrassing) phrase, to 'punch above one's weight'. The world of the late 1950s, in which 'summit meetings' meant a gathering of the Americans, the Soviets and the British (and when it caused a stir for Macmillan not to be invited to the Kennedy–Khrushchev meeting in Vienna in 1961) is now difficult to imagine. On the other hand the end of the 'special relationship' and of Britain's special global position has long been predicted. Yet here we are in the late 1990s, four years on from Britain having played much the same role as the US's principal support in the Gulf War as it did in the Korean War of 1950–53, still with a permanent seat in the UN Security Council (and with no obvious likelihood of losing it) and one of the five most powerful nuclear strike forces in the world. 'Plus ça change . . .'.

The second important change in emphasis of Britain's objectives in EPC over the last fifteen years has been the recognition that a selective approach – using the European system as a policy instrument when required, rather than as a source of fundamental global identity – has become much more complicated, even difficult. If British attitudes to European foreign policy are still schizophrenic, then the schizophrenia is now far less convenient.[24]

On the face of things Britain has fought a consistently effective battle to keep EPC intergovernmental and outside the legal constraints of the treaties which underpin the Community. This would be conceded by many disappointed enthusiasts for a common foreign policy, pointing to the separate nature of Title III of the Single Act, and the second pillar of Maastricht, both of which are outside the jurisdiction of the European Court of Justice. A deeper analysis, however, reveals a series of grudging concessions made by Britain under pressure from structural changes in the nature of European external relations, as well as from partner states. It is unlikely, for example, that Britain by itself would have felt the need for a 'treaty' on European foreign policy at all. It would certainly not have sought the introduction of majority voting or the merger of the EPC Secretariat with the Council Secretariat made possible by Maastricht.

Nevertheless the British have not adopted the full ostrich posture. They have been perfectly aware that politics and economics have an intimate relationship in international relations, not least in the Community's external affairs, and they have taken a relatively relaxed view over the Commission's greater participation in EPC – with the exception of Mrs Thatcher's strong reactions against Jacques Delors' more assertive personal diplomacy. Nor have the needs to create more 'consistency', and to locate security in its economic context, gone unnoticed in London. What has caused problems, and where Britain has not been able wholly to hold the line, has been the determination of many partner states to move away from an empirical, organic, and hortatory approach (comfortable for those who live with an unwritten constitution, but unsatisfying for those in the Roman law tradition), into a more formal set of rules and obligations whereby the challenge to state sovereignty is carried over into the hitherto sacrosanct sphere of foreign policy.

So far the constitutional base of European integration has not altered substantially, despite the change of nomenclature from European Community to European Union. But the debate on constitutional change has developed enormously, and probably irrevocably, as the implications of the agreement to go forward to monetary union have sunk in, and the pressures on the institutional functioning of the EC generated by enlargement have mounted. For Britain this has proved a two-edged sword: although favouring enlargement as a means of reinforcing cooperation over integration, London has thereby risked bringing the EU to a point of institutional crisis. Will a body of fifteen or more diverse states be able to function effectively without a 'qualitative leap' forward? If it cannot manage the latter, does not Britain then risk a decline in the EU's position in the world, and therefore losing the very advantages of solidarity and of mass for which it joined in the first place?[25]

This is particularly relevant to foreign policy. If the FCO did not set out deliberately to institutionalize a form of 'directoire' in foreign policy, it was certainly aware that a larger, looser EU would be dominated in external policy by the traditionally more powerful member states, given the difficulties of coalition building in international relations. Conversely, a smaller grouping in which a consensus might easily build up for the extension of supranationalism to foreign policy would then accentuate the roles of the Commission and the European Parliament, and states like

Britain would find themselves increasingly subject to various forms of irksome interference, whether from German pacifism, Irish human rights groups, or Belgian federalists.

Thus the contradictions of British foreign policy in a European context, which are inevitable to a degree, have become sharpened to the point of embarrassment. At the time of writing a head of steam has built up behind the demand for a further extension of majority voting in the CFSP in the Intergovernmental Review Conference which is due to start in 1996. Moreover even if Britain still maintains – as outlined above – an unusually salient position in broader international relations, the base on which this is founded has been further eroded. The number of British diplomatic missions in the world has now fallen behind that of Italy, and in the new states of the ex-Soviet Union Britain is largely dependent on Germany for assistance with representation.[26] The financial constraints on defence expenditure are tighter than they have ever been, and despite the Treasury's historical record of always finding resources at times of military crisis,[27] the sea change in Conservative Party attitudes, with the abolition of traditional Army regiments and the running down of the Royal Navy, makes it difficult to see where the next lobby for a 'strong defence' might come from. As the 1930s showed, when the Conservatives switch their concerns from national security to financial restraint, the impact on external strength can be difficult to reverse.

Given this, it is noteworthy that the Thatcher and Major governments did nonetheless not draw the conclusion that they should cooperate with their European partners to the extent of creating a genuinely common foreign and defence policy. The need for retrenchement was accepted without the corollaries that others should therefore take on some of Britain's international responsibilities and/or that all major actions in the future would have to be multilateral – and European. Britain has, it is true, gone some of the way down this road with its growing acceptance of the intertwining of the WEU and the EU, but it has also resolutely avoided drawing longer term conclusions about a reduced scope for national policy. Indeed, John Major remarked bullishly, launching his attempt to stimulate public debate on the future of British foreign policy, that Britain's first characteristic was that of being 'a Nation State in what, I firmly believe, will continue to be a world of Nation States for the foreseeable future'.[28] Ultimately, one has to ask whether Britain has any objectives in EPC/CFSP beyond the short term and the institutionally piecemeal, or whether it is, in effect, largely geared to events? The Bosnian crisis projects before us an image of a Britain caught halfway between a determination to accept its traditional responsibilities for shaping the European balance of power, and a helpless indecision in the absence of either an American lead or a powerful, mobilized, and truly collective European capacity for intervention.

SECURITY AND DEFENCE

Both the cutbacks in military capability ('the peace dividend') and the Balkan crises since 1991 have raised the issue of the relationship between defence policy and foreign policy, at the national and the European levels. A good deal has happened in the last five years to move forward the debate on a European defence capability, even if the movement has not been as far or as fast as some optimists have wished. Indeed, of all the areas of European integration, apart from that of money, this is now the most susceptible to growth.

It is possible to interpret the significance for Britain of the development of a European security dimension in two opposing ways. First, the fact that most of the other members of the Community are now willing to envisage going beyond pure diplomacy and into a commitment to cooperate on the provision of armed forces (note the gradual increase in the number of states wishing to associate themselves with the Eurocorps, and the willingness of the neutral states to soften their commitment to non-intervention) promises to narrow the gap between themselves and Britain and France, the two major military powers of the Union. It raises the question ultimately of whether Paris and London should put their superior resources at the disposal of the group (nuclear and conventional) and it also makes a more equal burden sharing conceivable. Now that the German Constitutional Court (1994) has made it possible for the Bonn government to send German forces abroad (albeit only after the consent of the Bundestag, and as part of a UN-legitimized multilateral action)[29] Britain is on the verge of having to face up to the practical consequences of its theoretical preference for a wider sharing of external responsibilities among the European powers.

Second and conversely, however, it can be argued that the very introduction of the security dimension to the EC project is more likely to highlight the gap between Anglo-French capabilities and the rest, given the improbability of either a significant German military role (Germany and Italy have significant self-denying ordinances as to where their forces can serve, arising out of the history of this century)[30] or a genuinely European defence community, with a single command centre and integrated multinational forces. The crises in ex-Yugoslavia and the importunate talk of 'the hour of Europe' raised expectations about EC military intervention which could not be and have not been fulfilled. It is clear for the present that if Britain and France (and probably also the USA) are unwilling to act then nothing can happen. To this extent Britain still possesses a negative form of international power: as one of only two European states with the capacity (i.e. the range of professional armed forces) to project military force well beyond its own borders, if it (or France) refuses to participate in a peace-enforcing action in Bosnia, then 'Europe' is paralysed.[31]

Britain has moved with the times to the extent that it accepts that some increased EC security coordination is necessary in the vacuum left by the end of the Cold War. In 1995 it tried to anticipate demands likely to be made in the 1996 IGC by launching an initiative to set up WEU Heads of Government meetings, back to back with the European Council meetings (thus blurring the issue of the differentiated memberships of the two organizations).[32] But it is still a first principle of British policy to preserve NATO and the American commitment to Europe. Indeed, it is arguable that London continues to be impaled on the horns of a diplomatic dilemma, between the 'coordination reflex' of EPC and the consultation impulse of what is left of the special relationship. In practice Britain attempts to maintain instant and open channels with both sets of partners, but there is considerable variation across issues, and according to which part of the Whitehall machine is involved. EPC has therefore made the Anglo-American relationship more complicated, and now the CFSP has breached the citadel of defence issues, it may in time force the fundamental reconsideration of the privileged London–Washington security nexus.[33]

This tension was already evident ten years ago, during the Westland affair, when two senior Cabinet Ministers resigned over the repercussions of a policy battle over whether a small British helicopter firm should secure its future with a European consortium or a predominantly American offer from the American United Technologies Corporation.[34]

In a strange echo in July 1995 of the Westland affair, British newspapers profited from full-page rival advertisements from American- and French-led firms seeking a British army helicopter contract, just as the Conservative Party was once again being wracked in a leadership contest between the Eurosceptic John Redwood and the marginally less sceptical John Major. History repeated itself in that the Americans won the contract (and the ultra-sceptic Michael Portillo became Minister of Defence). But this time the parameters have changed. A more pro-EU government may take over in Britain within two years; the Europeans are being forced as never before to give serious consideration to providing for their own collective defence; and the institutional structures of the EU and NATO now not only do not inhibit the evolution of a European pillar, they positively encourage it.[35] Britain may, therefore, find it much more difficult in the future to avoid choosing between the European and the transatlantic path for its security and defence policies.

CONCLUSIONS

In the 1983 version of this book I concluded that EPC as it stood 'worked too well for British foreign policy for Britain to seek a genuinely European alternative'. The passing of ten years means that this judgement must now be significantly amended. The continuing development of EPC, to the point where it has been nominally transformed into the CFSP and is actually at a decisive point of choice (between genuine supranationalism and a consolidated intergovernmentalism) has pushed Britain more clearly into the conservative camp. London can no longer pretend to progressive attitudes on the procedural evolution of a European foreign policy while also opposing any limitations on national freedom of manoeuvre. The British view of the CFSP is fundamentally that of thinking that even the new status quo of the TEU really goes too far; the trend which it represents no longer suits Britain so well.

Despite this, there is little willingness in London to project thinking very far into the future on the issue of how far continuing change inside and outside the Community might require a further deepening of the CFSP. It may well be that the present system of coordination will suffice for decades, despite the anxiety that this would induce in pathologically restless pro-integrationists. But if it does not, Britain will need to have a sense of the issues and options for change, including a view on what will follow from the choice to go it alone rather than to accept further significant restrictions on sovereignty. Although in this respect the problem is clearly part of the wider discussion of Britain's structural relationship to 'Europe', the particular implications of foreign policy cooperation have so far been neglected in the British debate, and few attempts have been made to delineate the options, at least in public.

Yet some reconsideration is inevitable. Britain itself has changed, both internally and in its international capacities. Together with an extensive set of bilateral relations, some of which go well beyond anything discussed in EPC, the country continues to shoulder a heavy – and largely self-imposed – burden in what might be called the executive management of international society. Britain is always prominent in multilateral decision-making and quick to take on costly responsibilities in crises, military or otherwise. This proclivity has endured for a surprisingly long time given the self-perception of internal decay, but the point of choice is fast approaching. It is only an historical or a principled sense of mission which will keep Britain active at a global level at all, for the final colonial ties are now being shed. And if a disproportionate global activity is to continue, then the costs will have to be met from some area of an already highly contested domestic budget.

Contradictions, or dialectical tensions, are an inevitable and to a degree a desirable characteristic of all politics. But when the contradictions becomed sharpened to the point of policy becoming either paralysed or unpredictable, then a crisis, with its promise of a resolution but risk of a disntegration, looms on the horizon. In Britain's case the contradictions in its relationship with EPC/CFSP have not yet reached crisis point, but they have been becoming steadily sharper over the last decade. To summarize, there are five manifest points of tension.

• The first is between the desire to lead European foreign policy and the de facto exclusion from the Franco-German partnership which is now the source of most initiatives in the EU.

- The second is between the acceptance in principle of the value of collective foreign policy-making and the tendency in practice to opt in and out of it on instrumental grounds.

- The third is between the continuing British commitment to intergovern-mentalism in the CFSP, and the increasing sense in other states that the CFSP cannot work without the introduction of more of the Community method.

- The fourth is between Britain's traditional attachment to NATO and the American partnership, and the newly evolving European defence dimension.

- The last is between the levels of process and substance in the CFSP; previously Britain tended to prefer procedural innovation (within inter-governmentalism) rather than intrude into sensitive policy areas. Now things are reversed, with procedural issues inevitably pressing up against the limits of intergovernmentalism, and London wishing for support in certain policy areas. The tension exists in the fact that whichever way round the British preference lies, the distinction between procedure and policy is ever more difficult to sustain – the operational level has been formalized in Article J of the TEU into 'common positions' and 'joint actions' and these are precisely the areas where the institutional battle over majority voting has been and will continue to be fought.

Britain needs a debate, or more fundamentally, a clarification at the level of domestic politics, on the whole European issue, if these contradictions are to be resolved. In structural terms the real issue is, how important is it for Britain to retain the freedom to diverge from general EU positions, procedures and instruments, when national necessity seems to demand it? In the particular context of the CFSP, the dilemma is very similar, namely, given Britain's interests and objectives in international relations, how important is the freedom to opt out of a common European approach, when weighed against the advantages of solidarity? Freedman put it another way, discussing Westland: 'Was European cooperation merely to be pre-ferred when other things were equal, or was it a high priority in all circumstances?'[36]

The British answer to these questions at present would be that the benefits of joint actions can only be judged on a case-by-case basis, whereas the freedom to decide for oneself is fundamental. More profoundly, the answer is rooted in the fact that most policy-makers in London, and even more the political opinions behind them, still find their identity in an idea of Britain first, and Europe a more distant second. Whether in this respect Britain is significantly different from the other nation-states which make up the European Union, the next ten years should tell.

NOTES

1 As shown in the *Basic Statistics* annually produced by the European Community, Eurostat, Office of Official Publications of the European Communities, Luxembourg. There has, of course, been a dispute over the accuracy of the figures, and whether they over or under state the black economies of the two states.

2 A recent example is the *New Statesman* sponsored conference on the foreign policy of the 'new' Labour Party, held at the London School of Economics on 16 June 1995, and discussed at length in the *New Statesman and Society* of the same date and that of 23 June. This followed on from the huge officially sponsored Chatham House conference on Britain's place in the world on 29 March 1995. See Note 28 below.

3 Since Britain joined the EC and EPC the following have held the office of Foreign Secretary: Sir Alec Douglas-Home (1970–74); James Callaghan (1974–6); Anthony Crosland (1976–7); David Owen (1977–9); Lord Carrington (1979–82); Francis Pym (1982–3); Sir Geoffrey Howe (1983–9); John Major (July–November 1989); Douglas Hurd (1989–95); Malcolm Rifkind (1995–).

4 For an early and perceptive example of this external analysis of the British approach, see Françoise de La Serre, *La Grande Bretagne et la Communauté européenne*, Paris, Presses Universitaires de France, 1987, particularly Chapter 8, 'L'Union européenne, un exorcisme réussi'.

5 For a survey of the foreign policy of the Thatcher years, see Peter Byrd (ed.), *British Foreign Policy Under Thatcher*, Oxford, Philip Allan, 1988.

6 In 1990 UK defence expenditure was 3.7 per cent of GDP, compared to 2.8 per cent for France and the Netherlands, 2.2 per cent for Germany, 1.8 per cent for Italy and 1.6 per cent for Belgium. See *The Military Balance, 1991–92*, London, Brasseys for IISS, 1991, p.212.

7 On the uses – and limits – of using the notion of nostalgia to explain British foreign policy, see Christopher Hill, 'The historical background: past and present in British foreign policy', in Michael Smith, Steve Smith and Brian White (eds), *British Foreign Policy: Tradition, Change and Transformation*, London, Unwin Hyman, 1988, pp.25–49.

8 On the dilemmas of Hong Kong, and the lack of cards in Britain's hand, see Michael Yahuda, 'Sino-British negotiations: perceptions, organization and political culture', *International Affairs*, 69, 2, April 1993, pp.245–66, and James T. H. Tang, 'Hong Kong's international status', *The Pacific Review*, vol. 6, no. 3, 1993, pp.205–15.

9 John Major, 'Europe – a future that works', second William and Mary Lecture, Leiden, The Netherlands, 7 September 1994, *Survey of Current Affairs*, vol. 24, no. 9, September 1994, pp.225–7.

10 Paul Kennedy, *The Realities Behind Diplomacy: Background Influences on British External Policy, 1865–1980*, London, George Allen and Unwin, 1981, p.379. But note that in his *The Rise and Fall of the Great Powers: Economic Change and Military Conflict from 1500 to 2000*, London, Unwin Hyman, 1988, Kennedy argues that we should not forget that 'there was also a critically important "continental" dimension to British grand strategy' and cites L. Dehio to the effect that Britain brilliantly pursued a Janus-faced strategy, 'with one face turned towards the continent to trim the balance of power and the other directed at sea to strengthen her maritime dominance' (pp.97–8).

11 Margaret Thatcher, *The Downing Street Years*, London, HarperCollins, 1993.

12 On the question of European relations with Britain on the Falklands War, see Stelios Stavridis and Christopher Hill (eds), *Domestic Sources of Foreign Policy: West*

European Reactions to the Falklands Conflict, Oxford, Berg, 1996, particularly the chapter by Geoffrey Edwards, 'The European Community level'.

13 Garry Clyde Hubauer, Jeffrey J. Schott and Kimberly Ann Elliott, *Economic Sanctions Reconsidered: Supplemental Case Histories*, 2nd edn, Washington DC, Institute for International Economics, 1990, pp.619–24.

14 For a full account of European policy on South Africa, see Martin Holland, *European Union Common Foreign Policy: from EPC to CFSP Joint Action on South Africa*, London and Basingstoke, Macmillan, 1995.

15 This is certainly the view of Bulmer and Edwards, whose 1992 survey barely notices Thatcher. See Simon Bulmer and Geoffrey Edwards, 'Foreign and security policy' in Simon Bulmer, Stephen George and Andrew Scott (eds), *The United Kingdom and EC Membership Evaluated*, London, Pinter, 1992, pp.145–60.

16 *The Downing Street Years*, p.309.

17 Thatcher's view was only 'broadly' realist because she combined (uneasily) a stress on national independence with an historicist belief in the ultimate demise of certain types (i.e. socialist) of state.

18 On the central place of the UK in EPC activities on terrorism, see Simon J. Nuttall, *European Political Cooperation*, Oxford, Clarendon Press, 1992, pp.302–7; also Christopher Hill, 'The political dilemmas for Western governments' in Lawrence Freedman, Christopher Hill, Adam Roberts, R.J. Vincent, Paul Wilkenson and Philip Windsor, *Terrorism and International Order*, London, Routledge/Royal Institute of International Affairs, 1986, pp.77–100.

19 The same analysis broadly applies to the evolution of the EC in general. See Françoise de La Serre, 'Comment être à la fois britannique et européen?', *Politique Etrangère*, I, 1993, pp.55–61.

20 See David Allen, 'The British presidency of the European Communities (July–December 1992): the impact on the Community', unpublished paper for the International Studies Association annual conference, 1994.

21 See Françoise de La Serre and Philippe Moreau Defarges, 'France: a penchant for leadership' in Christopher Hill (ed.), *National Foreign Policies and European Political Cooperation*, op.cit., pp.62–3.

22 De La Serre, *La Grande Bretagne et la Communauté européenne*, op.cit., pp.202–9

23 See Simon J. Nuttall, *European Political Cooperation*, op.cit., p.309

24 The title of my chapter in the 1983 edition of this book was 'Britain: a convenient schizophrenia', referring to the fact that London was enthusiastic about EPC, but bloody-minded on Community matters such as the budget, and that this Janus-faced approach turned out to be useful and successful – in the short term.

25 While Britain certainly applied for membership of the EEC in the hope of regenerating its economic performance, at least as important was the sense that, in the wake of decolonization, the country needed a new platform for the sustenance of its national foreign policy, particularly so as to ensure that Britain was not wholly dependent on the USA.

26 According to FCO data produced for the 1995 Chatham House/HMG Conference on 'Britain in the World', Britain has 215 overseas posts in total, while France has 286, Italy 253 and Germany 240. On 13 February 1993 the Italian newspaper *La Repubblica*, analysing Britain's difficulties in the ex-USSR states, headlined its report 'L'ambasciatore di Sua Maestà vive nel sottoscala' (HM Ambassador lives below stairs). Such financial constraints may explain why Sir Michael Franklin, a former Head of the European Secretariat in the Cabinet Office, was willing to recommend working towards a system of European embassies over 'a period of years'. See his *Britain's Future in Europe*, London, RIIA/Pinter, 1990, pp.33–7.

27 By repute Treasury orthodoxy governs British policy as a whole. But when it has

come to perceived national emergencies, the Treasury has never stood out against increased defence expenditure, whether in 1939, 1950, 1979, 1982 or 1990. On the historical background, see George Peden, *British Rearmament and the Treasury 1932–39*, Edinburgh, Scottish Academic Press, 1979. See also Michael Clarke, *British External Policy-Making in the 1990s*, London and Basingstoke, Macmillan/RIIA, 1992, pp.109–11.

28 'Opening Address' by the Rt. Hon. John Major MP, contained in *Conference Proceedings* of the RIIA/British Government Conference held on 29 March 1995 at the Queen Elizabeth II Conference Centre in London, and published by the two sponsors jointly. The Prime Minister's speech was global in its orientation, and did not refer to the CFSP.

29 See Reinhardt Rummel's chapter in this book, p.53.

30 Rummel, op.cit., p.53, p.65, note 30, on the 'Kohl Doctrine'.

31 That this 'national' perspective of European foreign policy (and an Anglo-French dominated perspective at that) is not anachronistic is born out by press analysis such as Mark Frankland's 'Humbled Europe learns its lowly place in the world', *The Observer*, 23 July 1995.

32 See *Agence Europe, Daily Bulletin*, 13–14 March 1995.

33 For salutary warnings from non-British sources not to write off the 'special relationship', see B. Vivekanandan, 'Washington must rely on London, not Bonn', *Orbis: A Journal of World Affairs*, Summer 1991, pp.411–22; Henry Kissinger, 'How do people outside Britain view our role in the world – the view from the United States', in RIIA/HMG *Conference Proceedings*, op.cit. pp.17–21. But it is notable how Kissinger tended to elide 'Britain' and 'Europe' in a way that must have disappointed his hosts.

34 On Westland see Lawrence Freedman 'The case of Westland and the bias to Europe', *International Affairs*, vol. 63, no. 1, Winter 1986–7, pp.1–19.

35 This dates from the NATO Summit of 6 July 1990 in London, whose communiqué said that 'the move within the European Community towards political union, including the development of a European identity in the domain of security, will also contribute to Atlantic solidarity and to the establishment of a just and lasting peace throughout Europe'. Cited in Franklin, *Britain's Future in Europe*, op.cit., p.38. Since then, there has been the TEU's placing of the WEU at the fulcrum of NATO/EU relations, and the agreement on 'Combined Joint Task Forces', aimed at making European operations compatible with the NATO command structure.

36 Freedman, 'The case of Westland and the bias to Europe', op.cit., p.2.

Chapter 4

Regional reassertion

The dilemmas of Italy

Gianni Bonvicini

Before analysing Italian assumptions about and interests in the European Common Foreign and Security Policy (CFSP, previously EPC) it is essential to address the issue of the country's present deep political transformation. Italy represents an important example of a radical renewal in domestic politics after the end of the Cold War (the other example being Germany).[1]

ITALY'S DOMESTIC CRISES AND THE EFFECT ON ITS FOREIGN POLICY ROLE

A new electoral law, more in line with those in use in other West European countries, has been approved. The old corrupt political class has collapsed, as a result of the 'clean hands' judicial operation and of popular referenda to change the electoral rules. New political forces have emerged, this fact having been confirmed by the long-awaited general election of 27 March 1994. A new government, headed by Silvio Berlusconi, a mass media entrepreneur, has opened the doors for the first time since the Second World War to a declared far right political party, Alleanza Nazionale (whose core was the Movimento Sociale Italiano (MSI), the old fascist party). Finally a process of constitutional adaptation, aiming to create a kind of federal state on the basis of traditional European models (more power to the Prime Minister or President, counterbalanced by greater autonomy to the Regions; a clearer division of competencies and roles between the Chamber of Deputies and the Senate, comparable to that between the Bundestag and Bundesrat) will most probably continue.

This has created, on the one side, high political expectations of deep internal change and, on the other, a considerable degree of political confusion in the country, aggravated by a difficult and ambiguous economic performance, except for those export-oriented sectors which took profits (at least in the short term) from the devaluation of the lira. Unemployment is giving no sign of easing, despite Berlusconi's promise during the electoral campaign, after one of the longest periods of economic recession experienced by the country. The new elections have not led towards the expected bipolar party system – on the contrary, the oldfashioned pattern of a coalition of parties with different political strategies and ideologies is weakening the potential for new and more efficient governing methods. In fact, some political forces are undermining national unity (the Lega), others recall nationalistic and state-oriented traditions, along with a neo-fascist vision of political life (Alleanza Nazionale). And finally, Berlusconi's political movement, Forza Italia (not yet transformed into a proper political party), expresses a wish for efficient management of the state and for its progressive 'privatization', which hardly coincides with the political priorities of its partners in government.

In this new domestic context, Italy's international relations are characterized by both continuity and change. At the international level there are also clear and important changes, such as the demise of political and strategic bipolarity and the growing number of local and regional conflicts not just outside Europe but right in the core of the old continent. Traditional multilateralism is facing growing problems, exacerbated by the deep and long-lasting international, especially European, economic crisis. It is within the context of this crisis that Italy's difficulties should be framed. Throughout the 1980s but still in 1991 and the first half of 1992 (i.e. just before the first monetary crisis) Italy had seemed eager to take up new international responsibilities and had played a significant role in relaunching the process of European integration. Yet, instead of a virtuous circle, we have witnessed the starting of a new vicious circle. The Italian crisis, mostly determined by internal causes, has thus been worsened by the international situation. The weakening of international relations at all levels, from NATO to the Europe of Maastricht, has thrown Italy's deficiencies and abnormalities into sharp relief. The stiff macroeconomic conditions set by the Maastricht Treaty have highlighted Italy's long-standing troubles with its economic policy, swollen bureaucracy and the political system. The repeated ERM crises have underlined the flaws of a domestic economic policy based only on the monetary level. Moreover, the ideological collapse in Eastern Europe has deprived Italy's political and institutional system of its connecting glue. Until recently, in fact, its governing system was based on a pact excluding the opposition (for ideological reasons), a 'conventio ad excludendum', accompanied by the consensual management of public affairs and working through the dominance of the legislature (where the opposition held around the half of the presidencies of parliamentary committees) over the executive. But one very positive feature of the old 'conventio' was that which allowed Italy to pursue a foreign policy which was attracting increasing national consensus. Today, with the potential for a regime of alternation in government, this consensus has to be ensured either by working out what the Americans define as a 'bipartisan' foreign policy (not easy in a system which is still multi-party) or by ensuring the necessary continuity on the constitutional and administrative levels (as in Germany or France).[2]

In this extremely volatile situation, at both international and domestic levels as well in their mutual relations, Italy runs the risk of playing an increasingly marginal role. In fact, the above-mentioned domestic factors have negatively affected Italy's foreign relations in that ongoing internal political, economic and institutional crises have led to the deterioration of her credibility and image abroad, to begin with in the financial community, due to the weakness of the lira and the appearance of an economic structural crisis, but more recently also among the political elites of Europe and the USA. For Berlusconi's decision to legitimize the neo-fascist party by taking it into the government could result in distancing Italy from its traditional European and transatlantic alliances.

This changing domestic and international situation can be contrasted with the continuity of the institutional and multilateral fora in which Italy participates. Although they were created in the context of the bipolar balance, they have not collapsed along with it. There may be uncertainty about the future role of NATO or of the policy that European Union has to adopt towards the new requests for enlargement or about the effectiveness of WEU in the managing of some military aspects of the Bosnian conflict, but participation in these institutions has not been put into question and they still constitute a stable point of reference for their member states.

On the other hand it is rather evident that Italy's role in these institutions has diminished: it has become a less essential ally in NATO, with the paradoxical result of being used as a forward base for NATO air strikes over Bosnia and at the same time being excluded from the Contact Group which decides the policies of the major powers towards the conflict in former Yugoslavia. Its ability to meet the macroeconomic criteria for Economic and Monetary Union is uncertain, as demonstrated by provocative proposals like that of the German Christian Democrats for a political–economic hard core inside the Union, which openly excludes Italy.[3] Its presence in the G-7 now seems less crucial, this question being unofficially raised when discussions about the enlargement of the Summit to Russia (and in the future to China) started, with the floated idea of letting the Summit coincide with a revised UN Security Council;[4] a line of reasoning confirmed by Italy's status inside the UN where it is not substantively equal to the other middle powers, namely Germany and Japan, which are the main candidates for inclusion in an enlarged Security Council – and this despite Italy's extensive engagement in UN peacekeeping operations, with the accompanying costs in terms of both financing and casualties. These developments do not mean that Italy has lost its ability to influence or act; they merely imply that it must carefully reassess its position.

For several years Italy has enjoyed a condition of geopolitical privilege

under the American protectorate and as an active member of the European
Community. NATO has granted external security and Europe a comfortable
internal and international context for the country's development. The end
of the bipolar world leaves Italy greater room for autonomous responsibility.
And the solution of the present economic and political crises could, at least
in theory, help to define the status of Italy among nations. Beniamino
Andreatta, the former Minister of Foreign Affairs, has stated that:

> The end of the Cold War has not caused a revision of the basic choices:
> Italy's membership in the EU and the Atlantic Alliance. It has implied,
> however, the end of a privileged position and of free riding. Membership
> is no longer enough in the new international conditions: one has to
> qualify oneself through presence and hard work.[5]

But, on the other side, the crisis of the Italian political and institutional
system comes at a time when Italy is increasingly becoming a front-line actor
(think of the Balkans and the Mediterranean) in the new European
environment. Consequently, this condition of political and institutional
transition compounds the ambiguity and lack of transparency in the
management and definition of Italian foreign policy in several ways.

In the first place it must be admitted that the seriousness of domestic
problems turns attention away from foreign policy issues; the domestic
political debate on foreign policy choices is practically non-existent and in
the long run this will produce confusion and, perhaps, a reversal in the list
of Italian priorities. It seems that foreign policy questions are just matters
for the government and more particularly for its Foreign Minister (his
colleagues and the Prime Minister focusing exclusively on domestic interests). In fact the new political forces, which gave birth after the general
elections of March 1994 to the first government of the so-called 'Second
Republic', made no real effort to specify their international interests and
have made only a few generic statements, except (as we shall see below),
for such specific issues as the quarrel with Slovenia and the negative reaction
to the above-mentioned CDU proposal for a core Europe excluding Italy.
Even these few declarations are contradictory and somewhat distant from
the reality of Italian international behaviour.

The Italian debate about participation in the EU or, more generally, on
its international attitudes is therefore an exercise that cannot be based on
continuity, in terms of clarity of political attitudes. It is more the outcome
of reactive and occasional actions in individual political episodes than the
result of strategic thinking at either the government or party level.[6]

In the event, despite the lack of attention to foreign policy, Italy has
continued with its international engagements and its military participation
abroad, under UN cover, is comparable to that of its major European
partners. But this armed presence in various crisis spots does not provoke
serious domestic debate, nor is it a means of getting advantages in terms of

a credible authority and prestige abroad; even in this respect, Italy remains a marginal international actor.

A crisis on Italy's borders, in the Balkans, has transformed the country, for the first time in many years, into a front-line player in a period in which, on the multilateral side, NATO and the CFSP are showing their limits in terms of decisional effectiveness, while on the domestic side a new national defence policy has not yet emerged. The combination of these two weaknesses is affecting confidence in the traditional pattern of foreign and security policy.

More generally, in order to sort out the current state of confusion, the new government will have to reassess the country's international engagements and priorities. But this can be done only through an analysis and evaluation of the tendencies which have emerged in the last years in the practical conduct of foreign policy with regard to both involvement in multilateral decision-making (particularly the CFSP) and to the country's basic international interests (particularly in relation to the USA, former Yugoslavia, and the Mediterranean).[7]

EUROPEAN FOREIGN AND SECURITY POLICY INITIATIVES: THE POSITIVE SIDE OF THE BALANCE SHEET

Starting from the multilateral decision-making aspects of Italy's international role, the most obvious point of reference for Italian action continues to remain its heavy involvement in CFSP, old and new. It is worth recalling that it was not by chance that the title of my chapter in the predecessor to this book about EPC and national foreign policies, written at the beginning of the 1980s, was 'Italy: an integrationist perspective'.[8]

It is useful to summarize the main reasons for the full and convinced support given by Italy, from the very beginning to the present, to the progressive reinforcement of a European foreign (and, later on, security) policy.

Since 1945 there has been a kind of 'natural' reflex in Italy's conception of foreign policy that has pushed the country to favour multilateral initiatives at the expense of purely bilateral approaches. From the outset, Italy's participation on EPC was considered the optimum way of underlining traditional political support for multilateralization on the basis of the original post-Second World War choices, to participate fully in both NATO and the Community.

This was not just the outcome of a new post-war 'philosophy', but also a very practical means of providing a stable incentive for the emergence of a bipartisan attitude (including the Communists as the major opposition party) on foreign policy issues under a common multilateral, and in this case, European 'umbrella'. Clearly multilateral choices and positions helped to minimize the chances of radical political confrontation over ad hoc international events (especially in a contiguous area like the Middle East), which could have disturbed the domestic political climate.

In addition, one has also to consider the great advantage for Italian national diplomacy, which in its bilateral activities often profited from the so-called 'cover function' provided by EPC in troublesome regions and towards those countries which posed a threat to the West as a whole, but where the limits of purely bilateral (or national) policy were all too evident. Typical, from this point of view, was Rome's line on the PLO, a very sensitive domestic political problem. Even those politicians (among others Giulio Andreotti, when Foreign Minister) who traditionally had been considered very close to PLO positions, had carefully avoided breaking European solidarity, especially in those years in which the peace process between Palestinians and Israelis appeared to be making progress. The discipline of European cooperation, in fact, was considered vital both to protect our own national interest and to promote the peace settlement.[9]

These first two considerations, which will be reinforced by what follows on Italy's traditional pro-European attitudes, help us to understand why, through practically the entire history of EPC, Italy has acted as a disciplined member, always giving priority to common interests (except in a very few and exceptional cases, like the second phase of the Falkland crisis, May 1982, when the Italian government withdrew from the sanctions against Argentina). Compared with other members of the Union our performance as a 'good pupil' could be given the highest marks. And this happened in a field where the basic rule was traditionally intergovernmental and therefore the possibilities of letting national preferences prevail were rather tempting.

This also has to do with a point of doctrine, that of working towards a more consistent process of European integration through the idea of adding a political dimension to the existing functional process in the economic field. The enlargement of the area of common competencies to include aspects of the foreign policy field was therefore seen as an essential element on the way to the strengthening of the supranational character of the Community (Union). This 'ideological' attitude explains the reasons why Italy always pressed for (or at least supported) a progressive movement of the cooperative method and decision-making structure of EPC towards that of the Community. Italy did in fact ask on several occasions (for example, with the original version of the Genscher–Colombo plan)[10] to 'communitarize' the decision-making procedures of EPC and, possibly, in the future also those in the security field. At the same time it wished to move towards more stable and common institutional mechanisms, like the Secretariat (which was first headed by an Italian diplomat, Giovanni Jannuzzi) at the time of negotiations on the Single European Act (1985), in addition to those run by the Presidency. In part, as we will see later, Italian diplomacy worked towards creating the conditions for adding a security dimension to EPC, again through the 1981 Genscher–Colombo initiative as a first stage and then through the relaunching of WEU in 1984. The same positive attitude towards the reinforcement of the security dimension was evident during the drafting of WEU Common Platform (1987). More generally in the 1980s, Italy strictly followed the traditional path of giving priority to those elements which would promote the 'communitarization' of common actions and policies. Typical, from this point of view, was the recourse for the first time inside the European Council to majority voting, under Art. 236, on the proposal of the Italian chairman Bettino Craxi to organize an intergovernmental conference for the revision of the Rome Treaty (Milan, June 1985): the main contentious point being the Franco-German plan for a Treaty on European Union, with a common foreign and security policy as one of its important aspects.[11]

Finally, through its committed participation in EPC's substantive activities, Italy tried to reinforce the international credibility of its own foreign policy and the functioning of its diplomatic mechanisms. Rome indirectly exploited this reinforcement, in order to be recognized as one of the main international actors in world affairs, from the Group of Seven to the many engagements in troublesome spots around the world under the UN umbrella. Paradoxically the positive record of participation, as a recognized and essential actor in EPC and more generally on the wider international stage, has helped to enlarge Italy's range of action and to reinforce its conception of distinctive national interests. This potential began to be exploited just before the great events of 1989, but it developed further in the new environment thereafter. Italian activism ranged from the naval participation in the first Gulf crisis (1987) to the Iraq war (1991), from Somalia (1992) to Mozambique (1993), from the patrolling of the Adriatic (1993) to the offer of its bases to NATO for air strikes on Bosnia (1994). In general, the country has tried to sustain what was termed 'an emerging profile' for its national foreign policy, which appeared at the beginning of the 1980s with the first important decision to deploy Euromissiles (1981).[12]

THE EMERGENCE OF THE NEW EUROPE AND ITALIAN MOVES TOWARDS GREATER SELF-ASSERTION

In the new geostrategic situation of the post-1989 world, Italy perceived almost immediately an important change in its international position: the country, as we have pointed out, is now less essential in terms of its traditional alliance duties, but at the same time even more 'front-line' in its position than before. As a consequence, in these first years of the post-Cold War period, Italy is living out the ambivalent perception of both having more room for manoeuvre and being less important, while at the same time it is subject to worrying new dangers. This perception, still unclear at the conceptual and political levels, will almost certainly stimulate diverse domestic political reactions due to the perverse combination of what used to be called the 'dual crises', internal to Italy and international at the same time.

In any case, in the first period, between 1989 and the end of 1992, Italian activism in international politics succeeded in affecting traditional partners, as new projects and foreign policy priorities emerged one after the other, such as the Central European Initiative (CEI), launched as the 'Quad-rangolare' in 1989; the so-called CSCM[13] for securing stability in the Mediterranean, an adapted version of the old CSCE for the Southern Region (1990); the new attention given to the Maghreb (the Five-plus-Five initiative, 1990); and more recently, in 1994 a proposal for reforming the UN Security Council. One of the characteristics of those plans was that of having been elaborated outside the framework of EPC, a rather unusual step given the recent tradition of Italian diplomacy. This created some nervous reaction among our partners (e.g. the Germans and even the European Commission were disturbed by the CEI, which was considered an element of confusion on the way to a new policy for the Community towards the Central and Eastern European Countries)[14] and the need to regain their confidence through an assurance of the strict linkage between Italy's own initiatives and the foreign and security positions of the Union. The attempt to attribute a more active and less traditional role to Italy can also be seen with respect to some European initiatives, such as the support given to the British point of view, through the so-called British–Italian Declaration, as opposed to the German–French 'entente'. This proposal about the future of European security policy was released at the end of 1991, on the eve of the Maastricht European Council, and its aim was to emphasize the nature of WEU as a pillar inside the Atlantic Alliance, in contrast with the Franco-German orientation to link it definitely to the EU. The move was seen as a break in the usual Italian preference for Germany or for the Franco-German entente. Italy here tried to play the role of mediator between the extreme positions of France and Germany, on the one hand, and Britain, on the other, with regard to the future of European defence and its relationship with NATO. Like Britain, it was particularly concerned with the negative American reaction to a plan which sought to allocate a strong autonomous role to WEU. In addition, Italy had some reservations on the idea of the Franco-German Brigade (today the Eurocorps), from which it was originally excluded, as the future military nucleus of WEU.[15]

In fact, Italy was also rather reluctant to accept the Franco-German offer to become part of the Joint Brigade. Here again Italian diplomacy rejected the idea of being offered only a second rank membership in an initiative which was considered too bilateral and in contrast with traditional engage-ments in the Euro-Atlantic collective security network. In fact, a great deal of Italian suspicion towards the Franco-German Brigade had to do with the traditional reluctance to isolate the USA from the European defence scenario. But this line did not hold up for long, and it developed into a full support of the 'spirit' of Maastricht with respect to the CFSP, that is in line with the French–German interpretation.

More recently, Italy has witnessed a progressive transition towards a greater emphasis on a more autonomous European contribution within NATO. During the Atlantic Council of January 1994, former Prime Minister Aurelio Ciampi underlined the need to rebalance the responsibilities shared by Europe and the USA in the European theatre.[16] The Bosnian case and, most probably, the bad experience in Somalia under US leadership may have convinced Italy about the appropriateness of a different share of responsibilities with the USA. In short, Italy has fully aligned itself with the group of those in favour of giving Europe a greater weight within NATO and the possibility of acting autonomously in the circumstances of an American decision to stay out of certain actions. Italy is still not in the Eurocorps, but this is likely to last for a short time only and for reasons which have nothing to do with the US attitude towards the old Franco-German initiative.

So far as Euro-American relations are concerned, the Ciampi government, and particularly its Foreign Minister Beniamino Andreatta, developed the idea of a full reconsideration of transatlantic links and expressed themselves in favour of a new pact between Europe and the USA, the so-called 'Transatlantic Charter Mark Two', a profound revision of Baker's original Charter, which would address the whole range of relations between the two parties, including the economic and political dimensions. The idea was to create preventive mechanisms and more stringent rules in order to avoid open conflicts between the two parties. This proposal, which never became an official request of the Italian government, reflects concern about a possible American retaliation against the protectionist attitudes of some European countries, as had been the case during the final stage of the GATT negotiations.[17]

Another sign of the new foreign policy assertiveness of Italy was a growing presence in multilateral military operations in out-of-area regions and the offer of troops for UN peacekeeping activities. Here again Rome tended to move, at least partially, outside the context of a strict European coordination, and in several cases domestic considerations dictated behaviour, as was clear in the case of Somalia. Italy's active role in UN peacekeeping operations gave birth to a debate on reforming the UN Security Council and on the Italian presence in it. The Berlusconi government officially adopted an old proposal of former Foreign Minister Andreatta, on the creation of a semi-permanent member's status in the Security Council, based on objective criteria, such as economic indicators, human resources, culture and mass communications.[18]

More generally, while maintaining a traditionally pro-European attitude, Italy has seemed to take a more independent role in the new international environment. Three key cases, those of Somalia, former Yugoslavia and Mediterranean security, will serve to illustrate this new tendency.

THE PRICE OF INDEPENDENCE: THREE CASE STUDIES

A bad experience in Somalia

As will be easily remembered, the original goal of the mission 'Restore Hope' of December 1992 was to ensure the distribution of humanitarian aid to the population of Somalia. The subsequent development of new and unclear goals highlighted the different national perceptions about how to deal with crisis management. Moreover, it offered a chance to rethink the role of the UN and that of individual countries in peacekeeping and peace enforcing. The participation of Italian troops in the UN contingent in Somalia (UNOSOM), which originally consisted only of American troops, was not initially welcomed by Washington because of Italy's historical and political involvement in the country and, especially, because it flowed from purely national concerns and not from a collective European decision.

In addition, the case of General Bruno Loi, the first Italian commander in Somalia, who did not want to take orders from the UN which conflicted with Italian perceptions of the aim of the peace mission, raised several delicate questions such as the role of the individual members of the UN, the source of authority over the military, and the frequent subordination of UN troops to the military concerns of the USA.

In Somalia the USA has demonstrated how difficult it is for a leading country not to be in a commanding position. This has added to the contradiction between national interests and the management of collective interests. Faced with the difficulties associated with the ambiguous US role and with an unclear mission, the UN proved unable to set up an efficient chain of command and could find no better way out than to put the blame on the Italians. The latter, who held largely justified misgivings about the US approach and about UN confusion, were unable to get their views heard through the formal decision-making mechanism and then gave in to the old Italian tendency of attempting an unsolicited mediation. Italy's complaints evoked no quick or full support from the other members of the Union present in Somalia nor from the CFSP process. Italy remained completely isolated and it had to bear the consequences of antagonism not just from its traditional ally, the USA, but also for the very first time from a multilateral institution like the UN. The Italian and the foreign press headlined the tensions between Italy, the USA and the UN over the intervention in Somalia as 'the conflict between Rambo and Machiavelli'.

An assessment of what has happened should help to avoid the repetition of such an unpleasant situation, in which Italian participation in peacekeeping received little reward. More generally, the Somalia case has highlighted the difficult relationship between the international institutions and national responsibility. In particular what has not yet been clarified is the extent of the transfer of sovereignty to international institutions in the management of peacekeeping operations.

In the case of Somalia, Italy tried to raise the question of the role of international institutions versus national responsibility, but finally decided to adopt a national stance, not least because nobody else fully supported its position. The collapse of a multilateral approach has thus led to the temptation of affirming national interests as a priority within a multi-national initiative; such oldfashioned concepts as the 'geopolitical approach' and 'spheres of influence' began to be seen again in the writings of the Italian press and of scholars in relation to Somalia.[19] Europe remained an abstract actor with no influence either on the domestic debate or on Italy's international behaviour.

Italy and former Yugoslavia: a power vacuum

In relation to the Balkan crisis no less than towards Somalia it is now felt in Rome that there is a need to reassess Italian policy on the basis of a clear definition of the national interests at stake. Nonetheless, in general Rome's behaviour has continued to emphasize the importance of giving full support to collective efforts, Italy being ready to accept any request for a contribution to the settlement of the conflict.

As a consequence, although Rome has always been very reluctant to consider military intervention in the absence of a global political agreement among the parties at war, Italy has repeatedly displayed its willingness to participate in humanitarian or peacekeeping missions. In the autumn of 1991 Italy was ready to participate in the UNPROFOR in Croatia with a force of 3,000 men and one year later an Italian contingent of 1,300 men was ready to be sent to Bosnia for a UN humanitarian mission.

In both cases, a veto from the Serbs kept these plans from being realized. Moreover, the UN continued to rule out the participation in military missions of countries bordering on the crisis area. Former Foreign Minister Andreatta declared that Italy was ready, should the UN request it, to participate in operations in Bosnia aimed at implementing a peace plan agreed on by the parties, and this still remains the general tendency among the new political forces. Moreover, it must be remembered that Italy made its most important contribution in the field of logistics, by offering the use of its airbases to NATO's various missions, including the bombing of the Serbs in Bosnia.

Italy's progressive transformation into a 'launch platform' for intervention in the former Yugoslavia naturally poses a number of problems. The Italian government insists that each operation departing from Italian soil must be under a UN flag and that it must be informed in detail of the plans of every mission to be carried out. Although Italian troops are not deployed on Yugoslav territory, Italy is providing a significant contribution to the implementation of the new measures adopted by the various international organizations and it therefore finds itself in a front-line position. Moreover, as it borders on the former Yugoslavia, Italy will eventually have to find a *modus vivendi* with all the successor states.[20]

This explains Italy's difficult position in the light of Washington's oscillations – first the US reluctance to enter the Yugoslav conflict, and second the contradictory US wish to launch the 'lift and strike' military action by air without a parallel engagement on the ground. Italy also had reservations about Warren Christopher's opposition to the European 'Safe Havens' plan.

In the Yugoslav case, although Italian national interests are fairly clear, Italy has normally supported the positions of its European partners while avoiding any self-assertion at the national level. At the same time it has expressed its frustration at the limited European role and at the 'failure' of CFSP. In other words, Rome believes that more of a European role is needed to prevent new manifestations of nationalism towards former Yugoslavia and here again the low profile of European policies is not helping to overcome nationalistic pressures. The risk is that of leaving too much room for manoeuvre to those political forces of the extreme right, now present in the government, which would like to transform this sense of disappointment into a national issue, by reopening – as they did first during the electoral campaign and then again once in the government – the question of Italy's eastern borders with Slovenia and Croatia.[21] It is particularly over Slovenia that the national issue has moved to the forefront. Under the pressure of Alleanza Nazionale, and of its more radical and nostalgic core, the old but still alive and kicking fascists of MSI, the new government has reversed the strategy of playing down the contentious elements in the relationship and has loudly declared that the solution of bilateral questions has to be considered a precondition of the opening of negotiations between the European Union and Slovenia. An attitude like this, so far from the traditional Italian habit of privileging multilateral interests over purely bilateral concerns, has provoked a lot of surprised reactions, to say the least, from our European partners. The case represents yet another important sign of changing Italian behaviour in foreign policy.

Italy's role as a Southern European

The Italian role in the Mediterranean has always been a source of conflict at both domestic and European levels. Post-war official policy was to link the country firmly to Europe and to play down the role of 'Mediterranean' state inside the EC. The first priority, on the other hand, was clearly Europe, or to use a famous Gianni Agnelli slogan 'to look over the Alps'. But some political parties and especially factions of the old Christian-Democrats and Communists did try on several occasions to bring the attention of the government towards the Mediterranean Basin, which had to be considered a vital national interest. It must be said that these few attempts remained rather marginal with respect to the focus on the building of a strong European Union, our full participation to NATO and on the defence of Europe from the Eastern threat. This pro-European attitude was seen by Italy's northern partners as an effective prophylactic against possible temptations to act nationalistically, as other Southern European member states, namely France and Greece, have done.

In the new post-Cold War world the situation has changed, and this time there is concern expressed from the Italian side over the Mediterranean policy of the European Union. There is in Italy a widespread feeling that Southern Europe seems to count less now than in the past, and far less than it should. This is especially true with regard to competition from Eastern Europe for economic assistance from the West, and particularly from the EU, which, in the opinion of the governments of Southern Europe, is depriving the Mediterranean of substantial resources.[22]

With the rise of nationalism and religious fundamentalism, accompanied by growing security concerns, one of Italy's main priorities is that of helping the creation of a cohesive framework which would facilitate some kind of aggregation: the assumption being that risks and rivalries are more easily solved in a multilateral framework. Italy's relations with the countries of the Mediterranean region have long ceased to be considered in narrow economic terms and now represent a facet of overall national security policy. Italy's Mediterranean policy is based on a comprehensive concept of security that regards political, cultural and economic factors as more important than purely military ones. Consequently, Italian foreign policy now strives to develop a strategy of cooperation with the countries of the area.

In line with the above considerations, the old CSCM project, which included four European countries (France, Italy, Spain and Portugal) and five Arab countries, all members of the Arab Maghreb Union (Algeria, Libya, Mauritania, Morocco and Tunisia), was formally presented by Italy and Spain at the Mediterranean environment conference of the CSCE in September 1990. The idea was to extend the logic of cooperation to the whole Mediterranean area, using the framework of rules and principles adopted in Europe with the CSCE as a model.

The CSCM failed essentially because the USA was more concerned with ensuring that the nascent peace process in the Middle East was not disrupted and because the Community adopted a rather cool attitude towards it. In particular, the leading position of the USA in the Mediterranean was realistically recognized by the Italian government which, if with some reluctance, officially withdrew the CSCM proposal.

Nevertheless, Italy has tried to launch new initiatives for the Mediterranean in the context of transatlantic relations. In fact, during the NATO summit of January 1994, Prime Minister Ciampi stated that the Alliance should contribute more directly to the establishment of stability in the Mediterranean. Italy proposed the creation of a high-level, non-governmental study group with the participation of the Allies and some non-NATO Mediterranean countries.[23] The purpose would be to promote stability and cooperation in the region. Of the same view was the Berlusconi government, which was among the more active promoters of the Mediterranean Forum, whose Agenda for the Mediterranean was officially launched on 3 July 1994 in Alexandria (Egypt), on the basis of a plan prepared in Rome.[24]

One of the perceived weaknesses of Italy's more assertive role in the Mediterranean is the fact that national actions are being pursued in the absence of a clear multilateral umbrella (e.g. the European Union or NATO). In a longer perspective there is a real risk of disagreements, particularly with the USA, to whom Italy could well be less even-handed and conciliatory than it has been in the past. A new wave of nationalism could more easily erupt, now that the bloc-to-bloc policy of the Cold War has ended. Again here what is clearly needed is a strong and credible European 'cover',[25] which is only emerging with some difficulty. The Italian government had to fight, on the eve of the Lisbon European Council of 1992, to include the Mediterranean on the guideline list of areas which could be considered for joint actions as provided by Article J.3 of the Maastricht Treaty. This illustrated both the reluctance of Italy's partners to consider the southern region among EU's priority interests, and the difficulties of linking the eastern and southern crises. As a result of this isolation, the possibility of unilateral Italian moves in the Mediterranean cannot be excluded.

CONCLUSIONS

For the time being, although there are several signs of change, it is difficult to perceive any radical reversal in the traditional Italian commitments of the post-war period. Europe and the Atlantic Alliance, still constitute the two main pillars of the official policy of the Italian government and attract general consensus among the principal political actors at home. But because of its internal crises, Italy senses the risk of losing credibility abroad and, therefore, of weakening its participation as an equal in the groupings of its traditional partners.

There is a fear in Rome of being excluded from the emerging core of the European Union, and of being marginalized in the G-7. The same risks of exclusion are felt over a reformed UN Security Council or in new defence initiatives (e.g. the Eurocorps), in which Italy, even if accepted, fears that it will be considered a second-rank country.

This means that if the multilateral framework continues to be considered the best way of serving Italian national interests, the perception of a certain marginalization (or even singularization) could foster the emergence of unilateral positions. We might witness in the near future the emergence of demands in Italy which are in contrast with both its original integrationist motives in the EC and the firm preference for a multilateral approach in foreign policy. The present combination of European with Italian internal crises has, in fact, helped to midwife the birth of new kinds of internal political tendencies,[26] of which three, interrelated strands can be identified:

1 **Neo-mercantilist** Proponents of this approach seek to exploit the relative advantage for trade of a policy of competitive devaluation of the lira. This is contrary to a long-standing conviction in the country that participation in the ERM, at any cost, would be a long-term advantage for the Italian economy. The reluctance of the then Prime Minister Giuliano Amato and the former Governor of the Bank of Italy, Aurelio Ciampi, to leave the ERM in September 1992, was a result of this integrationist philosophy. They were forced to do so, however, and at present there is no discussion about any re-entry into the ERM. Supporters of a neo-mercantilist tendency exist both inside the government and in the very large sector of small and medium-size enterprises, which for the first time for many years seem to view Europe as an obstacle to their plans of development.
2 **Neo-nationalist** The aim of this approach is to reopen some of the contested agreements signed after the Second World War, particularly those referring to Italy's eastern border. Slovenia is the easiest case to reopen. Proponents of this approach emphasize also the geopolitical concept of 'spheres of influence', as in the case of Somalia.
3 **Neo-neutralist** Advocates of this approach would like to see a lesser engagement of Italy in the Western camp, favouring a full assignment of authority to the UN, as a kind of world government.

The common elements in these three approaches are a policy of progressive disengagement of Italy from Europe and support for greater national freedom in international affairs. What must be underlined is that in comparison with the beginning of the 1980s, Italy is today suffering from a crisis of identity in relation to its famous pro-European outlook. For the time being, these positions do not represent real alternatives to Italy's traditional attachment to the EC. Rather, they are limited to a group of intellectuals who wish to add a geopolitical approach to Italian foreign policy and to a few political forces – such as the Movimento Sociale Italiano which takes a neo-nationalist position (the party voted against the ratification of the Maastricht Treaty); and the Rifondazione Comunista (the rump of the old Communist party) which still favours a neutralist view and disengagement from NATO. Even if not generalized, these tendencies provide a first important sign of a possible radical change in Italy's international behaviour. Their prospects for success are still very low, but they could gain ground in the future.

There are two preconditions for Italy to remain on its own traditional track of transatlantic and European engagement, despite the above tendencies:

- the solution of its domestic crises, including the creating of a more homogeneous and soundly based governing coalition;
- a favourable development of the international scene towards a higher degree of multilateralization; in particular, so far as Europe (and CFSP) is concerned, towards the renewed effectiveness of its 'cover' function and the creation of credible security mechanisms.

At the governmental level this second precondition, that of an effective transformation of the EU into a political entity, is being taken seriously. Foreign Minister Antonio Martino stressed in 1994 that the process of European integration had to be conditioned less by macroeconomic criteria and oriented more towards credible and effective foreign and security policies.[27] Ironically, this would act as an inhibitor against unilateral moves by Italy (and other European states) and against the strengthening of neo-neutralist and neo-nationalist attitudes.

In the light of the case studies which have been examined above, one important initiative which needs taking from the Italian viewpoint is that of clarifying the role of the EU in the Mediterranean and neighbouring regions. A strict linkage between the European and Mediterranean theatres has to be established. More generally, for a country strategically located at the crossroads between Europe and the Mediterranean, the end of the Cold War has to be accompanied by an additional strengthening of the cover provided by multilateral institutions, not just in Europe but also in the Mediterranean. Only under such a multilateral 'umbrella' might we ensure that the Italian contribution to the development of a common CFSP does not coincide with a period marked by considerable friction.

NOTES

1 See IAI Report 1992, 'The dual crisis', *The International Spectator*, no. 1, January–March 1993, pp.5–30.
2 G. Bonvicini, 'The new international order and Italy's role', *Lettera Italia*, no. 1–2, January–June 1994, p.53.
3 The CDU's proposal has been published in Italian: Riflessioni sulla politica europea, *Europe Documenti*, no. 1895/96, 7 September 1994.
4 C. Merlini, 'The G-7 and the need for reform', *The International Spectator*, no. 2, April–June 1994, pp.5–25.
5 B. Andreatta, *Una politica estera per l'Italia*, Bologna, Il Mulino, no. 349, May 1993.
6 The electoral platforms of the Italian political parties have been published in the IAI's Yearbook, e.g. *L'Italia nella Politica Internazionale, Anno Ventunesimo*, Rome, SIPI Publisher, 1994 edn.

7   C. Merlini, 'Six proposals for Italian foreign policy', *The International Spectator,* no. 3, July–September 1993, pp.5–20.

8   G. Bonvicini, 'Italy: an integrationist perspective', in C. Hill (ed.), *National Foreign Policies and European Political Cooperation,* London, Allen and Unwin, 1983, pp.71–82.

9   L. Guazzone, *The Evolution of the Italian Mediterranean Policy and the Italian Attitude Towards the Palestinian Question,* Doc 1A1 9209, 1992.

10 F. Lay, *L'iniziativa italo–tedesca per il rilancio dell'Unione Europea,* Padua, Cedam, 1983.

11 M. Neri Gualdesi, *L'Italia e la CE. La partecipazione italiana alla politica d'integrazione europea 1980–1991,* Pisa, Ets Editrice, 1992, pp.59–87.

12 R. Aliboni, 'Italy and the new international context: an emerging foreign policy profile', *The International Spectator,* no. 1, January–March 1985, pp.3–17.

13 Conference for Security and Cooperation in the Mediterranean.

14 M. Cremasco, *From the Quadrangolare to the Central European Initiative,* Doc IAI 9213, 1992.

15 M. Neri Gualdesi, op.cit., pp.144–54 on the negotiations towards Maastricht. NB: This was over two years before the Berlusconi government and its ideological sympathies for the British position on Europe.

16 The commitment of the United States to NATO, which we deeply welcome, finds a Europe willing to shoulder greater responsibility. I am convinced that the progressive development of a European security and defence identity, first in the framework of the WEU and then – I hope – as a part of the European Union, will prove to be its strongest asset.
    (From the speech of former prime minister Aurelio Ciampi at the NATO Summit, 11–12 January 1994)

17 B. Andreatta, 'La partecipazione dell'Italia al processo di integrazione europea nell'attuale momento della Communita internazionale', speech given at the University of Bologna, 12 July 1993, at which he presented the Atlantic Charter Bis Proposal.

18 B. Andreatta, Statement to the Forty-Eighth Session of the General Assembly, New York, 30 September 1993, in which he first mentioned the Italian proposal for the reform of the UN Security Council.

19 The geopolitical approach found its best expression in a new Italian magazine, *Limes: Rivista Italiana di Geopolitica,* published by the Editoriale l'Espresso.

20 E. Greco, *Italy's Policy Towards the Yugoslav Crisis,* Doc IAI 9316E, 1993.

21 E. Greco, 'Italy, the Yugoslav crisis and the Osimo agreements', *The International Spectator,* no. 1, January–March 1994.

22 R. Aliboni, 'L'Europa tra Est e Sud: sicurezza e cooperazione', *Collana Lo Spettatore Internazionale,* Milan, Angeli, 1992.

23 In his speech at the NATO Summit in Brussels, 11–12 January 1994, Prime Minister Aurelio Ciampi proposed:

    the establishment of a high level study group, initially with a non-governmental capacity, with the participation of our Allies and of some non-NATO Mediterranean Countries. Its purpose should be to define a political, economic and social concept, which would lead to a possible intergovernmental initiative aimed at promoting stability and cooperation in the Mediterranean Region.

24 IAI, 'Cooperation and stability in the Mediterranean: an agenda for partnership', *The International Spectator,* no. 3, July–September 1994, pp.5–20.

25 By 'cover' (or the 'alibi function') is meant the protection against domestic and foreign criticism which derives from locating a national policy within that of a wider group. 'Cover' both lowers a profile and provides diplomatic solidarity. See William Wallace, 'Introduction: cooperation and convergence in European foreign policy', in Christopher Hill, op.cit., pp.10, 199; Françoise de La Serre, 'The scope of national adaptation to EPC', in Alfred Pijpers, Elfriede Regelsberger and Wolfgang Wessels (eds), *European Political Cooperation in the 1980s: A Common Foreign Policy for Western Europe?*, Dordrecht, Martinus Nijhoff, 1988, pp.210–11.

26 C. Merlini, 'Six proposals for Italian foreign policy', op.cit.

27 A. Martino, 'Prepariamo subito la nuova Maastricht', *Il Sole 24 Ore*, 20 November 1994.

Chapter 5

Spain

The uses of foreign policy cooperation

Esther Barbé

Spain's accession to the European Community, and therefore to European Political Cooperation (EPC), has inside the country the significance of an 'historical solution'. In effect the participation of Spain in the Community means the end of a 'national trauma' which began in 1898. This date went down in Spain's history as the year of the big colonial defeat (Cuba and Philippines) and at the same time as the origin of an important cultural and intellectual movement.

The colonial defeat of 1898 implies the beginning of the Spanish twentieth century. In terms of foreign policy, the Spain of the twentieth century does not share the experience of its neighbours. Particularly relevant in this context were Spain's neutrality during the two World Wars and the maintenance of a fascist system until the death of Franco (1975). Thus, post-Francoist Spain had to surmount right away the diplomatic isolation in which the country had lived over several decades.

The colonial disaster of 1898, which transformed Spain into a small European state after several centuries of imperial power, gave rise to a moral crisis, which in turn generated a cultural and intellectual movement. Creativity in the arts went hand in hand with an intellectual debate about Spain's future. It can be said that from Ortega y Gasset's writings up until the accession of Spain to the European Community in 1986, an idea expressed by this philosopher at the beginning of the century has persisted all along: Spain is the problem and Europe is the solution.[1] Thus, Europe becomes an 'historical solution' for Spanish democrats. This is the explanation for the symbolism represented by the 1960s advertising hordings seen by thousands of tourists every summer: 'Spain is different' was a Francoist slogan that implied the political isolation of the country from the European democracies.

IS SPAIN DIFFERENT?

The accession of Spain to European Political Cooperation generated anxiety among European diplomats. What behaviour was to be expected from the new actor? The concept of 'enfant terrible',[2] noted by some analysts, throws light on the doubts that Spain evoked among its new partners. For this reason we shall analyse the distinctive elements of Spain's attitudes towards EPC.

First, it should be noted that Christopher Hill's latecomer label used for the Europe of the Ten (particularly for Britain, Denmark and Greece) does not fit Spain.[3] Spain shares some conditions with these countries: being geographically located on the margins, being a peninsula and joining the Community after the Luxembourg compromise. However, Spain represents a counter-argument to the apparent association between latecomer and opponent of supranationalism. In fact, Spain stands out right away because of its political programme on EPC, favourable to the most integrationist tendencies in institutional and organizational matters.[4] Therefore, a first distinctive feature is the particularity of the Spanish accession when compared to the overall pattern of the previous enlargements.

History and geography are two important factors which help us to focus on the distinctive elements of Spain's attitudes towards EPC. Simon Nuttall stresses clearly the historical factor when stating: 'Spain has emerged too recently from a long period of isolation to be other than a fervent unionist'.[5] In effect the political elites and the Spanish society of post-Francoism consider Europe the ideal goal: joining Europe is the historical solution to the problems of the country. In this field, the idea of Europe among Spaniards is more emotional than utilitarian,[6] and this should be understood as an 'emotional response to some of the vague ideals embodied'[7] by the Community system. The attachment to Europe is more linked to what the Twelve represent (ideals) than to what the Twelve do (outputs). Beyond the prospect of economic gains, the Community is seen as the solution to Spain's two historical problems: democracy and international projection. Once more, Spain differs from the mainstream of latecomers, those for whom the Community has essentially an utilitarian–economic interest. Therefore, EPC is an important element of the image Spain has of Europe: EPC is an instrument capable of facilitating Spain's international projection and hence making it possible to overcome the syndrome of isolation.

However, other historical and geographical factors signal the appearance of problems in Spain's attitude towards EPC; those which led many to presume that Spain, once in EPC, would behave like a 'new Greece'. We refer to the existence, for historical and geographical reasons, of a diplomatic agenda of its own that would lead Spaniards to adopt divergent positions from the majority in EPC, as happened in the Greek case. To this effect, it is worth recalling some of the characteristic tendencies of the Spanish diplomacy before the accession to EPC: 'Third Worldism', defined by good relations with the Arab world (Spain did not recognize the State of Israel until the entry into the Community in 1986; this was part of accepting the 'acquis politique') and Latin America (including Cuba); and nationalist rhetoric, focused on the decolonization of Gibraltar. The analysis of Spain's voting behaviour in the UN during the years immediately previous to its accession to the Community demonstrates that Spain votes as the Ten do (when they agree unanimously). However, Spain aligned itself with Greece (and often with Ireland) on certain issues that produce divergence among the Ten. The main issues in which the Spanish vote differs from the dominant line in EPC are: Palestine, disarmament, human rights and Western Sahara.[8]

Therefore, one of the principal questions about the Spanish participation in EPC centres on the combination of the traditional orientation of Spanish diplomacy with its adaptation to EPC. In short, to what extent has Spain's orientation towards Latin America and the Arab world made participation in EPC difficult?

The central hypothesis of this chapter is that Spain is not different. This is to say that, according to its attitude in EPC/CFSP, Spain may be defined as an engaged and responsible actor in organizational matters, a moderate Europeanist in institutional matters and pragmatic in political matters, provided that its vital interests are not affected. These definitions could broadly be applied to most of EPC's participating states.

Since Spain joined EPC, Spanish diplomacy has lived through two extremely different periods. Spain enjoyed a first period (between accession in 1986 and the fall of the Berlin Wall in 1989, including the first Spanish Presidency) especially favourable to its integration into the EPC machinery, since there was no crisis that could have obliged the Spanish government to choose between its own diplomatic agenda (particularly in Latin America) and the Twelve's diplomacy. The invasion of Panama by the USA in December 1989 constituted the first evidence of Spanish dissidence on international affairs. Furthermore, it took place in a changing international situation. Since 1990 however, the Spanish government's attitude towards political orientation of EPC/CFSP has suffered some changes. These changes, focused on the fact that both elites and the government realize the importance of Maghreb for Spain, must be understood as a counter-policy against the Twelve's majority orientation towards Central and Eastern Europe in the post-Cold War era. This orientation runs contrary to Spain's geographical constraints, defined by its peripheral situation.

As we will see, in the new international context Spanish diplomacy has sought its own profile, complementary to EPC's profile (Conference on Security and Cooperation in the Mediterranean, Latin American Conferences, United Nations, Peace Conference on the Middle East). Therefore the analysis of the relationship between Spanish foreign policy and EPC within the context of post-Cold War implies, as we will see, a broadly realist interpretation. In a symbolic manner, it may be noted that Fernández Ordóñez, Spanish Foreign Minister in 1990, stated that 'we are less ingenuous with regard to Europe',[9] referring to the supposed idealism responsible for Spain's integration into Europe. This chapter holds to the idea that, in diplomatic terms, Spain has reached a genuine middle power status over the last years owing to its diplomatic activity at both bilateral and multilateral levels.

EUROPE MEANS MODERNIZATION

Europe being the solution to Spain's problems involves, as has been noted above, democracy and internationalization. These two processes are seen as the foundations for the country's modernization, thus abandoning old attitudes characteristic of the traditional and isolated Spain. This idea, alive in the Spanish thought all through the twentieth century, constitutes one of the basic pillars of Felipe González's political programme. The Prime Minister's Europeanism is always associated with references to its modernizing potential.

Spain's entry into EPC is therefore seen as a positive factor for Spanish diplomacy, as an opportunity to modernize its structures. Accordingly integration into EPC, and particularly the demands of running the Spanish Presidency, became challenges for the Spanish administration. We might call them 'shock therapy' of a modernizing kind.

The Spanish government's overall Europeanist rhetoric is turned into activism in the organizational field of EPC. Indeed, Spanish diplomacy has been a leader in the mechanism. So it was that during the first semester of 1986 Spain was in third place as to the number of Coreus sent (just behind Luxembourg, the Presidency at the time, and the UK). The initial Spanish 'enthusiasm' persists if we consider that in 1992 Spain was in fifth place, having sent out about 700 Coreus from Madrid, behind the Big Three and the Netherlands'.[10] This leads us to think that Spain aligns itself, like the Netherlands, with the group of countries which stress the importance of the EPC mechanism as a form of information structure ('communauté d'information'). On the other hand, one of the main weaknesses of Spanish diplomacy was precisely its limited capacity in the communication field. It is very significant that the Spanish press refers to the positive impact of joining EPC as a way of escaping the limitations of an underdeveloped state's foreign policy administration.[11]

It is not surprising, therefore, that some Community partners express doubts about Spain's technical (not political) capacity to hold the EC/EPC Presidency. Thus the first Spanish Presidency (first semester 1989) became a 'challenge' for the government. As far as organization and coordination are concerned, it was defined by the Foreign Minister as 'the biggest task ever undertaken by the Government and the Spanish administration'.[12] It is seen as an impetus for democratic Spain towards modernization and full incorporation into its wider political environment. The Prime Minister has referred to the Presidency in terms of dignity and has underlined the

Spanish intention to increase its prestige'.[13] In the Spanish case, the Presidency of the Twelve became what Helen Wallace describes as 'a distinctive political objective'.[14] This objective was:

1 to make EPC more genuinely European;
2 to place Spain among the major countries of the Community in terms of will and commitment;
3 to take advantage of the prestige of the Presidency at a domestic political level (with a view to the elections eventually held in October 1989).

Since January 1989 Spain has fulfilled the functions assigned by Article 30 of the Single European Act to the Presidency in EPC matters (initiative, organization, coordination, representation, coherence with respect to the Community's external activity and relationship with the Parliament) via a clear strategy for Europe, as has been mentioned earlier. This means applying the Single Act with special care in order to favour consistency between EPC and the Community's external relations (Spain stresses this point *vis-à-vis* relationships with the USSR and Romania) and to improve the relationships with the European Parliament (an outstanding role was played by the Foreign Minister, Fernández Ordóñez, with several appearances before committees and plenary sessions of the Parliament). The activity of the whole EPC machinery is especially important during the Spanish Presidency, as will be seen below.

Spain took on the Presidency in January 1989, after a semester of the Greek Presidency damaged by the latter's domestic problems; it had therefore been an inactive Presidency, although some important international events had occurred (such as the proclamation of the State of Palestine).

After a 'low profile' European Council in Rhodes, Spain took over EPC. Now the Spanish Presidency had to establish its priorities in that field and very soon it was seen that they were ambitious (Latin America and the Middle East among them), with the particular aim of modifying the image left by Greece of a decaying interest in the EPC mechanisms.

Far more than the political programme of action put forward by the Spanish government, the Foreign Ministries of Europe were to follow with attention the capacity of the country to provide leadership in EPC. Fernando Perpiñá Robert, Political Director in 1989, wrote in respect to the function of the Presidency:

In the operation of the European Political Cooperation the Presidency plays a fundamental role. Since consensus is the rule, the Presidency obviously cannot impose a decision on the other member countries. But it can lead to discussions about certain issues, foster their treatment, put a brake on them, orientate them. Overall the Presidency has much room for manoeuvre, but it has to perform its activity with prudence so that it provokes no suspicion in any of its Community partners. The Presidency provides great influence but also enormous responsibility. Its main duty lies in fulfilling its functions in an integrating manner, trying to incorporate the points of view and attitudes of all member countries into the final decision, before submitting it to their approval. Were this obligation not fulfilled, the political credibility of the country holding the Presidency might be at stake.[15]

As for the Spanish administrative machinery in charge of the EPC Presidency, the Spanish Ministry had already suffered an internal reshuffle with a view to Spain's accession to the EPC mechanism. Before its full integration in January 1986, Spain had enjoyed special access to EPC from 1982 (meetings at the troika and Political Directors' level) and had participated as an observer (together with Portugal) since June 1985.[16] Thus in August 1985 a ministerial reshuffle took place, involving the creation of a General Secretary for Foreign Policy so that the structure of the Spanish Ministry would be compatible with the EPC needs. Hence the General Political Secretary performs the double function of general co-ordinator of foreign policy (the number two of the Ministry, after the Minister) and Political Director in the EPC mechanism. Therefore the Political Director acquires in the Spanish case a new and outstanding significance within the administrative structure, brought about by EPC.

In the case of the European Correspondent, Spain has opted for diplomats with previous experience in the UN or in EPC itself (via the Secretariat). In one case, the outgoing European Correspondent became an Ambassador immediately afterwards. Once more, this indicates that in organizational terms, Spain plays its Europeanist card with a model of organization and appointment of posts that 'revalues' EPC upwards. This model may therefore be considered closer to the Italian or German model than to the British one.

In technical and political terms, the Spanish Presidency maintains a coherent behaviour with respect to rhetoric (i.e. stressing the importance of EPC) and expectations (i.e. displaying the will to promote the mechanism). In order to evaluate the work done by the Spanish Presidency, we may look over the operation of the EPC machinery during the first semester of 1989. Broadly speaking, the Spanish Presidency aims at promoting EPC as a 'communauté d'information', 'communauté de vues' and 'communauté d'action'. A brief summary shows that the Spanish Presidency of EPC produced: 3,600 Coreus; about 200 meetings presided over by the Spanish delegation at the UN; 6 Political Committees (1 in Vienna and 5 in Madrid); the Gymnich meeting (in Granada); 44 meetings of EPC Working Groups; 21 EPC meetings (outside the Working Groups framework); multiple meetings with third countries (10 of the Minister himself, 5 of the troika and 18 at lower levels); 8 appearances of Fernández Ordóñez as spokesman; 239 diplomatic actions and 25 political declarations'.[17]

The effort made to organize the Working Groups was outstanding. During the Spanish Presidency there existed twenty-one working groups (among them: Africa, Asia, CSCE, CDE and other aspects of the Helsinki Final Act, Western Europe, Human Rights, Latin America, Middle East, Non-proliferation, UNO/Disarmament). Their tasks had to be directed and supervised from the Spanish Ministry, and particularly, by the state office concerned in each case. The volume of work involved in the mechanics of this operation, generating forty-four meetings during the Spanish Presidency, explains the fact that the Ministry had to take on about fifty new diplomats, among whom were those newly incorporated into the corps and provisionally appointed, and some already retired.

At the political level the Spanish Presidency stood out for the importance given to the function of the troika, which was easier to perform in operative terms for being a 'Mediterranean troika' (Spain was preceded by Greece and followed by France), and for the relationships established with the European Parliament. These relationships brought the Spanish Minister himself, Fernández Ordóñez, before the Political Committee of the Parliament on two occasions during the semester.

Thus it can be said that in organizational terms Spain's attitude, in a generic manner and especially during the Presidency, favours the 'daily' development of EPC through the so-called (political) 'reflection of consensus' and (administrative) 'esprit de corps' or, more plainly, the Europeanization of the states' foreign policies. In the Spanish case this has a positive parallel effect on the country itself. Spain, poorly internationalized until the 1980s, has increased its prestige and influence since its integration into the EPC machinery and especially during its Presidency. This idea will be developed more deeply when tackling the link between EPC and the Spanish diplomatic agenda.

CAREFUL EUROPEANISM

The above-mentioned mentality that sees in Europe the solutions to Spanish problems, implies that the Community will be a positive value among Spaniards. In fact, Spanish public opinion (and particularly its leaders) does show a clear Europeanist orientation. In November 1991 73 per cent of Spaniards (EC average 69 per cent) considered that their country's Community membership was 'a good thing' against 62 per cent in 1986. In November 1991, more than 80 per cent of Spanish public opinion supported the unification of Western Europe against 70 per cent in 1986. In the same way, the percentage of people who think that EC membership has benefited Spain increased from 20 per cent in 1986 to 55 per cent (EC average 56 per cent) in November 1991.[18] The leaders' opinion is overwhelmingly pro-Europeanist. Thus in 1991, 96 per cent of them considered Spain's membership of the community to be beneficial, against 2 per cent considering it to be prejudicial.[19]

Among the benefits obtained through Spain's membership of the Community, for Spanish public opinion the most outstanding is directly related to EPC, namely the international role of the country, as shown by the poll in Table 5.1.[20]

Table 5.1 Evaluation of the effects of Spanish EC membership on different fields (1988)

	Positive	Negative	NA
Spain's role in world	73	6	21
Social modernization in Spain	69	9	22
Operation of democracy	68	6	26
Development of Spanish economy	57	20	23

In accordance with the dominant opinion in the country, the Spanish government belongs, in its foreign policy dimension, to a group of integrationist countries, opposed to the group of the intergovernmentalists. The question dividing the two groups and repeatedly tackled from the failure of the European Defence Community in 1954 to the signing of the European Union Treaty in 1992 and through all significant moments of Europe's political construction (Fouchet Plan, Tindemans Report, Genscher–Colombo Plan, Single European Act), is the difference of view between those countries promoting a sovereign states' concert to express coordinated opinions in foreign policy matters and those other countries wishing to create a common foreign policy as the expression of the European Union.

Since the very moment of its accession to the Community, the Spanish government has maintained a rhetoric characteristic of the group of countries traditionally integrationist, like Italy, Germany or the Benelux states, and against the group of countries traditionally intergovernmentalist, like the UK or Denmark.

Following the orthodoxy of EPC's constitutional texts from the Davignon Report (1970) onwards, the Spanish government has defended the view that a common foreign policy is one of the basic elements of Europe's political construction. Thus since 1988 Felipe González has promoted the idea that the common foreign and security policy constitutes one of the pillars of the European Union, with the economic and monetary union, and the European citizenship.[21] And he defended it once the Community's reform process started, after the fall of the Berlin Wall.

The first relevant Spanish document in this regard, related to the summons of an Intergovernmental Conference on Political Union, is a letter from Felipe González to the President in office, the Irishman Charles Haughey (4 May 1990). In this letter, the Spanish Prime Minister sets out the notion of the three pillars. For this reason the CFSP became one of the central issues for Spain during the Intergovernmental Conferences.[22] Nonetheless, as the debate on European construction progressed, Spain insisted on her priorities relating to social and economic cohesion, and took a most resolute attitude, including veto threats during the Maastricht negotiations.

Although CFSP is not a vital element (as cohesion is) in the Spanish agenda, it is an important element in the global process boosted by Spain: that is, reinforcing the Twelve's international influence, both in economic and political matters. The fourth enlargement of the Community – generating suspicion in Spain – must be counteracted, among other instruments, by the reinforcement of CFSP. This was the basic philosophy of the Spanish negotiator during the Intergovernmental Conference on Political Union. Consequently, CFSP is, unlike cohesion (a fixed principle for the Spanish government), a negotiable issue within a wide framework.

The Spanish position when negotiating the creation of CFSP relied on two ideas:

1 the common foreign policy as a basic foundation for the Political Union;
2 the European fiasco in the Gulf crisis being explained by the lack of adequate instruments to cope with the situation.

Thus Spain considers that the creation of CFSP is a basic means on the way to European unification and that it should foster new mechanisms (diplomatic and military) between the Twelve in the international political arena. In this issue, the governmental policy counted on the support of the public opinion favourable to the development of a 'European identity' in the international system. Thus in February 1991 *Eurobarometer* indicated that 54 per cent of Spaniards were favourable to CFSP while 17 per cent were hostile.

Second, the Spanish position in the negotiation is positively affected by the domestic consequences of the Gulf War. For the first time in its recent history, Spain took part in an international naval operation in war time (Spanish warships participated in the naval blockade organized by the WEU). Moreover Spanish bases were used for bombing runs against Iraq (something of a pleasant surprise for Washington, given the difficulties over the bases negotiations in 1988). The Spanish public opinion's reaction (48 per cent of Spaniards were for participation while 35.4 per cent were against) was interpreted by Prime Minister González as 'the end of a century of Spanish isolationism'. Hence Spanish negotiators spared themselves one obstacle (on the domestic front): the traditional reticence of Spanish opinion over participating in multinational military projects. At the end of the war 62 per cent of Spaniards supported the government's approach.[23]

In the difficult negotiations about CFSP, up until the Maastricht summit itself, the Spanish government belonged to the group of countries in favour of progressing towards a common policy for the Twelve in the international sphere, a policy with resources and instruments of its own. Together with Germany, France and Belgium, Spain defended the introduction of the qualified majority vote into the Council when adopting Joint Actions, for those issues previously designated as candidates for Joint Actions, and also accepted in principle the inclusion of all foreign policy issues within CFSP. This position was, however, to vary slightly during the negotiation.

At the Maastricht summit, the question of how to take decisions (by unanimity or majority) as regards common actions constituted a 'veto issue'. The French–German–Spanish wish to adopt decisions by majority ran contrary to the British–Portuguese–Danish opposition to change. The final result, described by Jacques Delors as 'complex and paralysing', was due to the Spanish mediation between the two positions, according to Felipe González. As he stated before the plenary session of the Chamber of Deputies:

> I regret to admit that the resulting formula was the one suggested by Spain in order to break the deadlock, for there was no way to achieve an agreement. It was Spain who proposed it: viz. at least let's reach by unanimity an agreement about which issues will be decided by qualified majority. I know this is a bit of hair-splitting, but against the veto we used this formula; otherwise, there was no way that the minimal decision could be taken by any other procedure than unanimity on any question. It is absurd to establish it for Joint Actions, particularly during the first stage of construction of a common foreign and security policy; unanimity is inevitable to decide the direction of foreign policy, but afterwards, in order to develop these common actions, the qualified majority would be the sensible solution. We demanded this, but in fact many precautions have been taken.[24]

On this particular case, the Spanish position has been both 'careful' and 'confusing', according to the documents presented by Spain at other stages of the negotiation. Thus, for instance, the common foreign policy proposal that appears, together with other national options, in the report of the personal representatives of the Ministers for the General Affairs Council held on 4 February 1990. This proposal reflected two Spanish ideas maintained afterwards (the inclusion of all foreign policy areas within CFSP, but with mechanisms permitting the selection of specific areas, and the progressive incorporation of WEU elements into the EC), and Spain showed prudence about the decision-making mechanism through its preference for the maintenance of consensus. Implicit in this, according to Fernández Ordóñez's statements, was a concern for defending Spanish interests in Latin America. The Minister declared in Parliament for example that 'Spain must be very careful, we run great risks of finding Spain's interest areas included in qualified majority formulas.'[25]

A first document presented by Spain in November 1990 had already given the broad outline for the future: favouring an agenda of its own and adopting a moderately pro-European stance. Some areas liable to generate common positions were suggested, in particular the Mediterranean. As regards the decision-making mechanism, the possibility of using the qualified majority was included for the implementation of Joint Actions whose general principles had already been established by the European Council or the General Affairs Council.[26] Likewise, a non-exclusive right of initiative was suggested for the Commission in CFSP matters.

The outcome of Maastricht in relation to Joint Actions[27] and to decision-making (with its prudent mention of qualified majority voting) is not too far from the Spanish conception. Spain would have been more generous if given a free hand. But it would have never committed itself to the Dutch proposals of integrating the second pillar into the Community.

In short, the Spanish position as regards institutional options of EPC/CFSP may be broadly called integrationist (generic defence of the existence of a common foreign policy), although with respect to mechanisms it might be said that the Spanish position tends towards what in theoretical terms is called supranational intergovernmentalism,[28] focused on the political negotiation at the highest level (European Council). Thus Spanish officials value the role of the European Council and the Council of Ministers in EPC/CFSP, while reserving a respectable role for the Commission and the Parliament.

The various proposals and actions of the Spanish government show a progressively clearer tendency to specify its European policy, with a view to the future context of an enlarged Community, containing more smaller and Northern countries, through the adoption of Big Country positions. The Spanish participation in the Paris meeting of Three (with France and Germany) on 11 October 1991, in order to break the deadlock in the CFSP negotiating must be seen in this light. This meeting's Directory of Powers character radically clashes with the established institutional mechanisms where the initiative lies in the hands of the Presidency.

This meeting corresponds to a change in Spanish behaviour. The best example of this evolution was given by Felipe González himself when he suggested in May 1992, in line with the purest Gaullist tradition, the creation of a Directory of Powers (i.e. the Big Five, assuming of course the Spanish presence) in order to deal with EC/CFSP questions.

The subsequent development of CFSP, as handled by the Lisbon European Council (June 1992), deserves a mention since the Twelve accepted a Spanish proposal: the Mediterranean (Maghreb and Middle East) was listed as an area liable to Joint Actions. As far as the Maghreb was concerned, this represents a success for Spanish diplomacy, anxious as it was to 'Europeanize' its policy towards the Mediterranean. This point will be developed in detail when tackling the connection between the Spanish diplomatic agenda and EPC/CFSP.

SECURITY AND DEFENCE: A CONTROVERSIAL TOPIC

The topic of security and defence has been very controversial in the process of internationalization followed by democratic Spain. The only international topic giving rise to an important domestic debate has been that of Spanish options in security matters. Spain joined the Atlantic Alliance in May 1982, in a period of domestic difficulties (there had been a coup d'état attempt in 1981 followed by the break-up of the government party, the UCD) and against the opinion of an important part of the political forces (particularly the Socialists).

Whereas Spain's accession to the EC attracted consensus among the political parties, the accession to NATO aroused controversy. The political culture of the Spanish left had an important anti-American component. In the eyes of the public, Franco's relationships with the USA had transformed Spain into a penetrated political system.[29] Thus the relationships with Europe were seen once again as a solution, as an alternative to the dependence relationships with the USA (initiated by the unequal Spain–USA agreements on bases in 1953).[30]

Therefore, from the start (October 1982) the Socialist government tended to align Spain on security matters, in relation to the USA, with its French neighbour. Spain is, like France, a member which feels uncomfortable in the Alliance and formulates its security policy in Europeanist terms (explicitly mentioning the WEU), as an alternative to Atlanticism.

Felipe González's radicalism during the election campaign, offering to withdraw Spain from NATO, soon moderated once he became Prime Minister. In October 1984, González made public a 'Decalogue on Peace and Security' outlining the government's plans: the holding of a referendum to find out Spanish opinion on the topic (an electoral promise) and the Spanish preference for the WEU as a future framework for European security. The referendum about NATO, held in March 1986, gave a relatively narrow verdict in favour of Spain remaining in the organization (with the participation of 59.4 per cent of the electorate, 45.5 per cent voted for remaining in while 39.8 per cent voted against). The referendum result must be interpreted as a plebiscite in favour of Felipe González since the Prime Minister linked his remaining in office to the referendum result. We therefore face a paradox: a pro-Europeanist leader in defence matters who makes continual references to WEU as his final goal, but who defends the Atlantic Alliance (a US-run organization in Spanish eyes) before his own public opinion.[31]

This established the future line of Spanish behaviour in the debate, which traditionally occurred between Atlanticists (the UK and the Netherlands being the most obvious examples) and the Europeanists (led by France) with respect to defence institutions. This line, confusing for some allies, led some to label Spain as a free rider because of its behaviour. In fact, there was a first defining period up until 1988, when Spain signed the NPT, acceded to the WEU, defined its mode of participation in NATO (no integration into NATO's military structure) and signed the first *inter pares* agreements with the USA. The signature of these agreements implied the withdrawal of an important part of the US forces based on Spanish territory, and ran into US opposition. The Spanish policy, ambiguous for some allies, is a mixture of pragmatism (military hardware interchange-ability with the Atlantic allies) and symbolism (the withdrawal of the US from Spain).

The end of the Cold War faces the Twelve with a changing international situation. And this favours, within the framework of the IGC on Political Union, the opening of a debate on security and defence. Spain, logically enough, is one of the promoters of this debate. Together with France and Germany, it argued for the inclusion of the terms 'common defence policy' and 'common defence' in the text of the Treaty as well as the introduction of the WEU as an 'integral part of the European Union process and in charge of setting in motion the security and defence policy'.[32]

The Spanish struggle in favour of 'the European defence identity' – in the sense of common defence organized by the WEU/EU – is however formulated in terms of complement and not alternative. Thus Spain shares the dominant approach in the post-Cold War by defending the com-plementary character of common European defence policy (WEU/EU) and the other, already existing, institutions (NATO, CSCE).

Overall, the disappearance of bipolarity facilitated the participation of Spain in the debate on European security. Thus the reform of NATO in the Rome summit of November 1991 was welcomed by the Spanish government. Prime Minister González's adviser, Carlos Alonso Zaldívar, noted that 'after the Rome summit, the Atlantic Alliance becomes lighter and more flexible, less nuclear, more European, and more transparent and open. A reform in the direction Spain has been defending'.[33] The Spanish government's rhetoric in the field of defence organization is pragmatic, seeking a formula to participate fully in European security, without formally modifying its mode of integration into NATO. Thus, according to Carlos Alonso Zaldívar, 'the creation of multinational units in NATO, the Rapid Reaction Force among them, does not close the possibility of creating genuine European units, for instance in the WEU. Nothing impedes the WEU from creating its own force structure, nor every country from furnishing NATO and WEU with the same units. In fact this possibility of 'double-hatting' is defended by Spain, which considers NATO and EC–WEU to have a complementary character, and foresees the possibility of participating in both schemes'.[34]

The Spanish will to participate in the common defence was evidenced during the Gulf crisis. The first participation of Spain in a multinational operation (naval blockade), beyond the usual military manoeuvres, generated a new 'state of opinion' in the country. Spanish public opinion accepted Spain's participation in international military actions on the basis of its integration in a European, and not Atlantic, defence organization. According to Eurobarometer, in October 1990, 62 per cent of Spaniards were favourable to the creation of a common defence organization, while in the spring of 1993 the figure had risen to 71 per cent.

In view of the revision of the Treaty of European Union in 1996, it is predictable that Spain will combine a technical–military pragmatism in WEU–NATO ('double-hatting') with a political rhetoric favourable to the strengthening of WEU as the 'armed branch' of EU. To this effect, during 1993 Spain has integrated into Eurocorps, joining France, Germany and Belgium, and has constituted a Joint Naval Force with France and Italy.

In the field of security and defence, Spain has standardized its situation by becoming more similar to the other Community countries. The normalization of the relationships with the USA (agreements of 1988) and the international changes (disappearance of the East bloc, Gulf War, Balkan wars) have certainly favoured such a standardization. Spain is therefore less and less different.

BECOMING A MIDDLE POWER: PRESTIGE AND INTERESTS

Before 1986, the suspicions aroused by Spain as a future member of EPC were not only focused on the doubts about its management capacity. The diplomatic options of the country were also important. The terms 'new Greece' or 'enfant terrible' referred to Spain's distorting potential within EPC. This fear is not strange if we consider that Spain participated in the Conference of Non-Aligned Countries, held in Havana in 1979. However, the neutralist whims of the UCD government (its Prime Minister in 1979 being Adolfo Suarez) were swept away by the Socialists, in office from October 1982.

In general, there has been a progressive rapprochement between Spanish diplomacy and overall EPC positions on the more controversial issues such as Central America and the Arab–Israeli conflict. Thus the incorporation of Spain (and Portugal) into the European caucus in the UN does not have a distorting effect. On the contrary, the Spanish attitude in the UN favours the 'communauté de vues', both because it has reinforced the dominant line and because of the positive effect that the 'enfant sage' (in opposition to the alleged 'enfant terrible') attitude of the Spaniards may have had on the Greek change of direction of the late 1980s.[35]

As seen above, the Spanish period of adaptation to EPC was very positive.

In four years (between 1986 and 1989) there was no international crisis which compelled Spain to choose between its own agenda (Latin America and Arab World) and the will of the majority. On the contrary, the Europeanization of Spanish foreign policy constituted from the beginning an alibi for González's government, since it enabled him to redefine a highly delicate issue: the position of Spain in the Western Saharan conflict.

The EPC had not tackled this conflict before the Spanish accession. Indeed, it was under Spanish pressure that the first political declaration was made during the Greek Presidency (7 September 1988), announcing that the Twelve would join in the UN peace plan.[36] The Europeanization of the Spanish position enabled Felipe González's government to adopt a moderate attitude, without favouring any of the parties, which was something previously unthinkable (the PSOE had traditionally defended the struggle of the Polisario Front). Its European obligations (France has always supported Morocco in the dispute) were an excuse for distancing policy from the Polisario Front. Thus the 'realpolitik' of the Spanish government, interested in improving its relationships with Morocco, finds in the 'European commitment' an excellent alibi before Spanish public opinion (which was favourable to the Polisario Front).

The Spanish Presidency of EPC provides a good opportunity to examine the contents of Spanish adaptation to foreign policy cooperation. We have already seen that Spain gives a high priority place to EPC on the grounds that it increases international salience. The Presidency of EPC is the best opportunity to take advantage of that projection, that is to increase the country's prestige. Thus during the Spanish semester Felipe González held EPC in great esteem, so much so that some members of the Commission feared that Spain would give less attention to the Single Market negotiations than to diplomatic moves in the Middle East or in Latin America.[37]

As regards contents, the EPC agenda prepared by the Spanish Presidency was very tight, indicating a determined activism. When González took office, he established the Spanish objectives in EPC:

1 maintaining a common position in several frameworks (relationships with the USA and Canada, strengthening the Council of Europe, open relationships with Central and Eastern Europe through the Helsinki process, reduction of military forces in Europe, development of a common security based on WEU and development cooperation policy);
2 making concrete efforts in two crisis areas (the institutionalization of an economic and political relation with Latin America and opening a dialogue between all the involved parties in the Middle Eastern conflict);
3 operating jointly within the UN.[38]

This apparently ambitious programme intended therefore not only to reinforce the 'communauté de vues' (with explicit mention of the UN) but also to develop the 'communauté d'action' in two specific areas. This would then activate the San José Conferences and the meetings of the troika with Arab and Israeli representatives. However, no great progress was made in either of the two fields: the Madrid Declaration on the Arab–Israeli conflict was timid, and González' attempt to create a Guarantee Fund for the Indebted Countries (with Latin America in mind) failed. However, the Spanish Presidency was also taken up with responding to the changes in Eastern Europe, through such means as the interruption of negotiations with Romania and the dialogue with the USSR.

As a general rule, the Spanish Presidency aimed at linking political declarations to concrete actions. Thus it promoted consistency between EPC and the external relations of the Community, something demanded by the Single European Act, and it broke off negotiations with Romania for a trade agreement after the EPC condemnation of human rights abuses. To this effect, the Spanish Presidency was repeatedly congratulated. Jacques Delors stated that under the Spanish office 'political declarations were finally accompanied by facts',[39] and Giovanni Jannuzzi, head of the Secretariat for Political Cooperation, affirmed that:

> The Spanish Presidency had accelerated Political Cooperation. There has been made a remarkable effort to accelerate the reaction times with respect to events and to make Political Cooperation more concrete as, for instance, in the case of the Middle East, or the dialogue with the USSR. Everyone acknowledges the notable balance of this Presidency; the judgement is extremely positive[40].

Naturally González and Delors shared the same perspective to begin with, as Socialists and pro-Europeans.[41]

The Spanish Presidency represents the end of a first phase in the EPC–Spain relationships. The second phase begins at the end of 1989. On the one hand, the changes in the international system demand the adaptation of Spain to the new reality. In this process of adaptation, Spain identifies its own interests and accepts that they are not the 'hard core' of the EPC agenda. This process of adaptation had already started in December 1989, when Spain, together with the Latin American countries and distinct from most EPC countries, voted for a resolution of the UN General Assembly condemning the invasion of Panama by the USA. Fernández Ordóñez's summary of the situation was: 'We are alone in Europe.'

The turning point of 1989 reorientated Spanish diplomacy. Spain sought a place of its own apart from EPC while defining more precisely its own priorities (Mediterranean and Latin America), within it, against the general tendency to concentrate on Central and Eastern Europe. Two factors motivated the approach: the search for a higher international status as a middle power, and the perception of being a peripheral country in the New Europe.

Spain's middle power status since 1990 has been substantiated by its activity and achievements: the proposal for a Conference on Security and

Cooperation in the Mediterranean (stalled, but not an idea which Madrid will give up on), active participation in UN Peacekeeping Forces (see Table 5.2), promoter of the Latin American Conferences, member of the UN Security Council, international projection through 'Spain 92' (Olympic Games, Expo in Seville, Latin American Conference in Madrid), the holding of the Peace Conference on the Middle East in Madrid, and so on. All these activities have improved Spain's image, not least that of the Army; at the start of 1992 Spain was the country with the largest number of national officers involved in peacekeeping forces.

Table 5.2 Spanish participation in peacekeeping forces

UNAVEM	Angola (1989–91)
UNTAG	Namibia (1989–90)
ONUCA	Central America (1989–91)
Iraq blockade	Persian Gulf (1990–91)
ONUVEH	Haiti (1990–91)
UNAVEM II	Angola (1991–)
ALFA-KILO	Iraqi Kurdistan (1991)
ONUSAL	Salvador (1991–)
SHARP-GUARD	Blockade Serbia–Montenegro (Adriatic and Danube, 1992–)
UNPROFOR	Bosnia (1992–)
ONUMOZ	Mozambique (1993)

The Spanish desire to acquire international prestige is symbolically reflected in its hosting of the Madrid Peace Conference on the Middle East from November 1991, and in its participation, together with France, Britain, Russia and the USA, in the Four-plus-One Agreement on Bosnia-Herzegovina, reached within the UN Security Council in May 1993. To sum up, Spanish diplomatic activity, outside EPC, shows the Spanish wish to implement a middle power policy, but based more on diplomatic prestige than on resources. Thus Spain's promotion of consistency between EPC and EC instruments, which makes more resources available for diplomacy. In effect Spain has tried to 'Europeanize' its privileged areas (Mediterranean and Latin America), bringing pressure to bear in order to provide them with more EC resources. However, Spain still adopts a distinctive national attitude on these questions.

For example, with respect to the Mediterranean/Arab World, Spanish policy has been actively developed since the end of the Cold War. Spanish interests have been defined more closely with the help of the Gulf War, leading to the Maghreb becoming a priority goal by virtue of the perception of it as an area of risk for Spanish security. The strategy followed to defend Spanish interests may be labelled as 'tous azimuts' (bilateral relations, the CSCM proposal, supporting the Four-plus-Five Group, creating a pro-Mediterranean lobby in the Community). This strategy included the

Spanish pressure within the CFSP framework to select the Mediterranean as an area liable to Joint Actions (European Council of Lisbon, 1992). Of course, Spain has equally sought to locate its policy towards the Maghreb in a European context by encouraging the transfer of Community resources on the grounds that it is a conflict prevention mechanism.

As for Latin America, Spanish strategy has been different. Spain does not perceive Latin America as an area of risk (as is the case with the Maghreb), but as an area of prestige. That is to say, the relationships with Latin America do not affect Spain's security but rather its identity or values. Spanish ministers define their relationships with Latin American states as those of 'brotherhood' or 'family'.[42] Thus Spain pressured the Community to transfer more resources towards Latin America, for example through the San José Dialogue and at the same time tried to maintain its room for diplomatic manoeuvre in the region, as in the case of Panama.

CONCLUSION

The Spanish position with respect to the three tensions (organizational, institutional and political) which determines the life of EPC/CFSP may be summarized in two ideas: normalization and dynamism. On the one hand, Spain wishes to be and has become a normalized country that acts like the others. Spanish diplomacy has learned to use the EPC mechanism to heighten its prestige and as an alibi for taking difficult decisions which jar with its public opinion (as over Israel,[43] Western Sahara). Yet, the 'European-ization' of the Spanish agenda reaches its limits when an interest perceived as part of one's identity such as the 'family relationships' with Latin America is at stake. With a view to the future, the limits may also be reached in relation to the perception of Spanish security interests in North Africa (the case of human rights in Morocco is not to be lost sight of).

On the other hand, Spain has a dynamic perspective as regards the future development of CFSP. Two tendencies support this assertion. Spain has always considered CFSP, the current second pillar of the Union, to be an important opportunity for strengthening the Community. Spain's suspi-cions about a new enlargement by rich countries from the North have been subsumed into a resolute support for all processes of reinforcement, including the complete acceptance of the acquis by the newcomers, and the development of CFSP. Furthermore, Spain is committed to pursuing the implementation of a common defence policy, and even a common defence.

Events both outside and inside Spain (for instance, the end of the González era of Spanish socialism) will undoubtedly test the balancing act which Madrid pursues between European ideals and emerging national self-confidence, but there seems little likelihood of a wholesale reaction against the fundamentally European character of modern Spanish foreign policy.

NOTES

1 Commentary from 1910, cited in J. Ortega y Gasset, *Obras completas*, t. 1, Madrid, Revista de Occidente, 1966, p.521.

2 Reference to E. Regelsberger, 'Spain and European political cooperation – no enfant terrible', *The International Spectator*, vol. XXIV, no. 2, 1989, pp.118–24.

3 C. Hill, (ed.), *National Foreign Policies and European Political Cooperation*, London, Allen and Unwin, 1983, p.193.

4 We adopt Nuttall's logic referring to organizational, institutional and political tensions to analyse the tensions suffered by EPC which have affected its development. See S. Nuttall, *European Political Cooperation*, Oxford, Clarendon Press, 1992, pp.2–4.

5 Ibid., p.310.

6 The distinction is based on D. Easton, *A System Analysis of Political Life*, Chicago, Chicago University Press, 1965, p.177. I owe this distinction to A. Bosch, *Actituds envers la Comunitat Europea a España: tres tipus ideals per a l'analisi*, doctoral thesis, Universitat Autònoma de Barcelona, 1993.

7 L.N. Lindberg, and S.A. Scheingold, *Europe's Would-be Polity*, New Jersey, Prentice Hall, 1970, p.40.

8 Regelsberger, op.cit., p.121.

9 'Fernández Ordóñez: Ante Europa somos menos ingenuos', *El Pais*, 24 June 1990. All translations are by the author unless otherwise stated.

10 Data from 1986 in K. Saba, 'Spanish foreign policy decision making', *The International Spectator*, vol. XXVI, no. 4, 1986, p.32. Data from 1992, according to information from the Spanish Ministry for Foreign Affairs (interview with the European correspondent).

11 Special reference is made to the technical progress in the communications system of the Palacio de Santa Cruz, seat of the Spanish Ministry for Foreign Affairs. See 'España pone fin al subdesarrollo de sus embajadas', *El Pais*, 3 February 1989.

12 'Informe sobre la presidencia española de la Comunidad Europea', Madrid, Spanish Ministry for Foreign Affairs, 1 July 1989 (typescript), p.1.

13 See analysis of the Spanish presidency in E. J. Kirchner, *Decision-making in the European Community. The Council Presidency and European Integration*, Manchester, Manchester University Press, 1992, p.105.

14 H. Wallace, 'The presidency of the Council of Ministers', in C. O'Nuallain, *The Presidency of the European Council of Ministers*, London, Croom Helm, 1985, p.274.

15 F. Perpiña Robert, 'La Cooperacion Politica Europea', *Politica Exterior*, vol. III, no. 9, 1989, p.43.

16 On the procedure followed in the Spanish case, see P. Schoutheete, *La Cooperation Politique Européenne*, Brussels, Labor, 1986 (1st edn, 1980), pp.201–4; S. Nuttall, 'European political cooperation, annual surveys', *Yearbook of European Law*, 1985, pp.325–6. Enlarged and checked data through interview with the European correspondent in the Spanish Ministry for Foreign Affairs.

17 For more information see 'Informe sobre la presidencia española de la Comunidad Europea', op.cit.

18 Data from Eurobarometer in A. Gil Ibahez, 'Spain and European political union' in F. Laursen, and S. Vanhoonacker, (eds), *The Intergovernmental Conference on Political Union. Institutional Reforms, New Policies and International Identity of the European Community*, Dordrecht, Martinus Nijhoff, 1992, p.103.

19 S. del Campo, *Informe Incipe 1991. La opinion publica española y la politica internacional*, Madrid, Tecnos/Incipe, 1991, p.54.

20 CIS Poll (November 1988) cited by M. J. Rodriguez Caamano and A. Almarcha

Barbado, 'The consequences of EC membership for Spanish educational policy' in A. Almarcha Barbado, *Spain and EC Membership Evaluated*, London, Pinter, 1993, p.278.

21 See, for instance, the Prime Minister's speech in 'Les grandes conferences catholiques' (Brussels, 12 December 1988) in *Actividades, Textos y Documentos*, Madrid, OID, 1988, p.227.

22 For the Spanish position in the IGC, see E. Barbe, 'Spanien' in W. Weidenfeld and W. Wessels, *Jahrbuch der Europaischen Integration 1991/92*, Bonn, IEP, 1992, pp.361–8.

23 See C. Alonzo Zaldívar and M. Castells, *España fin de siglo*, Madrid, Alianza Editorial, 1992, p.215.

24 *Diario de Sesiones del Congreso de los Diputados*, no. 155, 17 December 1991, p.7788. By 'precautions' is meant that majority voting was hedged about with restrictions.

25 *Diario de Sesiones del Congreso de los Diputados* (Committees. Joint Committee for the European Communities), no. 169, 9 November 1990, pp.5087–8.

26 'Common foreign and security policy. Spanish contribution', Madrid, 26 November 1990, cited by Gil Ibáñez, op.cit., p.104.

27 According to the post-Maastricht agreements, the areas liable to Joint Actions were: CSCE; disarmament and arms control, including confidence-building measures; nuclear non-proliferation and economic aspects of security, particularly transfer control on military technology and arms exports, and various geographical areas.

28 See R. Keohane and S. Hoffman, *The New European Community. Decisionmaking and Institutional Change*, Boulder, Westview Press, 1991.

29 Concept used in the same sense as J. Rosenau, *The Scientific Study of Foreign Policy*, London, Pinter, 1990.

30 See Angel Viñas, *Los pactos secretos de Franco con Estados Unidos: Bases, ayuda económica, recorte de soberanía*, Barcelona, Grijalbo, 1981.

31 Spanish opinion's anti-Americanism is shown in a poll from 1991, during the Gulf War. When asked about the major danger for world peace, 22 per cent of Spaniards believed that it is the policy of the USA, while 13 per cent believed that it was Iraq's policy. However, the political élites held a completely different opinion (the major danger being Iraq, for 31 per cent of them, and the USA are not perceived at all as a threat to world peace). See del Campo, op.cit., p.76.

32 'Conference intergouvernamentale sur l'Union Politique. Le "communiqué conjoint" franco-allemand-espagnol', *Europe Documents* (Agence Europe), no. 1737, 17 October 1991, p.1.

33 C. Alonso Zaldívar, 'El año en que acabó un mundo. La política exterior de España en 1991', *Anuario Internacional CIDOB 1991* Barcelona, CIDOB, 1992, p.22.

34 Ibid., p.23.

35 See E. Regelsberger, 'EPC in the 1980s: Reaching another plateau?' in A. Pijpers, E. Regelsberger and W. Wessels (eds), *European Political Cooperation in the 1980s*, Dordrecht, Martinus Nijhoff, 1988, pp.35–6.

36 See A. de Urruela, *La Comunidad Europea y el conflicto del Sahara Occidental*, Universitat Autònoma de Barcelona, Memoria de Licenciatura (typescript), 1994.

37 See 'Delors y González muestran su optimismo por la CE bajo la presidencia española', *El Pais*, 9 January 1989.

38 See *La unidad europea. Intervenciones del presidente del Gobierno Felipe González*, Madrid, Spanish Ministry for the Government's spokesperson, 1988, pp.72–94.

39 See 'Mitterrand tiene un ambicioso programa de medio ambiente', *El Pais*, 4 June 1989.

40 'Jannuzzi: La Comunidad sigue siendo la piedra angular de la construcción europea', *El Pais*, 24 June 1989.
41 Following the argument of Guy De Bassompierre, *Changing the Guard in Brussels: An Insider's View of the EC Presidency*, New York, Washington Papers, 1988, p.81
42 M. Oreja, 'Discurso de Marcelino Oreja en la XXI Asamblea General de Naciones Unidas (27 September 1976)' in J. F. Tezanos, R. Cotarelo and A. de Blas (eds), *La transición democrática española*, Madrid, Sistema, 1989.
43 Spain recognized the State of Israel a few days after its accession to the Community, in January 1986.

BIBLIOGRAPHY

Almarcha Barbado, A. (ed.), *Spain and EC Membership Evaluated*, London, Pinter, 1993.
Alonso Zaldívar, C. and Castells, M., *España fin de siglo*, Madrid, Alianza Editorial, 1992.
Barbé, E., 'El año español de la Cooperación Política Europea', *Anuario Internacional CIDOB 1989*, Barcelona, CIDOB, 1990, pp.109–20.
——'Spanish responses to the security institutions of the new Europe', in A. J. Williams (ed.), *Reorganizing Eastern Europe*, Dartmouth, Aldershot, 1994, pp.57–72.
Cortada, J. W. (ed.), *Spain in the Twentieth-Century World. Essays on Spanish Diplomacy 1898–1978*, London, Aldwych Press, 1980.
Dezcallar, J., 'Las relaciones España–Magreb', *Anuario Internacional CIDOB 1991*, Barcelona, CIDOB, 1992, pp.37–56.
Fernández Ordóñez, F., 'The EC presidency experiences of Spain', *European Affairs*, no. 3, 1989, pp.18–20.
Gil, F.G. and Tulchin, J.S., *Spain's Entry into NATO. Conflicting Political and Strategic Perspectives*, Boulder, Lynne Rienner, 1988.
Gil Ibáñez, A., 'Spain' in F. Laursen and S. Vanhoonacker, *The Intergovernmental Conference on Political Union. Institutional Reforms, New Policies and International Identity of the European Community*, Maastricht, European Institute of Public Administration/Martinus Nijhoff Publishers, 1992, pp.99–114.
Grugel, J., 'Spain's socialist government and central American dilemmas', *International Affairs*, vol. 63, no. 4, Autumn 1987, pp.603–15.
Marquina Barrio, A., *España en la política de seguridad occidental 1939–1986*, Madrid, Editorial Ejército, 1986.
Morán, F., *Una política exterior para España*, Barcelona, Planeta, 1980.
Palou, J.,'El concepto de potencia media. Los casos de España y México', *Revista CIDOB d'Afers Internacionals*, no. 26, 1993, pp.7–36.
Pollack, B., *The Paradox of Spanish Foreign Policy. Spain's International Relations from Franco to Democracy*, London, Pinter, 1987.
Preston, P. and Smyth, D., *Spain, the EEC and NATO*, London, Routledge and Kegan Paul, 1984.
Regelsberger, E., 'Spain and the EPC. No enfant terrible', *The International Spectator*, vol. XXIV, no. 2, 1989, pp.118–24.
Rodrigo, F., 'The end of the reluctant partner: Spain and Western security in the 1990s', in R. Aliboni (ed.), *Southern European Security in the 1990s*, London, Pinter, 1992, pp.99–116.
Saba, K. 'The Spanish foreign policy decision-making process', *The International Spectator*, vol. XXI, no. 4, 1986, p.24.
Schoutheete de Tervarent, Ph. de, 'La politique étrangère de l'Espagne et la

coopération politique des Neuf', in *L'Espagne et les Communautés Européennes. Problèmes posés par l'adhesion*, Brussels, Editions de l'Université de Bruxelles, 1979.

Tovias, A., *Foreign Economic Relations of the European Community: The Impact of Spain and Portuqal*, Boulder, Lynne Rienner, 1990.

Viñas, A., *Los pactos secretos de Franco con Estados Unidos. Bases, ayuda economica, recortes de soberanía*, Barcelona, Griialbo, 1981.

Wiarda, H. J. (ed.), *The Iberian–Latin American Connection. Implications for U.S. Foreign Policy*, Boulder, Westview Press, 1986.

Chapter 6

The Commission

The struggle for legitimacy

Simon Nuttall

When Political Cooperation was set up in 1970, the idea that the Commission might one day come to play an independent part in matters of high policy would have appeared laughable. To grant a role to the Commission would have demonstrated acceptance of supranationalism. Even those member states most attached to the Community ideal accepted as a political reality the fact that this was inconceivable for France, soon to be joined by the UK and Denmark. And the foreign policy establishments of all member states, confidently reposing on their long-standing traditions of state diplomacy, were at best inclined to treat the Commission with the high courtesy of condescension.

Yet twenty years later the Treaty on European Union conferred on the Commission the non-exclusive right of proposal and reaffirmed the unique position it had acquired in Political Cooperation over the years. True, the member states had declined to apply to their common foreign policy activities the principle of supranationalism, but the change over two decades was remarkable. Condescension had given way to nervous respect. This chapter attempts to chart the Commission's long search for legitimacy in foreign affairs.

'Legitimacy' means a recognized place for the Commission within the Community's foreign policy process. Recognized, that is, within the Community; third parties were perplexed by the ambiguities and shifting nature of the roles of the Commission, the Presidency and the member states. And some third parties, while having a very clear idea of the state of affairs at any given time, nevertheless professed 'faux-naif' bewilderment in an endeavour to draw diplomatic advantage from the Community's uncertainties and ambiguities.

The confusion was compounded by the fact that the Commission's role varied not only over time, but also according to the area of policy concerned. It ranged from being the exclusive spokesman of the Community on questions regarding trade in manufactured goods (the French representative at the GATT Council in Geneva was once told by the GATT Director General to hold his peace, as the Commission had already expressed the Community's views), at one extreme, to questions like the Euromissiles, on which it would have been thought very odd if the Commission had spoken out at all, at the other.

The acceptance of the Commission by foreign countries as agent as well as spokesman of the Community did however increase over time, particularly after the collapse of communism in Europe in 1989 and the decision of the Western Economic Summit to entrust the Commission with the coordination of international aid to Poland and Hungary. This was the first time the Commission had been treated as an actor in its own right, being entrusted with a task by a body outside the EC.

The precedent was nevertheless confusing. It led to the presumption that the Commission enjoyed a personality which could in some way be assimilated to state power. This presumption was fostered by some quarters in the Commission, and deeply resented and feared by some member states. But the legal reality, borne out overwhelmingly by the facts, was that the Commission was but the agent of the Community, executing policies decided within the Community system. Admittedly the system was *sui generis*, and one in which the Commission played an important part in policy-making as well as enjoying a wide measure of flexibility in implementation. Nevertheless, if the Commission's role was autonomous, it was not independent, either in the traditional areas of exclusive Community competence or, still less, in the evolving area of high diplomacy.

The situation would have been different if, for instance, the Commission had enjoyed the type of legitimacy which comes from responsibility before a democratic assembly, in this case no doubt the European Parliament. But the Commission refrained from going down that road, as will be explained below. The result is that the Commission's 'actorness' is different from that of the member states, as described in this book. The Community foreign policy system, still evolving, can only be understood if the traditional bond between 'actorness' and national sovereignty is dissolved.

THE INTELLECTUAL BACKGROUND: DE GAULLE AND HIS LEGACY

To understand the issues, we must go back to the origins. Political Cooperation was set up as part of the deal done at the Hague Summit in 1969. In return for an agreement to admit the UK to the Community, President Pompidou secured budgetary stability in the agricultural sector and foreign policy cooperation on traditional Gaullist lines. These combined a burning ambition that Europe should have a greater voice in the world with the conviction that the necessary legitimacy could only be found if policies were expressed through the member states. His conversations with Prime Minister Edward Heath, which prepared the way for the accession of the UK, had convinced him that these views would be in no danger even from that British government which, more than any other before or since, best understood the continental European approach to European Union.

The main casualty of this approach was the Commission, which was seen as the embodiment of supranationalism. After all, Walter Hallstein's efforts to conduct a distinctively European foreign policy from his vantage point as President of the Commission (caricatured as the 'red carpet' syndrome) was reputed to have sparked off General de Gaulle's mistrust of the Commission and his attempts to put it under greater surveillance. It was therefore not surprising that the Luxembourg Report of 1970, which laid down the ground rules for Political Cooperation, foresaw only a limited role for the Commission. The operating procedures owed much to the experience acquired in the foreign policy Ministerial meetings which occurred sporadically between 1960 and 1963, and to the result of discussions in the Fouchet Committee before they were broken off. The Commission was not to be regularly associated with the Ministerial meetings, nor with the work of the Groups which were now set up, but 'should the work of the Ministers affect the activities of the European Communities, the Commission will be invited to make known its views'. This, and other restraints on supranationalism, were not welcome to member states whose views on the matter differed from the French, but, as German Foreign Minister Scheel said at the time, to insist on an ideal solution was to be condemned to failure.

The Commission's reaction was defensive. Far from seeking to play a high profile part in the foreign policy process, its first concern was to secure admittance to these high diplomatic councils, and, once in, to ensure that its Community prerogatives were not invaded. If the best way of doing this was to make itself indispensable, then so much the better.

The effect of these limitations and of the Commission's tactics can be seen in the early meetings of Political Cooperation. The first Ministerial Meeting at Munich in November 1970 had on its agenda the Middle East and the CSCE. For the discussion on the Middle East, the Commission was not invited at all. Nor was it invited to the first part of the discussion on the CSCE, devoted to general issues. It was only when the Ministers turned to the Community aspects of the question, for a discussion at the end of the day which lasted less than an hour, that the Commission delegation, led by President Malfatti, was admitted. Malfatti called for the participation of the Community as such in the CSCE. Although he was supported by Dr Scheel and by the Dutch Foreign Minister, Dr Luns, the call was opposed by France. M Schumann argued that the Conference would be more concerned with security questions than with economic ones, and would be between states, not blocs – a position which appeared to deny the very rationale of Political Cooperation as a system, but which had the merit of excluding the Commission.

The Commission was also excluded from the discussions on the Middle East at the Ministerial Meeting in Paris the following May, which led to the adoption of the first common position on the area by the Six. Continued work on the Middle East ignored the Deniau plan for economic cooperation in and with the region put forward by the Commission, acting by virtue of its Treaty powers; it was only brought in when discussions turned to the possibility of increased financial assistance for the refugees.

In both these areas it was not long before the impossibility of making a clear distinction between the political and economic aspects of external relations and the need to respect the Commission's powers under the Treaty of Rome obliged even the French to soften their attitude on Commission participation in EPC discussions. As work on the CSCE progressed, it was discovered that the economic aspects could not simply be shunted to one side. Already at the Ministerial Meeting in Paris in May 1971, President Malfatti had suggested that the study of the substance of the economic questions should be entrusted to the Community. This ran into objections because of the risk of thus strengthening the position of Comecon. The alternative proposal that the Commission should be represented in both the Political Committee and the appropriate group for all points of Community competence was blocked by the French Foreign Minister, M Schumann, from his position in the chair. A compromise was reached whereby the Commission should address its comments in writing to the group, through the Political Committee, and be invited to take part in the meetings of a new group, set up for no other purpose than to provide a forum in which the Commission's presence was acceptable. The first step had been taken along the long road towards full Commission association with EPC.

A similar road was travelled some years later on the Middle East. Alarmed by the immediate and longer term implications of the October War of 1973, France launched in Political Cooperation a high profile initiative aimed at carving out a distinctive European position. This was based on the idea of entering into a political dialogue with the Arabs. The initiative foundered on the reef of American opposition, and could only be saved at all by concentrating on economic cooperation. The assistance of the Commission thus became indispensable, and its representatives had to be admitted to the various bodies set up to prepare and conduct what became the Euro-Arab Dialogue.

These distant events have been recounted in some detail not only because they show the very different view taken of the Commission at the time – it is sometimes forgotten that this was only twenty years ago – but also because they exerted an influence on the way the Commission itself saw its role. The Commission did not attempt to inject an independent political appreciation into the debate. Instead, it tried by asserting its own powers under the Community treaties to secure a place for itself at the conference table and prevent the member states from usurping its Community functions. Such legitimacy as there was was provided by the Treaty of Rome.

The organization of work in the Commission reflected this approach. Since the question was one of exceptional political sensitivity, it was handled by the President with the assistance of the Commission department directly responsible to him, the Secretariat General. Other departments were called on to help as the Commission was required to provide technical input and expertise. Thus DG I (external relations) took part in the meetings of the CSCE group; the Euro-Arab Dialogue, however, continued to be handled by the Secretariat General under the guidance of the Deputy Secretary General.

FULL ASSOCIATION: THE VIRTUES OF USEFULNESS

As the years went by, the member states became more accustomed to the Commission's presence in their meetings. Their tolerance was made easier by the Commission's careful avoidance of any behaviour which might cause diplomatic eyebrows to be raised. Its representatives did not venture to express an opinion on the political issues of the day, but they were always available to explain the implications for the Community of any matter under discussion and to provide technical advice where appropriate. This function was recognized in the Copenhagen Report of 1973, which noted the participation of the Commission in discussions of the economic aspects of the CSCE and the future role of the Council of Europe.

This did not mean that the association of the Commission with Political Cooperation became total and trouble free. It was still not admitted, on principle, to certain groups. Its representatives attended meetings of the Political Committee but not those of the European Correspondents. It was always invited to the United Nations Working Group, never to the Middle East Working Group, and on a casual and unpredictable basis to the Mediterranean Working Group. It received some COREUS (cypher telexes exchanged among Foreign Ministries in EPC), but not all; it could send them, but only through the Belgian Foreign Ministry. At any moment, its participation in a meeting could be vetoed by any member state. France usually did, from time to time, just to keep its hand in.

This situation was to persist until the London Report of 1981. The full association of the Commission with EPC was then admitted, but only after difficult discussions and a change of government in France. Nor was France the only country to have doubts. The curious language used to mark the Commission's emergence from purdah ('Within the framework of the established procedures the Ten attach importance to the Commission of the European Communities being fully associated with Political Coopera- tion at all levels') was at the request of Denmark, as reluctant as France to see any mingling of the genres of Political Cooperation and the Community.

Indeed, Lord Carrington had some innocent fun at the expense of the Danish Foreign Minister at the Ministerial Meeting in London which adopted the Report. He accused the hapless Charles-Ferdinand Nothomb, who as Belgian Foreign Minister was the last person in the world to put obstacles in the Commission's way, of being responsible for the remaining reservation. K. B. Andersen was obliged to admit in some embarrassment that the reservation was Denmark's, before lifting it.

The details of the Commission's full association with EPC were subject to further difficult negotiations. The member states had accepted the principle, but real or feigned doubts about the extent of its application still had to be put at rest. If the presence of the Commission at all meetings in the capital of the Presidency was now accepted without question – the Commission representatives were admitted to the Correspondents' Group and the dinner of Political Directors, for example – the participation of the Commission's Delegations in EPC activities abroad and its connexion with the COREU network were at first contested.

Member states wanted adequate assurances that the Commission was in a position to guarantee confidentiality. In particular, they were not convinced that its cypher communications were up to scratch, and that the distribution of papers inside the Commission would not lead to leaks. In fact, the Commission had for several years been running a professional cypher communications network with its more important Delegations, and had the means of restricting the circulation of papers on a 'need to know' basis, but it was only after it had submitted a memorandum setting out its internal arrangements in considerable detail that member states gave the green light for full participation in all activities. The European Correspondent of the Commission, now admitted to full status with his colleagues, oversaw these arrangements from his post in the Secretariat General. He retained his previous responsibilities as head of confidential communications, and by way of derogation from the general rules of the Commission, operated a separate distribution system for EPC correspondence which bypassed the normal channels and offered better guarantees of security.

The Commission had sought and found a new legitimacy. In the first stage of EPC, it had relied upon the legitimacy conferred by its Treaty powers; now, to justify and make possible its full association with EPC, it had had to provide itself in addition with the legitimacy of traditional diplomatic procedures.

FOREIGN POLICY THE COMMUNITY WAY: THE KEY TO ACCEPTANCE

The Commission deliberately adopted a low profile following the London Report, in order not to imperil its newly accorded full association. Its representatives were on their best grown-up behaviour, sitting up straight at table and speaking only when they were spoken to. The wisdom of this attitude was demonstrated by an incident which occurred when the London Report was adopted: the Commission Spokesman had made bold to announce to the world that the Commission now had a part to play in EPC, calling down the wrath of France and causing grief to the UK, which had played an important part in ensuring full Commission association. A great deal of oil had to be poured on troubled waters before a more equable situation could be restored.

The counterpart of this modest and retiring approach towards a political role was rigorous insistence on respect for the Commission's prerogatives under the EEC Treaty in matters of Community competence. Paradoxically, but not unsurprisingly, the Commission's warmest supporters in this were those countries like Denmark which were determined to maintain a clear distinction between EPC and the Community. Conversely Belgium, whose integrationist credentials were second to none, expressed irritation at what it saw as the Commission's excessive legalism in defending Community powers. In fact, although few realized it at the time, the issue of whether EPC was to remain both intergovernmental and separate or be incorporated into the overall Community framework had already been joined.

The role of the Commission in EPC developed in parallel with the growing acceptance by member states that they needed to have recourse to Community instruments in order to give effect to foreign policy decisions. In many cases, the Commission's institutional involvement was indispensable, and its bridging role between the EPC and Community machines provided valuable oil in the works. The Commission was nevertheless commonly viewed by the member states as their servant in these matters rather than as a body entitled to its own views. There were difficult moments when views diverged, as also when the member states sought to share the Commission's management powers, particularly in the execution of the budget and the carrying out of aid schemes. As the years went by, however, the Commission became a familiar partner in the diplomatic apparatus of Political Cooperation, opening the way to recognition of its special role, first in the Single European Act and then in the Maastricht Treaty.

The process was given a significant boost by the succession of crises which befell EPC in the months after the London Report. In rapid succession, martial law was declared in Poland, Argentina occupied the Falkland Islands, and Israeli forces invaded the Lebanon. In each case the reaction of Political Cooperation could only find material expression through sanctions applied by the Community.

This had not previously been admitted. In the cases of Rhodesia, Iran and Afghanistan the possible use of Community sanctions had either not been considered at all or had been rejected by the large majority of member states. When martial law was declared in Poland in December 1981, the Ten were at a loss what to do. They came under pressure from the USA to join them in imposing economic sanctions, but Germany was reluctant to sacrifice the hard won benefits of *détente*. The final spanner was thrown into the works by Greece, which declined to join the consensus which had evolved by January to consider economic measures. The solution was found in the Community framework, and was only possible within that framework: a general measure limiting trade with the Soviet Union was accompanied by a specific derogation for Greece. Both measures took the form of Council Regulations, which accordingly had to be formally proposed by the Commission. The Commission's right of initiative was not in this case politically significant, but it provided the influence on events traditionally conferred on the wielder of the pen.

The practice gained was put to good use only two months later when Argentina occupied the Falkland Islands. The decision to respond by Community sanctions was nevertheless only taken after long discussions. There were two questions, which were closely linked: should sanctions be applied, and if so should they be adopted by member states individually or by the Community as a whole? The Commission took the latter view, not only to reinforce Community powers to conduct a common commercial policy but also to avoid the chaos which would ensue on the Community market if each member state adopted its own measures. The Commission was supported by Germany and Belgium; Denmark was in difficulties because of the domestic drubbing it had recently received over the use of Community measures to impose politically inspired sanctions on the Soviet Union; and countries like Ireland and Italy were glad enough to place at one remove the responsibility for decisions required by Community solidarity but which would command doubtful domestic support. The Commission, while taking its cue on the political substance of the issue from the views expressed by member states, was able to play a significant role in the procedural outcome. The process was greatly facilitated by the fact that the Political Committee and Coreper were both, by the happy accident of the Belgian Presidency, meeting in Brussels. The Commission representative, the only participant to have institutional access to both bodies, was able to shuttle constructively between the two.

The Community response to the Israeli invasion of Lebanon in June 1982 was less clear cut. No economic sanctions were applied; EPC limited itself to issuing a declaration which was condemnatory of Israel's action while admitting the provocation. Possibilities of 'future action' were referred to, in the event of Israeli non-compliance with the Security Council Resolution. More significant in Community terms was the action taken following Israel's rejection of the Ten's request for assurances on a number of items including the admission of international humanitarian aid and the observance of a cease-fire. Having consulted the President of Coreper, the Commission decided not to sign the new Financial Protocol with Israel and to submit to the Council the question of whether to postpone the scheduled meeting of the Joint Cooperation Council. (It was postponed.) These were political decisions taken by the Commission, albeit inspired by the Political Cooperation discussions which it had attended. The political and economic sides were beginning to rub off on each other. Had the Commission not been fully associated with Political Cooperation, it would no doubt have taken the same decisions, but the fact that it did so as a participant in EPC gave them an added dimension. Here, the Commission was drawing legitimacy for its political decisions, not from any independent source enhancing its own standing, but from its association with the deliberations of member states. It has to be recognized, however, that the question was one of internal organization. It must be doubted whether Israel, though aware of them, gave special attention to these subtleties, or attributed a particular political stance to the Commission rather than to the Community as a whole.

The decision to impose economic sanctions on South Africa was more difficult than in the cases of the Soviet Union and Argentina. Already in the 1970s the issue had been ducked by the adoption of a Code of Conduct; by 1985 it could no longer be postponed. How the overall policy would turn out was clear from the beginning of the summer of that year, when Mr Genscher proposed a two-pronged approach combining restrictive and positive measures, but it took Political Cooperation two bites at the cherry and a full twelve months before the policy was agreed in all its details. The first round of restrictive measures, in 1985, was applied by member states on a national basis, even though it included such typical Community actions as the cessation of oil exports. The Commission made the appropriate proposals to the Council, using its right of initiative, but they were not adopted because of the opposition of the UK, Denmark and Germany. It was only a year later, when the second round of restrictive measures was decided on, that some of them, in particular the ban on the import of gold coins, were applied through Community instruments.

The South African case was a difficult one for the Commission, and put its developing foreign policy legitimacy under strain. It was under pressure from the European Parliament to use its Treaty powers to propose Community sanctions, and as a result took an unusually active and public role in the sanctions debate. This in turn attracted criticism from the member states, which were not ready to accept that the Commission was entitled to express independent foreign policy views. The Commission decided that discretion was the better part of valour. It chose to forego the legitimacy it might have acquired from acting in Political Cooperation as the spokesman for the majority view in the European Parliament. It no doubt reflected that the final policy decision would in any event be taken by the member states independently and that the likely outcome of a political initiative by the Commission would have been to impair the latter's growing standing in EPC. The Commission therefore limited itself to making those formal proposals which were needed in order to translate into Community action the foreign policy decisions taken in EPC. This orientation was confirmed in the 'Declercq doctrine', which subsequently served as a guideline for Commission conduct in similar cases. Mr Declercq, who was Commissioner for external relations at the time, announced to Parliament that, in the area of foreign affairs, the Commission would only use its right of initiative if there was consensus in Political Cooperation. In the view of the Commission, this referred to consensus on the substance; the Commission did not accept the view of some member states that the consensus should also extend to the question of whether or not it was appropriate for a foreign policy decision to be implemented by a Community measure. This was a question on which the Commission was anxious not to limit its Community prerogative, in order to keep open every possibility of interaction betweeen EPC and the Community.

The Commission's role in EPC was not limited to the negative one of go-between in the imposition of Community sanctions. It was also responsible for the conception and management of aid programmes financed by the Community budget and the EDF (the separate fund set up in connexion with the Lomé Convention). During the 1980s member states increasingly saw the advantages of exploiting these programmes to give an added dimension to their EPC foreign policies. This gave the Commission a new legitimacy: that of the cheque book. It also gave rise to tensions and the contesting of legitimacy, as member states fought for a greater say in the way that programmes, especially those with high political implications, were managed.

To hold the cheque book is of limited value when the balance of the account is low. The Commission attempted to exploit political interest to secure additional funding in the Community budget for actions which might not have been undertaken without the political impulsion coming from EPC. A good example is the case of Central America. From the beginning of the 1980s, EPC's policy towards the area had been based on the principle that political instability there was the consequence of economic and social backwardness. The acceptance of this principle logically required the Community to contribute to overcoming this backwardness. The Commission therefore made suggestions in 1981 for an aid programme for the region as a whole, but it pointed out that money was tight and that additional funds would be necessary. The Political Committee hesitated to back the request for more money, and it was not until November 1982 that agreement was reached on increasing the allocation for Central America by ECU 30m, less than half what the Commission had proposed. Again, the region probably would not have received additional funds in the 1985 budget had the Community, for political reasons, not concluded an Agreement with Central America that year.

The conception and management of aid programmes can be of great political sensitivity. The more these programmes were prayed in aid by

Political Cooperation, the more member states attempted to have a say in the details of operations. Since the conception of aid programmes is the responsibility of the Commission, in association with member states according to recognized Community procedures, and since the execution of the budget is the sole responsibility of the Commission, there was scope for the exercise by the Commission of something resembling a political role, which gave rise to frequent tensions with member states. Central America is a case in point. The 1982 funding decision was held up for several months because the UK objected to the inclusion of Nicaragua among the beneficiaries. The Commission, supported by several other member states, was able to press successfully for its de facto inclusion because the discussion took place in the Community, not in EPC. This was an important political decision to which the Commission contributed by virtue of its Treaty powers. Once the decision had been taken, the Commission had a relatively free hand in how the programme was carried out.

The case of South Africa demonstrates even better the de facto political powers of the Commission in this area. It will be recalled that EPC policy was based on a two-handed approach combining restrictive and positive measures. The positive measures depended largely on Community action through a special programme to assist the victims of apartheid. This was set up and administered by the Commission. Four non-governmental channels were used for the distribution of aid, of which one, the Kagiso Trust, had been created by the Commission to cover non-church and non-union beneficiaries. The UK in particular objected to the use of this channel, which it claimed was a cover for assistance to the ANC and in any case unjustifiably excluded Inkatha. The Commission was not swayed from its purpose, and in the light of subsequent developments may be forgiven for displaying some pride in its political judgment at the time.

The Commission also ran into trouble with member states for the way in which it administered humanitarian and development aid in some countries which for the time being happened to be political footballs – once memorably described by a member state official as 'the Commission's proclivity to afford comfort to international pariahs'. Commission decisions to grant even emergency and humanitarian aid to Vietnam were frequently criticized, as was the apparent tolerance of the Ethiopian government's schemes for agricultural resettlement and collectivization. The Commission for its part argued that it was better to maintain contact with governments even when their policies were repugnant, in order to be able to exert discrete and therefore more effective pressure behind the scenes.

During this period of rapid expansion of the Commission's presence and activities in EPC, its own internal organization remained basically unchanged. The unit in the Secretariat General dealing with EPC was somewhat enlarged, but remained small. Its role was that of a go-between, linking the Commission departments with the machinery of EPC, although it was beginning to collect and exploit information from various sources, including the Commission's Delegations, in a first move towards setting up an autonomus input capacity. The Delegations themselves now took part in EPC activities abroad, although patchily, reflecting the unevenness of EPC outside the capitals.

FROM THE SINGLE EUROPEAN ACT TO MAASTRICHT

The Commission had a double objective regarding the foreign policy section of the negotiations leading up to the Single European Act of 1987. In line with the policy followed since the London Report of 1981, on the one hand it wished to secure the greatest possible connexion between the EPC and the Community frameworks, and on the other it was determined to avoid any encroachment by the member states on its Treaty powers. It achieved both these aims.

In the Opinion which it delivered in July 1985 the Commission stated that it was 'necessary, in the general context of transition to European Union, to make fresh progress not only on economic and social integration but also on foreign policy. Indeed, the fact that the two form an indivisible whole should be recognized by incorporating the proposed new provisions in a single framework'. This view was eventually accepted by the member states, resulting in the adoption of a *Single* European Act, meaning one containing both EPC and Community provisions in one instrument.

Whatever its views on what would be desirable in the long term – indeed, the same July Opinion declared that 'at the end of the day only unified institutions – one Council, one Parliament, one Commission – will prove effective and speed progress towards European Union' – the Commission accepted that the time was not ripe to seek a special status in Political Cooperation. Its representatives in the Political Committee, which nego-tiated Title III of the Act dealing with EPC, therefore limited themselves to upholding Community prerogatives. In this they were frequently aided by member states which also wished to maintain the separation between EPC and the Community, but for the opposite reasons.

A case in point is the wording on consistency. Consistency was a term of art referring either to fruitful interaction between EPC and the Community, or to the need to keep a close watch on the Commission, depending on one's point of view. Article 30.5 of the Act provides that 'the external policies of the European Community and the policies agreed in European Political Co-operation must be consistent. The Presidency and the Commis-sion, each within its own sphere of competence, shall have special respons-ibility for ensuring that such consistency is sought and maintained'. Earlier drafts had placed responsibility for ensuring consistency on the member states collectively. The Commission had successfully resisted this, on the grounds that it would be unworkable in practice. Its representatives could not believe their luck when the Danish delegation insisted that, if the Commission was to share any institutional role with the Presidency, it should be within the limits of its existing powers. They were happy to assent to this formula, which in reverse protected the Commission's existing powers from any raids by the Presidency or the member states collectively. Thus it came about that the Commission acquired a role in Political Cooperation which was based on its Treaty powers, but confirmed in an EPC legal text. It thereby gained a new sort of legitimacy, which foreshadowed the future Maastricht Treaty.

The position of the Commission in foreign policy questions was transformed between 1987 and 1991. This was less the result of the Single European Act than of the earth-shaking events in Central and Eastern Europe and the Soviet Union from 1989 on. Practically overnight, the Commission found itself coordinating the international aid effort to Central and Eastern Europe, playing a crucial role in the unification of Germany by ensuring the trouble-free absorption of the former East Germany into the Community, and negotiating successive agreements with the former Communist countries which defined their future relationship with the Community. Institutional hazard put the Commission centre stage, at a time when the spotlight was trained there. This was the old legitimacy of Treaty powers, but given fresh importance by the size of the political stake. Events moved fast; member states working in the intergovernmental mode found their machinery too slow. It was small wonder that, as this period drew to a close just when the Intergovernmental Conference on Political Union was beginning its work, some were tempted to believe that the time had come to make a push for the single institutional framework with recognized powers for the Commission which had been foreshadowed in the Commission's Opinion of July 1985.

Perhaps the single most striking event to enhance the status of the Commission was the decision of the Western Economic Summit Meeting in Paris in July 1989 to entrust it with the task of coordinating international assistance efforts to Poland and Hungary, extended the following year to other countries of Central and Eastern Europe. This was a new kind of legitimacy: the Commission received a mandate from a body outside both the Community and the EPC frameworks. In the conduct of its coordinating role it was therefore not subject to the control of either, although of course the presentation of EPC–EC positions in the so-called 'G-24' group was coordinated in advance with the member states. For the first time, the Commission was a foreign policy actor in its own right. This development can be seen with hindsight to have been inherent in its presence at the Economic Summits, as often as not as the only visible representative of the Community. The seeds which Roy Jenkins had sown nearly fifteen years earlier when as President of the Commission he secured admission to the Summit meetings were now bearing full harvest.

The Commission's role in negotiating the Community's agreements with the countries of Central and Eastern Europe also conferred on it greater political weight. More so than the traditional trade and cooperation agreements with third countries, these agreements had global political significance at a time when both East and West had lost the bearings which had kept them on course for more than a generation, and were facing with foreboding the prospect of an uncertain future. Furthermore, the Community made it plain in 1990 that 'coordinated assistance should be provided on the basis of commitments from the countries concerned to political and economic reform'. This new element of conditionality was an important political factor: the missions to the countries concerned to receive the necessary commitments were carried out by the Commission, which thus became responsible for the preeminently political task of verifying compliance with the requirements of conditionality.

These developments speeded up a change of attitude towards EPC with which the Commission was already experimenting. Instead of erecting fences around Community powers, the Commission now sought to blur the boundaries between EPC and the EC, at least in presentation. It was hoped thus to encourage the emergence of a common foreign policy combining regular input from both sides. An early example of this switch is the wording used in EPC declarations. Under the old approach, any reference to the 'Community' would have been extirpated by the Commission representatives on grounds of constitutional impropriety. Now, the received terminology was 'the Community and its Member States' in all cases, regardless of the subject matter of the declaration.

The drawback to this from the Commission's point of view was that it became more difficult to engage in the still necessary defence of the Community's powers. Member states not unreasonably argued that, if there was to be a blurring of distinctions, it should work both ways. They were insensible to the argument that only Community procedures could guarantee efficient decision-making. Similar difficulties arose regarding responsibility for the presentation of policy. While the Commission was still unable to act as the spokesman for EPC, the Presidency increasingly acted as spokesman for both EPC and the Community, as the two were conflated. The Commission faced a dilemma: it could not use its association with EPC to build up an autonomous political role without at the same time paying the price of permitting some encroachment on its Treaty powers. It was uncomfortably straddled between legitimacies.

The greatly increased foreign policy activities of the Commission and its change of approach towards EPC brought about changes in its organizational arrangements. A full-time Political Director was appointed in the Secretariat General, with a Directorate under his command which included the European Correspondent's service, the cypher communications service, the human rights service, and a policy planning unit. The Commission's autonomous input capacity was thus further increased.

THE MAASTRICHT TREATY ON EUROPEAN UNION

It might have been expected that this strengthening of the Commission's position would be reflected in the Maastricht Treaty. It was not, or not to the extent that was at one stage hoped for. The Commission ended up with a non-exclusive right of initiative and a shared responsibility for ensuring consistency that was rather more blurred than in the Single European Act; it had no part in the all-important function of representing the Community externally. There were no doubt various reasons for this. The atmosphere of crisis which had been all-pervading in the immediate aftermath of 1989 was subsiding, and it seemed safe to return to comfortable old ways. The old quarrel between intergovernmentalism and integration, in which the position of the Commission had always been at the centre of debate, could be resumed without fear of the consequences. The Commission had been too successful for its own good, and was beginning to be seen as a rival, if not a threat; it was scarcely to have been expected that a Conference composed of career diplomats would enhance the standing of an organization which might one day put into question their *raison d'être.*

These hesitations and suspicions may be seen from the positions taken by the member states in the preparatory phase and in the Conference itself. The Belgian Memorandum of March 1990, which launched the process with some imaginative ideas which member states would have been well advised to follow up, said of the Commission no more than that '[its] role ... should be better defined, so as to secure the desired consistency' – a Sibylline recommendation, which could be taken either way. The European Parliament, on the other hand, called in July 1990 for the Commission to have a right of initiative in proposing policies and a role in representing the Community externally. Denmark took the view that the Commission's 'current position as an equal partner in EPC should be confirmed in the text of the Treaty'. Portugal thought that the Commission 'should be formally accorded a non-exclusive right of initiative in foreign policy matters'. The UK was opposed to a greater role for the Commission in EPC. The Commission itself took the view, in its Opinion of October 1990, that together with the Presidency and the other member states, it should be given the right of initiative in the field of the common foreign and security policy.

The maximum to which it seemed likely member states could be brought to agree was the non-exclusive right of initiative for the Commission. This was therefore included in the guidelines with which the Rome European Council of December 1990 launched the IGC. The discussions which followed throughout 1991 did not materially change this view, which was incorporated into the Maastricht Treaty. At one stage during the conference proceedings (March 1991) the Commission tabled a draft for the foreign and security section of the Treaty with the object of considerably enhancing its own role and making it an equal partner with the Presidency in the conception and management of policy. While not technically going much beyond what was finally agreed, the Commission succeeded in presenting itself in such a lurid light that the member states took fright, and the Commission's contribution did not become a basis for discussion.

The Commission was thus left, on the entry into force of the Maastricht Treaty, with a position of which it could make as much or as little as it pleased. It undertook a significant reorganization of its departments in order to be better prepared for the tasks which lay ahead. The new Commission which took office in January 1993 had decided to divide among three Commissioners the responsibility for external relations which had previously been exercised by two. Mr van den Broek, previously Dutch Foreign Minister, was made responsible for external political relations and the common foreign and security policy (CFSP), while Sir Leon Brittan and Mr Marin were made responsible for external economic relations with developed and developing countries respectively. At the same time, the decision was taken to set up a new Directorate General for external poltical relations built around the old Directorate for relations with EPC in the Secretariat General. This, with some 300 staff manning geographical desks as well as running the Commission's overseas Delegations, was designed to provide the Commission with the sort of raw material for its participation in the CFSP which member states get from their Foreign Ministries. (The experiment did not last: two years later the political and economic desks were merged once again, although Mr van den Broek retained responsibility for the CFSP as a whole.)

But how far would the Commission be allowed to play an effective role in CFSP? It had gained a new legitimacy in the intergovernmental section of the Maastricht Treaty and thus separate from its previous Treaty powers. But the question remained whose foreign policy views it purported to represent. The member state governments could at least claim to represent their electorates, however remote the connexion in practice on most foreign policy issues. The Commission is appointed by governments, and dismissed (in theory) by the European Parliament. Parliament is determined to exploit to the full its new powers to be consulted on the choice of the President of the Commission, but the debate on the appointment of Mr Santer did not turn on the Commission's position as foreign policy actor. We have seen in the case of South Africa that the Commission chose not to seek legitimacy from Parliament, preferring to preserve its relationship with the member states. This approach is now changing, at least to the extent that Commission representatives engage in a full dialogue with the appropriate Parliament committee on CFSP questions. This relationship is appreciated by Parliament, but it has not yet developed to the extent that the Commission would feel able to be the champion of Parliament in CFSP discussions. So does the Commission draw its legitimacy, as it does in the Community, from its role as the representative of the Community interest? This will be difficult so long as its right of initiative is non-exclusive – for what makes its position more respectable than that of any member state with an equal right to put forward proposals? – and so long as the CFSP is not a genuine common policy but rather, as in the days of EPC, a highly coordinated collection of national policies. The question of the legitimacy of the Commission and its effective power to play a foreign policy role is bound up with the question of the future institutional development of the European Union, which the Intergovernmental Conference of 1996 may – perhaps – resolve. It will not do so if the discussions on foreign policy are limited by the assumption that only states are foreign policy actors, and that the European foreign policy actor must therefore be a European state. There is room for a *sui generis* system, in which functions are shared, and this is probably the only politically realistic way forward.

BIBLIOGRAPHY

Allen, D., Rummel, R. and Wessels, W. (eds), *European Political Cooperation*, London, Butterworths, 1982.

Bourrinet, J. (ed.), *Le Dialogue Euro-Arabe*, Paris, Economica, 1979.

Cloos, J., Reinesch, G., Vignes, D. and Weyland, J. *Le Traité de Maastricht*, Brussels, Bruylant, 1993.

Couste, P. and Visine, F. *Pompidou et l'Europe*, Paris, Librairies techniques, 1974.

De Ruyt, J., *L'Acte unique européen*, Brussels, Editions de l'Université de Bruxelles, 1987.

Doutriaux, Y., *Le Traite sur l'Union européenne*, Paris, A. Colin, 1992.

Edwards, G., 'Europe and the Falklands crisis', *Journal of Common Market Studies*, vol. 22, no. 4, pp.295–313.

Edwards, G. and Regelsberger, E. (eds), *Europe's Global Links*, London, Pinter, 1990.

Edwards, G. and Spence, D. (eds), *The European Commission*, London, Cartermill, 1994.

Etudes européennes, 'Un défi pour la Communauté européenne: les bouleversements à l'est et au centre du continent', Brussels, Editions de l'Université de Bruxelles, 1991.

Fonseca Wollheim, H. da, 'Zehn Jahre Europaische Politische Zusammenarbeit (EPZ)', *Integration*, February 1981, pp.17–66.

Greilsammer, I. and Weiler, J., *Europe's Middle East Dilemma: The Quest for a Unified Stance*, Boulder, Westview Press, 1987.

Heisenberg, W. (ed.), *Die Vereinigung Deutschlands in europaischer Perspektive*, Baden-Baden, Nomos, 1992.

Holland, M., *The European Community and South Africa*, London, Pinter, 1988.

Ifestos, P., *European Political Cooperation*, Aldershot, Avebury, 1987.

Laursen, F. and Vanhoonacker, S. (eds), *The Intergovernmental Conference on Political Union*, Maastricht, EIPA, 1992.

Nuttall, S., *European Political Co-operation*, Oxford, Clarendon Press, 1992.

Pijpers, A., *The Vicissitudes of European Political Cooperation*, Leiden, University of Leiden, 1990.

Pinder, J., *The European Community and Eastern Europe*, London, Pinter, 1991.

Pryce, R. (ed), *The Dynamics of European Union*, London, Pinter, 1989.

Schoutheete, P. de, *La Cooperation politique européenne*, 2nd edn, Brussels, Labor, 1986.

Part II

The smaller countries

Chapter 7

Belgium

The importance of foreign policy to European political union

Christian Franck

Right from the beginning of the construction of Europe, Belgium has supported developing a common foreign and defence policy in order to add elements of a political union to those of economic integration. According to a former prime minister these elements consist of 'an extension of Community competencies, the reinforcement of its democratic legitimacy and of the efficiency of its institutions . . . [as well as] including within the scope of community action foreign and security policy'.[1] At the Twenty-fifth Anniversary of the signing of the Treaty of Rome in March 1982, Leo Tindemans, Minister of Foreign Affairs, recalled that 'economic integration should one day lead to political unity' and suggested 'the development of the systematization of European Political Cooperation' as one of the main ways of putting political union 'at the level of that which has been realized in the economic sphere'.[2]

The evolution of a foreign policy does not only contribute to the political construction of Europe but also gives the European Community a voice and a role in international politics. In order for this role to be effective, it is important to ensure that there is a coherence between external economic relations and European Political Cooperation.

This is the second priority which the Belgian government gives to European Political Cooperation. A declaration emanating from the government on 9 May 1988 illustrates this by calling for 'strengthened common action on the part of the member states in the international arena by means of upgrading EPC and by establishing greater coherence between the external activities of the European Community and those of EPC'.[3]

Analytically the Belgian position on the development of a European foreign policy presents itself in the form of three equations. The 'coherence' equation applies to economic relations and political positions; it legitimizes taking economic sanctions. The security equation extends foreign policy to the domain of 'security' policy resulting eventually in a common defence; it excludes neutrality. The 'political union' equation makes foreign security policies an essential element of a political union with federal aims; this means that it is destined to move from a strictly intergovernmental procedure towards a Community procedure.

THE COHERENCE EQUATION: SANCTIONS

In the first half of 1982 the Belgian Presidency of the Council initiated the first trade sanctions resulting from decisions in Political Cooperation. In March a regulation based on Article 113 of the EEC imposed restrictions on Soviet imports as a result of the role played by the Kremlin in imposing martial law in Poland on 13 December 1981. On 19 April 1982 a second regulation concerning trade imposed an embargo on Argentine products for a month as a result of the Argentinian army's invasion of the Falklands. Simon Nuttall remarked that the fact that EPC had used EEC measures was 'attributable in part to chance, in part to the predisposition of the Belgian Presidency to look for Community solutions, and in part to the convenience of having EPC meetings in the same city'.[4] If this latter point applies to communication channels between the Political Committee, which because of the Belgian Presidency was meeting at that time in Brussels, and COREPER which has a permanent seat in that city, the second refers to Belgian doctrine on European policy. In contrast to countries that wish to separate EPC and external economic relations due to the heterogeneity of the procedures involved, the one side intergovernmental and the other Community (a position supported by France), or to the tension between the principle of economic cooperation with third countries and political attitudes towards them (the Danish concern), Belgium felt that it was necessary to bring together these two elements of external action. During the speech to the European Parliament in which he presented an assessment of the Belgian Presidency, Leo Tindemans described the imposition of sanctions against the Soviet Union and Argentina as 'the realization of the principles of convergence between European Political Cooperation and Community action' which is 'a basis of European union'.[5]

Even though the Single European Act established the principle of 'coherence' instead of 'convergence', it nevertheless established a link between political positions and economic action which meant that there would never be any contradiction between the two; What is more it also strengthened the credibility of Political Cooperation by supplying it with the means to impose economic pressure. The Belgian government has always insisted that economic sanctions should be taken by the Community and not left to the discretion of national governments. When, in 1986, the Twelve discussed imposing sanctions against the policy of apartheid in South Africa, Prime Minister Wilfred Martens and Minister of Foreign Affairs Leo Tindemans opposed the suggestion that they be national measures. 'The measures will not be sanctions if they are not taken by the Community as a whole', explained the former.[6] In an article published in *De Standaard*, the latter said: 'History has shown us that national measures have hardly ever been uniform across all the Member States ... when considering applying economic pressure on the South African government, it soon became apparent that each Member State interpreted the proposals in a different way and made little or no effort to adapt their position.'[7] The Community finally undertook very limited measures in October 1986. An ECSC Decision suspended imports of iron and steel whereas an EEC regulation suspended imports of gold. As the Community's treaties did not provide any legal basis for suspending European investment measures, this was done on a national basis. The Belgian government contacted La Fédération des Entreprises de Belgique and asked Belgian contractors, as it had no power to compel them, to suspend investments.

The Iraqi invasion of Kuwait also led to the adoption of Community sanctions: first there was the cancellation of the Generalized System of Preferences and then an embargo was imposed on the aggressor state. What is more, in applying Resolution 661 of the Security Council of 6 August 1991, Belgium immediately blocked Iraqi assets on its territory (amounting to approximately 100 billion dollars). In accordance with an EPC decision, Belgium along with its partners maintained this freeze as long as Iraq did not fully conform with the demands drawn up in April 1991 by the Security Council (Resolution 687) which dealt with the recognition of Kuwaiti borders and with the destruction of all chemical, ballistic and nuclear weapons belonging to Iraq.[8]

During the 1980s EPC did not only use commercial sanctions (or the related decisions to suspend financial aid, as with regard to Syria in 1987); it also applied political sanctions on countries such as Libya and Syria which were suspected of being involved in acts of international terrorism. Over and above national measures which put an end to exports of arms and military equipment, diplomatic sanctions were also imposed on Tripoli and Damascus. In April 1986 Belgium applied a Political Cooperation decision by reducing the diplomatic personnel at the Libyan Embassy in Belgium by half and limiting Libyan personnel movements to within the zone of Brussels. When similar measures against Syria were being contemplated, the Belgian Minister felt that it was necessary to distinguish between state terrorism as conducted by Libya and the involvement of 'certain Syrian groups' in the terrorist attack on the Boeing El Al at London's Heathrow Airport.[9] But by November 1986 high level political contacts with Damascus had been suspended. As a result, when the Belgian Presidency in the first half of 1987 was trying to revitalize the mediation role played by European Political Cooperation in the Middle East conflict, Leo Tindemans was unable to visit Damascus during his travels around the region.

THE SECURITY EQUATION

In 1976, the Tindemans Report on European Union asked that 'security should not be left outside the scope of the European Union'.[10] Having become Minister of Foreign Affairs, after having been Prime Minister from 1974 to 1978, the author of the Report noted that this request had been ignored. Both the London Report on European Political Cooperation of October 1981 and the Stuttgart Solemn Declaration on European Union of June 1983 limited themselves to allowing EPC to deal with the 'political aspects of security'.[11] As it was obvious that no progress could be made in this field, Leo Tindemans proposed in an article published in *Le Monde* on 23 December 1983 that cooperation in and coordination of defence policies which related to the dimension of European security, should be undertaken with the framework of the Western European Union. The article by the Belgian Minister was published just before the Franco-German proposal of February 1984 was tabled with a view to relaunching the WEU which culminated in the Rome Declaration of 27 October 1984. It is not clear whether Belgium was influencing or reflecting the positions of its larger neighbours on the question.

The support given to the idea of relaunching the WEU constituted a U-turn for Belgian European policy. For the first time Brussels had supported an initiative which would take place outside the framework of the Ten. In his article published in *Le Monde* Leo Tindemans wrote that it introduced 'a notion of a differentiated Europe in the security domain similar to that which the EMS established in the monetary domain'. According to Cahen, Brussels made this choice with 'resignation'. However it was obvious that several member states – Greece, Denmark, Ireland – were not inclined to extend the scope of Political Cooperation to the military aspects of security. 'In choosing between a standstill and a solution which was not satisfactory but had the merit of providing – even if in a more narrow framework – necessary European consultations on security problems, the advocates of a relaunch of the WEU chose the second path.'[12] However the Belgian government did not give up on the idea of 'one day restoring European security problems to their appropriate framework: at the level of the Ten and later of the Twelve'.[13]

The prospect of a Soviet–American agreement on Euromissiles in 1987 encouraged, moreover, Prime Minister Martens to propose that the Twelve should debate this strategic question. After Gorbachev had announced the reversal of the Soviet position on the zero option with respect to the dismantling of Euromissiles, Commission President Jacques Delors appealed on 15 March for an extraordinary meeting of the European Council so as to reach a common position and to lay down the foundations of a common security policy.[14]

Holding the office of President of the European Council, Wilfred Martens, no less than President Mitterrand, had reacted positively to M Delors' proposal. The Belgian Prime Minister declared that he would tackle the problem of a strengthening of the ties between the Twelve in respect of defence at the time of a meeting on 19 March with the French President.[15]

Leo Tindemans, however, the Foreign Minister, insisted that the Single European Act, which had not yet entered into force, did not permit the Twelve to tackle the military aspects of security in Political Cooperation. He added that Ireland would refuse to participate in a meeting on such a theme, by virtue of its neutrality. 'A discussion between the Eleven is no longer a Community discussion'[16] concluded the Minister of Foreign Affairs, thus reining in the Prime Minister's instincts for boldness.

A former Director-General of Political Affairs within the Belgian Ministry of Foreign Affairs, Ambassador Alfred Cahen became the first Secretary-General of the reactivated WEU. The doctrine which bears his name establishes membership of the Community as the condition of membership for the WEU. Thus a future of compatibility between the WEU and the European Union was made possible. Although this doctrine was supported by Belgium it was not passed unanimously in the WEU. The UK envisaged that Turkey might join the WEU which would render an eventual integration of the WEU into the EU problematical. Nevertheless the Maastricht Treaty made just such an integration possible. Not only are security questions fully linked to foreign policy in the framework of the CFSP but Pillar Two also establishes the eventual goal of 'a common defence policy, which might in time lead to a common defence' (Article J.4.1). At the intergovernmental conference in 1991 the Belgian delegation contributed to this 'pleonastic' formulation which allowed for the eventual integration of the WEU ('Common Defence Policy') within the EU as well as the integration of national military forces into a 'common defence'.

The foreign policy–security equation has two consequences. The first is a logical consequence. If the European Union develops jurisdiction over security including defence the countries which wish to join the Union will not be able to preserve any active neutrality. Mark Eyskens, who succeeded Leo Tindemans at the Foreign Ministry in July 1989, therefore had reservations about Austria's application for membership which included its intention to maintain its neutrality.[17] Jean-Luc Dehaene, who has been Prime Minister since March 1992, went on record once again – notably for the benefit of Sweden, Finland and Austria – saying that neutrality was not compatible with membership.[18]

The second consequence is practical. As a means of showing its interest in the idea of 'common defence' Belgium decided on 25 June 1993 to join the Franco-German Eurocorps. This decision, which was announced only a few days before Belgium took over the Presidency of the Council, was intended to act as a positive political signal with regard to common defence initiatives. The integration of some 11,000 men within the Eurocorps had previously been agreed between the heads of government of France, Germany and NATO on condition that the Eurocorps would belong both to NATO and the WEU.[19]

THE CFSP–POLITICAL UNION EQUATION

During an official visit to Paris in December 1992 King Baudouin delivered a speech at the Elysée Gala Dinner which was devoted to the idea of a 'more democratic' Europe, a Europe which would 'influence the course of history'. He reminded listeners that Belgium favoured the 'federal option' for Europe and that political influence internationally required 'the transfer of competences to a federal European level where they could be exercised most efficiently'.

With this in mind the King described the Maastricht Treaty as 'an essential stage . . . [for] the development of a common foreign and security policy'.[20] The Belgian doctrine sees political union culminating in a federal union in which the CFSP would be a 'federal' competence. During the course of the 1980s and even in the post-Maastricht Treaty era, Europe remained far removed from reaching these objectives. However, Belgian diplomacy has worked devotedly, with more pragmatism than doctrinal rigidity, towards promoting the development of a foreign policy system in this direction.

The Belgian government ardently supported the principle of giving legal codification to European Political Cooperation as was done in the Single European Act. On the eve of the Milan European Council of June 1985, Belgium opposed the Franco-German proposal to reduce the concept of a European Union solely to this legal codification.[21] For the same reason Belgium refused to allow European Union to figure in the title of the Single European Act as this only represented a degree of progress towards the European Union.[22] The importance attached to the way in which the concept of European Union was used was designed to preserve its real meaning, one which would apply to strengthened institutional structures and a deepening of policies.

In March 1990 the Belgian government presented a 'memorandum on European construction' to the Irish Presidency.[23] The memorandum called for progress to be made in terms of improving institutional efficacy and reducing the democratic deficit, of affirming the principle of subsidiarity as well as the strengthening of European Political Cooperation. This Belgian initiative was motivated by the wish to reinforce Community institutions and to improve the functioning of EPC in order to avoid the risk of seeing the construction of Europe undermined by pan-European cooperative structures linked to the CSCE. The memorandum shows that the Belgian proposals aimed at 'bringing the Community ever closer to a political union'. They moved in the direction of a 'deeper Europe', but do not stand in the way of the construction of a 'wider Europe' involving the countries of post-communist, Central and Eastern Europe. However the priority remained the consolidation of the European Community. As far as European Political Cooperation is concerned, the Belgian text suggested that the 'General Affairs' Council be the centre of policy decision-making of the Community and that it should endeavour to 'implement policy rather than merely increase the number of declarations it issues'. It also argues that EPC should be able to debate security questions 'without restriction'. Finally it envisages the revision of Article 30 of the Single European Act and the progressive assimilation of foreign policy within the Community institutional framework which most significantly would entail the use of majority voting.

The Maastricht Treaty has satisfied only a limited number of suggestions included in the 1990 Belgium Memorandum. Philippe de Schoutheete, the major figure behind the scenes on Belgium's EPC policy, and a noted author on EPC,[24] feels that it is undeniably 'important that the Union has established the objective of implementing a common security policy'. However apart from the conceptual breakthrough with regard to security and defence 'progress has been extremely modest'. As far as the CFSP generally is concerned, the supporters of the status quo have prevailed over those who desire substantial progress, notably by recourse to the use of majority voting.[25] This can at present only be used for decisions relating to the development (i.e. in practice the implementation) of Joint Actions, Article J.5.2. In order to keep open the prospect of a 'communitarization' of the CFSP, Belgium was one of the delegations which introduced in Article B.0.5. the possibility of applying to it 'the effectiveness of Community mechanisms and institutions'[26] when the Treaty is revised in 1996.

Although the progress made by Maastricht in the area of the CFSP may be judged only modest, Belgium seized the opportunity of its Presidency in the second half of 1993 to start implementing straightaway the provisions of Title V. After the Extraordinary European Council of 29 October which celebrated the entry into force of the Maastricht Treaty on 1 November, the Belgian Presidency launched five Joint Actions. Conforming to the procedure laid out in Article J.3, the European Council requested 'that the Council should develop as a matter of priority the conditions and modalities of Joint Actions'[27] in the following areas: the Pact of Stability in Europe (problems of the protection of minorities and of the inviolability of frontiers in Eastern and Central Europe); the support of the peace process in the Middle East by the mobilization of the diplomatic, economic and financial resources of the Union; support for the process of democratic and multiracial transition in South Africa; search for a negotiated solution and support for humanitarian action (corridors for humanitarian convoys) in Bosnia; support for the democratic process in Russia (sending of observers for the elections of 12 December 1993).

With the transformation of EPC into the CFSP the EPC Secretariat created by the Single Act was incorporated into the Council Secretariat. The Belgian Ambassador Pierre Champenois, who had succeeded the Italian

Giovanni Jannuzzi as Head of the Secretariat in April 1991,[28] thus became Director of the CFSP Section in the Council's General Directorate of External Relations.

The three equations, relating to coherence, security and political union, highlight the Belgian position with regard to the evolution of the Common Foreign and Security Policy. The contribution which Belgium makes towards the implementation of such a policy is most important in those areas where Belgium's foreign policy is most actively involved: Africa, the Mediterranean and the Middle East, and the two security frameworks, European and international. We shall examine these areas in turn.

AFRICA

The economic crises and political instability which are prevalent right across the African continent affect Belgian policies in Central Africa. The two crises over Kinshasa in 1988 and 1990 – put an end to bilateral cooperation with Zaïre. Since 1990 the Belgian government has been waiting for the results of the Zaïrean National Conference, itself dealing with the very long process of constitutional revision, in order to resume cooperation. In Rwanda both Belgium and France have encouraged and supported the 1993 Arusha agreement which aimed to end the civil war between the regime headed by President Hibyarana representing the Hutus and the Rwandan Patriotic Front representing the Tutsis. In Burundi Brussels encouraged the transition from a single party regime dominated by the Tutsis towards a multiparty regime. The presidential and parliamentary elections which took place in the summer of 1993 gave concrete expression to this multi-ethnic process of democratization. Then the reaction of the army in October and the assassination of the new President nullified these efforts. At the same time civil war broke out again in Rwanda, and in Zaïre right through 1993 and 1994 the process of constitutional reform continued to be deadlocked.

Due to its traditional links with these three central African countries, Belgium plays a leading role when decisions to undertake international action in these countries are taken. An established trilateral process of consultation between Brussels, Paris and Washington closely links Belgian, French and American diplomatic initiatives towards Zaïre. However Belgium, like France, also plays an influential role in defining European Political Cooperation positions with regard to Zaïre, Rwanda and Burundi. This is not to say, of course, that harmony and cohesion between Paris and Brussels on Central African issues is assured. But disputes and misunderstandings have been less sharp than in the late 1970s, the last occasion when the region caused concern in Europe.

With regard to Zaïre, following a decision in EPC, the Community suspended all its aid programmes (with the exception of humanitarian assistance) on 22 January 1992 due to the fact that President Mobutu's government was hindering the Zaïrean National Conference's attempt to draw up a new constitution.[29] In October 1992 EPC welcomed the conference's election of Prime Minister Tsishekedi who led the transition government.[30] However the Community decided to delay a decision to restore its aid to the country until it was convinced that democracy had taken firm root there. The democratization process suffered a new setback in 1993. President Mobutu formed a second Birindwa government which claimed to be replacing the Tsishekedi which had been installed by the National Conference. At the Brussels EEC–ACP Council on 17–18 May, the Zaïrean delegation was made up of representatives of the Birindwa government. The Belgian government made it clear at this meeting that Belgium did not recognize this government. At the opening session of this joint council the President of the Council of the Community read out a political declaration on behalf of the Twelve which stated that the EC did not recognize the Birindwa government as it had been set up in contravention of the democratization process taking place in Zaïre.[31] The ACP countries then decided to allow the Zaïrean delegation to remain seated at the Council. The Delegation refrained, however, from making any verbal contribution to the proceedings.

With regard to Burundi, an EPC declaration issued in July 1993 congratulated President Ndadaye on behalf of the Twelve as he had been democratically elected as a result of an 'exemplary process of democratization'.[32] However on 20–21 October a military coup put an end to the first shoots of democratization. President Ndadaye was assassinated and the Community suspended its aid programme to Burundi although it did supply aid to the Hutu refugees who fled to Zaïre and Rwanda.[33]

Apart from its important interests in Central Africa, Belgium has also been involved in Operation Restore Hope and in UNISOM 2. Some 700 men were sent to Somalia between December 1992 and December 1993. These men were deployed in the south of the country in the Kismayuo region. The Belgian soldiers ensured the distribution of humanitarian aid and endeavoured to separate and disarm the rival factions. In March four Belgian soldiers died when a mine exploded. It is interesting to note that the European Development Fund undertook to finance the Belgian military mission, an example less of 'consistency' than of overlap.

The Belgian soldiers who were pulled out of Somalia in December 1993 were redeployed in Rwanda in order to reinforce UNAMIR, the UN's peacekeeping force, as the country was being torn apart when civil war broke out again after the Arusha agreement was violated. In April 1994 ten Belgian paratroopers were disarmed and brutally executed by Hutu militia. This occurred after the Presidents of Rwanda and Burundi had both died when an assassination attempt had caused their plane to crash at Kigali Airport.

THE MEDITERRANEAN AND THE MIDDLE EAST

Although its geographic position does not make it an obvious choice, Belgium's foreign policy has nevertheless focused constant attention on the problems in the Mediterranean and the Middle East during the course of the 1980s. Cooperation and development agreements signed in the 1970s created ties between Belgium, and Morocco, Tunisia and Algeria. The last-mentioned is an important supplier of natural gas. In the early 1990s the three countries of the Maghreb have consistently constituted one of the zones in which Belgium concentrates its bilateral aid. In 1989 Morocco played a mediatory role between Brussels and Kinshasa in order to put an end to the Belgo-Zaïrean crisis of 1988. Belgian Presidencies of the Community Council tend to pay great attention to relations with Mediterranean countries. The Belgian Presidency in the first half of 1982 called for 'the concerns of the Mediterranean countries regarding the consequences of enlargement' (to Southern Europe)[34] to be taken into account. In March 1987 Leo Tindemans urged the Council to adopt the third financial protocol which would accompany the cooperation accords between the EEC and the Mediterranean countries.[35]

Belgian Presidencies also endeavour to encourage EPC to take a stand on the Israeli–Palestinian conflict. In the first half of 1982 Belgium tried to get the Community to follow up the Venice Declaration of June 1980 which had recognized the legitimate rights of the Palestinian people. Five years later the Belgian Minister for Foreign Relations in a speech to the European Parliament declared that: 'If one wants to avoid giving the impression that the Ten are abandoning their efforts to help produce a global negotiated peace settlement it is important that they should devote themselves to following up European action in the Middle East.'[36] Noting that the European Council held in London on 6 and 7 December 1986 had not referred to the Middle East in its final communiqué, Leo Tindemans warned his colleagues that the Belgian Presidency in the first half of 1987 would propose adopting a new declaration on behalf of the Twelve. This Belgian initiative had received a particular stimulus as a result of a meeting between Tindemans and the King of Morocco in Rabat. Against the backdrop of the Iran–Iraq War and a new low-profile stance taken by Washington as a result of Irangate, King Hassan II stated that 'in this period of doubt and in the absence of any credible leadership many people hoped that the Twelve would show the way'.[37] A declaration by the Twelve on 23 February 1987 called for 'an international peace conference to be held under the aegis of the United Nations involving the participation of interested parties.'[38] The Belgian Prime Minister tried to use his good offices in an attempt to reconcile the positions of the various parties involved in order for such a conference to be convened. After talks with Israel which took place in January during a meeting of the EEC–Israel Cooperation Council, Mr Tindemans visited Amman, Cairo and Riyad in mid-April, but did not visit Damascus due to the diplomatic sanctions which had been applied against the Syrian government and which banned high level political contacts with the country.

The Belgian Presidency of the second half of 1993 was to try its best once again to reactivate the Mediterranean policy. It exercised 'a very strong pressure aimed at getting the negotiation mandate relating to the Euro-Maghreb agreement approved'.[39] In parallel to the Israeli–Palestinian peace process, it also worked to specify the negotiation mandate for a new agreement with Israel.

SECURITY STRUCTURES

Belgium's security policy underlines its constant commitment to NATO, to the reactivated WEU and to action undertaken by the UN as a result of Security Council Resolutions. Belgium has never seen its membership of the Atlantic Alliance running in contradiction to the strengthening of the WEU nor to its membership of the Eurocorps. The Belgian position on this subject is reflected in Declaration No. 30 of the Maastricht Treaty: 'WEU will be developed as the defence component of the European Union and as a means to strengthen the European pillar of the Atlantic Alliance.'[40] Before joining the Eurocorps Belgium sought an assurance that it would serve a dual function both within NATO and within the WEU.[41]

However Belgium's commitment to NATO is not without limits and Belgium does have reservations about the degree to which the USA wishes its partners to participate in military exercises. The decision to authorize the stationing in Belgium of the first sixteen CRUISE missiles (out of a total of forty-eight) was taken with great difficulty in March 1985 by a centre right coalition government which had to overcome fierce opposition to it, even within the ranks of Prime Minister Martens' party, the Christian People's Party (the CVP). The missile crisis triggered the development of a pacifist movement which was capable of exerting great pressure on the Belgian government all through the 1980s. In April 1986, Belgium refused to deploy in peacetime the so-called 'binary' chemical weapons whose production was authorized by the American Congress in 1985 in order to counterbalance Soviet chemical weaponry. In October 1988 and again in May 1989, the Defence Minister of the Centre Left coalition government, Guy Coëme, told NATO's Nuclear Planning Group that Belgium had great reservations about modernizing short-range nuclear weapons, an idea that was being examined within the Alliance.

When the war in the Gulf broke out Belgium felt that this did not concern NATO as such. In September 1990 Defence Minister Coëme explained: 'Our action must be determined within the framework of the UN and the WEU and the support we give must fulfil concrete needs which again must be defined by the UN and the WEU.'[42] The Belgian government did not want to participate in offensive missions. Instead it provided naval support to implement the embargo which had been imposed by the Security Council against Iraq. Belgian minesweepers formed part of the naval force put together by several WEU countries. *Matériel* and troops of WEU partners were transported to the Gulf by C130 cargo planes. It is true that in November 1990 the Belgian government refused to provide Britain with shells which were destined for British forces stationed in Saudi Arabia, but Prime Minister Martens later said that this had been a mistake. Disagreements within the Centre Left government in which the Socialists were very reluctant to follow American leadership explain why Belgium's military commitment in the Gulf crisis was so 'low profile'. Here, as in the Cruise Missiles problem, Belgium was glad to have membership of the European foreign policy system to fall back on, even if EPC could not strictly address the question.

Belgium's military commitment is, however, very high profile when it comes to UN peacekeeping missions. Belgium forces participated in operations 'Restore Hope' and UNISOM II in Somalia, in the UNPROFOR mission in Eastern Slavonia (the Croatian zone of Baranya) and in Bosnia, as well as in the UNAMIR in Rwanda. The Belgian government rejected the idea of going beyond the 'peacekeeping' level of commitment in Bosnia. However, after the bombing of the Sarajevo market in February 1994, Willy Claes, Minister of Foreign Affairs and soon to be Secretary-General of NATO, came to support the idea of 'peace enforcement' to be undertaken by NATO airstrikes. However the Belgian government is realizing, as its European partners also involved in Bosnia are, that 'peace-keeping' and 'peace enforcement' strategies are gradually cancelling each other out.

ASSESSMENT

The creation and development of a Common Foreign and Security Policy has, then, received the constant support of Belgian diplomacy. The extension of the scope of this policy to the military aspects of security is asserted to be a literal necessity for the realization of a political union. Thus, since the Fouchet Plans at the start of the 1960s, Belgium has argued that the procedure applied in the domain of foreign policy should leave pure intergovernmentalism behind and draw closer to the procedures and institutional framework of the Community. Majority voting, an increased role for the Commission, a single decision-making centre for Community external relations and for CFSP, are all considered to be significant steps in this direction.

In certain circumstances, Belgium has contributed to reinforcing the original character of the positions of the Twelve. The Belgian initiative of a declaration by the Twelve on the Middle East in February 1987, just as the support for a solution to the internal conflicts in Nicaragua and El Salvador made in the framework of the EC–Central American Cooperation Agreement, also at the time of the Belgian Presidency of 1987, demonstrated the capacity for initiative and the autonomous actorness of EPC. Likewise, while seated on the UN Security Council in 1991, Belgium ensured that the interventions of its representative, Ambassador Noterdaeme, consistently reflected the positions taken by the Twelve.

By comparison with those of its partners, Belgian policies converge with those of France on Black Africa; they are more attuned to what is at stake in Euro-Arab relations than are the Netherlands, with their closer ties to Israel. Similarily, Brussels differs from The Hague in pushing the idea of a common European defence – of which participation in the Eurocorps is a concrete expression – whereas the Dutch tend to fear the weakening of NATO. It is necessary, moreover, to underline the fact that Belgium insists on the compatibility between European structures, such as those of the WEU and the Eurocorps, and those of NATO. Moreover, it has made the 'dual use' (NATO/WEU) of the Eurocorps the condition of its entry into this multinational force.

Officially a 'federal state composed of Communities and Regions' since February 1994 (Article 1 of the revised Constitution) Belgium has understood for more than twenty years the importance of asserting the bi-national character underlying the new federal-type unity. The successive constitutional revisions have progressively conceded to the Communities (Flemish, French- and German-speaking) and to the Regions (Flanders, Wallonia, Brussels) a degree of participation in external relations. They now have an international treaty-making power on cultural and socio-economic issues corresponding to their domestic competences. Under this heading the Regional and Community Ministers can henceforth represent Belgium at the Council meetings of the European Union, as they are further authorized by the EC Treaty Article 146 revised by the Treaty of Maastricht. In March 1994 the Federal State, the Communities and the Regions signed a cooperation agreement organizing the participation of the federal and the federated executives in the ministerial meetings of the EU. Four situations were distinguished: those which come under the respective exclusive competences of the federal and federated entities, and two of mixed competence, one where the federal power is dominant and one where the Regions and Communities hold the upper hand. The General Affairs Council of the EU and particularly the CFSP come exclusively under the competence of the federal executive.

Thus Belgium's unique internal conformation affects its external relations in that growing grey area between what used to be known as 'high' and 'low' politics. Up to the time of writing, and for the foreseeable future, the subject matter of the CFSP is still an area, by contrast, where Brussels directs most of its attention to external consensus building with its partner governments. In this respect, while there are certainly tensions in some of

Belgium's positions, Brussels shows no sign of relinquishing the commitment to extending integration to the foreign policy sphere which has become its trademark within EPC and its successor, CFSP.

NOTES

1 Speech given by Wilfried Martens, Prime Minister, 7 March 1991; text published in Wilfried Martens, *L'une et l'autre Europe*, Brussels, Racine, 1994, p.35.
2 Speech of the President of the Council, Twenty-fifth anniversary of the signature of the Treaty of Rome, Brussels 29 March 1982 (press release).
3 Government Declaration of 9 May 1988, Chapter 4 (press release).
4 Simon Nuttall, *European Political Cooperation*, Clarendon Press, Oxford, 1993, p.201.
5 In the European Parliament, 16 June 1987.
6 Remarks of the Prime Minister cited in *Het Laaste Nieuws*, 13 October 1986.
7 *De Standaard*, 23 September 1986.
8 Bulletin of Questions and Replies, Chamber of Representatives, 1991–2, no. 3, cited in 'La pratique du pouvoir exécutif et le contrôle des Chambres législatives en matière de droit international', *Revue belge de droit international*, vol. XXVI, no. 2, 1993, p.598.
9 Remarks reported by *L'Agence Belga*, 28 October 1986.
10 *Bulletin of the European Communities*, supplement 1/76, pp.17–18.
11 The Solemn Declaration of Stuttgart talks of 'the political and economic aspects of security'.
12 Alfred Cahen, 'La coopération politique européenne et la sécurité', in *Belgique, Communanté européenne et sécurité occidentale*, Textes et Documents, collection 'Idées et Etudes', no. 334, 1986, Ministère des Affaires étrangères, du Commerce extérieur et de la Coopération, p.50.
13 Ibid.
14 *Agence Europe*, no. 4510, 16–17 March 1987.
15 *Agence Europe*, no. 4511, 18 March 1987.
16 *Agence Europe*, 19 March 1987.
17 Mark Eyskens, *Buitenlandse Zaken*, Lannoo, 1992, pp.122–5.
18 Jean-Luc Dehaene's speech at Heverlee, 4 May 1993 to 'The European Bridge' (roneotext).
19 This is the agreement of 21 January 1993 between Shaliskashvili (Saceur), Lanxade (the French Chief of Staff), Neumann (German Chief of Staff). The terms of this agreement were classed 'confidential defence'. Furthermore, the Council of Ministers of the WEU recognized the Eurocorps on 19 May 1993 as 'the WEU's dependent force'.
20 The text of the speech appeared in *La Libre Belgique*, 1 December 1992.
21 Paris and Bonn submitted a draft of the Treaty of European Union covering only foreign policy. See Jean De Ruyt, *L'Acte unique européenne*, Brussels, ULB, Coll. Etudes Européennes, 1987, p.60.
22 See Jean De Ruyt, op.cit., p.87.
23 Text published by *Agence Europe*, in the Europe – Documents series, no. 1608.
24 Ambassador de Schoutheete, currently Belgium's Permanent Representative to the European Communities, wrote *La Cooperation Politique Européenne*, Brussels, Labor, 1980, (2nd edn, 1986).
25 Paper given by Philippe de Schoutheete de Tervarent, Belgium's representative to the European Communities, workshop of 21 February 1992, the document

published by l'Institut d'Etudes Européennes de l'Université Libre de Bruxelles and the Groupe d'études politique européennes, pp.25–6.

26 See the commentary in J. Cloos, G. Reinesch, D. Vignes and J. Weyland, *Le Traité de Maastricht*, Brussels, Bruylant, 1993, p.117.

27 *Bulletin of the European Communities*, 10/93, pp.8–9.

28 He had been nominated by the informal meeting of Ministers of Foreign Affairs held at Mondorf les Bains in Luxembourg in April 1991.

29 *Bulletin of the European Communities*, 1–2/92, 1.5.13.

30 *Bulletin of the European Communities*, 9/92, 1.4.3.

31 *Agence Europe*, no. 5982, 17–18 May 1993.

32 *Bulletin of the European Communities*, 7–8/93, 1.4.4.

33 *Bulletin of the European Communities*, 11/93, 1.3.52.

34 *Action programme of the Belgian Presidency*, Strasbourg, 21 January 1982, text published in the press review of the Ministry of Foreign Affairs.

35 The dossier remained in suspension for many months. Mr Tindemans says that he put pressure on his colleagues in the Foreign Affairs Council to conclude the matter. See L. Tindemans, *Europa zonder Kompas*, Antwerp, Standaard Uitgeverij, 1987, p.167.

36 *Action Programme of the Belgian Presidency*, op.cit.

37 Cited in L. Tindemans, *Europa zonder Kompas*, op.cit., p.61.

38 See Mokhtar Lamani, 'La présidence belge des Communautés européennes et la conférence internationale sur la paix au Moyen-Orient', in C. Franck and L. Roosens (eds) *La politique extérieure de la Belgique, 1987–88*, Louvain-la-Neuve, Academia, 1988, pp.43–55.

39 'The Belgian Presidency of the European Union', texts and documents, Ministry of Foreign Affairs, of External Trade and of Development Cooperation, Brussels, June 1994, p.18.

40 Declaration no. 30 relating to the WEU.

41 See the agreement between SACEUR and the French and German Chiefs of Staff, January 1994.

42 See C. Franck, 'Du désarmement en Europe aux engagements militaires dans le Golfe et en Afrique', in C. Franck, Cl. Roosens and T. de Wilde d'Estmael, *Aux tournants de l'histoire. La politique extérieure de la Belgique au début de la décennie 90*, Brussels, De Boeck University, 1993, pp.18–40.

Chapter 8

Denmark

A new activism in foreign and security policy

Bertel Heurlin

INTRODUCTION

The security policy implications for Denmark of the international sea changes which took place between 1989–90 were profound and extensive. This was the case for almost all countries in the world. The position of Denmark was in many ways improved, given that Denmark was left on the winning side once the Cold War ended. Furthermore Denmark's basically universalist approach to its own security and that of the international system as a whole was reinforced by the boost given to norms such as collective security, the rule of law, democracy, free trade, market economics, human rights and individual freedom. These are norms which are now at least formally aimed at in practically all major states and they accord fully with the ideals and world view of a small state like Denmark.

The fact is, however, that this new 'universalization' of security policy has also left Denmark in a relatively weakened situation, at the same time as it seemed to outline new possibilities for a new foreign policy activism. One of the reasons for this was developments directly caused by the sea change, namely the increasing – at least in an institutional sense – 'Europeanization' of national foreign and security policy. The new term – coined by the USA acting as the leader of NATO – is the 'European Security and Defense Identity'.[1]

What are the direct structural impacts of these two important developments – internationalization and Europeanization – on Danish security and foreign policy, and what are the basic attitudes of the government and Denmark's political élites to the new situation. What has changed, and why, in respect of Denmark's position in the process of European foreign policy cooperation? And what are the prospects for the future?

This chapter will try to answer these questions in the following way: First, four structural and process level implications of the new 'universalization' will be presented. Then one of them, namely Europeanization, will be analysed in a more comprehensive way. A crucial factor in the whole game is the democratic factor (i.e. the internal, domestic scene). The next step will be to examine the parameters of Denmark's new foreign and security policy. The findings are summarized in the conclusion.

FOUR NEW IMPLICATIONS FOR DANISH SECURITY

What then are the implications of the global structural changes which imply a change from bipolarity to unipolarity? And what is the impact of this unipolarity in terms of a general universalization of the values, norms and regimes of the winners, that is the USA and the West?[2]

First, Denmark's relative position in terms of security is weakened. Second, structures giving Denmark a certain freedom of action have been fundamentally altered. Third, Denmark has now chosen to an increasing degree actively to participate in international military activities affecting the security of other states. In this way Denmark appears to have changed its role from being mainly a consumer to being also a producer of security. Fourth, and as a consequence of the transformation, choices which with the overlay of the Cold War could be avoided, are now all too visible. The choices are inherently painful, but Denmark has to face them. Such choices have a great deal to do with the emergence of the European Union. The EU implies an increasing Europeanization of foreign policy.

We shall now analyse in more detail the implications for Denmark of the seismic shift in international politics which has occurred over the last decade.

The relative weakening of Danish security

During the Cold War Denmark, although a front-line state, enjoyed some privileges, being perceived as part of a Nordic low tension area, manifested in a policy of no nuclear weapons, in the absence of foreign troops and in certain territorial restrictions. Denmark followed a security policy of reservations *vis-à-vis* the USA's nuclear policy, the general tendencies towards rearmament and the West's confrontational policy of the 1980s. Emphasizing a continued *détente* was considered an important part of Danish security policy. In certain ways one might characterize this policy as non-provocative towards the main enemy, the Soviet Union, even if it did not go half so far in that direction as a more vulnerable Scandinavian state, Finland.

The Nordic low tension situation and policy was, however, more or less accepted by NATO, including the USA.[3] This enabled Denmark to have a rather low level of military expenditure compared to other NATO allies and to neutral Nordic countries. Furthermore the concept of a certain cohesion in security terms among the Nordic states, often labelled 'the Nordic Balance', was implicitly accepted and taken into consideration by the allies.

With the disappearance of the Cold War, this condition of relatively high security has vanished. The whole of Central Europe, that former powder keg with the clear military line of confrontation, now enjoys the same low tension status as Denmark during the Cold War. The former privileges of sanctuary have gone.

But if the structural changes have left Denmark with a relatively weakened security situation, since the game is not zero-sum this new position primarily affects Danish self-perception. In absolute terms the situation has been enhanced, as the one and only threatening enemy, the highly militarized Soviet empire very close to the Danish borders, has vanished. Then again this transformation has triggered off unexpected events, leaving scattered and diversified, mutually unrelated islands of unrest and chaos behind all over Europe.

Changing structures

In terms of broad political and institutional structures, while a clear bipolarity persisted, Denmark was an undisputed part of the Western pole, militarily wholly integrated in the northern part of Germany through BALTAP, the joint NATO command. At the same time it was part of the Nordic Balance – from NATO–Norway in the West to the committed neutral in the East, Finland. NATO was the unchallenged organizational unit, linking the fate of the USA to Western Europe, and vice versa. This provided Denmark with a certain freedom of action in political and military terms.[4] For example, under these circumstances Denmark could play a role as the semi-reluctant NATO member, allowing itself to have severe reservations as regards the general NATO policy towards the Soviet Union (for example the 'footnote policy' in the 1980s). Moreover, at the same time Denmark felt free to have its own policy on *détente*, by trying to promote what could be identified as common East–West values over and above the limits of military confrontation.

This extra freedom of action is now non-existent. The new world structure is based on a *primus inter pares* situation, even unipolarity, with the USA as the only universal state able and willing to be a political and military manager. In the long run the structure may transform itself into a multipolar world, leaving new roles to Europe.

The specificity and room to manoeuvre of Denmark in this new international environment have changed dramatically. Denmark is now a small state among all the new small states in Europe exposed to fresh threats arising from the collapse of empire, particularly in the chaos and even war of South-eastern Europe. Denmark has to look for new ways both to protect and to express itself internationally. This can, for example, be done by promoting a new universalizing approach to security and stability, as indicated below.

New responsibilities

The concept of a change from a consumer to a producer of security deserves to be examined closely, not least because it sounds like an exaggeration: how could tiny Denmark with a very limited number of armed forces, stigmatized in the 1980s as a free rider in NATO, leading to the label of 'Denmarkization', come to 'produce' security? This is, however, a relevant description of recent developments, and in three different ways.

1   As part of NATO's new strategy the whole reinforcement structure has been changed. Previously, as a front-line state, Denmark was designated to receive innumerable reinforcement combat troops and military equipment. Obviously this is no longer the case. The new strategy implies that all member states should be prepared to provide reinforcements. Denmark is now organizing and structuring her armed forces to meet the new demands from NATO in the form of rapid reaction forces, and has therefore become a reinforcement delivering country.

2   Denmark has – as the revitalization of a long-term policy – increased and maximized its potential for participating militarily in OSCE/UN peacekeeping operations, which hints also in the direction of peace *making* operations. It is now the position of the Danish government that NATO can play an active role in such operations so long as it acts as a kind of 'entrepreneur'. Danish personnel have for some time been operating in the former Yugoslavia. At present some 1,500 are serving in the UNPROFOR MISSION, the EU-Observer Mission, the Red Cross and the UNHCR.

    Recently the establishment of a Danish international reaction brigade to be used in the UN as well as in OSCE, NATO–UN operations or national missions, and also to be part of the new NATO rapid reaction forces has been agreed by the Danish Parliament. The brigade will be fully operational in 1996. The Danish International Brigade will consist of 4,500 soldiers, 80 per cent of whom will be fully trained discharged conscripts who after their service will have a three-year contract to be on call. The other 20 per cent will be regulars. The brigade can participate (either as a whole or in part) in military operations dealing with conflict prevention, peacekeeping, and peacemaking. Humanitarian operations are also foreseen. Part of the brigade will be allocated to the UN's stand-by forces, once the forces are organized.

3   The new situation in the Baltic Sea also seems likely to require a far greater role for the Danish armed forces, as the Germans are concentrating their efforts in the North Sea. This is not just the result of NATO arrangements and strategies, but also the product of cooperation with the reborn Baltic states. Denmark has informally been assigned by the Western countries the role of being coordinator *vis-à-vis* the Baltic states. This has materialized through unilateral agreements between Copenhagen

and the individual Baltic states (Estonia, Latvia and Lithuania) according to which officers and soldiers will get some military education and training in Denmark. Some deliveries of equipment, but not weapons, are included. In this connection Denmark's role is envisaged as that of assisting and coordinating the setting up, organization and training of a new Baltic peacekeeping unit on a multilateral basis.[5] An agreement between Denmark and the Russian Federation concerning bilateral military cooperation has also recently been signed.[6]

Choices

The structural transformation of world politics has severe implications for Denmark concerning its role in a Europe where a (Western) European security identity is increasingly possible. The need for entirely new organizing principles for the international system has given impetus to the Europeanization of security matters.

Denmark is now left with crucial choices which it cannot avoid. In the long run Copenhagen cannot cling exclusively to the membership of NATO which has served Denmark so well as the only route to security. Denmark's main choice is whether or not it wishes to accept some sort of European defence identity and some sort of a 'separate, but not separable' European defence.[7] In the background lies the idea of Nordic defence cooperation – perhaps in one way or another connected to a broader European structure. As yet nothing indicates any widespread willingness to face the choices, let alone to cope with them.

In a recent Danish White Paper (June 1993) about security policy the following sentence is emphasized several times: 'Even if the threat of a comprehensive military attack on Denmark has disappeared, Denmark's membership of NATO will remain the irreplaceable guarantee for the territorial integrity of Denmark'.[8]

Denmark is now the only EU member besides the neutrals which is not a member of the WEU. Norway is now an Associated Member with the right to participate in the decision-making processes, but with no veto or obligation to accept the clause on military assistance. Central and Eastern European states have also been given Associated Partner status. By contrast Denmark is merely an Observer. Any changes in this status seem unlikely, as the detachment from WEU was a very important part of the exceptions made for Denmark in the Maastricht Treaty by the Edinburgh Summit. These exceptions were later accepted by the Danish population in the referendum of 18 May 1993.

But why is NATO so important to Denmark? The principal explanation is the fact that the USA participates – and more importantly that it is Washington which leads the alliance. The USA can be considered – in the famous phrase of Joseph Joffe – to be 'Europe's pacifier'. The USA is the geographically distant balancer which brings about a situation where Denmark becomes less dependent on Germany. The role of the USA ensures that Denmark is not confronted with the situation where it has to accept everything that a Franco-German defence and security policy can come up with.

Furthermore, as the only European country with a territorial attachment to the American continent – namely Greenland – Denmark must necessarily have a special relationship with the USA. And this can take place most comfortably inside the NATO framework.

MAASTRICHT AND THE CFSP

Here we arrive at the core of the question: what are the distinctive elements of Denmark's attitudes towards European Political Cooperation and towards what now has been extended into the Common Foreign and Security Policy?

Normally Denmark is pictured as the foot-dragging European, isolationist in relation to all the Europe embracing countries to the South. It is seen as a country which is preoccupied with and desperately clinging to the maintenance of its national sovereignty.

In this way Denmark was also considered by its fellow members to be a threat to the fragile construction called the Maastricht Treaty. Denmark was the country, in a formal sense at least, which seemed to be capable of stopping the EC from becoming a European Union.

In the June 1992 Danish referendum on the full Maastricht Treaty the no votes just topped the 50 per cent mark. Denmark had rejected the European Union treaty. But after almost another year had passed a previously scrapped Danish draft, excluding four specific areas, was accepted in a new referendum. The new version – referred to as the 'Edinburgh agreement' – was based on what in Denmark was called 'the national compromise'. It has the following exclusions, accepted by the other eleven member states:

1 The third phase of the Economic and Monetary Union is omitted. Denmark is, however, participating fully in the first two phases, and is following an economic policy fully in accordance with the EMU targets.
2 The principle of a superordinate EU citizenship is omitted. This has, however, no practical purpose, as Denmark has legally secured the stipulated rights for citizens from EU countries.
3 The internal and juridical issues of Pillar Three are omitted. Denmark will, however, participate in all relevant areas as long as the cooperation stays at the level of intergovernmental relations. Denmark will not follow the possibilities in the Maastricht Treaty for transforming aspects of intergovernmental cooperation into supranationalism.

4   The fourth exception is of specific importance here. It refers to cooperation on defence policy. Denmark does not want to participate operationally in any possible cooperation on defence whether it is referred to as 'defence policy' or as a 'common defence'. It might, however, join in with discussions. When Denmark is President of the EU, however, it will leave the chair when defence matters are being discussed, decided or implemented. Moreover Denmark will remain an Observer (albeit an active one) in WEU; this as mentioned is the only possible status for the country at present.

Again it is crucial to emphasize that Denmark will in no way give up its commitment to European cooperation in political and security related areas. This is explicitly stated in the Edinburgh agreement.

Why does Denmark have these problems with the Union, and why do these problems include defence policy, leaving the CFSP as it currently stands as an efficient, valuable and attractive alternative?

EXPLAINING ATTITUDES AND POLICY

The fundamental explanation for Danish policy is to be found in the country's basic position. Position is here to be understood in terms of relative placement in the international and regional system, referring to geopolitics, resources and size and population, as well as economic and military strength, political system and culture.

For a small country like Denmark a fundamental and lasting dilemma exists between, on the one hand, the need to integrate into the international and regional system in order to survive (given that geography does not permit isolation), and, on the other hand, likewise in order to survive, to avoid an integration which will dissolve the country as an independent unit.

On the basis of an analysis which takes as a point of departure the geopolitical position of Denmark one can arrive at the assertion that Denmark – reflecting the views of the government, social élites and the wider population – is striving towards five integration projects simultaneously in order to cope with the ever-changing external environment. The words 'integration projects' could lead to a misinterpretation. The term integration is here, however, restricted to characterizing the process of pooling sovereignty in international organizations such as is foreseen in the Danish constitution. The five projects are not necessarily competing. On the contrary, for the most part they may be considered complementary.[9] The five are as follows.

First is the universalist project, the point of departure for which is the UN. The membership of the UN has always been assigned a high priority in Danish foreign policy. As the Danish constitution after the Second World

War was in the process of being transformed – the new constitution entered into force after a referendum in 1953 – the debate around Section 20 of the draft, which referred to the conditions for transferring sovereignty to international organizations, also included obligations – not least in the field of security – towards the UN.

Second, a pan-European project has been promoted as a long-term goal, rather vague in character and mostly introduced as an alternative or a supplement to the geographically restricted integration process in Western Europe. Originally, in the late 1940s, Denmark supported some of the federalistic, integrative elements in the drafts of the charter of the Council of Europe, which was designed to cover the whole European continent. During the Cold War Denmark continued to support initiatives to bring the whole of Europe together, for instance the Soviet concept of what later became known as the CSCE. Now Denmark is among the most active supporters of the widening processes inside EU, including the bringing of Central and Eastern European countries into pan-European security arrangements.

Furthermore it has to be emphasized that the so-called anti-European forces in Danish society, the anti-Marketeers, had only one target in bringing their guns into position: the European Community as a closed Western institution. Their negative picture is that of a rich, aggressive, and protectionist Western Europe where French nationalism is elevated to the European level and where Germany's latent great power dreams can thrive behind a European disguise. On the other hand these same anti-European forces often supported the idea of an integrated pan-European unit with regard to North–South relations, in terms of being able to help the South more effectively.

Third, one has to mention the project of Nordic integration. Increased Nordic cooperation has been a constant factor during the years following the Second World War. This process has been labelled 'the process of parallel national action'.[10] The basic idea behind it can essentially be characterized as resting on the 'spider's web' concept of integration. This predicts that as cultural, administrative, economic and functional integration increases – as it seems to be doing in many ways – the web might one day turn out to be sufficiently strong to be able to carry the weight of the necessary structures of political federalism.

The creation of a Nordic Federal Unit has been, and will stay, a dream. But a constant strengthening of Nordic cooperation has been the declared policy of every government since the Second World War. The Nordic identity is for the Danes both obvious and natural. A (Western) European identity is not. It is common to refer to Norway, Sweden, Iceland and Finland as sister or brother nations. The same vocabulary would never be used in connection with other European countries. Surveys indicate that, asked what nationality they woud prefer if they were not Danish, up to 90 per cent of Danes refer to Scandinavian countries, and the rest to England, but almost nobody wants a continental European nationality.

Fourth is the existence of a North Atlantic project, based on NATO. Formally speaking there are no federal features in the Washington treaty, nor are there any such aims in the alliance. NATO's strength has been its strictly intergovernmental structure. Nevertheless its organizational frameworks and its political–military processes reveal many federative and integrationist features. This is, for example, the case in the mixed, international military hierarchy which is supposed to function in a highly integrated manner in wartime, but which is also at work in peacetime.[11]

In the case of Denmark it is characteristic that the country has been assigned to the most integrated and the best functioning command unit inside NATO: BALTAP. Since the 1970s Denmark has enthusiastically promoted integration in this field, through an intensified cooperation in BALTAP and still more through reliance on the designated reinforcements coming principally from the UK and the USA. This policy continued, curiously enough, following its own logic, during the 1980s, the years of 'Denmarkization' and NATO 'footnotes'. 'Denmarkization' was used by critics to refer to Denmark's relatively limited contribution to the common defence, enjoying protection at a very low price. The footnotes were due to the strange situation of having a minority centre right government which on security matters was dependent on an 'alternative security policy' majority, including one of the small parties. This produced footnotes on the biannual NATO communiquées. The Danish reservations mainly pertained to the alliance's nuclear strategy and policy on nuclear weapons acquisition.

The problem arises, however, of whether NATO will continue as a central institution now that the Soviet empire has disappeared and accordingly deprived NATO of its common enemy. Given that the Alliance has functioned not solely on the basis of a clearly defined and mighty enemy, but also as the only transatlantic organization binding the USA and Western Europe together, there are reasons for predicting its continuing central role. The NATO summit in Brussels in January 1994 foresaw a NATO as strong as ever. It is certainly a magnet for the states of Central and Eastern Europe.

Thus Denmark has put all its eggs into the NATO basket. NATO will continue to provide 'the irreplaceable guarantee for Denmark'.[12] Denmark does however participate fully in all other European and universalist organizations relevant to its security, even if NATO is considered second to none. The one exception, in a condition of dynamic change, is the WEU, and the question of an EU common defence policy. And this is the rub for Denmark.

THE WESTERN EUROPEAN PROJECT

This problem arises from the fifth project: that of Western European integration and organization. Starting with the ECSC, through EEC and the EC to the European Union, European cooperation has always been a project as well as a process. The idea of interpreting integration as a project is crucial, in the sense that there is a clear objective: the process of creating 'an ever closer union among the peoples of Europe'.[13]

Logically this means a union which will cover all areas, ending with a new political unit, whether the European Union or even a United States of Europe. But politics is not logic. And Denmark has never adhered to the logic of the ultimate objective of cooperation. The 'still closer union' notion has been ignored – or rather seen simply as the formal invocation of the good principle of cooperation between peoples, without having any connotations of a final federal union. The interpretation which has been accepted refers only to close cooperation, which is fully compatible with Denmark's basic foreign policy goals: the more functional, regulated and legally binding cooperation with like-minded nations, the better.

Once Denmark became a member of the EC in 1973 (after the referendum of 1972) the concept of 'union' played a minor role. The Danish translation of the term was the incorrect 'sammenslutning', which corresponds to the English word 'association' (i.e. indicating a looser organization). As in Britain the European Community was almost exclusively referred to as 'the Common Market'. This continued to be the case until recently. Parliamentary control of EC policy took place in the 'Market Committee', which only changed its name to the 'Europe Committee' as late as October 1994.

Going back to Denmark's accession to the EC in 1973, there were no objections towards EPC, which had been set up in 1970 and which was organized outside the Community on a purely intergovernmental basis. Denmark was certainly no reluctant member of EPC, supporting without hesitation the presentation of common positions each year at the UN General Assembly – where, in September, the Presidency expresses the general views on international politics of all the member states. Denmark also actively participated in the formulation of EPC's (not always uncontroversial) decisions on such sensitive areas as the Middle East, South Africa, and later the Gulf and Balkans, without noticeably behaving as a maverick.

The changes in EPC as part of the SEA did not in the long run cause any fundamental problems for the Danish support of foreign policy cooperation so long as this cooperation was based on intergovernmentalism. Even the principle of decisions based on majority voting which was eventually accepted in the Maastricht Treaty has been adopted, no doubt because it depends on a unanimous acceptance beforehand that the issue in question should be subject to majority voting.

The notion of the 'European Union' was introduced in the Paris Conference of October 1972 together with a plan of action for the rest of the decade to implement it. Denmark accepted the federal notion without debate, the reason being that there were no fixed obligations and there was no clear definition of the content of 'union' as indicated above.

The official Danish view in the 1970s of a European Union in general is to be found in the memorandum submitted to Tindemans in connection with his report of 1976. This official document indicates that Denmark prefers a pragmatic, functional form of cooperation including, however, extensive pooling of sovereignty on certain areas. Foreign policy was to be a pragmatic area of cooperation which, moreover, took place outside the Community. Any ambitious political superstructure was to be avoided.

The characteristic feature of the memorandum was the emphasis on the independence of the Commission as a protector of the interests of the small countries. Consequently the declining role of the Commission was deplored. Denmark even suggested an extended use of majority voting. There was a further proposal for intensified cooperation between Council and Parliament, although the Parliament was not to develop into a proper legislative body. The precondition for further integration was (and is, in the Danish view) that all countries fulfil in the most comprehensive way their legal obligations on the basis of EC decisions. Common rules and common policies in the areas covered by the treaties – be they agriculture, fishing, transport, energy, economy – were generally seen as in the interest of a small country like Denmark.

This process of common policy on selected, functional areas including foreign policy and some security related issues, but more or less ignoring the project of a political superstructure, seemed to be continuing in connection with the adoption of the SEA.

Generally it can be stated that although the fundamental rationale of European integration was security, its manifestation was largely economic. During the Cold War there was not much space for an independent European security policy, with the exceptions of the short period of *détente* in the 1970s and the beginning of the end of the Cold War from the mid-1980s on.

Denmark had, as mentioned above, no objections in principle towards the EPC. On the contrary it was considered beneficial that the Western European countries in general and specific areas of foreign policy could speak with one voice. The precondition of support was the preservation of EPC's intergovernmentalism. Supranationality in this area was not acceptable. Therefore there were no real problems with the new formulations of the SEA, except during the process of negotiation in relation to minor differences over the permanent EPC secretariat and over making EPC a full part of the treaty.

As the EPC developed during the 1980s it became increasingly difficult to uphold the dividing line between politics and economics in European external relations. An example is the EPC condemnation of the Soviet invasion in Afghanistan and the follow-up policy by the EC with economic sanctions against the Soviet Union. This development created problems for the Danish policy of maintaining a clear distinction between pure foreign policy in the EPC and the general Community commercial policy.

This problem became pertinent in 1982, when Denmark opted out of Community sanctions over Poland on the grounds that this was not an appropriate use of Article 113 of the Treaty of Rome, but it became more evident after 1989, once economic instruments became central to the new Western policy towards the newly liberated states of Central and Eastern Europe.

Here we can see a clear shift in policy. As early as the October 1990 Memorandum Denmark was suggesting a common structure along the lines of what was to become the solution in the Maastricht Treaty, namely giving the Council competence *vis-à-vis* all three pillars, including Pillar Two, the CFSP. This can be interpreted as a clear expression of Denmark moving from a limited 'Market' policy to a wider 'Europe' policy. The same shift is to be found in the position towards the intergovernmental conferences. Denmark was against the convening of the 1985 Conference which resulted in the SEA, but in favour of that which was to lead to the European Union. Moreover Denmark had no problems in accepting that security matters and not just foreign policy could be discussed in what was later designated the CFSP.

Denmark could not, however, go along with implementation where a military action might be part of a 'Joint Action'. On the other hand the procedure where WEU can be asked to act on behalf of the Union (see Article J.4) was considered unproblematic given Denmark's lack of full membership of the WEU.

Why then was there a negative attitude to the European Union at all, as demonstrated in the 'no' vote in the 1992 referendum? To the Danish population the concept of 'union' had become synonymous with that of a federal, centralist, great power Europe. This view should be seen against the background of an electorate which looked upon the EC as a Common Market. The population had not forgotten the famous dictum of the then centre right Prime Minister Poul Schlüter in 1986: 'the Union is dead; stone dead'.

This rejection of a political superstructure for the EC was a fundamental part of Danish attitudes to Western European integration. So Denmark had a problem once the idea of a Union once again came on to the European agenda in earnest after the sea changes of 1989–90. Further integrative provisions on functional areas – especially the environment and the labour market (the social dimension) – were in accordance with Danish policy. The main problem was the revitalized European Union. The new edition of the EU seemed now to have a federally inspired political structure which threatened national sovereignty in high policy areas with great symbolic value, such as those of citizenship, the common currency and bank, a common defence policy leading to a common defence, and common policing.

The population rejected this apparently federalist scheme. In order to persuade them to swallow it, it was necessary, as we have already seen, to remove the contentious elements of defence, EMU, cooperation on legal and internal affairs, and citizenship. The Danish rump treaty was then ratified after the referendum of 18 May 1993.

Another important feature was that the combination of Maastricht and Edinburgh created a new situation. The general image of a European federation as a serious project faded. What ensued was the political realization among most EC member states, that federalism – and the subsequent transformation of the nation-state – was not the relevant answer to the process of European integration. The notion of subsidiarity – which had been considered part of the federal vocabulary – could now be interpreted as a restraint on the federal process.

The Danish way of coping with the concept of subsidiarity (which was a totally new and alien term in Denmark's political vocabulary) was to translate it into 'the principle of nearness', a term signalling decentralization and autonomy. This understanding implies that the centre (the Council and the Commission) should not interfere in affairs which can be dealt with on a national, regional or local level.

Subsidiarity is not directly connected to the question of the CFSP. But it is a principle which, given that it is mentioned explicitly in the preamble to the Treaty of European Union, will also certainly influence questions of foreign policy.

THE DOMESTIC ENVIRONMENT

Never before in the history of Denmark has the political consensus on foreign and defence policy been more extensive. All parties in the parliament are now supportive of NATO. Even the left-wing Socialist Peoples Party, a traditional anti-NATO party, has now changed its position. It is a paradox that the disappearance of military threats towards the Danish territory has coincided with the achievement of full parliamentary support for NATO. The explanation is twofold:

First, the way in which to deal with the former Soviet and Eastern threat not least during the 'Second Cold War', divided the political parties, and the common denominator which kept them together was the continuation of some sort of a *détente*.

Second is the fact that after the disappearance of the threat, the real choices became evident: the only alternative to NATO seemed to be a European solution, which would provide the EC with security and defence powers. Only a small fraction of the parties – including those on the right wing – supported membership of the WEU. And due to the 'National Compromise' official Danish policy for some time to come will be based on the consensual understanding of the Edinburgh decisions.

Furthermore the population in general seems to support Danish membership of NATO. Polls have indicated that the support since the end of the 1970s has been over 50 per cent. An opinion poll in May 1992 found 73 per cent of respondents to be pro NATO, 15 per cent against and 12 per cent undecided. A result like this seems to indicate that Denmark is among the principal supporters inside the alliance.

Another expression of positive attitudes towards the alliance is the fact that over the years a considerable part of the population has joined the Danish Home Guard. These voluntary forces – keeping their weapons in their private homes – enjoy constant support and recruitment from the Danish population. On the other hand the Danish people seem not yet ready to defend Europe in the sense of subscribing to the WEU. But they are ready to support UN, Atlanticist, or pan-European interventionism to stop local wars in Europe.

DANISH SECURITY POLICY IN THE 1990s

Denmark is unwilling – as we have seen – to accept European integration in the area of defence, be it in the EU or in the WEU. For itself Denmark will not follow its partners by consenting to the principle of dual WEU–NATO membership. But Copenhagen has no intention of obstructing such an integration process among the other EU states. And Denmark generally welcomes more intensive foreign and security policy cooperation.

To Danish policy-makers the European security and defence policy setting has, however, changed. WEU is not what it used to be. Although the notion of a European defence, and certainly that of a European defence identity, seems to be strengthened through the entering into force of the Maastricht Treaty, it would be reasonable to argue that the time when it was necessary to make a choice between Europe and the USA has gone. And so perhaps the situation for Denmark has been eased, at least in the short run.

The WEU is undergoing a process of 'NATOization'. France is no longer striving desperately to develop WEU as a fully independent organization. The countries involved have accepted that the WEU is primarily the European pillar of NATO, thus satisfying the wishes of the USA, which urged the Europeans to set up such a pillar more than thirty years ago in the Kennedy era. Inside this pillar a European Security and Defence Identity can be nursed, but certainly not against the interests of the USA. As was stressed in the NATO summit declaration of January 1994: 'The United States and Europe have the same strategic interests.'[14]

In Denmark the WEU used to be a bogey institution which was seen as being fully in accordance with chauvinist, interventionist and Euro-nationalist ideas and principles of mainly French provenance. These principles were considered to be based on more crude nuclear strategies than NATO,[15] on more automatic military involvement procedures than NATO and finally on a clear out-of-area strategy in contrast to NATO's restrictions. All in all the somewhat distorted picture was of a WEU which from the outside could be looked upon as the military arm of a militarist, fortress Western Europe, following a policy entirely independent of the USA and against common American–European interests.

In practice all the bogey-like characteristics of WEU have now vanished. The old nuclear deterrence strategies have lost their relevance, interventionist policies without the consent of UN or OSCE acting as a regional UN are a remote possibility, pointing to the fact that the universalist institutions have gained new influence and legitimacy on the basis of structural changes internationally. The activist policy of the revitalized WEU from 1983–4 has been more than modified and with the French move towards NATO, WEU is now almost integrated into the Atlantic Alliance. So why does Denmark hesitate to join WEU as a full member, as all its EU partners except Ireland and the three recent entrants have done?

There are two main reasons for Danish reluctance: one is structural, relating to Denmark's position in the international system. The other is domestic, having to do with internal political structures and processes. The first factor has already been dealt with in some detail above.

The second factor has two aspects. The first relates to the universalist perspective which is widely found in both the Danish population at large and in governing circles. From this viewpoint the WEU gives the EU – as seen from outside – an image of a militarized unit which is a threat to the rest of the world, and particularly the Third World. The WEU is considered an organization which has not taken up the ideas of 'soft security' which have become fashionable after the Cold War.

There is evidence of this view in Danish policy. It is, for example, a fact that the public spending on 'soft security', namely aid and assistance to developing countries, humanitarian and disaster assistance, economic aid to Eastern Europe, aid to refugees – in sum which everything that can be labelled as Denmark's contribution to international society – exceeded expenditure on national defence in 1993. The figures are approximately DKr 16 billion for soft security and DKr 14 billion for defence. This may be the only such case worldwide.

The second aspect arises out of the relation between the politicians and the general population. In the first referendum of 1992 the voters were presented with a treaty which envisaged the creation of a European Union with a common defence. This Union looked very much like a federal construction, thereby nullifying Denmark's four approaches to multilateralism.

The great majority of the parliament supported the EU, as they assessed the Union to be more rhetoric than reality. On the other hand the general population, who had to decide if it accepted a treaty presented as more than 300 pages of complicated, indigestible and partly incomprehensible paragraphs, simply gave up, and in order to be on the safe side voted against by a figure of 51–49. The slogan 'if in doubt, vote no', had been effective. In the next, and no less complicated referendum, most of the factors considered the reasons for voting no were removed. This political solution convinced the population. They delivered the merchandise: a comfortable majority. But by this time the popular credibility of the politicians had worn thin.

Although the discussion in Denmark concerning the crucial question of European defence has barely begun a possible solution is another referendum in 1997. But this will not necessarily happen. The new role of WEU is still not clear, as it is based on a broad compromise. Moreover it is certainly not an attractive task for the politicians to present the population with a third referendum on the same issue inside a very short timespan. A vast coalition of parties from the right to the left including the former anti-Marketeer Socialist Peoples Party had agreed on the 'National Compromise' that became the point of departure for the Edinburgh agreement, and this would be difficult to replicate.

A realistic assessment would also point to the fact that Denmark, which is a member of practically all the existing universal and regional security-related organizations, will not miss much influence by not being a full member of WEU in the period up to 1997, or after, given the still embryonic character of this organization.

CONCLUSIONS

As a small, democratic, open, highly industrialized, rich and welfare-oriented country Denmark has undergone remarkable changes in the 1980s and 1990s which have had impressive effects on its foreign and security policy. Up to well over halfway through the 1980s Copenhagen had serious problems in coping with the 'Second Cold War'. Denmark's goal was to sustain what was left of the East–West *détente*. In this it was close to Germany, but in policy terms there was a significant difference: Denmark tried – as a lone voice – to continue a policy based on arms control, *détente* and no provocations towards the USSR. This was manifested in the 'footnote' policy in NATO, soon labelled by critics 'Denmarkization' or free riding. As the Cold War ended with the voluntary surrender of the USSR this policy lost its meaning. Denmark now found itself in a new international system tending towards unipolarity.

This implied a wholly new security situation, where the direct threats had disappeared and there was almost no need for either deterrence or *détente*. In security terms Denmark now had the best of all worlds: a new world order with dramatically reduced military threats, and a trend towards the spread of common values and the revitalization of the UN.

Yet the liberation of Eastern Europe and the removal of part of the American 'overlay' in Europe leaving a greater part of the European security to the Europeans created a situation of unpredictability and instability, not least due to the dissolution and the delegitimation of the socialist empire. The result was partly war arising from neo-nationalism and partly general economic, political and societal insecurity due to the lure of freedom. In Denmark this challenge was met with a new foreign policy activism, to be embedded in broader regional and international frameworks.

But which international and regional frameworks? The new development is that Denmark's five multilateralist projects – the international, trans-atlantic, all-European, Western European and the Nordic – are now increasingly converging on one project (i.e. the European), primarily due to the end of bipolarity. And even in Europe one can identify a regional 'pole' – the EU – although the pole consists of a union between what are in principle fully sovereign states.

Denmark has supported EPC since its beginnings and has accepted, without much reluctance, its practical and formal development (i.e. the SEA and the TEU, with the exception of the military dimension). To Denmark it seemed wholly compatible with the national interest to operate together with Western European countries on specific European issues, so long as any decisions taken were not directly contrary to transatlantic or Nordic interests.

With the EU as an at least formally strengthened player, Denmark is now positioned in a process which could expose her national policy to a more direct challenge. This could involve giving up specific, narrow concerns and may be the price Denmark has to pay in order not to be marginalized in the inevitable stratification which would follow the creation in Europe of an EU core surrounded by a number of concentric circles. An indication of Denmark's interest in being in a core position can be seen in recent economic and diplomatic moves in relation to the EU – a policy which is being pursued in defiance of the Edinburgh opt-outs.

Apart from tracing the evolution of Denmark's concerns about EPC and its transformation into the CFSP this chapter has also sought to identify the main problems and the hard decisions to be taken in connection with Danish defence and security policy in the 1990s. The reasons for Denmark being in a more exposed situation than during the Cold War have been given. In many ways all Denmark's longstanding objectives in the field of security policy have been fulfilled. The problem is that in consequence the tough choice between Europe, WEU and NATO is threatening. The obvious answer is to go for all three. But in the long run Denmark cannot avoid a more direct engagement in European defence. If it could be embedded in a transatlantic framework Denmark would have the best of all worlds. There are three possible trends or scenarios.

1 Certain changes in the institutional structures are bound to take place in Europe in a foreseeable future. The enlargement of the EU with most of the EFTA countries has led to the Central and Eastern European states knocking at the door. The inclusion of new 'associate partners' into the WEU (i.e. the Central and Eastern European states) could make the WEU even more influential. As to the transatlantic link it is possible that changes will take place in the direction of a Partnership-for-Peace (PfP) enlargement of NATO, which in the longer run will result in a closer relationship tantamount to membership for the PfP countries. Together these developments will ease and perhaps solve Denmark's problems.

In this respect the three most important integration projects – the all-European, the Western European and the transatlantic – could be united. The crown could be the overall universalism of the UN, to which the new Danish International Brigade is primarily dedicated – at least at the declaratory level.

However, if this solution is to have real value for Denmark, the condition will be a NATO which is as strong as it is now. A primary Danish interest in the long run continues to be a unipolar world where the USA retains its organizing role in Europe. This is not least because the German problem with its European and international implications, will still be solved in the best way, from the Danish viewpoint, if it is embedded in a strong transatlantic institution. But a strong NATO does not any longer exclude a strong European pillar manifested in WEU. In the long run Denmark cannot avoid membership of this organization, or if it is to be dissolved, of a succeeding EU-based military organization.

This would be particularly true bearing in mind the possible change of the international system into a multipolar world, although this transformation is not immediately round the corner, and indeed, has been wrongly predicted for several decades.

2 The second scenario relates to the currently dormant debate on Nordic defence cooperation. Will some sort of agreement materialize? In 1992 an agreement of mutual defence assistance, possibly containing some secret paragraphs, was agreed between Sweden and Finland. From Norway some positive, if cautious, signals have been delivered. Denmark has officially rejected the possibility, but with some indications that the implications and problems will have to be analysed. It is, however, evident that as an isolated phenomenon a Nordic solution has no future.

3 The third, and seemingly ultimate solution is the combination of all five

Danish integration projects – all of them surviving according to their own merits. This is more a dream presupposing a general transformation in the direction of a dissolution of the anarchic structure of international relations.

Projects in the real world, and in a Europe still liable to be torn apart by wars (even if so far they are only occurring in relatively peripheral areas with little risk of proliferation) will necessarily be interconnected and require managing on the basis of clear priorities. In the real world the order of priorities is national, regional and then international security. For Denmark in the foreseeable future national security is best served by a high priority to NATO, and supported by a strong commitment to the regional, European security to be found not necessarily in WEU but in a more militarily oriented EU.

NOTES

1 See, for example, Communiqué from the NATO summit, 12 January 1994.
2 As to the use of the term unipolarity, see, for example, Bertel Heurlin, 'The United States, the Soviet Union and the transformation of Europe 1989–91', in Morten Kelstrup, (ed.) *European Integration and Denmark's Participation*, Copenhagen, Copenhagen Political Studies Press, 1992, pp.59–88, and Birthe Hansen, *Unipolarity and the Middle East*, Copenhagen, 1995, Chapter 3.
3 For an analysis of the specific role of Denmark during the Cold War see Bertel Heurlin, 'Danish security policy' in *Cooperation and Conflict*, no. 2, 1989; no. 4, 1992 and 'Danmark som et lavspændingsområde', in Bertel Heurlin and Christian Thune (eds), *Danmark og det internationale system*, Copenhagen, Copenhagen Political Studies Press, 1989, pp.115–34.
4 On the general Danish security policy see SNU (The Danish Commission on Security and Disarmament), *Danish Security Policy*, Copenhagen, SNU, 1993.
5 See Agreement between the Ministry of Defence of the Republic of Estonia/Latvia/Lithuania and the Ministry of Defence of the Kingdom of Denmark on the development of relations in the field of military cooperation and contracts of March 1994/January 1994/March 1994. See also *Memorandum of Understanding Concerning Cooperation on the Formation of a Baltic Peacekeeping Battalion* between Denmark, Estonia, Finland, Latvia, Lithuania, Norway, Sweden, United Kingdom of 11 September 1994.
6 Agreement of 8 September 1994.
7 The term separate but not separable refers to the significant passage in, for example, the Brussels communiqué from the NATO Summit of January 1994, indicating the compromise over the position of WEU as the European military arm of NATO.
8 Udenrigsministeriet, *Principper og perspektiver i dansk udenrigspolitik. Dansk udenrigspolitik på vej mod år 2000*, Copenhagen, 1993. See also *Danish and European Security*, Copenhagen, SNU, 1995.
9 See Bertel Heurlin, *Federal Conceptions in Denmark: Traditions and Perspectives*, Working Paper, Institute of Political Science, University of Copenhagen, 1993/14.
10 See the article by Gunnar Nielsson in A. J. R. Groom and Paul Taylor (eds), *Frameworks for International Co-operation*, London, Pinter, 1990, pp.78–108.

11 See Bertel Heurlin, *NATO, Europa, Danmark*, Copenhagen, SNU, 1990.
12 See note 8.
13 See Treaty of Rome, first sub-paragraph of the preamble.
14 See the NATO Summit Declaration, 12 January 1994.
15 See WEU-traktaten, Copenhagen, SNU, 1992, p.62.

BIBLIOGRAPHY

Burgess, Michael, *Federalism and the European Union*, London, Routledge, 1989.
Groom, A. J. R. and Taylor, Paul (eds), *Frameworks for International Cooperation*, London, Pinter, 1990.
Hedetoft, Ulf (ed.), *Nation or Integration?*, Aalborg, Aalborg University, European Studies, 7, 1993.
Heurlin, Bertel, *NATO, Europa, Danmark*, Copenhagen, SNU, 1990.
Kelstrup, Morten (ed.), *European Integration and Denmark's Participation*, Copenhagen, Copenhagen Political Studies Press, 1992.
Lyck, Lise, *Denmark and the EC-Membership Evaluated*, London, Pinter, 1992.
Øberg, Jan (ed.), *Nordic Security in the 1990s*, London, Pinter/Transnational Foundation for Peace and Future Research, 1992.
Petersen, Nikloaj, *Game, Set and Match: Denmark and the European Union from Maastricht to Edinburgh*, Aarhus, University of Aarhus, 1993.
—— *Denmark and the European Community 1985–92: An Interpretation*, Aarhus, University of Aarhus, 1993.
SNU (The Danish Commission on Security and Disarmament), *Danish Security Policy*, Copenhagen, SNU, 1993.
—— *Danmark efter den kolde krig*, Copenhagen, SNU, 1993.
—— *Dansk og europaisk sikkeshed*, Copenhagen, SNU, 1995.
—— *Danish and European Security*, Copenhagen, SNU, 1995.
Thomsen, Birgit Nüchel (ed.), *The Odd Man Out*, Odense, 1993.

Chapter 9

Greece

The limits to convergence

Panos Tsakaloyannis

INTRODUCTION

The signing of the Treaty on European Union, in Maastricht was hailed in Athens as the harbinger of a new era in Europe and as a national success of historical proportions. Most elated by the event was Greece's octogenarian President, Constantine Karamanlis, who saw in the Maastricht Treaty his reward and vindication for thirty-five years of tireless efforts to anchor Greece to 'Europe'.[1] Yet, within a remarkably short time enthusiasm for Maastricht waned and nagging doubts appeared about the value of the results reached there. As clouds thickened over the Balkans, such doubts multiplied, so by the time Greece's turn came to chair the Presidency of the EC Council in January 1994, euphoria had given way to a profound pessimism. The reasons for this change of mood will be discussed below. Suffice it to say here that events in the closing months of 1993 have left Greek 'Europeanists', including the normally phlegmatic President of the Republic, bewildered, embarrassed and in need of time to recover themselves. And while they confined themselves to elliptical statements,[2] public opinion began to question first principles and to feel unease about Greece's precise place in the EU.

Greek peculiarities within the EU, as well as political uncertainties in the Balkans, evidently demand a somewhat different methodological approach to that adopted in the first edition of this book, written in more tranquil times and in a different domestic and international setting. A broader political and historical perspective is necessary to understand Greek attitudes to the EU, especially with regard to its Common Foreign and Security Policy (CFSP). This is the more so as Greece is situated in the Balkans where presently 'stupendous forces are loose, hurricane forces'[3] whose effects on Greece might be chilling.

This chapter, therefore, claims neither to be exhaustive, nor strictly 'scientific' as some of the questions raised here are of such complexity that they defy scientific scrutiny. It is more an exercise in interpretation from a sceptical historical standpoint. In more practical terms this means that no effort will be made here to present an exhaustive account of facts, an exercise which might lead either to pedantry, whereby more and more could be said about less and less, or worse, to wrong conclusions, supported by a seemingly unassailable array of evidence. This means that some aspects concerning Greece's record in EPC, like her voting pattern at the UN, or sundry other matters, will be left out of the discussion.

In short, the approach to be adopted here has drawn its inspiration from an earlier intellectual genre. This claims that the quality of the work depends on the researcher's skill in evaluating and interpreting the ocean of facts at his/her disposal. This, especially during times of political convulsions like the present ones in the Balkans, when the field is flooded by a myriad of new unexpected considerations, makes ignorance the first requisite of social analysis. Ignorance which, as an earlier writer put it, 'simplifies and clarifies, which selects and omits'. The investigator's strategy, therefore, should be subtle. He should:

> attack his subject in unexpected places . . . fall upon the flank, or the rear . . . shoot a sudden, revealing searchlight into obscure recesses, hitherto undivined . . . row over the great ocean of material, and lower into it, here and there, a little bucket, which will bring up to the light of day some characteristic specimen, from those far depths, to be examined with a careful curiosity.[4]

The main objective here, therefore, is not to prove a theory but to present an intelligible interpretation of reality.

A final caveat is that a deeper insight during periods of historical convulsions in which 'the world jumbles its catalogue', as Lamartine put it in the early nineteenth century, can only be acquired by historical analogy. Life, after all, as a philosopher has put it, 'is lived forwards but understood backwards'. This may present a problem here as most studies concerning the EC, including EPC, either keep history at arm's length, or tend to present a sanitized version of it. Arguably, while this attitude to Europe's troubled past might have been justifiable in the 1970s and the 1980s, in the present circumstances, it blinkers our vision. This is because today, in A. D. Smith's apt words, 'we are thrown back on history, and specifically on political and legal traditions and cultural heritages and symbolisms'.[5] Such considerations can no longer be ignored by students of EPC, and certainly not where Greece is concerned.

GREECE AND THE EC: FROM THE FALL OF THE BERLIN WALL TO THE MAASTRICHT TREATY

The momentous events in Europe, in the autumn of 1989, found Greece in a sad, melancholic state. As the Berlin Wall crumbled, Greece was in the grip of a grave political, economic and moral crisis. The general elections in that month, the second within five months, not only failed to break the deadlock, but produced a spineless all-party government, which included even the Stalinists, headed by an octogenarian technocrat. Absorbed in their own world, most Greeks still hailed enthusiastically the changes in Europe. After all, it should be recalled, most Greeks strongly resented 'Yalta' which they blamed not only for the bloody civil war in 1946–9, but also for much of Greece's post-war malaise, like the imposition of the military regime, or the Cyprus problem. This, in conjunction with the colossal economic problems Greece had accumulated by 1989, like spiralling public deficits, a swelling external debt, low productivity and high inflation, inclined most people to look for salvation in the promising pastures of the new 'European architecture' in which the European Community was to be its centrepiece. This became an attractive proposition to all political parties, save the Stalinists, the more so as it promised greater transfers of cash from Brussels at a time they were urgently needed to bail out the Greek economy.

The decision in Dublin, in April 1990, to proceed with the convening of an IGC on 'Political Union', coincided with another election in Greece which this time produced a Conservative government of New Democracy headed by Constantinos Mitsotakis, a pragmatist, with impeccable credentials in other EC countries, above all in Germany. The new government in Athens, no doubt as a gesture to affirm its strong commitment to the EC, not least to political union, was the first to submit a Memorandum after Dublin, on 15 May 1990.[6] The details of this Memorandum need not detain us here as it is evident that it was written in a hurry and it covers familiar ground of the themes discussed in the second half of the 1980s, especially in the context of SEA, the completion of the Internal Market and parallel developments, like the inception of a Secretariat, and the adoption of a security 'Platform' by the WEU, in October 1987, which Greece aspired to join. Its most pertinent part, for the purpose of this chapter, is its last section headed 'External Policy and Defence'. It should be born in mind that this Memorandum was submitted well before the outbreak of the Gulf crisis, which played an important part in elevating security as a prime objective of the IGC.[7] The Greek paper came close to calling for a common security of an 'organic' form, although this was worded rather elliptically. It proposed a definition of the Community's role 'in the field of defence and the security of its territory, with the concept and extent of Community frontiers being defined' and 'for the establishment of "Community solidarity" as the basic principle governing the behaviour of the Member States when dealing with these problems'.

Athens' eagerness to become part of an 'organic' political union, even if that meant relinquishing its veto, grew as the IGC shifted its attention to devising a common security of a federal type. Greece joined the 'maximalists', headed by Germany and Italy, and threw its weight behind calls for a 'Federal Europe'. For Greece the enterprise was particularly attractive as the realization of this objective would have settled her perennial security concerns which, if anything had been compounded by events in neighbouring Yugoslavia.

The cooption of the Western European Union into the European Union, which according to the Maastricht Treaty was to become the Union's military arm, made the prospect even more appealing to Athens, in view of Article 5 of the modified Brussels Treaty, which stipulates that should one of its members become a victim of aggression, the other parties should 'afford the party so attacked all the military and other aid and assistance in their power'. Therefore, for Athens, the presumed advantages to be derived from a 'federal union' outweighed the sacrifices entailed in it, including the renunciation of the national veto.[8] It should be stressed that such optimistic assessments and expectations from Maastricht, were not confined only to the government, the politicians, the press and the mass media. They were also backed by the overwhelming majority of Greek academics, including students of international relations, and analysts of the EC.[9]

PASOK'S LEGACY IN THE 1980s

Greece's position in the IGC on EPU undoubtedly appears a remarkable U-turn from the perspective of the 1980s, during which the Papandreou governments had doggedly dug in their heels on this issue, be it on the Genscher–Colombo plan, the Stuttgart Declaration, or the Dooge Committee and the SEA. For, besides Greece's lonely stance on particular themes, like the resistance to the imposition of EC sanctions on the Soviet Union and Poland, pro-Palestinian positions on the Middle East, or the case of the Korean KAL007 aircraft, which was shot down by the Soviet Union in early 1983 over Soviet airspace, mistakenly identified as a military jet,[10] a more permanent feature of the period is PASOK's adamant insistence on the preservation of the national veto in EPC when vital political or security interests were perceived to be at stake.[11]

Yet this does not imply that PASOK's position remained immutable over the decade. Far from it. For as we shall examine below, there was a fundamental evolution in its attitude to EPC, and later to security. First PASOK's use of the veto changed from an almost indiscriminate application in the early 1980s, on issues where the invocation of 'vital national interests' was virtually indefensible, like the case of the Korean airliner, in early 1983, to a more careful use by the mid-1980s. For instance, while Athens declined to impose sanctions against Syria, following the Hindawi affair in 1986, it did not block a decision by the rest. Moreover, the impression often given, even by students of the EPC, that Greece was the odd man out in EPC on international terrorism,[12] does not stand up to close scrutiny.[13] Broadly speaking Athens' application of the veto, in the first half of the 1980s, was

ィriably linked to East–West issues and hardly at all to non-European ィsues, including the Middle East.

Another subject where the veto has been invoked is with regard to Turkey, but this does not apply only to PASOK. Here the Greek position, be it on the granting of financial assistance to Ankara, or on Turkish membership of the EC, is that the Cyprus problem should be settled first. However, even here Greece's position has been less irreconcilable than it appears as certain compromises have been struck, mainly on financial or environmental projects, funded by the EC, from which Turkey has been a beneficiary. Moreover, while Greek–Turkish differences do complicate EC–Turkish relations, it would be facile to make Greece the scapegoat for such problems. For as the Commission's 'Opinion' on the Turkish application makes clear there are sizeable road blocks on Ankara's route to Brussels and not all of them have been erected by the Greeks. Indeed, it could be argued that Greece provides a convenient alibi for some other member states' objections to Turkish membership.

It should be recalled that the preoccupation with Turkey had played the most decisive role in Karamanlis' efforts, in the mid-1970s, to join the EC.[14] Therefore, it was crystal clear that the EC, by spreading its wings into the Eastern Mediterranean, was bound to be saddled with intricate political, security and other problems, which even NATO had been unable to settle. Apart from vague allusions to the effect that the EC's closer relations with Greece and to a lesser extent with Turkey, should have contributed to reducing tensions in the regions, it never became clear how Brussels could tackle such thorny problems, the more so as there was bound to be a major divergence of perspectives on this issue between Athens and the majority of its partners in the EC,[15] not dissimilar to those faced in NATO.

A far more important change in PASOK's attitude towards EPC was on security arrangements in Western Europe. When it was in opposition, and during its early years in office, PASOK had viewed any security engagements in the EC as detrimental to its 'proud and independent foreign policy'. This point was most forcefully stressed during the Genscher–Colombo plan discussions in 1981–3. This, and Greece's idiosyncratic attitude in the EPC in the early years of PASOK's administration, played a role in the decision to reactivate the WEU in 1984. Athens' initial response to these developments in 1984 was low key and non-committal.[16] The fact that in the Dooge Committee, Athens took a 'minimalist' stance on security, and that it reaffirmed in no uncertain terms its strong opposition to any arrangements in the EC that might have prejudiced its freedom on security matters, suggests that at that stage Athens did not value highly the potential of the reactivated WEU, or its value for Greece, perhaps, therefore, under-estimating the moves of the bigger states to outflank 'troublemakers' such as Greece or Denmark. Yet, within two years, in 1987, Athens had applied to accede to the WEU.

This was a remarkable U-turn in PASOK's attitude to the EC with far-reaching consequences, some of which will become more apparent below. First, however, let us briefly examine the main reasons for PASOK's conversion. This will also enable us, I hope, to acquire a clearer insight into PASOK's current attitudes in the EC. The first reason has to do with Greece's perennial security concerns which reached a new crescendo in March 1987, when Greece and Turkey came within a whisker of armed conflict in the Aegean. This event had had considerable political side-effects which have not yet been fully worked out. Weeks after the incident Turkey submitted an application to join the EC. Greece then applied to join the WEU. In the light of this incident the apparently rejuvenated WEU, became a very attractive proposition for Athens, not least because of Article 5, which implied that, once Greece had become a full member of WEU, she could count on the other members to provide support in case of war with Turkey.[17] The net effect of this development was to bring the Greek–Turkish dispute into the heart of the muddled debate on security in the EC, EPC, WEU and NATO, in the late 1980s and early 1990s. The most pertinent point here, however, is to note PASOK's conversion to Karamanlis' and New Democracy's thesis that the EC could provide the answers to Greece's security prayers.

A second reason for PASOK's conversion has to do with developments in East–West relations in the early 1980s. The 'Second Cold War' was hoisted on 'The Threat From the East' banner, just as the first one had been on 'the Communist threat' in Greece.[18] This new 'arc of crisis', stretching from Afghanistan to Lebanon, via Iran and the Gulf, greatly upgraded, in the eyes of the security establishment in Washington and NATO, Turkey's value for the Alliance, which was seen as the bulwark of the new containment policy. Therefore, as with Karamanlis in the 1970s, PASOK's conversion to 'Europeanism' was to a very large extent prompted by frustrations with NATO and by a desire to counterbalance Turkey's edge in the Atlantic Alliance. A third reason has to do with developments in the Gulf and in the Middle East which dampened PASOK's earlier enthusiasm for the Arabs, as the actual political, diplomatic, and economic advantages derived from this source fell well short of PASOK's inflated expectations.[19]

This recognition brought about a gradual and low-key shift to a more balanced policy towards the Arab–Israeli conflict. This was manifested in two ways, from the mid-1980s on: first, in an unwillingness to use Greece's position in EPC to champion the cause of radical Arab states, not least Syria, and a corresponding improvement in relations with Israel. While such relations lacked a diplomatic veneer before 1990, when Athens eventually recognized Israel on a *de jure* basis, nonetheless this should not detract attention from the remarkable growth of cooperation between the two countries. While this was largely confined to cultural, economic and tourist sectors in the 1980s, by the early 1990s it had been extended to military and internal security cooperation, including exchange of information on terrorism. Indeed, the expansion of links with Israel in recent years, can be described as one of the most remarkable readjustments in post-war foreign policy. This means that Greece can become a valuable asset for the EU in the Middle East peace process as she commands at the moment excellent relations with both the Palestinians and the Israelis, as attested by the flow of high level visits to Athens from each side since moves towards the peace treaty were initiated.

On the other hand, by the mid-1980s, the EC was undergoing a major recovery with the adoption of the SEA, the first steps towards the creation of an internal market and the settlement of chronic problems, like enlargement and the budget. This, in conjunction with a gradual easing in East–West relations in the mid-1980s, and a growing preoccupation with trade and economic issues, helped enhance considerably the EC's image in Greece, which was seen now as a 'civilian power' and a paragon of peace and stability in Europe and the world. This enabled a convergence of views on most issues discussed in EPC, not least on regional issues, like Central America, South Africa, and EC's relations with ASEAN. Indeed, the EC's growing involvement in intraregional cooperation, and its positions on issues like Central America and South Africa struck a positive chord in Greece and they were in tune with public opinion, which normally sided with underdogs and with peoples subjected to colonial rule. No wonder that Athens gave its full support to the Community's involvement in peace efforts in Central America as well as to economic sanctions on South Africa. Indeed, by the late 1980s Greece was in line with the mainstream opinion in the EC and Britain was taking over the role of 'the odd man out'.

This new attitude found expression in PASOK's handling of the second Greek Presidency, in the second half of 1988, which bore little resemblance to the first in 1983. Thus whereas in December 1983, in the Athens European Council, Papandreou had refused to release the Ten's statement on international issues, on the justified grounds that the poor state of affairs in the EC hardly justified their rather pompous pronouncements on major international issues, five years later he took pride in presiding over a European Council meeting at Rhodes which marked the apogee for the EC, just before the historic changes in Europe.[20]

The net effect of such developments was a more pliant Greek attitude to institutional and security innovations in the EC from the mid-1980s. Thus, while Athens did not repudiate its position in the Dooge Committee to use the right of veto, nonetheless, following the ratification of the SEA, Greece, for reasons mentioned above, invoked the veto mainly with regard to Turkey and more specifically with regard to the granting of financial assistance.[21] At the same time Athens made an effort to associate itself with institutional innovations, like the creation of an EPC Secretariat to which it sent a diplomat at its inception, under the rule of five-country representation, that is one from the Presidency, plus two from the previous Presidencies and two from the succeeding members.[22]

It should be noted that this more accommodating Greek attitude in the EC was also dictated by Athens' desire to accede to the WEU. To accomplish this objective Athens had to drop some of its earlier rhetoric and to demonstrate its readiness to abide by the strictures of the nine members of the WEU, not least their 'Security Platform', adopted in October 1987 in The Hague. This reincarnation as a 'good European' could be performed by Papandreou, who in his 'apophatic' style[23] could now claim that developments in the EC since the mid-1980s called for a major revision of Greek attitudes within the Community. In this his task was made easier by the affinity which existed at the time between Athens and Paris, and by the feeling general to the Mediterranean states that the Community was moving in a direction favourable to their interests.

Of course, PASOK's conversion to the status of good Europeans was also lubricated by the transfer of large sums of money from Brussels to Greece, which by the mid-1980s could make a lot of difference to the beseiged Greek economy. Therefore a turning-point in PASOK's attitude to the EC can be identified as having occurred in the autumn of 1985, when the Greek government adopted an emergency economic programme known as the 'Stabilization Programme', whose aim was to curb an uncontrolled public deficit and galloping inflation. Part of the package was a devaluation of the Greek Drachma, a freezing in wages and salaries, plus economic assistance from Brussels to the tune of two billion ECUs. Henceforward PASOK's 'battles' with Brussels would consist not so much in lonely arguments in EPC, but rather in debate over how to optimize Greece's economic benefits. This new tack was in line with changing economic conditions in Greece. PASOK's stronghold in the previous decade (mid-1970s to mid-1980s) had been the rural voters, as well as city dwellers of recent rural origin. As farmers were the main beneficiaries from the EC transfers, their attitude to the Community changed perceptibly.

This evolution also found expression in public opinion's attitudes to the EC, which in the 1980s underwent a remarkable transformation with the percentage of those in favour of the EC nearly doubling from 38 per cent in October 1981, to 73 per cent a decade later, while that against the EC dropped from 21 per cent to 6 per cent, in the same period.[24] These figures suggest that the bulk of PASOK's supporters had been converted to the EC by the end of the decade, helped by receipts from the EC and in particular from the CAP.[25] They also suggest that party allegiance plays a significant role in people's attitude to the EC. This is worth noting, especially in view of the fragility of Greece's political institutions, which in conjunction with the explosive situation in the Balkans, offer great opportunities to demagogues. The results of the last general elections lent credence to this point and raise certain doubts as to the solidity of this pro-EC sentiment in Greece.[26]

GREECE, MAASTRICHT AND THE NEW EUROPEAN DISORDER

The gist of the above remarks is that Greek attitudes in EPC have been defined by security concerns, to a much greater degree than in any other member state. This security concern, until 1991, was almost exclusively confined to Turkey. By the late 1980s a broad consensus had emerged to the effect that security links with a robust Western Europe, could provide an answer to Greece's security dilemmas – hence the gratification with Maastricht. However this should not lead to the conclusion that differences in perceptions, or specific tactics, completely disappeared. Far from it. This would have been virtually impossible given the individualistic style of Greek politics and the almost wholly contrasting temperaments of Mitsotakis and Papandreou.[27]

Nonetheless, in spite of certain nuances, most Greeks believed Maastricht had laid the foundations for a united Europe in which they were fortunate to be full members. This was also strengthened by the considerable increase of funds which Greece was to receive from Brussels in the 1990s, in order to enable her to meet the stringent conditions on convergence stipulated in Maastricht. This created a rather idyllic picture about the future whereby Greece, almost miraculously, would have ridden herself of chronic problems.[28] Such a euphoric mood was also encouraged by the outbreak of the Gulf crisis in August 1990 which the recently elected government in Athens used in order to improve its credentials in the West. Greece gave her full support to the coalition forces in Operation Desert Storm and she joined in the WEU-coordinated naval blockade of the Gulf. This position was facilitated by the fact that Saddam Hussein was opposed by countries like Egypt and Syria, with whom Greece has traditionally enjoyed good relations. At the same time the outbreak of the Gulf crisis in August 1990 contributed to a blurring of Greek perspectives in the early 1990s as some drew the hasty conclusion that Greece's security challenges had shifted, after the end of the Cold War, from her northern to her southern borders.[29]

Such euphoria, however, did not take into account the new political realities in Europe. To begin with, the end of the Cold War set in motion a scramble for influence and a proliferation of ad hoc initiatives which presumably were to provide the bricks for the building of the 'new European architecture'. The disturbing thing, for Greece, however, was that she was excluded from most of these initiatives, like the much discussed 'Mediterranean Conference on Security and Cooperation', which was to emulate the CSCE. Equally unnerving for Athens was that Greece could not fit into any of the geometrical shapes which Italy's Foreign Minister, Gianni de Michelis, was devising so energetically at the time, whether 'pentagonale' or 'hexagonale'. At the same time old ghosts had begun to reappear in the Balkans including a race for influence in the region by outside powers.

Such developments were embarrassing to the Conservative government in Athens which could take solace in the IGC and in the belief that with Maastricht such problems might disappear. The fact that Greece had given her full-hearted support to the federalist cause, plus Mitsotakis' excellent relations with Bonn,[30] were supposed to be enough to convince Athens that it was on the right track. To be sure in June 1991, bad omens made their appearance, with the secession of Croatia and Slovenia from Yugoslavia. In 1991 Athens was in the forefront of those countries, which included the USA, Britain and France, urging caution on the question of recognition. This was the first major point of friction with Bonn. The second was on the question of military intervention by the WEU in former Yugoslavia, which caused heated and acrimonious arguments in the autumn of 1991.[31] However the turning point, the 'moment of truth', for Greece came on 16 December, 1991, with the Twelve's decision to proceed with the recognition of the two break-away republics of Yugoslavia. This and subsequent events left Athens bewildered and in total disarray.

It is true that Greece did in fact follow suit in Brussels on 16 December 1991, even if with great misgivings. Having displayed such enthusiasm for Maastricht and aligned itself so closely with Bonn, in the course of the IGC, Athens did not dare to rock the boat in Brussels. Greek concerns with the Brussels decision became vocal in early 1992, when it realized the implications of that decision, especially on Macedonia. Since early 1992 there has been an overwhelming consensus among Greeks of all political persuasions that the Brussels decision was wrong and that Greece was coerced to go along with it against her better judgement. Even Mitsotakis, in an interview in early 1994 with *Der Spiegel*, expressed this view. This brought a retort by Genscher that after all the Greek Foreign Minister had raised no objections in Brussels. In any case what is most important to bear in mind is that the decision in Brussels on recognition has soured relations between Athens and Bonn.

It would be impossible to present here even an outline of Greek reactions in their full complexity. Suffice it to say that developments in neighbouring Yugoslavia rekindled Greek fears which had lain dormant for more than forty years. Greece's Achilles heel, before 1945, had been its Macedonian region which had always been up for grabs.[32] The question now was whether the EC, in which Greece had placed all her hopes, could act as a prophylactic against a repetition of this tragic past. The problem for Greece was that the Twelve, for want of military solutions, and as a device to conceal the deep rift in their ranks, not least between Paris and Bonn,[33] resorted to legalistic measures as the fig leaf for concealing their disarray. The unpalatable reality had to be well wrapped up, otherwise the Treaty signed in Maastricht would have been blown to pieces even before the celebrations were over. The fig leaf was the appointment of the Badinter Committee of jurists to examine the criteria for recognition.[34]

Considering Greece's legalistic approach to political and social issues, whereby problems are swept under the carpet by putting them under the auspices of a judge, normally with a pompous title, as well as intoxication with 'Maastricht', it was no surprise that Athens raised no objections to this process but confined itself to inserting, in the Badinter Committee, certain additional criteria for recognition, like a pledge to respect current borders, the removal of clauses in the republic's constitution stipulating territorial claims, etc. Yet the Twelve's decision of 16 December 1991 had opened a can of worms which almost immediately began to gnaw at Greek entrails. A new order was in the making in the Balkans and the Greeks, in spite of their participation in the West's most exclusive clubs, not least the EC and NATO, felt insecure.

For enthusiasts of a brave new world, convinced that history had at long last gone to sleep, or for zealots of a new 'European architecture', Greek fears could be summarily dismissed as a predictable reaction of a people incapable of catching up with the times and renowned for its paranoia and neurosis. While such criticisms contain a great deal of truth, nonetheless they do not take into account the Balkans' heavy historical baggage which most of Greece's EC partners, especially those with little interest in the region, did not want to know about. Indeed, some of them, in 1990–91, would easily have ascribed to Bismarck's aphorism of 1876 that 'the Balkans were not worth the healthy bones of a Pomeranian grenadier'. Thus Greek concerns, derived from their historical experience, could be dismissed as the hysterics of the one Balkan and 'Balkanized' member of the Community. It is a moot point whether Greek reactions to events in the Balkans could have been more 'European' if the country had been in better economic and political shape. Yet, it would be expecting too much of the Greeks to disregard centuries of historical experience which has moulded their collective consciousness, just because of a decade-long membership of the EC. This historical experience reminded them that whenever there is a political earthquake in the world, Greece is invariably at its epicentre. This has occurred three times in this century, in the First and Second World Wars, and in the outbreak of the Cold War.[35] In other words, in the case of Greece, historical experience could not be disregarded in order to conform with a CFSP which had just been dealt a heavy blow in the Balkans, and was preoccupied more with appearances than reality.

Such misunderstandings were compounded by Athens' confusion and its incoherent and spasmodic reactions, fed from domestic and outside pressures. Domestically, stunned by the speed of events in the Balkans, Greeks interpreted them as a prelude to the return of a past, characterized by the perception of Turkey's megalomania to construct a new imperium stretching 'from the Adriatic to Xinjiang'; by a scrabble for influence in the region among outside powers, including some of Greece's partners in the EC; and, last, but not least, by the (re)discovery of cultural and religious fault lines between Western and Orthodox Christians. This gave vent to a nationalist backlash and to a stiffening of Greek attitudes on the Macedonian question which led to its further isolation, not least in the EC.[36] An apparent return to power politics in the Balkans stirred up unhappy memories for many Greeks.

For two years Athens had gone through the agony of fighting a diplomatic battle against recognition which it had no realistic prospects of winning. The only thing in which it succeeded was to isolate itself from its partners and seriously to impair its place in the Community. As a Greek critic put it in 1992, Greece's behaviour inside the EC, with regard to the crisis in the Balkans was that 'not of a Community member who happen to be located in the Balkans, but that of a Balkan country who happened to be a member of the EC'.[37] Yet this was a self-inflicting punishment as it cost, besides a lot of ill-feeling with its EC partners and some other countries, the squandering of tremendous energy and assets plus damage to its broader political, economic, diplomatic and security interests in the region.

Yet to leave things at that would be one-sided and simplistic. To begin with, it is questionable whether Greece and her partners in the EC would have lived in complete harmony, even if Athens had not chosen the wrong ground, that is diplomatic pressure, to abort the recognition of the new state as Macedonia. This formalistic–legalistic approach did not quite correspond to Balkan realities, whereby Wittgenstein's logic is often more applicable than 'formal logic'.[38] Greece's problem is that she had been answering 'five' to a question whose answer was either four or, perhaps, ninety-seven.

This evolution is best illustrated by Mitsotakis' predicament. He staked virtually everything on Maastricht and on his cordial relationship with Bonn. He went out of his way to prove his allegiance to his EC partners, by even making public, in the autumn of 1991, President Milosevic's offer to carve up Yugoslav Macedonia between Greece and Serbia, which Mitsotakis rejected out of hand. By making public Milosevic's offer, an extraordinary move considering the close historical, political and cultural links between Greece and Serbia, Mitsotakis wanted to demonstrate his allegiance to his EC partners, even if that meant seriously impairing Greece's relations with her traditional friend in the Balkans. He also wanted to send a message that Greece had no territorial ambitions in the Balkans. One year later, in November 1992, Mitsotakis took the initiative to hold a meeting among FYROM's neighbours in Athens to extract a pledge that they would observe its territorial integrity. Yet, not only did his gestures receive little encouragement from his EC partners, but he also had to face an international public opinion, 'almost as often wrong headed as [it is] impotent',[39] which was quick to castigate Greece for almost everything, from breaches of sanctions against Serbia, to harbouring aggressive designs in the Balkans, not least towards former Yugoslav Macedonia. He also had to face a public opinion at home which made him a scapegoat for problems for which it was largely responsible. His defeat in the October 1993 general elections was largely due to this predicament.

Papandreou's return to power and the recognition, in December 1993, of FYROM by half the twelve EC member states, including the four most important states, marked a new phase in Greece's relations with the EC. Its three main features are a strengthening of relations with the USA, which was now viewed in Athens as a stabilizing element in the Balkans; a corresponding scaling down of expectations of the EC, particularly as regards foreign policy and security; and a reexamination of Greece's position towards FYROM where PASOK has tacitly accepted the diplomatic *fait accompli*.[40] With regard to the first point, Athens professes to believe that the USA is not only the sole superpower, but that it is also more attuned to the nature of the problems in the Balkans. With their experience in Vietnam, in the Middle East and elsewhere, the USA can have a more down-to-earth approach of the problems in the Balkans than the Twelve, whose lack of collective will leads only to 'a balance of impotence'. And as an historian has put it 'if absolute power corrupts, so does absolute impotence'.[41] Last, but not least, the USA, for a number of reasons, including distance and a less troubled historical record in the Balkans than some West Europeans, can be relied on more to act as an 'honest broker' in the region. This turn towards Washington is a volte-face considering Greek disputes with the USA in the 1980s. It could be a tactical manoeuvre, but is more likely to betoken deep Greek concerns about vulnerability in the Balkans and the consequences of estrangement from Bonn and other European partners.

Certainly, the EU's structures, and not least its putative CFSP, look much less attractive than they did in 1992. This also applies to the WEU, which was seen as the ultimate prize for Greece during the IGC. Today expectations from the WEU have been scaled down to a more realistic level.[42] This stems from a dual realization, first that the WEU, for want of political will, is largely a defence organization without a nervous system and, therefore, incapable of addressing problems like those in the Balkans today. Second, even if the WEU did possess real muscle, it is far from certain whether it would have rushed to Greece's side. The rescinding of Article 5 of the modified Brussels Treaty, where Greece and Turkey are concerned, in one swoop has virtually nullified the security value of the WEU to Greece. If Athens cannot count on the WEU's support in case of conflict with Turkey, it is hard to see in what circumstances it might be of any real value. For, in Athens' view, apart from Turkey, none of Greece's northern neighbours pose a direct security threat.

Such considerations lie behind the new tendency to look outwards to the Atlantic. Papandreou's turn to Washington was much advertised during his meeting with President Clinton in Brussels, in January 1994, where he went out of his way to present the view that both leaders saw eye to eye on major international issues, from world trade to Bosnia-Herzegovina, on which, in another U-turn, Papandreou backed NATO's decision in principle of August 1993 to use air strikes, not least over Macedonia. He acquiesced in the US military presence there and, more significantly, he acknowledged that FYROM's national integrity was in Greece's national interest, for in the event of outside interference, most likely from Albania, events might lead to another Balkan war.[43] These facts are well known; the point here is that Papandreou tried to give the impression that, in contrast with the EC, he was acting in unison with Washington and that both sides shared a common perspective on the Balkans.

CONCLUSIONS AND PROSPECTS

The EC debate in Greece started in the early 1970s, triggered by a domestic political and social crisis and above all by security concerns which NATO could not meet. Hence, the EC, which was perceived to be on its way to becoming a major power, became a panacea for solving Greece's problems. Twenty years later the same story was to be repeated in the IGC, but this time in a completely transformed European setting. The overall conclusion, therefore, is that EC membership has had marginal socio-political and cultural effects on Greece. The economic effects have been more pronounced by the free circulation of goods, capital and persons, and by the transfer of cash to Athens from Brussels. Yet, even here Greece's defective bureaucracy, statism, and archaic social structures, which have been affected only marginally by EC membership, have combined to produce some deformities. For example, instead of acting as the stimulus to economic modernization, membership of the EC has led to a decline in Greek productivity, especially in agriculture and manufacture, while it has encouraged the Greeks' insatiable consumerism.

The net effect has been an explosive public and external debt and a trade deficit, unique among the OECD members. This feeble eudemonism has made Greece not only more dependent on handouts from Brussels, but has had corrosive social and political effects. Arguably, Greece and her EC partners can live happily with such a mutually beneficial arrangement as it ensured the Greeks a life-style beyond their means, and her partners the tapping of the Greek market, an exporter's paradise where invisibles in 1992 from shipping, tourism and remittances of Greek expatriates well exceeded Greece's total export earnings. However, this cosy arrangement might be shaken up by the political convulsions in the Balkans which might play the serpent to such precarious economic arrangements.

By dint of geography, history and culture, Greece was to be the EC's weakest link which, once the Balkans exploded, was bound to create tensions in Greece's relations with her EC partners and even pose unpalatable dilemmas for the Greeks themselves. This has been exacerbated by Greek bitterness about the flippancy with which some of her EC partners have trampled upon her interests in the Balkans, and by counter-accusations of Greek intransigence, 'Balkanization' and a retreat into isolation. This, in conjunction with Greece's legacy in the 1980s, has set in motion a process of drift and alienation which, if anything, Maastricht has compounded as it has confused the picture even more, with the Greeks now feeling that their glittering prize at Maastricht was not what it looked, and the eleven EC partners feeling irritated by Greek stubbornness and a failure to 'catch up with the times'.

In other words Greece's record in the EC has been saddled by gross misunderstandings and inflated expectations, not least on political–security matters. For no other EC member has staked so much on the EC to solve intractable security problems than Greece, yet no other member has stood fewer realistic chances of accomplishing their goal. Athens believed in 1990–91 that this objective was within its reach with the Treaty on European Union which promised to have transformed the Community from a 'Gesellschaft' to a 'Gemeinschaft', that is from an organized to an organic entity. Had this occurred it would have made a tremendous qualitative difference, not least for Greece. For, as Ferdinand Tonnies put it, in a 'Gemeinschaft', its members 'remain essentially united in spite of all separating factors', whereas in a 'Gesellschaft' 'everybody is himself and isolated, and there exists a condition of tension against all others'.[44]

The above definition describes very accurately not only Greece's present position in the EU, but also the current state in the EU as a whole which, in spite of Maastricht, still remains 'a nerveless body, incapable of regulating its own members, insecure . . . and agitated with unceasing fermentations in its own bowels'.[45] Whether this state of restlessness in the EU could be brought to an end in the coming years is highly doubtful as, to change metaphors, the way ahead has become foggy, the vehicle is getting overcrowded and the engine is rattling without any clear notion as how to fix it. What is evident by now is that the IGC on PU has not closed the gap between capabilities and expectations in the EU, hence 'the status quo in European policy is clearly unsatisfactory and even dangerous'.[46] As far as Greece is concerned this implies, most probably, a scaling down of expectations from the EU, especially on political–security matters. This in itself could have only positive effects on both sides because the current state of inflated expectations can cause only harm and misunderstandings.

A good way to proceed, therefore, would be for the Greeks to cease demanding from their partners things which they have neither the means nor the will to deliver and for Greece's partners to realize that ten years of EC membership is hardly enough to lift Greece above her Balkan vocation. Nor is it enough to erase those Greek characteristics imprinted over a long historical process of isolation from the rest of Western Europe. This implies that both sides would need more freedom of manoeuvre, especially on the crises in the Balkans. The sad story over the recognition of FYROM suggests that, Maastricht's stipulations for a joint CFSP notwithstanding, such a close embrace might be harmful to all parties concerned, not least to Greece which, being in the crisis zone, should be able to define her own responses. This is more so as there is not an EU common voice but a cacophony on the Balkans.

The aim should be threefold: first to preserve the economic aspects concerning Greek membership, hoping that this process might gradually ease Greece's way to the more demanding socio-economic levels of her West European partners. Second, to explore what Greece and her partners can do together in the Balkans. For example, Greece's economic weight and her relatively advanced infrastructure, compared to her Balkan neighbours, make it a natural candidate for the coordination of Community aid and development programmes. Last, but not least, to show more mutual understanding about each member state's views and policies on the crises in the Balkans. It is unrealistic and counter-productive for Greece to expect the rest to see the Balkans through her own looking glass; and it is equally objectionable for Greece's EU partners to demand that Athens dance according to their own dissonant tune. Whether this low-key approach would lead to a gradual convergence of views on the Balkans is not certain. But it is the only way to avoid further frictions and misunderstandings. Beyond that it is hard to go at this stage, given the chaotic situation in the Balkans as well as uncertainties about the EU's own development. This may be criticized as a hopelessly cautious and sober analysis, and as contrary to the prevailing attitude in recent years which has laboured for bold solutions to extremely intricate problems, sometimes even before the nature of the problem was properly understood, as in former Yugoslavia. Yet the lesson to be learned, not only from Yugoslavia but also from the Twelve's rush in 1990 to construct 'Political Union', is that such a *fuite en avant*[47] in the present world, is counter-productive and dangerous. Hence, rushing from one blueprint to another, a natural bureaucratic reflex, exacerbates more than alleviates problems. As a critic of this approach has put it, when one blueprint fails, 'the technocratic mind, rather than deal with failure, simply wipes the slate clean and writes a new definition'.[48]

Invariably this approach, based as it is on voluntarism and on preserving the form regardless of reality, without a clear notion of the consequences of the proposed solutions, leads to further failures and disappointments. For as the same critic points out, zealots of this approach, in their hurry to solve problems, can hardly afford time for reflection and for digesting the nature of the problem under consideration. Yet, allowing time for thinking and working out what is to be done, especially at times of crisis, is an indispensable feature of most societies.[49] Arguably, this point is worth bearing in mind on the eve of the next IGC scheduled to open in 1996. And while it is too early at this stage to attempt even a preliminary assessment of the IGC and its effects on Greece, one thing is certain: it is hard to see how the most fundamental political issues can be evaded this time. This is borne out by the controversial CDU–CSU Paper for the 1996 IGC, and the reactions to it in some other EU countries, not least France and Britain. As for the so far rather lukewarm reaction in Greece, the state of Nirvana concerning the IGC should be attributed mainly to bewilderment mixed with embarrassment (particularly given the Paper's stress on the need for the EU to develop a 'strategic partnership with Turkey'). Hence it would be a mistake to interpret current Greek difficulties in articulating its position on the forthcoming IGC as a sign of compliance. This is the more so given the fact that both the Balkans and the EU are today in the political melting-pot. Judging by the past there is no reason to assume that Greece's response to political union issues in the next IGC will be any les erratic than it has been up to now.

NOTES

1 Karamanlis sent a message to President Delors congratulating him for his 'courageous and persistent contribution to the success at Maastricht which, at long last, has laid the foundations for a United Europe'. *Macedonia*, 12 December 1991.

2 For example, President Karamanlis, in his New Year address to the nation, castigated the 'thoughtless intervention of foreign powers in the Balkans', which 'by their incoherent and irrelevant initiatives, have exacerbated tensions among the Balkan nations'. *Kathemerini*, 1 January 1994.

3 Anthony Eden's expression in the late 1930s cited by E. H. Carr, in *The Twenty Years' Crisis, 1919–1939: An Introduction to the Study of International Relations*, London, Macmillan, 1939, p.53.

4 Lytton Strachey, *Eminent Victorians*, London, Chatto and Windus, 1918, Preface. See also E. H. Carr, *What Is History?*, Harmondsworth, Penguin, 1964, p.14; On the 'ignorance principle' see Paul K. Feyerabend, 'How to be a good empiricist: a plea for tolerance in matters epistemological', in P. H. Nidditch (ed.), *The Philosophy of Science*, London, Oxford University Press, 1968, pp.12–39. As this approach might appear idiosyncratic, or 'unscientific', or even capricious, it is useful to supplant it by John Lewis Gaddis' recent advice to the effect that while students of international relations should not jettison the scientific approach to the subject, nonetheless, it is vital 'to bring it up to date by recognizing that good scientists, like good novelists and good historians, make use of all the tools at their disposal in trying to anticipate the future. That includes not just theory, observation and rigorous calculation, but also narrative, analogy, paradox, irony, intuition, imagination, and – not least in importance – style'. In 'International relations theory and the end of the Cold War', *International Security*, vol. 17, nos. 3–4, Winter 1992–3, pp.57–8.

5 A. D. Smith, 'National identity and the idea of European unity', *International Affairs*, vol. 68, no. 1, January 1992, p.70.

6 *Greek Memorandum*, 'Contribution to the discussions on progress towards political union', Brussels, 15 May 1990. Full text in Finn Laursen and Sophie

Vanhoonaker (eds), *The Intergovernmental Conference on Political Union: Institutional Reforms, New Policies and International Identity of the European Community*, Maastricht, EIPA, 1992, pp.277–81. The next national paper submitted to the IGC was Italy's, the President of the Council, four months later.

7 This was the kernel of the Italian proposal, submitted on 18 September, whose opening paragraph stated that the primary objective of the IGC on PU should be 'the elaboration and implementation of a common foreign and security policy'.

8 There is an interesting twist to this affair. In the run up to the meeting in Maastricht, Athens threatened to veto the whole package unless its demand to join the WEU was met, *Financial Times*, 29 November 1991 – a demand which was met three years later (Greece joined the WEU officially on 6 April 1995). Later on, following the disintegration of former Yugoslavia, when it became clear that Greece was being isolated in the EC on the recognition of the former Yugoslav republic of Macedonia, Athens sought refuge in the provisions of the veto powers, which it had been so willing to relinquish in the IGC.

9 For example, the President of ELIAMEP, an Athens-based institute of foreign and security policy, described in 1992 Greece's future 'optimal defence and security profile' in terms of concentric circles. Its inner core would have been 'served by a healthy and competitive economy'. The next circle, 'represented the remarkable functionalist experiment of the EC which solidifies and supplants Greece's defensive/deterrent/status quo stance. Needless to say, Greece's potential adversaries will think twice before attempting to challenge its territorial integrity in the sense that they will be challenging, in addition to the country, the gradually integrating European Union'. Furthermore, the author stressed, Greece would be 'counting on the WEU to provide the value of collective security. In fact, the WEU could assume quite substantial dimensions in the unlikely and undesirable contingency that US policy-makers would opt for a neoisolationalist stance'. Theodore A. Couloumbis (with Prodromos Yannas) 'Greek security in a post-Cold War setting', *Yearbook 1992*, Athens, ELIAMEP, 1993 [in English], p.53.

10 Athens, which held the Presidency at that time, refused to discuss a Community response to this incident. See Panos Tsakaloyannis, 'Greece's first term in the presidency of the EC: a preliminary assessment', in Colm O'Nuallain (ed.), *The Presidency of the Council of Ministers of the EC*, London, Croom Helm, 1985, pp.111–12.

11 For Greece's position in the Genscher–Colombo plan see Pauline Neville-Jones, 'The Genscher–Colombo proposals on European Union', *Common Market Law Review*, vol. 20, December 1983, esp. p.678. To the 'Solemn Declaration', Greece entered two reservations to the final text, both related to the question of consensus in the Council on political matters. The first stated that 'discussion on a subject must continue until a unanimous decision has been reached when vital national interests are at stake and written modification has been given to this effect'. The second stated that 'in signing this statement, Greece declares that nothing can restrict its right to determine its own foreign policy in accordance with its national interests'. Similar reservations were expressed in the Dooge Committee. One of Greece's fourteen reservations stated that she was, in principle, in favour of a more extensive use of majority voting, nevertheless she felt that the Presidency should not call for a vote before 'reasonable time has been devoted to the search for consensus'. Moreover, Greece, backed by Britain and Denmark managed to insert the following counter proposal in the final document: 'When a Member State considers that its very important interests are at stake, the discussion should continue until unanimous agreement is reached'.

Greece's insistence on the preservation of the veto was also reiterated by Papandreou at the June 1985 European Council: 'for a whole series of reasons', he said, 'Greece could not give up the right to use the veto.' For further examples on this theme see Arthur den Hartog, 'Greece and European political union', in Finn Laursen and Sophie Vanhoonacker (eds), *The Intergovernmental Conference on Political Union*, Maastricht, EIPA, 1992, esp. pp.83–90.

12   For example, Elfriede Regelsberger has argued that although Greece's position had softened on a number of issues by the mid-1980s, nevertheless Athens was still isolated on certain issues, including state-supported terrorism. 'EPC in the 1980s: reaching another plateau?', in Alfred Pijpers, Elfriede Regelsberger and Wolfgang Wessels (eds), *European Political Cooperation in the 1980s*, Dordrecht, Martinus Nijhoff, 1988, p.35.

13   See Christopher Hill, 'European preoccupations with terrorism', in ibid.

14   Panos Tsakaloyannis, 'Greece: Old problems, new prospects', in Christopher Hill (ed.) *National Foreign Policies and European Political Cooperation*, London, Allen and Unwin, 1983, pp.121–36.

15   As Françoise de La Serre has put it, 'Athens has exposed the dangers which threaten EPC should there be any fundamental difference in national policies. The problem has been largely created by the fact that in the vital field of security, Greece and its partners have greatly differing conceptions on the nature of the external threat.' 'The scope of national adaptation to EPC', in Alfred Pipers *et. al.* (eds), ibid., p.204.

16   Panos Tsakaloyannis, 'Greece and the reactivation of the WEU', in P. Tsakaloyannis (ed.), *The Reactivation of the WEU: Its Effects on the EC and its Institutions*, Maastricht, EIPA, 1985, pp.97–102.

17   In the event, the Petersburg Declaration of June 1992 contained an explicit disclaimer that the WEU guarantees might apply to the Greco-Turkish dispute.

18   See for example, Fred Halliday, *The Threat From the East?* Harmondsworth, Penguin, 1982.

19   Panos Tsakaloyannis, 'Greece and the Arab–Israeli conflict' in David Allen and Alfred Pijpers (eds), *European Foreign Policy-making and the Arab–Israeli Conflict*, The Hague, Martinus Nijhoff, 1984, pp.107–20.

20   Notably, the first pilot edition of *The European* was produced from Rhodes, by Robert Maxwell. On the top half of the first page it carried a huge photograph of President Mitterrand and Chancellor Kohl holding hands and at the bottom the caption: 'We Have a Dream'. Most Greeks were eager, indeed proud to be part of such historical events which seemed to be fully vindicating Karamanlis' choices in the 1970s.

21   On the issue of Turkey's application for membership, submitted in 1987, Greece did not need to cast a veto as the Commission's 'Opinion' on the matter was negative.

22   In a visit to the Secretariat of EPC in Brussels, a few months after its beginning on 21 September 1987, this author was impressed by the good working relationship between its Secretary, Giovanni Jannuzzi, and the Greek diplomat accredited to the post.

23   This term is borrowed from Steven Runciman's *The Great Church in Captivity: A Study of the Patriarchate of Constantinople from the Eve of the Turkish Conquest to the Greek War of Independence*, Cambridge, Cambridge University Press, 1968. Although Runciman was referring to the Orthodox Church's distrust of scientific enquiry and to its intolerance of demonstrable error, residues of this attitude are evident in contemporary Greek political culture. This makes possible sudden switches on fundamental principles without a prior debate or explanation. Thus Papandreou, while strongly against the presence of US bases in Greece in the 1970s, once in power could assert that there was new evidence in his possession

which justified their stationing in Greece. More recently, while Papandreou violently castigated Mitsotakis for his 'sell-out' on the Macedonian issue, once in office he again discovered new 'evidence' which made a compromise with FYROM possible on the grounds that preventing FYROM from collapsing, and escalating the Balkan war, was in Greece's national interest.

24 Arthur den Hartog, 'Greece and European political union', op.cit., p.85.

25 A study of the economic effects of Greek membership in the first decade has concluded that 75 per cent of receipts from the EC between 1982 and 1985 and more than 60 per cent in the following five years 'came from the guarantee section of FEOGA and [were] mainly used for consumption purposes by farmers'. T. Georgakopolous, 'Greece in the European Community: the experience in the first ten years', *Discussion Paper 93–04*, Department of International and European Economic Studies, Athens, 1992, p.1.

26 I refer here to the appearance on the Greek political scene of a new populist party, the 'New Spring', which polled 5 per cent. Its leader, Antonis Samaras, Foreign Minister in Mitsotakis' government, was sacked for his stance on the Macedonia question, which, according to Mitsotakis, had put in grave jeopardy Greece's position in the EC. Interview in *Economicos Tachydromos*, August 1993. While it is too early to judge this party's prospects under PASOK, it is certain that its appeal is among disaffected nationalists.

27 Papandreou's personal assessment of the results reached in Maastricht was cautious. While admitting that Maastricht was a major event, nonetheless he expressed serious doubts about its political–security value for Greece. Papandreou described the results on CFSP. While he welcomed the decision in Maastricht to accept Greece as a member of the WEU, he nonetheless warned against complacency as the putative benefits for Greece were almost cancelled out by the WEU's parallel decision to suspend Article 5 of the modified Brussels Treaty in the case of Greece and Turkey. This, from Greece's vantage point, automatically took away the most valuable benefit Greece expected to have gained from accession to the WEU. As Papandreou put it in Parliament, 'our interest in applying to join the WEU [in 1987] was in order to be able to face Turkey as a non-ally'. This objective, Papandreou argued, was not attained in Maastricht. 'Andreas Papandreou: PASOK's views on foreign policy', Hellenic Parliament, 20 December 1991. Reproduced and translated by *ELIAMEP Year Book 1991*, ELIAMEP, Athens, 1992, pp.283–5.

28 For example, Stefanos Manos, New Democracy's Minister of Economy and Finance, in the parliamentary debate on the ratification of Maastricht, claimed that by 2000 the EC would have a common currency, the ECU. And he added: 'We will then substitute our drachmas for ECUs. As a result of that, Greece will become overnight a country with low inflation, stable prices, low interest rates and currency stability. We will accomplish what we have been trying to since the creation of the Greek state: a country with economic and monetary stability.' *Hellenic Parliament, Minutes of Parliamentary Session, II*, 27 July 1992, p.19.

29 See, for instance, article by the then Foreign Minister, Antonis Samaras, in *Kathemerini*, 7 September 1990.

30 Greek enthusiasm in the IGC, not only on political but also on monetary union, seems to have infuriated Mrs Thatcher, who comments in her memoirs: 'I became all too used to a Greek chorus of support for whatever ambitious proposals Germany made.' *The Downing Street Years*, London, Harper Collins, 1993, p.763.

31 On this issue, see Panos Tsakaloyannis, 'The EC's IGC on political union and new conflicts in Europe: the case of Yugoslavia', *Quaderni Forum*, Anno VIII, no. 2, 1995.

32 In 1940–41 Greek Macedonia was offered first by Mussolini and later by Hitler to Yugoslavia and to Bulgaria if they had joined them in smashing the Greeks. In the post-war period there had been a 'subversive war of words' between Yugoslavs and Bulgarians as to who was the proprietor of the whole Macedonian region, including its Greek part which is invariably referred to as 'Macedonia of the Aegean'. For a revealing and accessible guide to this murky world see Svetozar Vukmanovic (General Tempo), *Struggle for the Balkans*, London, Merlin Press, 1990. In the Orwellian realities of the Balkans nothing is what it appears, and on closer inspection it transpires that the 'Struggle for the Balkans' is in fact the 'Struggle for Macedonia' including its Greek part, between Yugoslavs and Bulgarians. This book is a typical example of the huge propaganda effort of a Stalinist vintage conducted by both sides over the years.

33 Paris tried hard, in the second half of 1991, to restrain Bonn from recognizing unilaterally the break-away republics, by means of persuasion or outright threats. Roland Dumas, for example, warned in October 1991 that Bonn's recognition of the republics, would set back Franco-German relations by twenty years. Hans Stark, 'Dissonances franco-allemandes sur le fond de guerre serbo-croate', *Politique Etrangère*, vol. 57, no. 2, 1992, pp.339–40.

34 The decision on recognition, on the strength of the Committee's report, was deferred until 15 January 1992. Bonn, however, went ahead with recognition on Christmas Eve.

35 For a competent historical presentation of Greek apprehensions along the lines suggested here see Stephane Yerasimos, 'L'autre Alexandre', *Politique Etrangère*, vol. 57, no. 2, 1992.

36 Thus, whereas in the past a compromise on FYROM's name had appeared possible – a left-wing journalist and writer on the Balkans had suggested 'Slavo-Macedonia' in early 1991 as a compromise to get out from this strait-jacket – by 1992 even such a compromise was regarded as a climb-down. Stavros Lygeros, *Winds of War in the Balkans – Anemi Polemou sta Balkania*, Athens, 1992.

37 Ibid., p.143.

38 'If you ask a man how much is 2 plus 2 and he tells you 5, that is a mistake', Wittgenstein argued.'But if ask another man the same question and he answers 97, that is no longer a mistake. The second man you are talking with is operating with a wholly different logic from your own.' Cited by Thomas L. Friedman, *From Beirut to Jerusalem*, New York, Doubleday, 1990 p.431.

39 E. H. Carr, *The Twenty Years' Crisis*, op.cit. pp.50–1.

40 The imposition of a trade embargo on the former Yugoslav Republic of Macedonia, in February 1994, the 'counter-measures', which was a euphemism of sorts, was if anything a manifestation of the bankruptcy of Papandreou's policy on this issue. This led to Greece's further estrangement from her Community partners and to the addition of another knot in an already tangled problem.

41 Steven Runciman, *The Great Church in Captivity*: op.cit. p.viii.

42 For example, the Minister of Defence, Gerasimos Arsenis, was reported to have said in a press interview that Greece's real benefits from the WEU would be mainly from her participation in the WEU's 'European Armaments Group'. He also said that he did not 'wish to disturb the waters in the WEU' before Greece had ratified her Treaty of Accession to it. *To Vema*, 28 November 1993.(The Treaty was ratified by Parliament in early January, 1994.) It is worth noting that Arsenis, who was also a senior minister in PASOK's government between 1982–5, belongs to the 'Eurosceptics'. See his *Politiki Katathesi* [Political Statement], Athens, 1987, esp. pp.168–74 and 190–4.

43 For a disturbing account of this aspect of the Balkan imbroglio see Robert Fox's

article 'Albanians and Afghans fight for the heirs to Bosnia's SS past', *Daily Telegraph*, 29 December 1993. The moslem mujahedins in Bosnia, Fox reports, 'are trained and led by veterans from Afghanistan and Pakistan', according to US sources. 'The strong presence of native Albanians is an ominous sign. It could mean the seeds of war are spreading south via Kosovo and into Albania, thence to the Albanians in Macedonia'. It should be recalled that the Albanians in former Yugoslav Macedonia form about 35 per cent of the population and given current demographic trends, they are expected to be a majority in twenty years.

44 Ferdinand Tonnies, *Community and Association*, London, Routledge, 1974, p.74.
45 J. Madison and A. Hamilton, 'The Federalist Papers', no. 19, New York, Mentor, 1961, p.130.
46 Christopher Hill, 'The capability–expectations gap, or conceptualizing Europe's international role', *Journal of Common Market Studies*, vol. 31, no. 3, September 1993, p.326.
47 This was defined by Andrew Shonfield as 'a headlong flight into an unknown future, in order to escape from a fearful present'. *Europe: Journey to an Unknown Destination*, Harmondsworth, Penguin, 1973, p.18.
48 John Ralston Saul, *Voltaire's Bastards: The Dictatorship of Reason in the West*, New York, Free Press, 1992, p.107.
49 Ibid., p.585.

Chapter 10

Ireland and common security
Stretching the limits of commitment?

Patrick Keatinge

Of the three new member states which composed the EC's first enlargement in 1973, Ireland probably enjoyed the clearest gain from its overall terms of membership. Accession to the Common Agricultural Policy was the most obvious single advantage, after decades of dependence on a British market characterized by low price levels. More generally, Irish policies were now able to benefit from the opportunities afforded by a multilateral policy process which reduced the effects of political marginalization. The reservations about membership seen in the UK and Denmark – and more decisively in Norway – were thus largely absent in the case of Ireland.

Participation in EPC was bound to be more problematic. This was not simply because 'Political Cooperation' was itself an unknown quantity in the transitional years of Irish membership; indeed, it may be that being involved in the pioneering stage of the process was more of a help than a hindrance in making the necessary adjustments. Ireland's difficulty lay rather in the distance it had to travel from the outer margins of international life to involvement in a diplomatic network with pretensions to a central role in world affairs. Prior to joining the EC Irish foreign policy consisted of two main pillars; the first was the bilateral relationship with the UK (entailing considerable tensions given the reemergence of the conflict in Northern Ireland in 1968), while the second was the UN. An 'activist' profile had been established in the latter setting in the late 1950s, but this rather abstract and selective profession of policy principles hardly reflected a wide range of interests. So far as the international politics of 'Europe' were concerned, there was an enormous gap – Ireland came into the Nine as the only member state which had neither signed the North Atlantic Treaty nor established diplomatic relations with the Soviet Union.

Starting from this state of innocence, Ireland's initial adaptation to EPC proved to be something of a success story.[1] Any apprehensions about the maintenance of formal sovereignty were allayed by the strictly inter-governmental nature of the process. It also became apparent that the distinctive elements of the state's UN profile were not seriously threatened. The original support for decolonization was transformed into a broader advocacy of Third World issues, in which Denmark and the Netherlands were also prominent. The credibility of Ireland's vocation as a consistent contributor to UN peacekeeping operations was sustained, in a context which favoured the image of the Nine as an embryonic 'civilian power'. This compatibility of national policy and EPC was matched by an enhancement of Ireland's foreign policy capabilities.[2] High level access to the major governments of both partners and third parties became a matter of routine, and the Presidency offered a unique opportunity for a small state to demonstrate its new status. The machinery of national diplomacy, with regard both to its representation abroad and its specialization at home, was transformed.

However, this successful adaptation was marked by modesty in its presentation and caution in its execution. Irish governments were rarely keen to force the pace in EPC. Indeed, the converse is nearer the truth, with the insistence on what might be called the 'doctrine of parallel integration'; political integration, including the development of EPC, should only proceed at the same pace as economic integration, as measured by a general convergence in living standards across the Community.[3]

Partly such caution reflects the prudence which might be expected of any small state playing in the big league, but it is also based on a reservation peculiar to Ireland – its policy of 'military neutrality'. This refusal to enter into formal military commitments was originally motivated by a general desire to avoid British domination, and its credibility was enhanced for most Irish voters by the government's success in escaping the ravages of the Second World War. The policy was continued in the very different Cold War system, though with a decidedly parochial flavour in the late 1940s, when NATO membership seemed to be contingent on moves towards the unification of Northern Ireland with the Irish state. After applying for EC membership in 1961 Irish governments played down the imperatives of neutrality, by making general commitments to eventual political union. However, on the implicit assumption that defence competences would only be agreed at the eleventh hour, they maintained neutrality in the interim.

It has been argued that 'neutrality', as a technical term in the discourse of international politics, was never justified in the Irish case; even the more permissive interpretations show that Ireland deviated from many of the norms of neutrality policy adopted by Austria, Finland, Sweden and Switzerland up to 1989.[4] Nevertheless, however it was defined, neutrality was ignored by Irish governments at their peril. In 1981 the combination of neutrality and EPC made its debut in the arena of domestic politics, as a consequence of three separate developments which became curiously linked in political debate. The heightened interest in security arising from the New Cold War led to suggestions that European defence cooperation might come earlier rather than later; a crisis in relations with London over Northern Ireland reflected a similar proposition at the bilateral level; and last, but not least, governmental instability led to three general elections within eighteen months.[5] The overall effect of these events was to politicize neutrality at home, and, in the case of the Falklands conflict in 1982, to insert it divisively into the EPC response.[6] Thus Ireland entered its second decade as a member of EPC with its neutrality reservation reinforced.

THE NEUTRALITY FOOTNOTE (1983–7)

The evolution of EPC depends on developments at three levels of political activity: the broad international system within which the EPC bloc tries to be an 'international actor', the European Community itself, and the domestic politics of the member states. On the first level, the mid-1980s were marked by a significant change in East-West relations, from the New Cold War to *détente*; indeed, in retrospect this period may be seen as the beginning of the end of the bipolar system initiated in 1945. EC integration also advanced, from yet another 'relaunch' in 1984 to agreement on the single market programme and its institutional corollary, the Single European Act (SEA), in 1985. However, the domestic politics of a small, peripheral member state would not necessarily be pulled directly into the mainstream of such general forces, and this proved to be the case for Ireland.

The Irish government between late 1982 and 1987 consisted of a coalition of Fine Gael (affiliated to the Christian Democrats) and the Labour Party (affiliated to the Socialists). Although the latter were the junior party in the coalition, a strict adherence to neutrality was a *sine qua non* of their foreign policy profile, and this position was also adopted by a Fianna Fail opposition which had little time for bipartisan scruples. The Fine Gael Taoiseach (Prime Minister), Dr Garret FitzGerald, might in other circumstances have adopted a more open approach to security issues; in the event his generally positive attitude to EPC had to find other forms of expression.[7]

Irish involvement in major international issues during this period was most evident with regard to the Middle East and South Africa.[8] As a contributor to the UN peacekeeping operation in southern Lebanon (UNIFIL), Ireland's relations with Israel were often difficult. Although the immediate context was not within the purview of EPC, the existence of a long-established focus on the Arab–Israeli dispute by the Nine and later the Twelve may have provided some support in bilateral confrontations.

Policy towards South Africa, on the other hand, evolved very much within the EPC framework.[9] Ireland had no diplomatic relations with South Africa, not very much in the way of commercial interests, and a well-established anti-apartheid lobby. Thus it was hardly surprising to find Ireland at the 'activist' end of the EPC spectrum on the issue of economic sanctions when the South African situation deteriorated in 1985. Advocacy of firmer sanctions by the Twelve did not succeed, and the Irish government was then accused by its domestic critics of using the stalemate in EPC as an excuse for not undertaking more vigorous unilateral sanctions. In short, the 'alibi' or 'cover' function of EPC did not seem altogether effective at the domestic level.

It may, however, have had some effect at the international level, when the American campaign against 'international terrorism' led to sustained pressure on its European allies to take action against Libya early in 1986. Ireland was particularly dependent on American goodwill at this point, as promised financial support for the Anglo-Irish Agreement of 1985 was still subject to Congressional approval; commercial interests in Libya and participation in UNIFIL might also have been affected by the outcome. The requirements of EPC consultation and solidarity provided some relief from the demands of American friendship, as well as from a domestic public opinion which was not convinced of the merits of Washington's case. In the event no substantive damage was done to Irish–US relations on Northern Ireland; indeed this issue area has generally been successfully kept apart from broader considerations of West–West relations, suggesting that the USA had little difficulty with Ireland's absence from the Western alliance proper.

On the whole, then, the FitzGerald government projected the image of a 'helpful partner', and the third Irish presidency in 1984 exemplified this role. The exception to this rule lay in the realm of security policy. The Stuttgart Solemn Declaration of 1983, with its minimalist concept of security, reflected Irish interests at a time when it became clear, in the first opinion polls on the issue, that there was widespread public support for neutrality. However, the relaunch of integration the following year, in which it fell to the Irish presidency to follow through President Mitterrand's initiative, meant that the Solemn Declaration was not going to be the last word on security. The report of the Ad Hoc Committee on Institutional Affairs, chaired by the former Irish Foreign Minister, Senator James Dooge, included a formal reserve on the whole section on 'security and defence' – Ireland's 'footnote' was thus made quite explicit. In similar vein a cross-party parliamentary report at this time referred to neutrality as a foreign policy principle, which should not be 'bargained against material advantage'. Yet among the Ten Ireland was not isolated on the security issue, since the domestic politics of Denmark and Greece led to a similar position. Whatever irritation was felt by those governments anxious to develop the 'European' dimension of military security was deflected by the concurrent reactivation of the WEU, which seemed to circumvent the reservations of these three states which conveniently were not members of the latter organization.

The initial reaction of the Fianna Fail opposition to Title III of the Single European Act in December 1986 was to present it as an abdication of neutrality. The government rejected this proposition, but delayed the process of parliamentary ratification until late the following year, by which time the coalition parties were on the point of ending their partnership. Nevertheless, the parliamentary arithmetic seemed to suffice, the Labour Party being satisfied with informal affirmations that neutrality was not affected, when the whole ratification process was halted by the anti-EC lobby's recourse to legal action. Its leader, Raymond Crotty, claimed that the terms of the SEA required a constitutional amendment, and hence a referendum. Although the High Court rejected his case, he won on appeal to the Supreme Court, the whole procedure delaying the implementation of the Single Act by six months.

An interesting feature of the final decision was that the Supreme Court was in two minds on the legal significance of the new treaty base for EPC. Two of the five judges accepted the conventional wisdom that it did little more than codify existing practice, and by implication excluded military aspects of security; on the other hand, the majority argued that EPC had acquired a more binding character, and might, in some undefined way, impinge on Irish defence policy.[10] So far as the Irish government was concerned, it was now necessary to hold a referendum on the SEA, which was held in May 1987. This gave the anti-EC lobby the opportunity to advance their thesis that the end of neutrality was nigh – with characteristic hyperbole they described the Community as a 'nuclear alliance' – but the referendum approved the Single Act by more than two to one in a low turnout.

The outcome of this untidy series of events (in many ways a foretaste of the confusion which would attend the ratification of the Maastricht Treaty five years later) is at least partly explained by the change of government which occurred shortly before the Supreme Court decision. It was a new Fianna Fail minority government, suddenly bereft of its apprehensions about neutrality, which put the case for the SEA, supported by Fine Gael and faced by a Labour Party so divided on the issue that it did not even articulate an agreed position. Ireland's acceptance of Title III was accompanied by the most formal statement yet made of its neutrality reservation, in a national declaration appended to the instrument of ratification. However, this proved to be the highwater mark of this stance, for the change in the domestic balance of power in 1987 was an important factor in subsequent changes in attitude towards the compatibility of neutrality and EPC.[11]

HIGH DÉTENTE AND CHANGING ATTITUDES (1987-9)

The year of 1987 also marked a turning point in East–West relations. The successful negotiation of the Intermediate Nuclear Forces treaty was the first fruit of a short but intensive period of 'high *détente*' between the superpowers, before the bipolar system itself began to dissolve in 1989. Significant arms control measures, covering conventional as well as nuclear forces, were on the agenda not merely of Washington and Moscow but of all the members of the two alliance systems. The limited involvement of non-alliance states, through the confidence and security building negotiations in the CSCE framework, now became more closely meshed with the general move towards 'building down' the military confrontation in Europe. In this context, Ireland had been in a somewhat anomalous position so far as Irish supporters of neutrality were concerned; as a party to EPC solidarity in the Stockholm conference in the mid-1980s the Irish delegation seemed to be associated with the NATO caucus, yet could not be formally identified with that of the neutral and non-aligned countries.[12] Now such concerns – which in any case were more a matter of form than of substance – lost much of their relevance. Anecdotal evidence suggests Irish representatives had usually turned a blind eye (though not always a deaf ear) to informal discussion of the high politics of security, so long as such topics were excluded from public statements. With a change of emphasis in the subject matter, from deterrence to arms control, this degree of restraint might be relaxed.

When, in 1988, the new *détente* went beyond the sphere of arms control to significant consensus in the UN Security Council and moves to resolve major regional conflicts, the conditions for a revival of a 'civilian power' EC seemed more favourable than at any time since the early years of Irish membership of the Community. This matched the prospects for a more general revival of integration, and with the new emphasis on cohesion policy in favour of the poorer peripheral countries, it was a form of integration which was very much in Ireland's interests. The Fianna Fail government of Charles Haughey, at a time of considerable financial retrenchment, put its European policy at the centre of its medium- to long-term strategy. 'Europe' was the *deus ex machina*, the single market was presented as an opportunity rather than a threat, and full economic and monetary union was regarded as an essential element in Ireland's economic development.

Against this background, the proposition that neutrality must be main-tained at all costs received much less emphasis. Mr Haughey still repudiated the image of a 'superpower Europe' in general terms, but his overall approach to the 'political finality' of integration by implication represented a return to the 'defence last' thesis which had been conventionally held by Irish governments, rather than the 'defence never' position he had recently espoused. Two opposition parties moved even further, by expressing a mildly revisionist line on neutrality. In 1988 a Fine Gael policy document conceded, without making very much of the matter, that further integration might be at the cost of neutrality, perhaps in the context of two-tier integration. The foreign affairs spokeswoman of the recently formed Progressive Democrats (composed mainly of former Fianna Fail members) was more outspoken, referring to neutrality as 'bogus'.[13]

Irish positions on the major issues within EPC were not noticeably affected one way or another by such hypothetical considerations. In 1988 the Palestinian National Council's acceptance of UN Resolutions 242 and 338, a matter of 'particular importance' for the Twelve, was given an additional gloss as a 'very historic step' by the Minister for Foreign Affairs, Brian Lenihan. Domestic pressure to impose unilateral sanctions against South Africa continued, but the government stayed within the parameters of the Twelve's approach. With regard to issues in Central America, an area in which Washington's policies since the early 1980s had provoked criticism from the development lobby and the Irish left in general, the San José process moved in a direction favoured by Irish governments. In some respects Ireland was prepared to move beyond the mainstream. President Daniel Ortega of Nicaragua received a warmer welcome in Dublin than in some other EC capitals. More pointedly, Ireland was in a minority of three which did not vote against a General Assembly resolution condemning the American intervention in Panama in December 1989.[14] By the autumn of 1989, however, such nuanced variations (or even particular instances of dissent) in the national positions of the Twelve with regard to non-European conflicts aroused little comment at home or abroad. The one issue which attracted attention was decidedly European and arguably more fundamental – the dissolution of the Eastern bloc. Ironically, for a small state with a rather slight tradition of relations with that part of the world, Ireland was now to become more closely involved through the rotation of the Presidency of the Council of Ministers. Fortunately, given the operation of the troika system, Irish ministers and diplomats were reasonably well prepared for what would prove to be their most intensive Presidency so far as political cooperation was concerned. A change of government in the middle of 1989 – there was now a Fianna Fail–Progressive Democrat coalition – made little difference to Ireland's diplomacy, in which the Taoiseach, Mr Haughey, played an increasingly active role.

A NEW EUROPEAN ORDER? (1989–90)

The principal question on the agenda of the fourth Irish Presidency was the unification of Germany.[15] While the acquiescence of the Soviet Union was negotiated in bilateral talks and in the 'two-plus-four' framework, a special European Council in Dublin on 28 April 1990 gave the Community's seal of approval for what was in effect a further round in its enlargement. Another strategic decision was taken formally on this occasion, with the agreement to convene an Intergovernmental Conference on Political Union to complement that already envisaged for Economic and Monetary Union. It would be an exaggeration to say that there was no apprehension in Ireland about these momentous events – an eastward-looking German economy was an obvious worry – but there was none of the *realpolitik* frisson experienced in Paris or London. In the event, German unification was presented as the most natural thing in the world; in a country where national unification has been a prominent leitmotif this was not altogether surprising.

The Irish Presidency was also the bearer of good news on some of the more conventional routines in EPC. The release of Nelson Mandela in February 1990 was a breakthrough which led the British government to argue strongly for the immediate end of sanctions. There was no consensus at a foreign ministers' meeting, and when the Presidency publicly criticized the British approach as a precedent for sanctions busting, British references to the Falklands experience in 1982 testified to some tension on the matter. However, the Irish government succeeded in maintaining a more gradual and conditional approach to the reduction of sanctions.

The Middle East was another perennial issue, the Minister for Foreign Affairs, Gerard Collins, making no less than four visits to the region during his term as President. An emphasis on the rehabilitation of relations with Iran, which had deteriorated since the Rushdie affair in 1989, was also evident. This coincided with a particular Irish concern, the efforts to obtain the release of Brian Keenan, one of the Western hostages in Beirut. Keenan, technically a British citizen as a native of Belfast, was by the same token an Irish national, and his possession of an Irish passport proved to be a critical element in the long and intensive campaign for his release. This occurred in August 1990 and the Irish government may have derived further advantage from the status of the Presidency. Another positive result for the government was the first EPC declaration on nuclear non-proliferation at the second Dublin summit in June. France's position outside the NPT regime had hitherto precluded putting this issue on the agenda, but if any military questions were to come within the Twelve's purview it was precisely this sort of 'soft security' topic which would prove most acceptable to Irish opinion.

So far as EPC procedures were concerned, the Irish presidency introduced two innovations. The conventional distinction between the General Affairs Council and meetings of foreign ministers in Political Cooperation was dropped on two occasions, in 'special meetings of foreign ministers'. In addition, Mr Haughey and President Bush agreed the more systematic procedure for high-level contacts between the Community as such and the USA, which was to be formalized the following November in the Transatlantic Declaration.

Ireland thus entered the post-Cold War era with an unusually high diplomatic profile, offering the most a small state can to a multilateral process like EPC – a 'helpful' Presidency. The external environment was also helpful to Ireland, being conducive to the projection of civilian power and measures of soft security in the sphere of preventive diplomacy and disarmament; the elevation of the CSCE in the Paris Charter in November merely seemed to underline the point. Mr Haughey came away from the Rome European Council in December 1990 – the opening of the Political Union Intergovernmental Conference – claiming that the distinction still stood between 'security' (an admissible subject, at least in its SEA form) and 'defence' (still a taboo).

COPING WITH DISORDER (1990–91)

The euphoria surrounding the unexpectedly rapid unification of Germany, and the accompanying rhetoric about the 'new security architecture', could not disguise the fact that 1990 was not a *tabula rasa* so far as international security was concerned. Iraq's annexation of Kuwait was a reminder that the use of force in international politics was not such a transient phenomenon as the Cold War had proved to be.

Ireland's direct interests in the ensuing Gulf crisis were unusually significant for a small state outside the region.[16] Exports of beef to Iraq were immediately curtailed, leading to a financial crisis for the Goodman group, then the largest Irish – and European – beef exporter. More than 400 Irish nationals were trapped in Iraq, proportionately the largest group of hostages from among the Twelve. Ireland was also still involved in the troika, the crisis starting little over a month after the Irish Presidency.

The initial moves by the Twelve, consisting of declaratory policy and economic sanctions, did not arouse controversy in domestic politics. However, the position of the hostages posed a dilemma for the government, which was anxious to maintain the Twelve's stance of not bargaining for their freedom; although a parliamentary delegation did travel to Baghdad before the Iraqis abandoned the hostage ploy altogether, this was discouraged by the government and pressures by the hostages' families were resisted.

The prospect of being involved in military measures against Iraq was more problematic. The government refused an invitation to attend a WEU ministerial meeting as an observer early in the crisis, and opinion polls showed little support either for an early resort to force or for Irish participation in direct enforcement. Government statements expressed general support for an emphasis on continued economic sanctions and attempts to mediate, even after the Security Council Resolution 678 on 29 November 1990 in effect demonstrated that the decision between war and peace was essentially an American one.

Notwithstanding this delegation of authority by the UN, the imperatives of collective security had emerged more clearly than at any time since Ireland joined the organization in 1955. Policy had to be based on the presumption that the obligations of UN membership took precedence over considerations of neutrality. Resolution 678 did not require direct participation in the American-led coalition, but it requested 'appropriate support' from all states. When hostilities began in January 1991 Mr Haughey agreed to grant logistical facilities at Shannon airport, but arguing that this was not 'of sufficient degree or substance to constitute participating in the war', he avoided any significant domestic challenge from a public opinion which was clearly uneasy.

The Gulf War of 1991 was hardly the epitome of solidarity among the Twelve.[17] The minimalist expression of EPC support for the coalition during the brief land war caused no difficulty for the Irish government, and the rapid end to hostilities was matched by an equally rapid end to visible public concern. Nevertheless, the Gulf conflict as a whole did represent something of an innovation in Irish foreign policy. For the first time, however reluctantly, an Irish government formally accepted the legitimacy of the actual use of force; membership of the UN, up to that point associated with the constrained concept of peacekeeping, now seemed to require more far-reaching commitments.

The demands for 'humanitarian intervention' to protect Kurdish refugees in northern Iraq were a further confirmation of this trend. The Twelve's decision to support the establishment of sanctuaries on Iraqi territory, agreed at a special meeting of the European Council at Luxembourg on 8 April 1991, met with no evident reserve by the Irish government, even though the coordination and implementation of the measures were associated with the WEU. Indeed, on this occasion criticism of government policy at home reflected the view that not enough was being done. When the Yugoslav civil war broke out less than three months later Irish support for an activist approach by the Twelve was also apparent. The government authorized participation in the EC monitors' attempts to mediate at local level, and seemed to subscribe to the main lines of the Twelve's policy. However, there was little domestic debate at the key stages of the Yugoslav crisis during 1991. The early strategy to keep Yugoslavia together, and the controversial change to the recognition of the secessionist republics at the end of the year, were not matters which aroused significant comment either at the parliamentary or general public levels.

Nevertheless, there was an important departure in Irish policy when the government agreed that the Minister for Foreign Affairs would attend WEU meetings on 19 and 30 September as an observer. The decision was justified on the grounds that Irish participation in the Twelve's attempt to find a peaceful resolution to the conflict, and its contribution on the ground, gave it a 'significant and continuing interest in what takes place in Yugoslavia'. This apparently pragmatic reversal of attitude towards the WEU was welcomed by the Fine Gael opposition, but criticized as the abandonment of neutrality by the Labour Party.[18]

THE POLITICS OF MAASTRICHT (1991–2)

The evolution of Irish positions on security issues at this time, however tentative and pragmatic they appeared, must also be placed in the context of the Intergovernmental Conference on Political Union which led to the Treaty on European Union at Maastricht in December 1991. The commitment to the IGC accelerated the EPC review process agreed in the Single European Act and, because it was accompanied by inflated expectations of the deepening of integration in general, the whole range of Ireland's EC interests, including the much-prized cohesion policy, was at stake. Moreover, following the Supreme Court's decision in 1987, it was almost certain the outcome would have to be ratified by a third referendum. Ireland's negotiating stance at the IGC was thus influenced by the prospect of the difficult test of direct democracy.

The government's strategy was to table explicit proposals on cohesion, for which obvious allies (Spain, Greece and Portugal) were at hand, and to say nothing at first on security. Other member states' proposals for defence, it was assumed, would fall on issues other than Irish neutrality. By the middle of April 1991 there were already signs that this assumption was justified; divergence during the Gulf War reflected much older divisions on defence, between 'Atlanticists' and 'Europeanists'. In July Sweden's application to join the Community, and the Commission's opinion on Austria's earlier application, were further indicators that the new disciplines of Political Cooperation were unlikely to be much more rigorous than those of Title III. The government could thus contemplate a gradual extension of its security involvement, and its ad hoc presence at WEU meetings in the autumn may be partly explained in this context.

When it came to the final phase of the negotiations, Ireland could balance its general commitment that the Common Foreign and Security Policy (CFSP) should include 'all questions related to the security of the Union' with the fact that commitment to defence remained an aspiration, to be returned to at a further intergovernmental conference in 1996. Furthermore, although Ireland agreed to accede to WEU observer status on a permanent basis following ratification of the treaty, the latter's provisions on security, Article J.4, includes the somewhat opaque qualification that the policy of the Union 'shall not prejudice the specific character of the security and defence policy of certain Member states'.[19] The provisions for qualified majority voting, an issue on which Irish policy-makers are generally sceptical, were explicitly excluded from defence-related issues. As we shall see below, this outcome did put the hard question of a defence commitment on the agenda in a way which would require a substantive response from Ireland, rather than the traditional neutrality reservation, but the response could be delayed until 1996.

On this basis, and with an extension of cohesion policy, the Irish government prepared to sell Maastricht to its public. A study of public attitudes to neutrality and related issues between the mid-1980s and the 1992 referendum points to neutrality as a 'salient political symbol but [with] . . . an ill-defined content'.[20] The author found no clear political or social profile, and suggested that the large majority who think well of neutrality in the abstract would be much reduced by the cross-pressures of economic interests, leaving a minority for whom neutrality was associated with more general opposition to EC integration.

This proved to be the case, after a campaign which was seriously distorted by the issue of abortion, and not a little disrupted by the negative Danish vote two weeks before the Irish referendum. Ireland's decision for ratification was 69.1 per cent to 30.9 per cent, with a reasonably high turnout by Irish standards of 57 per cent. So far as neutrality and security were concerned, the referendum was hardly a model of informed debate. Opponents of the CFSP, imaginatively linking a maximalist interpretation of Article J with the provisions for citizenship, claimed it was the European superpower's instrument for raising a conscript army to fight resource wars in the twenty-first century.[21] (Actual wars in the former Yugoslavia and former Soviet Union received surprisingly little attention.)

The government's position, that the substance of a common defence policy awaited the 1996 review conference, deprived it of anything very concrete to say in the meantime, but the new Taoiseach, Albert Reynolds, did argue that the Cold War rationale for neutrality had disappeared, and that Ireland ought to be involved in the search for new security structures.[22] Thus, although many substantive issues had hardly been aired in the referendum campaign, and the ultimate demise of neutrality had not been conceded, there was a very important difference between this referendum and its predecessors – security was now a legitimate concern in public life, and the taboo on even discussing neutrality had been broken. Shortly after the referendum, in an unusual address to both houses of the Irish parliament, President Mary Robinson emphasized the point by calling for an open debate on the balance between neutrality and the state's responsibilities to its EC partners.

TOWARDS ENFORCEMENT? (1992–3)

While the focus in the IGC and the Maastricht referendum was on amendments to the rules of the game, it sometimes seemed as if the game itself, being played so incoherently in the former Yugoslavia, merited little attention in Irish political life. Ireland was, nevertheless, involved in the continuing debate on whether the international community in general, and the EC in particular, should engage in peace enforcement. As a state with a long tradition as a UN peacekeeping contributor, it was not surprising that it would insist both on UN authority and UN control as prerequisites for legitimating any escalation of military measures. The European Council's statement on the Bosnian war on 29 June 1992 bore the marks of this concern, and the government's preference for a negotiated settlement was a feature of its subsequent contributions to the debate on Bosnia. However, the possibility of enforcement was accepted in principle, even by the Labour Party leader, Dick Spring, when he became Foreign Minister in the new Fianna Fail–Labour Party coalition in 1993.[23]

However, for Ireland the debate on peace enforcement was not mainly focused on Bosnia. There were fewer direct Irish interests in the Balkans than there had been, for example, in the Gulf. No significant economic interests were evident; cultural ties were represented mainly by a recently developed interest in the Catholic shrine at Medugorje in Bosnia. Ethnic conflicts with religious overtones suggested uncomfortable parallels with the intractable conflict much closer to home. Although a diplomatic and military presence on the ground may attract domestic political and media attention, in this case Ireland's contribution to the EC monitors and UN missions was on a small scale, the bulk of peacekeeping assets being deployed in southern Lebanon.

Ireland's experiment in peace enforcement took shape in what seemed at the time to be the more propitious circumstances of Somalia. This accorded with the Irish public's long-established 'humanitarian vocation' in Africa, and the overall position of Third World issues in Irish foreign policy.[24] There was no significant Bosnian lobby in Dublin in the summer of 1992, but development cooperation groups succeeded in impressing the Minister for Foreign Affairs, David Andrews, with the need to respond to the famine in Somalia. The government accepted this as a priority for humanitarian relief, and the public was further mobilized by a visit to Somalia by the President, Mrs Robinson, in October.

When the international community, and the USA in particular, recognized that the restoration of public order was a prerequisite for famine relief in Somalia, the Security Council authorized an interim intervention. Since this was under American command an Irish contribution was precluded; the legal base for deploying troops outside the state requires UN control. By contrast, the continuation of the intervention, UNOSOM II, which took over in May 1993, was a full UN operation, and Ireland became one of six EC states to participate. Nevertheless, this commitment still required an amendment to the original legislation of 1960, because its mandate went beyond the restrictions of peacekeeping. As an innovation in multilateral peace enforcement, UNOSOM II posed political as well as military risks to the contributing countries .

That became all too clear, well before Ireland's eighty-man transport unit was sent to Somalia. Parliamentary approval for the change in legislation, to cover an enforcement mandate, was debated against a background of violence in Mogadishu, including UN and civilian fatalities, and mounting controversy about the evident weaknesses in UN command and control. The government persisted with its commitment, but was at pains to reassure the public that its troops did not have a combat role, and that outside the context of UN multilateralism the policy of military neutrality still stood.

The fatalities incurred by American troops at the beginning of October 1993, and the Clinton administration's consequent loss of enthusiasm for UN collective security, suggests that UNOSOM II may prove to be an isolated experiment. By the spring of 1994 Ireland was the only EU member state remaining in Somalia, out of the original quite considerable presence also provided by France, Italy, Germany, Belgium and Greece. Even this involvement depended on an amelioration of the Somali civil war. Nevertheless, Ireland's participation in an enforcement action, however tentative, does represent an extension of its commitment to collective action which would have been inconceivable only a few years previously.

CONCLUSIONS

In many respects Ireland's response to that element in Political Co-operation where it was hitherto most reserved – the field of security – has been more positive since the late 1980s. The objectives of Maastricht, including taboo words like 'defence', have been accepted in outline, and the legal base of military involvement has been modified in the context of peace enforcement. The Department of Foreign Affairs now has designated officials specializing in security both in Dublin and Brussels (where the ambassador to Belgium serves as permanent representative to the WEU) as well as a separate delegation to the CSCE in Vienna. These recent administrative changes, largely a consequence of observer status in the WEU, may serve as a direct link between the Irish political system and the realities of European security. Irish politicians will thus be confronted by substantive issues, and the need for concrete choices, and can no longer rely solely on the mantra of 'neutrality' to avoid taking positions. Ireland's adaptation to the exigencies of the post-Cold War international system is at least under way.

At the same time, this new openness in thought and deed should not be exaggerated. Ireland has not so far subscribed to the disciplines of military alliance. The programme for the Fianna Fail–Labour Party government which came into power in January 1993 contains a balance between the traditional reserve, in an explicit denial of membership of either the WEU or NATO, and acceptance of the possibility that a future negotiation might involve Ireland in a common defence policy.[25] The Intergovernmental Conference in 1996 will be just such a negotiation, but the content of a 'common defence policy' is not self-evident; it remains to be negotiated. The first preference of an Irish government may well be a minimalist approach, accepting such measures as a common assessment of risks and closer cooperation in peacekeeping, but leaving a mutual assistance guarantee – the Rubicon of Irish neutrality – for the ultimate stage of security integration, a 'common defence'.

The viability of that approach would depend to a large extent on the general political context of the 1996 review conference. The persistence of attempts to develop a cooperative security regime, encompassing a weak but reforming Russia, would favour a gradualist development of EU security integration, in which a loose form of variable geometry continued to be the norm. In those circumstances Ireland might find partners in procrastination, now that Austria, Finland and Sweden are member states and in no hurry to abandon the last vestiges of their neutrality. A more threatening security environment, on the other hand, might persuade the latter states, which are potentially much more exposed than Ireland to security threats, to undertake alliance commitments; it would also presumably increase incentives to reinforce such commitments by those countries which had long since made them. If Ireland were isolated in the Intergovernmental Conference in this way, it would prove very difficult to avoid a linkage between security and economic interests. This dilemma would be particularly acute in the context of a simultaneous move towards a clear-cut form of two-tier integration, in which for economic reasons Ireland aspired to membership of the first tier. The price of continuing solidarity in the economic sphere might have to be paid by subscribing to mutual assistance guarantees; if so, Ireland would be making the most significant foreign policy change since joining the EC more than twenty years ago.

However, that eventuality would have to be endorsed in a referendum – the third submission of European policy to popular approval in ten years. The increasing influence which domestic politics is likely to have on Irish foreign policy has also been reinforced by the establishment of a parliamentary Foreign Affairs Committee in the summer of 1993. Though not particularly well endowed with investigative powers by international standards, this body nonetheless represents a more systematic means of parliamentary scrutiny than that which existed during the first twenty years of Ireland's membership of the EC. In these circumstances, Irish governments are not likely to encourage proposals for a development of 'hard security' actions in the CFSP, nor are they likely to become advocates for the development of procedural experiments such as qualified majority voting. They will, however, feel compelled to rationalize their positions more fully in the public domain. Indeed, this is already happening, with a commitment to produce a comprehensive White Paper on foreign policy and public meetings to debate in 1995. It may be that a more open, systematic, and to some extent proactive, policy style is in the making. Already the Irish government is deliberately preparing for the next round of the CFSP debate, the IGC, in 1996 when Ireland will also be holding the Presidency.

The hallmark of the Irish approach to the future of the CFSP nevertheless remains one of caution and gradualism. In that respect there has been a remarkable continuity between the mid-1980s and the mid-1990s.[26] The reservation on defence obligations puts Ireland near the minimalist end of the spectrum, even if as a 'constructive minimalist'. Yet the increasing uncertainties associated with the post-Cold War international system represent a very different setting from that prevailing ten years ago, and the traditional basis of Irish foreign policy, as well as the style of policy-making, may be subjected to a more fundamental adaptation than at any time since 'Europe' became the focus of Ireland's external relations.

NOTES

1 See Patrick Keatinge, 'Ireland: neutrality inside EPC', in Christopher Hill (ed.), *National Foreign Policies and European Political Cooperation*, London, Allen and Unwin, 1983, pp.137–52.

2 See Patrick Keatinge (ed.), *Ireland and EC Membership Evaluated*, London, Pinter, 1991, pp.149–51.

3 Irish policy style is not much given to formal 'doctrines', but the proposition contained in 'parallel integration' has been a constant theme. See, for example, the formulation of a former Political Director: Padraic MacKernan, 'Ireland and political cooperation', *Irish Studies in International Affairs*, vol. 1, no. 4, 1984.

4 For the severest critique, see Trevor C. Salmon, *Unneutral Ireland: An Ambivalent and Unique Security Policy*, Oxford, Clarendon Press, 1989. An analysis of recent changes in the positions of European neutrals is Patrick Keatinge, 'Ireland and European neutrality after the Cold War', in Ronald J. Hill and Michael Marsh (eds), *Modern Irish Democracy: Essays in Honour of Basil Chubb*, Dublin, Irish Academic Press, 1993.

5 See Patrick Keatinge, *A Singular Stance: Irish Neutrality in the 1980s*, Dublin, Institute of Public Administration, 1984.

6 See Ben Tonra, 'The internal dissenter (II): Ireland', in Stelios Stavridis and Christopher Hill (eds), *Domestic Sources of Foreign Policy: West European Reactions to the Falklands Conflict*, Oxford, Berg, 1996, pp.132–50.

7 Dr FitzGerald, as Minister for Foreign Affairs from 1973 to 1977, was an 'old EPC hand'. See Garret FitzGerald, *All in a Life: an Autobiography*, Dublin, Gill and Macmillan, 1991, especially Chapters 6 and 18.

8 For annual reviews of Ireland's foreign relations, see Patrick Keatinge, 'Ireland's foreign relations in 1984 [and subsequent years]', *Irish Studies in International Affairs*, vol. 2, no. 1, 1985 [and subsequent editions].

9 See Brigid Laffan, *Ireland and South Africa: Irish Government Policy in the 1980s*, Dublin, Trocaire, 1988.

10 See Paul McCutcheon, 'The legal system', in Patrick Keatinge (ed.), *Ireland and EC Membership Evaluated*.

11 For the neutrality declaration attached to the Single European Act, see Patrick Keatinge, 'Ireland's foreign relations in 1987', *Irish Studies in International Affairs*, vol. 2, no. 4, 1988, p.98.

12 For an Irish participant's view of the CDE conference in Stockholm, see Philip McDonagh, 'The strengthening of security in Europe: the Stockholm Conference, 1984–6', *Irish Studies in International Affairs*, vol. 2, no. 3, 1987.

13 See Patrick Keatinge, 'Ireland's foreign relations in 1988', *Irish Studies in International Affairs*, vol. 3, no. 1, 1989, p.109.

14 Ireland and Greece abstained, and Spain voted for the resolution.
15 For the official record, see *Irish Presidency of the European Communities, January – June 1990*, PL. 7479, Dublin, Stationery Office, 1990.
16 See Patrick Keatinge, 'Ireland's foreign relations in 1990', *Irish Studies in International Affairs*, vol. 3, no. 3, 1991, pp.153–7; Liz Heffernan and Anthony Whelan, 'Ireland, the United Nations and the Gulf Conflict', ibid; Patrick Keatinge, 'Ireland's foreign relations in 1991', *Irish Studies in International Affairs*, vol. 3, no. 4, 1992, pp.80–3.
17 See Trevor C. Salmon, 'Testing times for European political cooperation: the Gulf and Yugoslavia, 1990–1992', *International Affairs*, vol. 68, no. 2, 1992.
18 See *The Irish Times*, 19 September 1991.
19 For interpretations of the legal base of the CFSP from an (orthodox) Irish point of view, see Patrick Keatinge (ed.), *Maastricht and Ireland: What the Treaty Means*, Dublin, Institute of European Affairs, 1992, p.6475; White Paper, *Treaty on European Union*, PL. 8793, Dublin, Stationery Office, 1992.
20 See Michael Marsh, 'Irish public opinion on neutrality and European Union', Occasional Paper 1, Dublin, Institute of European Affairs, People First/Meitheal, 1992.
21 See Joe Noonan and John Maguire, *Maastricht and Neutrality*, Cork, People First/Meitheal, 1992.
22 See the speech by Mr Reynolds on 18 May 1992, in European Documents Series, no. 1, Spring 1993, Dublin, Institute of European Affairs, 1993, pp.1–5.
23 See the Irish statement at the Security Council debate on Bosnia in April 1993, where it is accepted that if negotiation fails the Security Council has to consider 'all options' under the Charter: European Document Series, no. 2, Summer 1993, pp.65–6.
24 Ireland's policy towards the Third World has been described as 'the poor relation', but it has been a good deal more substantial than that with the former Second World: see Michael Holmes, Nicholas Rees and Bernadette Whelan, *The Poor Relation: Irish Foreign Policy and the Third World*, Dublin, Trocaire and Gill and Macmillan, 1993.
25 For the programme for government, see European Document Series, no. 2, Summer 1993, pp.68–9.
26 See Patrick Keatinge, 'Ireland: neutrality inside EPC', in Hill, op.cit., p.151.

BIBLIOGRAPHY

FitzGerald, Garret, *All in a Life: an Autobiography*, Dublin, Gill and Macmillan, 1991.
European Document Series, quarterly from Spring 1993, Dublin, Institute of European Affairs.
Heffernan, Liz and Whelan, Anthony, 'Ireland, the United Nations and the Gulf conflict', *Irish Studies in International Affairs*, vol. 3, no. 3, 1991.
Holmes, Michael, Rees, Nicholas and Whelan, Bernadette, *The Poor Relation: Irish Foreign Policy and the Third World*, Dublin, Trocaire and Gill and Macmillan, 1993.
Irish Presidency of the European Communities, January–June 1990, PL. 7479, Dublin, Stationery Office, 1990.
Keatinge, Patrick, 'Ireland: neutrality inside EPC', in Christopher Hill (ed.), *National Foreign Policies and European Political Cooperation*, London, Allen and Unwin, 1983, pp.137–52.
—— *A Singular Stance: Irish Neutrality in the 1980s*, Dublin, Institute of Public Administration, 1984.
—— 'Ireland's foreign relations in 1984 [and subsequent years]', *Irish Studies in International Affairs*, vol. 2, no. 1, 1985 [and subsequent editions].

—— (ed.), *Ireland and EC Membership Evaluated*, London, Pinter, 1991.

—— (ed.), *Maastricht and Ireland. What the Treaty Means*, Dublin, Institute of European Affairs, 1992.

—— 'Ireland and European neutrality after the Cold War', in Ronald J. Hill and Michael Marsh (eds), *Modern Irish Democracy: Essays in Honour of Basil Chubb*, Dublin, Irish Academic Press, 1993.

Laffan, Brigid, *Ireland and South Africa: Irish Government Policy in the 1980s*, Dublin, Trocaire, 1988.

McDonagh, Philip, 'The strengthening of security in Europe: the Stockholm Conference, 1984–6', *Irish Studies in International Affairs*, vol. 2, no. 3, 1987.

MacKernan, Padraic, 'Ireland and political cooperation', *Irish Studies in International Affairs*, vol. 1, no. 4, 1984.

Marsh, Michael, 'Irish public opinion on neutrality and European Union', Occasional Paper 1, Dublin, Institute of European Affairs, 1992.

Noonan, Joe and Maguire, John, *Maastricht and Neutrality*, Cork, People First/Meitheal, 1992.

Salmon, Trevor C., *Unneutral Ireland: An Ambivalent and Unique Security Policy*, Oxford, Clarendon Press, 1989.

Salmon, Trevor C., 'Testing times for European political cooperation: the Gulf and Yugoslavia, 1990–1992', *International Affairs*, vol. 68, no. 2, April 1992.

Tonra, Ben, 'The internal dissenter (II): Ireland', in Stelios Stavridis and Christopher Hill (eds), *Domestic Sources of Foreign Policy: West European Reactions to the Falklands Conflict*, Oxford, Berg, 1996, pp.132–50.

White Paper, *Treaty on European Union*, (PL. 8793), Dublin, Stationery Office, 1992.

Chapter 11

Luxembourg

New commitments, new assertiveness

*Pierre-Louis Lorenz**

INTRODUCTION

In a contribution to a book by the same editor on national foreign policies
and EPC ten years ago, I noted that Luxembourg's foreign policy drew
substantially on the dynamics of collective European foreign policy-making.
It appeared in the early 1980s that a decade of European Political Cooperation had been instrumental in lifting the foreign policy involvement
of the smallest EC member state to an internationally more rewarding level.
I furthermore ventured to state that in the long run Luxembourg's very
capacity to maintain its identity in the international community would
depend on its ability to play a real part in the formulation of what might
turn out to be a common European foreign policy.[1]

Luxembourg's national foreign policy formulation over the following
decade and its participation in the intergovernmental framework of European Political Cooperation, and subsequently the Common Foreign and
Security Policy (CFSP), and its signature and ratification of the Treaty on
European Union, have validated this observation. While the 1970s were the
period of the 'upgrading' of the Grand Duchy's presence in European and
international politics, the 1980s, under the influence of domestic factors
and foreign developments, confirmed its place as an equal in the circle of
its European partners. Finally the 1990s with new and far-reaching challenges will put questions of a different kind to Luxembourg's foreign policy
establishment.

'Small' has been and will remain the epithet attached to any description
of the Grand Duchy. Demography, territory, GNP, military resources: all
objective parameters point to the category of the small and medium-sized –
some might feel tempted to think 'mini' or 'extra small'. Luxembourg is
indisputably the smallest member state of the present EU Twelve by these
criteria. Weighted voting patterns in the Council and representation in the
European Parliament reflect this position.

(*) The author alone is responsible for any views expressed in this chapter.

Luxembourg's own assessment of its smallness has changed since the very first days of EPC. Its national and foreign policy establishments have moved away from the low-key, 'conciliatory-at-all-costs' attitude so characteristic of its post-war period politicians. As former Prime Minister Pierre Werner once described it, Luxembourg's leaders' 'main contribution to the affairs of the Community has always been one of good will, of sympathetic understanding of divergent viewpoints, of attempts to reconcile them and to defend the provisions of the treaties'.[2]

Today's generation of policy-makers is following a more self-confident and active style of policy. According to Minister of Foreign Affairs Jacques F. Poos:

> Le Luxembourg a su tirer profit de sa situation d'Etat souverain au sein d'une Communauté intégrée où il peut jouer un rôle certain.
>
> Nous sommes déterminés à garder et à défendre cette position. Si de temps à autre des voix s'élèvent même au sein d'institutions communautaires pour s'interroger sur la position des petits Etats dans une Communauté élargie, je dois dire ici clairement que pour nous il ne saurait être question d'accepter une quelconque diminution de notre statut actuel.[3]

Support for this view and the appreciation in general of the international community for this active approach towards regional and international matters was expressed by the then Secretary General of the UN when he told Luxembourgers that their country plays an even more important role in international cooperation by being an active member of the EC.[4]

In general and interestingly enough, small country theory in international relations research has simultaneously registered some new perspectives. Instead of focusing exclusively on objective and quantifiable data, like size, demography and wealth, present-day research has shifted to studying the small state's interaction with other kinds of often more 'powerful', players and neighbours.[5] In applying these latter criteria, one might assess Luxembourg's case, and that of other small states, differently. The Grand Duchy seems to have managed its case well in the toughening competition of harmonization and integration. This assessment applies, moreover, not only to the present European and international communities, based on the rule of law. It would also be valid in the historical context. After all, a small state like Luxembourg has succeeded in surviving for more than 150 years in its present configuration in an often very adverse political environment.

Building on the aforementioned chapter of 1983, what follows assesses how Luxembourg's institutions have been reacting to changes generated by the European integration process over the last decade and how they have tried to influence this evolution. It analyses the adaptation of the instruments of foreign policy formulation and uses case studies by way of illustration.

REACTIONS TO THE CHANGING ENVIRONMENT OF THE 1980s

Several factors have distinguished the society and economy of Luxembourg during the 1980s and early 1990s. First, the country's economy has made steady progress throughout this period, a trend shared with most European partners. Growth has been generated mainly in the services sector, notably in banking and financial engineering, communications and audiovisual media, and in transport. Foreign investment was attracted by active promotion of the country's basic advantages as well as by its proven social stability.

Second, the last decade has seen remarkable political stability. General elections in 1984 brought a change from a liberal–conservative coalition government to a conservative–socialist majority. This centre left government was re-elected in 1989 and has, over its two tenures, provided the solid framework for the country's economic, social and political evolution throughout the last ten years. It also contributed to continuity and cohesion in foreign policy formulation. The elections of June 1994 did not disrupt this pattern of remarkable stability.

Third, there is the immigrant factor and the growing societal awareness of it. Economic growth has been accompanied by a considerable creation of jobs, very often in rather specialized sectors such as electronic media and financial services, which has caused a still increasing influx of residents, mainly from other EC member states. At present, seven out of ten new jobs are taken up by non-Luxembourgers. Unemployment nevertheless remains low at some 2.1 per cent. About one-fifth of the total workforce is composed of non-nationals, whereas about 31 per cent of the total resident population are foreign nationals.[6]

The immigration question has, therefore, begun to surface and to provide nationalists with a distinctive argument in the domestic political debate. The main political groupings, however, have stayed aloof from these considerations and have not let them influence their attitudes on foreign policy and European integration. On the other hand the question of foreign European residents' participation in future local elections remains high on the domestic political agenda.

Fourth, the awareness of Luxembourg's own distinctive national interests has sharpened in the debate on the modalities of further integration as it emerged in the 1980s over the negotiation of the Single European Act and later in the two Intergovernmental Conferences leading up to the Maastricht Treaty.[7] The tendency of larger member states to reassert themselves in the fabric of European architecture, the prospect of the admission of new members and the subsequent proposals for a rebalancing of national representation in the decision organs of the future Union, as well as the never-ending debate on the final location of some existing and some still to be created common institutions touched a raw nerve in this small member state.

As in other countries among the Twelve, all these elements combined to diffuse a feeling of scepticism, which surfaced during the process of ratification of the Maastricht Treaty.

Luxembourg was not left untouched by these developments, the more so as the discussion was affected by two more specific elements in which it considered it had a particular stake. The one pertaining to the presence of an ever-growing foreign community has already been mentioned. The other is a direct consequence of the enlargement of the Communities over the years and the aspirations of those who joined later, in the 1970s and 1980s, to host some of the still to be created common institutions. A major goal of Luxembourg's European strategy since the foundation of the Coal and Steel Community has been the consolidation of its position as host to a number of common institutions. Over the last decade, however, the smallest member state has lost out to Brussels and Strasbourg in its tireless efforts to remain one of the three locations of the European Parliament.

Nor did it succeed in making its partners respect the commitments it had received from the original six founder members on the location of any future legal and financial institutions in the Grand Duchy. These aspirations were betrayed at the Brussels extraordinary Council of Heads of State and Government in October 1993, notably on the future location of the European Central Bank and the Trademark Institute.

These events have inevitably affected the attitudes of Luxembourgers and led to more differentiated views about the European process. Opinion polls in recent years have never shown the levels of indiscriminate support (i.e. at 80 per cent or even 90 per cent) for a 'unified' Europe that was the rule up to the early 1980s. Today favourable opinion rarely gets past the 50 per cent mark.[8]

In terms of political culture, this represents something of a sea change. The designation, however, by the extraordinary European Council on 15 July 1994 of Prime Minister Jacques Santer as successor to Jacques Delors as next President of the European Commission from January 1995 will undoubtedly have an impact on Luxembourgers' perception of European affairs and may well put the negative trend into reverse.

Fifth, a major turning point for people's attitudes crystallized around the spring 1989 celebrations of Luxembourg's 150 years of independence as a sovereign state. Despite unanimous agreement on that solemn occasion that Luxembourg's present independence, stability and prosperity can only be secured by its membership in regional and international organizations, the commemorations could not bridge the gap between the abstract ideal of the independence of the small nation and the reality of the unavoidable compromises imposed by the European integration process.

In neighbouring countries critical voices on the European project have found ever-growing expression in the media and in public opinion. In Luxembourg, however, parliament and government have deliberately acted to filter and muffle these attitudes. Intent on ensuring that its pro-Europe position was borne out by deeds, the Luxembourg government succeeded in avoiding any controversial debate on the Maastricht Treaty. Indeed, the text of the Treaty was largely negotiated during its 1991 EC Presidency. The Chamber of Deputies voted to accept it in July 1992.[9] Luxembourg was then the first member state to ratify.

The foundations of Luxembourg's foreign policy consensus, however, have remained virtually untouched by these more recent developments. Throughout the 1980s the central principles have been supported by the majority as well as by the opposition parties in parliament, and by public opinion. The media have also never called them into question. They are the product of the lessons which a small state has drawn from an often anguished past, conditioned by its geopolitical situation.

It is the profound belief, firmly established in the mind of the foreign policy establishment since the First World War, that final and reliable stability and security can only be provided by the rule of international law, represented by intergovernmental or supranational organizations such as the UN, the North Atlantic Treaty Organization, the Council of Europe and above all the European Community (today, the European Union).[10] What might appear to be idealism in a large state is necessity for a small one like Luxembourg.

Yet it has become a truism for all European Union member states to admit that there is no credible and viable alternative to cooperation in an integrated Europe. Even the larger member states hold to this basic assumption as a tenet of political realism, and it naturally applies all the more to the smaller members.

THE DOMESTIC ENVIRONMENT

Inasmuch as Luxembourg does not strive for a fully fledged, global foreign policy of its own, it has never found itself at odds with common or consensual foreign policy formulation over the last decade, be it among the Twelve in European Political Cooperation or among the Sixteen in the framework of the Atlantic Alliance.

There are several domestic reasons, characteristic of the small nation-state, that might help to explain this situation, although the domestic environment is itself closely connected to Luxembourg's geopolitical situation.

One important factor is that, as is sometimes observed, in the absence of an identifiable national interest, Luxembourg's diplomacy has a tendency to rally to the majority view of its partners and allies. This is well demonstrated by Luxembourg's voting pattern in the General Assembly of the United Nations. Over the last ten years (i.e. since 1984), Luxembourg has on all but two occasions voted with the majority of EPC member countries.

Its voting pattern in the UN has been the most consistent with the EPC majority pattern of all the EC states.

This solidaristic behaviour, which is indeed pronounced, can be traced to some basic elements of Luxembourg society, which values very highly the consensual approach as the model for societal cohesion and government. This low controversy model has been internalized by the entire nation and is respected throughout political and economic life, including the political opposition and the labour unions.

The conciliatory approach has also emerged as a fundamental lesson taught by Luxembourg's own history of interaction with the neighbouring countries of the region. The approach has worked well during the post-war years. Although geography is sometimes thought less and less relevant in the electronic age, the fact remains that the further the physical distance of a third country, the less likely the possibility that Luxembourg might have any quantifiable national interest at stake, be it of an economic or commercial nature or through the presence of a sizeable expatriate community. The immediate neighbouring countries are, by contrast, of considerable importance to the small state. With them levels of inter-dependence and dependence are most developed.[11]

A common foreign policy, however, on the basis of intergovernmental cooperation, applies to third countries only and excludes relations among the members themselves. Luxembourg's bilateral political, economic and cultural links, intensive as they are, particularly with its neighbours, there-fore do not interfere with EPC/CFSP.

Another factor facilitating Luxembourg's consensual approach to com-mon policy-making is that the spheres of common foreign policy and of Luxembourg's own bilateral aspirations very rarely meet. The kind of domestic compromise resulting from diverging national interests on the one hand and common majority positions on the other, which has to be faced now and again by larger member countries, is virtually unknown to Luxembourg's small state. It has, therefore, been possible for Luxem-bourg's foreign policy-makers to deal with sensitive issues – arms exports, economic sanctions, a common attitude towards South Africa, the Middle East, and a solution to the war in former Yugoslavia – in a fairly serene domestic political climate. In the case of the FYROM (or Macedonia), for example, out of consideration for Greece, its EU partner, but with a domestic opinion not unsympathetic towards the newly independent repub-lic, Luxembourg managed, despite its earlier recognition, to proceed to the establishment of full diplomatic relations only after the end of the Greek EU Presidency, in September 1994.

Domestic tranquillity certainly helped Luxembourg's EC and EPC/CFSP Presidencies to run so smoothly in 1985 and 1991. Luxembourg's experts could always concentrate, at least in the foreign policy field, on reaching the best possible compromise among its partners, that is on acting as a broker and mediator. The Single European Act was negotiated mainly under a Luxembourg Presidency,[12] in 1985, as was the Treaty on European Union, and in particular Chapter V of the CFSP,[13] in the framework of the Intergovernmental Conference in 1991. The Luxembourg government and parliament alike welcomed the strengthening of EPC into CFSP which brought the possibility of Joint Actions and resorting in certain cases to majority voting, a compromise formula that suited the smaller member state well.

The Luxembourg government therefore also never had to defend at home any major foreign policy approach that might have been controversial to its own electorate. The additional level of domestic coordination, always present in other member states, is virtually absent from the Luxembourg scene.

This widespread national attitude of detachment on most international issues, with the notable exception of those involving human rights and development aid, is also reflected in the debates of parliament, the unicameral, sixty-member 'Chamber of Deputies'. Members of parliament are 'generalists'; none is an expert in international questions as is common in parliaments of larger countries. There are also no specialist expert staff to support MPs in their tasks.

Again as a direct consequence of size, all MPs are members of several, generally four or more, parliamentary committees. They obviously get more closely involved with those which deal with domestic questions of direct interest to their electorate. MPs' questions on foreign policy matters are rarely of an urgent nature and seldom have an immediate impact on policy formulation. Although the Chamber of Deputies Foreign Affairs Committee, together with the Defence ('Public Force') Committee, is considered among the most prestigious, its real role is less significant, at least in the field of foreign affairs proper. In the absence of any major domestic pressure groups and substantial interests abroad, the interaction between parliamentary committees and Government departments (the Ministry of Foreign Affairs in particular) is consequently of a very pragmatic, informal nature.

The main attention of the foreign policy establishment is focused on questions relating directly to EC or European Union matters which might affect the domestic situation. Objects of particular scrutiny include the Common Agricultural Policy, banking legislation, harmonization of fiscal legislation, steel industry, company law, transport, free movement and immigration, and location of common institutions.

It was the decision-making process of EPC/CFSP that raised the interest of a wider audience, much more than any substantive question of common foreign policy.[14] An adequate and equal participation in common foreign policy decision-making, as well as in the EC/EU decision process, is viewed as the residual core of national sovereignty and independence. Luxembourg politicians and MPs have become more and more outspoken since the prospect of enlargement and the possible restructuring of participation in the executive levels of the common institutions have put a question mark over the principle of the equal representation of all (especially the smaller) member states. On this issue, the Minister of Foreign Affairs stated that:

> L'égalité en droit entre Etats membres est un des éléments constitutifs de notre système constitutionnel communautaire. . . . Ce serait une grave erreur de vouloir modifier un système qui a bien fonctionné et qui, reposant sur l'égalité dans la diversité a permis à la Communauté d'avoir un tissu de relations internes empreint de confiance et respectueux du statut d'un chacun.[15]

A recent illustration of this attitude, one of the cornerstones of Luxembourg's European policy, occurred over the negotiations on adjusting the minority blocking in the EU Council upwards from twenty-three to twenty-seven votes, in response to the latest round of enlargement. During this debate in March 1994, which saw the UK and Spain oppose the remaining member states, Luxembourg sided strongly with the majority position on the ground that the smaller minority of twenty-three votes would have increased the weight of large member countries.

Luxembourg's newly elected government expressly referred in its July 1994 policy declaration to parliament to the necessity of avoiding 'a dangerous polarization' by discriminating between large and small member states.[16] By the same argument Luxembourg politicians criticized proposals put forward in a paper by the German Christian Democrats in early September 1994, exploring the two-tier Europe idea, despite the fact that Luxembourg itself was identified there as one of the five members supposed to form the 'inner circle'.

This debate marks a turning point. There are limits to the attachment of the small member state to pragmatic consensus formation, and the limit is approached when the expansion of the Union seems likely to place in jeopardy the formal equality of its member states.

At the other end of the spectrum of public interest in a common foreign policy, parliament's pragmatic attitude is matched by the aloofness of Luxembourg's media, at least so far as national positions are concerned. The press and the audiovisual media report extensively on international affairs, and have a reputation for doing so in a rather neutral and factual fashion. They almost never dispatch their own correspondents abroad, except to cover major regional or international events that might have an immediate domestic impact, such as European Council meetings.[17] Instead, they tend to rely on news agencies for their international reporting, abstaining from adding comments of their own. This attitude adequately reflects the limited national interests at stake in most foreign policy decisions.

THE FOREIGN POLICY APPARATUS IN THE 1980s

In the 1970s Luxembourg's foreign policy was mainly a reaction to the awakening dynamics of EPC.[18] The growth of EPC during its first decade stimulated the Grand Duchy's small but adequate diplomatic service to expand far beyond its traditional sphere of interest and to develop an organizational structure modelled on those of its larger partner states.

The second decade of EPC, the 1980s, saw the consolidation of Luxembourg's foreign policy as well as the practical adaptation of its foreign policy instruments, staff and material resources. Luxembourg evolved during its EPC membership from a local to a regional actor in the late 1970s and early 1980s, and has been progressing since then to an internationally recognized position.

Its EC/EPC Presidency of 1985 was a major factor in this latest adaptation. However, in contrast to the 1970s, when expansion was more clearly a response to external, albeit EPC, dynamics, the phenomenon as witnessed more recently seems to be more complex. Luxembourg's foreign policy, which had already become more active during the early 1980s, notably in the 'all-out diplomacy'[19] of Gaston Thorn, had in return started a chain reaction of responses by third states, thus moving Luxembourg gradually into the mainstream of international interactions.

The internationalization of Luxembourg's foreign policy was acquiring a momentum of its own as Luxembourg's diplomats found themselves more and more often approached with regard to matters in which they might not have a direct interest but in whose discussion they could participate by virtue of their membership of organizations such as the UN, the CSCE and the EC. Moreover, at the time of the change of government in 1984, domestic factors such as the dynamic growth of its national economy and the prospect of the forthcoming 1985 EC Presidency led the foreign policy establishment to put forward a more activist diplomatic agenda.

On a more material and organizational level, Luxembourg's diplomacy during its two Presidencies drew on the resources of its two Benelux partners only very modestly in 1985 and even less in 1991. Support was obviously needed and welcomed from the network of embassies that the next country in line for the Presidency, the Netherlands, could provide for establishing direct contacts or organizing visits in third countries where Luxembourg might not have been represented.

On matters of policy formulation however, the Presidency proved, in the words of appreciation of its partners, perfectly able to do the job that was expected. By virtue of the limited size of their domestic bureaucracies, small countries may even, as some suspect, have advantages in terms of flexibility and speed of response.

Both the Presidencies drew obvious benefits, and proportionally more than a larger country would, from the rampant institutionalization that had taken place in EPC over the years. In 1985 the presence, in its own Presidency cell in the Ministry of Foreign Affairs, of the secretarial support team of the so-called 'troïka' proved highly valuable. Luxembourg felt less inhibited than some of its partners and integrated this small European team fully into its own. As a consequence it turned to the troïka secretariat not only in procedural and organizational matters, but also on questions of policy.

By 1991, this itinerant formula had been exchanged for the sedentary EPC Secretariat in Brussels, better staffed and upgraded by the appointment of a formal head. Again, as a small member state, Luxembourg was able to use the full potential of this intergovernmental tool. Consultations on matters of substance with the head of the team became an integral part of any policy initiative. Breaking with the pattern of previous Presidencies, which had been entirely based in one location, this new formula divided up intergovernmentalism between the country's capital and Brussels. Bridging this distance, although a matter of routine with modern communications, put some additional stress on a country with few diplomatic staff.

Had there been any pervasive doubts as to the capacity and efficiency of the smallest member state, these past two Presidencies, it is felt in Luxembourg, must have brushed them aside. On the other hand Luxembourg is finding that yesterday's accomplishments do not inevitably ensure recognition tomorrow. This theme has been recurrent in policy-makers' foreign policy statements and it has been one reason why Luxembourg has not shied away from running its WEU Presidency (from July 1993) for a whole twelve months on the same political guidelines and flexible organizational scheme as it has done for its EC/EPC Presidencies. Since the WEU moved to Brussels in January 1993, the basic Presidency team and the secretariat of the organization have been co-located in the headquarters of the organization, also facilitating contacts with the Atlantic Alliance – as foreseen by the Treaty on European Union. Not only Luxembourg but also its WEU partners have felt sufficiently confident as to confirm the implementation of the decision of the European Council of October 1993 to reduce it to a regular period of six months in line with the EU Presidency, only after the completion of Luxembourg's full term in July 1994.

Over this last decade (1984–94), Luxembourg has increased the number of its embassies and missions abroad by almost half and has added some 50 per cent to its permanent diplomatic staff. A further expansion, albeit more moderate, is envisaged over the years to come. This is certainly a most atypical development at a time when all other members of the international community have been downsizing their foreign policy machineries, sometimes significantly.

This increase in personnel, material resources and representations abroad also exceeds the average increase in the size of Luxembourg's domestic administration over the same period.

Luxembourg's growing salience on matters of policy has generally preceded the adaptation of the tools of its diplomacy. While embracing in the framework of the EC those major questions it considers essential in the light of its national interest, Luxembourg, a founder member of the Atlantic Alliance and the WEU, but basically a civilian state, has been aiming simultaneously to give tangible proof of its solidarity with its partners on common foreign policy initiatives.

An enhanced visibility and presence on the international scene has thus become crucial to the credibility of this small member state's diplomacy. It has had to stretch its human and material resources to extraordinary limits to achieve this goal. Luxembourg's credit as a competent actor, on the basis of the substance of its European policies and its domestic achievements, has been steadily on the rise in EC partners' capitals, as in Vienna, Oslo, Stockholm, Helsinki or Bern, but also Washington and elsewhere. The increasing frequency of bilateral visits and contacts, as well as the regular reports in the international media of Luxembourg's views support this claim.

The most visible sign of appreciation by its immediate neighbours and other European partners, however, crystallized in July 1994 in the nomination of Luxembourg's newly elected Prime Minister to head the next EU Commission. Media coverage of the decision and comments by European and allied governments were in agreement quoting the country's widely appreciated track record in the field of European integration, as well as the specific achievements of its last EC Presidency. Many even mentioned the fact that Luxembourg's draft of what was to become the Maastricht Treaty had been so widely acclaimed by most of its partners that the succeeding Presidency's attempt to rewrite it only led to dramatic failure. Luxembourg, by contrast, had been able to satisfy leaders like John Major, François Mitterrand, Helmut Kohl or Felipe González, who are not always able to agree among themselves on questions of European integration. There was also considerable praise for Luxembourg's own domestic achievements, and for the fact that it was the only EU member already satisfying the economic and financial convergence criteria.

Contrary to former Luxembourg Prime Minister Gaston Thorn's bid for the EC Commission's chairmanship fifteen years ago, this time Luxembourg's candidate was chosen not only because he seemed personally less objectionable and therefore a potential mediator, but also because his country's policies during his years in office had convinced his peers that Luxembourg had become a credible player in the EU team.

NEW INTERESTS, MORE MISSIONS

Examples of Luxembourg's diplomacy foraying into uncharted terrain abound over the last decade. The motivation sprang first from a voluntarist approach to defending and strengthening its position in EPC/CFSP and then from a desire to secure relationships built up through fast-growing economic activity and ensuing across-border interdependencies. Further encouragement then came from public opinion, which showed a greater readiness to contribute to common causes in the framework of international organizations. Finally, the end of the Cold War and the ensuing revival of the UN has opened new opportunities for small country participation.

As an active member in the CSCE process since the days of the Helsinki Final Act, Luxembourg has engaged in arms reduction and arms control efforts since the Stockholm Conference and the Treaty on Conventional Forces in Europe (CFE). This, and later the breakup of the Soviet Union, was the starting-point for developing a new orientation for its armed forces.

As a signatory of the CFE treaty and the treaty on Open Skies, Luxembourg set up special units to participate in multinational missions of verification. It joined with Belgium and the Netherlands in 1993 to sign a cooperation agreement on joint participation in the Open Skies regime. At the end of the Gulf War it participated with a military unit in the UN humanitarian mission in northern Iraq to help the Kurdish population. It sent EC monitors to Croatia and Slovenia and assigned a contingent to the UN peacekeeping force (UNPROFOR) in Croatia (Slavonia). It received some 2,000 refugees from former Yugoslavia, more per capita than any of its partners in the EC or NATO. Last, its monitors participate in the sanctions enforcing WEU mission on the Danube.

The first common action to which Luxembourg contributed, if in the particular case only in a financial sense, was the mine clearance operation in the Persian Gulf in 1987–8, organized in the WEU framework.[20] During the Gulf War in 1991 it contributed substantially to the Allied Coalition effort, individually and again under the auspices of the WEU. These missions represent a considerable effort for a country with an army the size of a battalion.

The policy-makers and population of the country have both realized, with the country's increasing involvement in international affairs, that equal participation in the international community, and in regional European circles for that matter, might have its price. Having a voice on the board and making it heard needs the credibility which comes from actual solidarity and the taking of responsibility in the field. As a consequence Luxembourg has become anxious in recent years to be seen to be contributing on a regular basis and often even more than its share.

The most visible symbol of this new orientation is the participation of units of Luxembourg's army in multinational operations abroad and outside the scope of contingencies foreseen by the Washington Treaty. This has indeed been the first time Luxembourg has ever actually joined in any activity of this kind, whether on or outside (in the case of protecting the Kurdish populations) the European continent.[21]

A major legislative effort was necessary to permit such a contribution, as there was no solid legal basis to send troops abroad other than for defensive purposes in the framework of the Atlantic Alliance or the Western European Union. In 1992 the Chamber of Deputies passed a law allowing for participation in peacekeeping missions under the authority of the UN or the CSCE.[22] It is no surprise, then, that the report by the Parliamentary Defence Committee commenting on the proposed law considered it a form of practical solidarity with its European and Atlantic partners after Luxembourg's 1991 EC Presidency.[23] It raised no controversy among MPs, who adopted it by a solid fifty to three votes.

THE YUGOSLAV CASE

The Yugoslav crisis, once it had turned into war, could not leave a small member state like Luxembourg indifferent. The public and its representatives in parliament have reacted strongly and emotionally to a tragedy happening relatively close at hand in Europe. A high note was struck when the Chamber of Deputies passed the law on participation in peacekeeping missions in July 1992. Up to that moment Luxembourg had only been participating in the EC monitoring mission in former Yugoslavia.

In April 1992 it contributed a military unit of its regular forces to the UNPROFOR I contingent stationed in Croatia (Slavonia). This decision was widely supported by the public and parliament (even though it anticipated the actual change in the law).[24] The Minister of Foreign Affairs described it as boosting Luxembourg's position in the UN as well as reorienting the role and tasks of the Grand Duchy's armed forces. Even a modest Luxembourg contribution would be proof of the country's ability to function as a fully fledged member of the UN, while the new task could further motivate its armed forces and enlarge their experience.[25]

At the same time Luxembourg was quite clear on the conditions regulating its involvement in former Yugoslavia. It had to take place under the overall authority of the UN, its Security Council and its Secretary General. This was of course the position both of its EC partners and of NATO's members. It was all the easier for Luxembourg to support this approach as it had always spoken out in favour of strengthening the rule of international law and those organizations that are an expression of it. What was new was the changed international security environment, in which Luxembourg, bound by solidarity to its EU partners and NATO allies, felt it both safe and worthwhile to participate in UN peacekeeping missions.

SECURITY, DEFENCE AND THE CASE OF THE WEU PRESIDENCY

Since the 1940s the bedrock of Luxembourg's foreign and security policy orientation has been membership of regional and international organizations. In particular Luxembourg prides itself on being a founder member of the Atlantic Alliance and the Western European Union. Ever since the days of nineteenth-century emigration to North America and, more recently, its liberation from foreign occupation in 1945, Luxembourg as a nation has valued transatlantic ties with special warmth.

The new double role for the WEU that the Maastricht Treaty (and the October 1993 European Council) defined as the defence component of the European Union and the European pillar in NATO therefore places a member state like Luxembourg, which is equally pro-European and pro-Atlanticist, in a potential dilemma over which course to follow. The partners with more clearcut views had generally already made their preferences known when the Single European Act was adopted and again during the negotiations on the Political Union texts.

Ever since the days of its 1985 EC Presidency, Luxembourg has been trying to build bridges between the two sides, supporting the transatlantic partnership on the one hand while promoting the European project on the other. In this it has not been alone; at least Belgium and Italy, and perhaps also Germany and the Netherlands, find themselves in the same position.

Throughout the last Luxembourg Presidency decision-makers stayed in very close contact with their North American allies and exchanged views on the progress of the discussions in the Intergovernmental Conference on the Political Union. This cooperative attitude of 'transparency' was later practised with equally positive results during Luxembourg's year-long presidency of the WEU, from July 1993 to June 1994. It proved instrumental, before and after the North Atlantic Alliance Summit in January 1994, in fostering the acceptance of the European Security and Defence Identity (ESDI) by the North American allies.

The desire to avoid choosing between the two certainly facilitated the task of the Luxembourg Presidency of the WEU. This became particularly apparent at the NATO Summit in January 1994 when Luxembourg's Prime Minister presented the position of the WEU (on the ESDI and its relationship with the Atlantic Alliance) in the name of its member states. He did so without referring to any national Luxembourg position.[26]

However, this episode cannot help but stress the diffuseness of a national policy aiming to achieve the best of both worlds and in the process shying away from taking sides. The field of security and defence policy might not be the best in which to exercise such an approach. Yet in his yearly declaration to parliament on 27 January 1994 the Foreign Minister stated that, in taking on the Presidency of the WEU, Luxembourg is striving to assert a stronger European identity in the realm of military security, suggesting that the government is teetering towards making a choice.[27]

The limits of indecision became apparent when France and Germany created the Franco-German corps and later, in Strasbourg in early November 1993, when they proceeded to inaugurate it as the Eurocorps with the participation of Belgium. The Eurocorps consists primarily of forces to be put at the disposal of the WEU, with the consent of NATO's Supreme Commander.

Despite its sympathy for such a Europeanist initiative, Luxembourg refrained throughout its genesis from assigning forces or even observers to it. Some would consider that the size of its own armed forces might put a limit on how thinly its available resources could be stretched between its NATO commitment and the other new tasks it has been embracing so eagerly. Only towards the end of its WEU Presidency did Luxembourg feel confident enough to announce its intention to join the Eurocorps. This decision, taken on 13 May 1994, was explained two weeks later by the Minister of Defence to his NATO colleagues and subsequently to the press as flowing from 'la politique européenne que le Luxembourg, membre fondateur de la CE et de l'OTAN, a menée depuis le début de la construction européenne. Cette décision reflète la volonté du Luxembourg d'assumer sa part de responsabilité en Europe, y compris sur le plan militaire'. And the Minister concluded by reassuring the Alliance that his country's armed forces' obligations towards NATO would not be compromised by this decision.

This political decision reflects Luxembourg's desire once again to keep the delicate balance between its foreign policy and security commitments in the Atlantic Alliance framework on the one hand, and its support for a crucial initiative from its immediate European neighbours on the other hand.

COOPERATION IN BENELUX

The traditional cooperation between the three Benelux countries (Belgium, the Netherlands and Luxembourg)[28] has evolved considerably since it was created as a customs union, and later upgraded into an economic union.

Officials of the three countries meet frequently at various levels to raise matters of mutual interest. These now include EC, foreign policy, security and defence questions. The Ministers of Foreign Affairs and their Defence counterparts normally meet twice a year. Matters recently or currently on the agenda include consultation on certain institutional aspects of the Treaty on European Union,[29] cooperation with the Visegrad countries of Central Europe and with the Baltic states, and practical cooperation among the three in the field of arms control, notably the verification aspects of the CFE and Open Skies treaties.

This closeness also enables Luxembourg to associate on a preferential basis with its Benelux partners for humanitarian and peacekeeping missions abroad. Luxembourg's contribution to the UNPROFOR force in Croatia was not sent independently, but was integrated with the Belgian contingent.

This pragmatic cooperation, useful for questions of transport, communications and logistics in general, can make up for the practical deficiencies Luxembourg might experience in projecting its forces beyond its borders.

As recently as December 1992 the three Ministers of Foreign Affairs agreed to give a new dimension to political cooperation in the Benelux framework in order to enhance their input into common foreign policy formulation at the EC level.[30] Although it can take place on an almost daily basis at all levels of the CFSP process, this politically oriented cooperation has limits which are difficult to cross. The three governments have not seen eye to eye on the future of security and defence policy and on the role which the European defence component might come to adopt.[31] There are signs however that the new Dutch government which came into office in August 1994 might readjust its position and inch away from its predecessor's rather rigid Atlanticist credo.

The potential of Benelux political cooperation is substantial. The experience of forty years of very close cooperation and shared views and values cannot easily be dismissed. This nucleus could go far beyond the actual CFSP process and its potential 'Joint Actions',[32] into security and defence matters, given the pioneering role they have demonstrated so successfully in community integration matters. Three countries are always likely to be closer than twelve, and these particular three have a great deal in common.

A shadow was, however, cast over the future of Benelux as an organization when the Belgian parliament voted the new federal Constitution in early 1994. Responsibility for the economy will fall under the new regional competences. The core of the Benelux union, economic cooperation, might wither away as a result. Paradoxically this could give an additional boost to political cooperation between the three, a field left untouched by the new Belgian federalism.

CONCLUSIONS

Luxembourg's policy-makers have not wavered in their favourable attitude towards European integration. The benefits have been real. They might however, together with a more critical public opinion, have grown more sceptical about its final objective. Total integration carries the inherent risk of breaking up the small country's identity.

So far the globalization of EPC has led Luxembourg from a reactive to an active and voluntarist foreign policy, which has contributed successfully to maintaining its identity. The national stocktaking that took place in 1989 on 150 years of national sovereignty proved conclusive on that point.

A strong and closely knit regional and international community, governed by the rule of law, has been Luxembourg's belief system since the day of its independence. Support for European integration in general has remained strong, albeit less unconditional than for European Political Cooperation, a field where a small nation-state has had far fewer axes to grind.

During its participation in the early phase of EPC, up to the 1980s, Luxembourg was anxious to be seen to be carrying its share of responsibility alongside its larger partners. As a direct consequence of this collective experience, it enlarged its diplomatic resources, material and human, throughout the last decade. In this process it became aware of a phenomenon which recent small country research has been confirming: the attributes of size alone do not determine the position in which the small state might find itself; more significant is the quality of the interaction which it has developed historically with its partners.

Luxembourg's participation in EPC reads thus far like a success story. It has thrown a new light on the commonly held axiom that a 'small' country only needs a 'small' foreign policy to look after its 'small' interests. Luxembourg's foreign policy establishment consequently felt encouraged after its 1985 Presidency to engage fully in the ascending and fast revolving spiral of EPC diplomacy. A stronger participation in foreign policy matters was deemed necessary to secure its own identity in a more competitive environment. Its higher visibility on the international scene has been generating new expectations. Today Luxembourg is caught in the middle of this dynamic which initially was supposed to be the squaring of the circle and which might have created something more vicious.

Growth is limited by the parameters of size. Resources are a fixed variable everywhere, and more evidently so in a small state. The actions and ambitions of EPC are so far the unknown variable. Sooner or later the optimal point for the allocation of available resources is reached. The small state, however, arrives there earlier than the larger one.

When does it reach this crucial moment? When does further growth in activity cause its resources to be spread so thinly that the small state's very identity is called into question, not this time by external aggression but from within? This kind of lesson on diminishing returns might be the experience that the 1990s have in store for the small states in the EU. Yet past history suggests that Luxembourg is well equipped to take on yet another new challenge.

NOTES

1 'Luxembourg: the upgrading of foreign policy', in Christopher Hill, *National Foreign Policies and European Political Cooperation*, London, Allen and Unwin, 1983, p.163.
2 Pierre Werner, 'Luxembourg's challenge of smallness', in *The Atlantic Community*, Spring 1977, p.83.
3 Minister of Foreign Affairs Poos in his yearly address to Parliament, 28 January 1993, p.31.
4 On the occasion of the celebration of Luxembourg's 150th anniversary of independence, 'Séance académique du 18 avril 1989', the Secretary General of

the United Nations, Javier Perez de Cuellar, so stated in his speech: 'Le rôle du Luxembourg et des petits et moyens Pays aux Nations Unies'.

5 Smallness of states as an expression of size and in relationship with other states in international relations is a concept still very much disputed in international relations theory. Today researchers from smaller or medium-sized countries are proposing to open new perspectives to students of international relations. The quantifiable criteria predominant in the early research (e.g. Rosenau, Katzenstein) have been abandoned in favour of a more historically and politically oriented approach. The emphasis is now on how the nature of smallness might manifest itself in its time and geopolitical context.

A recent 'official' definition of smallness was given by the Luxembourg Minister of Foreign Affairs, Jacques F. Poos in his 'Declaration on Foreign Policy to the Chamber of Representatives', in 1987:

> Le rôle d'un petit pays dans les affaires internationales consiste à suivre une ligne de force dont le point de départ est son existence en tant qu'entité souveraine, et l'aboutissement son intégration – dans le respect de son originalité propre – dans les différentes sphères de solidarité dans lesquelles il se trouve intégré.

Contrast Gilbert Trausch, in his speech on the occasion of the celebration of Luxembourg's 150th anniversary of independence, 'Séance académique du 18/04/89' gave some insights into the historic dimension of smallness:

> Le Luxembourg est un Etat particulièrement sensible à l'environnement international. Longtemps il était pris dans le champ des tensions franco-allemandes et à chaque crise internationale – 1867, 1870, 1914 et 1939 – il a dû trembler pour son existence.

6 For some background information on the growing financial 'industry' in Luxembourg, as related to the specific characteristics of smallness, see: Rupert Bruce, 'Luxembourg thrives . . .', in *The International Herald Tribune*, 13–14 November 1993, p.14. See also: Ministère de l'Economie, ECO, Information letter, 7 January 1994 and 'Un portrait statistique du Luxembourg' *Eurostat*, Luxembourg, EC Publications, 1992. In 1989 the three main sectors of activity in Luxembourg employed respectively 3.8 per cent of the total active population in agriculture, 29.2 per cent in industry and 67 per cent in services. Of these, in 1993, agriculture added 1.3 per cent to GNP, industrial production 28.6 per cent and services 69 per cent. These figures have since been steadily growing for the service sector. For all other data, see *Luxembourg en Chiffres*, Statec – Service central de la statistique et des études économiques, Luxembourg, 1991, 1992, 1993, 1994.

7 Minister Poos, in his yearly address on foreign policy to Parliament, 28 January 1993 in *Bulletin d'Information et de Documentation*, Luxembourg, Service Information et Presse, 1, 1993, p.25, 'Ne soyons pas dupes: le grand rêve fédéraliste n'est plus guère d'actualité'.

8 See *Eurobarometer*, 12, 1991, after the Luxembourg EC Presidency of the first semester, 1991. To the question, 'are you in favour of a European Government?', Luxembourgers answered 48 per cent in favour and 23 per cent against. The average for the Twelve being 56 per cent in favour, 20 per cent against, the extremes being the Italians: 75 per cent in favour (9 per cent against) at the positive end, and the UK (35 per cent in favour, 40 per cent against) and the Danes (25 per cent in favour, 60 per cent against) at the sceptical end of the spectrum.

9   The Chamber of Representatives ratified the Treaty on the European Union on 2 July 1992, with 56 votes in favour and 6 against. The official arguments in favour can be read in a booklet edited by the Luxembourg Government, Department of Information and Press, *Traité de Maastricht*.

10   Minister Poos on 28 January 1993 before the Luxembourg Parliament in *Bulletin*, p.25. Also Prime Minister Jacques Santer on the occasion of the 150th anniversary of Luxembourg's independence, on the foreign policy pursued by Luxembourg since 1839: 'On nous créditera d'une expérience approfondie dans le domaine des organisations qui réunissent des nations. Nous avons acquis la connaissance des bienfaits que nous pouvions attendre de ces organisations et des abandons de souveraineté que nous devions leur consentir.'

11   See also 'Un portrait statistique du Luxembourg', *Eurostat*, 1992. In 1990 figures, Luxembourg's main trading partner for its exports is Germany, whereas its first address for imports is Belgium. On a more general level, 86.6 per cent of its total exports go to European Economic Area member countries and 95.6 per cent of its imports come from these same countries.

12   The Single European Act was adopted by the Chamber of Representatives by a 59 to 4 vote. The report of the Committee on Foreign Affairs of the Chamber commented 'Fidèle à une longue tradition en faveur de la construction de l'Europe, la Commission des Affaires étrangères ne saurait apercevoir dans l'Acte Unique a priori de nouveaux dangers pour l'exercice de la souveraineté nationale'. Chambre des Députés, *Projet de Loi*, no. 3014, p.11.

13   The Chamber of Representatives however reacted sharply when in the run-up to the two intergovernmental conferences and especially that on political union, the European Parliament attempted to strengthen its own powers. All three major parties, conservative, liberal and socialist, rejected any attempt to break the existing institutional balance which would weaken the national parliaments in favour of the EP. See Vincent Fally, *Le Grand-Duché de Luxembourg et la Construction Européenne*, vol. II, Luxembourg, Ed. Saint-Paul, 1992, p.388 ff.

14   This approach is reflected in domestic journalistic and research literature on Luxembourg's foreign policy, which rarely discusses political substance, but always the formal decision-making process.

15   The Minister of Foreign Affairs in his yearly address to Parliament on the role and situation of the small member state in *Bulletin*.

16   See also: Déclaration à la Chambre par M. Jacques F. Poos le 16 mars 1994, p.4: 'Cette difficulté concerne la minorité de blocage en cas de vote à la majorité qualifiée. . . . L'enjeu est qu'une minorité de blocage plus faible donne plus de poids aux grands Etats membres disposant de dix vois.' And: 'Conseil de gouvernement du 31 mars 1994', *Luxemburger Wort*, 1 April 1994, p.3. See also: Déclaration Gouvernementale prononcée par M. le Premier Ministre, le 22 juillet 1994, à la Chambre des Députés, p.49: 'Le Luxembourg n'accepte pas une polarisation dangereuse entre grands et petits Etats membres qui risquerait de menacer la cohésion de l'Union.'

17   Public interest and related media coverage may then rate very high: see *Eurobarometer*, nos. 35–6/91, 36–12/91 and 39–6/93) when 82 per cent of Luxembourgers considered themselves well informed on EC matters and 74 per cent judged the presidency of the EC as an 'important event'. Generally speaking, Luxembourgers considered all EC matters as of great importance. The media coverage of the EC during this period has been the highest in all EC countries. The figures remained identical two years later in the June 1993 poll.

   On the other hand, a mere 48 per cent of Luxembourgers rated the European citizenship project in 1991 as a good thing; only Denmark ranked lower with 28 per cent, while at 78 per cent Spanish citizens were strongly in favour. Two years later in mid-1993, Luxembourgers' support for the Maastricht Treaty had fallen by 11 points to some 45 per cent.

18 See Hill, op.cit., pp.158–63.

19 Gilbert Trausch, 'The Ministry of Foreign Affairs in the Grand Duchy', *The Times Survey of Foreign Ministries of the World*, London, Times Books, 1982, p.356.

20 Decided by the WEU Ministerial Council on 20 August 1987 under the Dutch Presidency.

21 A contingent of Luxembourg origin took part in the Korean war on a voluntary basis, backed by the government.

22 Loi du 27 juillet 1992 relative à la participation du Grand-Duché de Luxembourg à des opérations pour le maintien de la paix dans le cadre d'organisations internationales, *Memorial*, Recueil de législation, A no. 56, 5/08/92, pp.1744–9.

23 The draft law was discussed on several occasions on the level of the Parliamentary Commission on Defence Matters ('Commission de la Force Publique'), between April and July 1992. In its report of 7 July 1992 to the Plenary, the Commission made a direct link between this law, the Luxembourg EC Presidency of the first semester 1991 and the subsequent outbreak of the Yugoslav conflict.

The report then refers to the fact that this law represents a new stage in Luxembourg's foreign policy: 'Cette mission s'inscrit dans le cadre des nouvelles missions qui vont revenir à notre armée à l'avenir. Elle revêt plus qu'une valeur symbolique.' *Rapport de la Commission de la Force Publique*, Chambre des Députés, no. 3607, p.3.

24 See *Eurobarometer*, 6/93. However on the question of intervening in Yugoslavia, asked in March–April 1993, a European average in favour of intervention of 55 per cent was registered, whereas 52 per cent Luxembourgers were in favour. In comparison 64 per cent of Italians, 62 per cent of Dutch, 44 per cent Germans and 39 per cent of Danes approved intervention.

25 Minister Poos in his yearly address to Parliament 1993, in *Bulletin*, p.28.

26 See *Luxembourger Wort*, 11 and 12 January 1994.

27 Foreign Minister Poos in his yearly declaration to Parliament on 27 January 1994: 'En assumant aujourd'hui la Présidence de l'UEO, nous travaillons à l'affirmation d'une identité européenne plus forte dans le domaine de la sécurité militaire'.

28 It came into force on 1 January 1948 as a customs union and had developed by 1 November 1960 into an economic union.

29 Notably the common memorandum on the enlargement of the EC, as well as the one on transparency and subsidiarity. See also: Joseph Weyland, 'Le rôle des pays du Benelux dans l'élaboration du Traité de Maastricht', in *Bulletin d'Information et de Documentation*, 7/92, p.86–8.

30 At a ministerial meeting on 2 December 1992, the three countries adopted a position on coordination on foreign policy matters: 'Il s'agit en fait de donner au Benelux une vocation plus politique en permettant ainsi aux trois pays d'accroître leur influence au sein de la future Union européenne comme sur le plan international', Minister Poos in his yearly speech on foreign policy to Parliament, 28 January 1993.

31 Minister Poos in an interview with *Le Monde*, 9 December 1992:

Il y aura un autre domaine que le Benelux devra mieux couvrir, c'est la mise en oeuvre de la politique étrangère et de sécurité commune, où j'ai remarqué que les trois pays étaient souvent sur différentes longueurs d'ondes. Par exemple, pour ce qui est de la défense, la Belgique et le Luxembourg sont plus proches des thèses françaises alors que les Pays-Bas sont plus proches des thèses britanniques. Donc il reste une marge de manoeuvre pour coordonner les positions préalables.

32 Eight have already been undertaken since the entry into force of the European Union, for example the French proposal for a Stability Pact in Europe.

BIBLIOGRAPHY

Fally, Vincent, *Le Grand-Duche de Luxembourg et la Construction Européenne*, Luxembourg, Eds Saint-Paul, 1992 (2 vols).

Gambles, Ian, 'L'intégration européenne de sécurité dans les années 90', *Chaillot Papers*, no. 3, 1991.

Hoscheit, Jean-Marc, 'La présidence du Conseil des Ministres des CE: les présidences du Grand-Duché de Luxembourg', in Colm O'Nuallain (ed.), *The Presidency of the European Council of Ministers*, London, Croom Helm, 1985, pp.187–208.

Hrbek, R. and Läufer, T., 'Die Einheitliche Europäische Akte. Das Luxemburger Reformpaket: eine neue Etappe im Integrationsprozess', *Europa-Archiv*, 6, 1986, pp.173–84.

Kamp, Karl-Heinz, 'Ein Spaltpilz für das Atlantische Bündnis? Das deutsch-französische "Eurokorps"', *Europa-Archiv*, 15–16, 1992, pp.445–52.

Kasel, Jean-Jacques and Hoscheit, Jean-Marc, 'Le statut international du Luxembourg', *Memorial 1989. La Société Luxembourgeoise de 1839 à 1989*, Luxembourg, Les Publications Mosellanes, 1989, pp.133–43.

Mahncke, Dieter, 'Parameters of European security', *Chaillot Papers*, no. 10, 1993.

Schmuck, Otto, 'Der Maastrichter Vertrag zur Europäischen Union', *Europa-Archiv*, 4, 1992, pp.97–106.

Spang, Paul, 'La représentation diplomatique du grand-Duché de Luxembourg et l'étranger de 1815 à 1947', *Hemecht*, no. 43, 1991, pp.563–70.

Vogel, Heinrich, 'Integration and Desintegration: das europäische Dilemma', *Europa-Archiv*, 15–16, 1992, pp.433–8.

Werner, Pierre, 'Luxembourg's challenge of smallness', *The Atlantic Community*, Spring 1977, pp.80–4.

——'Le Luxembourg et l'idée européenne', *Memorial 1989*, op.cit., pp.167–78.

Chapter 12

The Netherlands

The weakening pull of Atlanticism

Alfred Pijpers

INTRODUCTION

After a long period marked by somewhat unbalanced, partly contradictory attitudes (ranging from being a very faithful NATO ally in the 1960s, to becoming a 'critical' ally in the 1970s, with strong sympathies towards the Third World), Dutch foreign policy has assumed a more stable pattern since the mid-1980s.

The rather uneven record of the 1960s and 1970s was to a certain extent due to the traumatic loss of its colonial status, which The Hague sought to offset by developing alternative overseas outlets through NATO and the Third World. Over the years, however, the Netherlands has learnt to adapt itself to the reality of being mainly a prosperous 'smaller medium–large' trading nation on the edge of the European continent. European Political Cooperation (among other things) has been instrumental in this process of adaptation and 'normalization'. In recent years the end of the Cold War has further helped to give Dutch foreign policy a more European, continental outlook (although still within a nominally Atlantic framework), with inside the European Union an increasingly economic, political (and partly even military) orientation towards Germany, and an active, middle-of-the-road contribution to the evolving CFSP. But this adaptation has not yet been completed, and the combination of a salient overseas past with a new 'continental commitment', does from time to time still create serious dilemmas for Dutch foreign policy[1].

In order to trace this 'Werdegang' [progression] from a strongly global foreign policy tradition to a more European–continental orientation, we shall first review, in the second section, the Dutch 'trauma of decolonization', and the mechanisms put into place to compensate for the loss of a colonial status during the 1960s and 1970s. In the third section a brief survey is given of the normalization and 'Europeanization' process which since the early 1980s has been increasingly characteristic of Dutch foreign policy and Dutch policy in EPC (with some notable exceptions). The fourth section deals with some characteristic elements of the Netherlands' European policy on the eve of 'Maastricht', while in the fifth section an analysis is presented of the various current foreign policy dilemmas of the Dutch 'province'[2] of the European Union.

POST-COLONIAL FOREIGN POLICY

The 'trauma of decolonization'[3]

The largest shock for Dutch society and Dutch foreign policy this century (apart from the German occupation) came from the loss of the Dutch East Indies, taking effect during a prolonged military and diplomatic struggle between 1945 and 1962.[4]

Through the centuries a very close relationship had grown up between Holland and the East Indies (the West Indies were less important in this regard). The very origin of the Dutch state had been related to the process of overseas expansion, and Dutch security inside Europe was always perceived as being connected with the balance of power in Asia, giving Dutch foreign policy an automatically global concern and outlook. In financial, cultural and psychological respects the colonial status was considered of vital importance. Indeed, the East Indies formed an integral part of the Dutch national identity and a major source of international rank and prestige. Only an intellectual and political minority cherished some doubts about the right to colonial possessions.

Small wonder, then, that the proclamation of the Indonesian 'Republik' in 1945 was felt as a tremendous blow. It was widely feared that without its colonies Holland would soon be reduced to just 'a farm by the North Sea', while the foreign policy élite was haunted by the prospect of declining to what was called 'the rank of Denmark'.[5] Decolonization, therefore, did not just incur the loss of trade or profits, but, more fundamentally, the amputation of an important part of the Dutch nationhood.

In particular, the transfer of West New Guinea (now West Irian) to the Indonesian authorities in 1962 encountered strong resistance, though the area in itself possessed hardly any economic or strategic value for the Dutch. As the last remnant of the former Dutch East Indies, however, it represented in the minds of many people, as Arend Lijphart has pointed out, 'the symbol of Holland's continued national grandeur, power and moral worth'.[6]

Quite understandably, the Netherlands sought compensation for this traumatic loss. To this end the EEC was, of course, very useful in economic respects, but NATO, and the Third World in particular, provided the channels through which the Netherlands could continue one of the more distinctive traits in its foreign policy: a strong overseas orientation.

Compensation in NATO

As a mainly transmaritime league (in geopolitical terms) NATO was in this respect very useful. The Royal Dutch Navy, for instance, traditionally the most prestigious element of the armed forces, lost with the East Indies the greater part of its area of operations, but thanks to the alternative employment offered in North Atlantic waters it was able to remain one of the largest navies in Western Europe. Joseph Luns, Foreign Minister from 1952 to 1971, particularly favoured strong relations with NATO countries such as Britain or Portugal for the sake of security, but also because he had a weak spot for seafaring nations with a proud colonial past. The Dutch preference for NATO was reflected in its adoption of the role of a faithful ally, with great trust in the American (nuclear) security guarantees, the rejection of independent European security arrangements, a relatively high defence contribution and (compared with other member states) a very slow rapprochement with Eastern Europe when *détente* set in during the mid-1960s. Moreover, being allied with an overseas superpower enabled The Hague to steer away from continental European power politics and security blueprints. Underlining the American predominance also served to blur the inequality between the larger and smaller European countries and provided the Dutch with extra leverage *vis-à-vis* France or the Federal Republic.

The primacy of Atlanticism in those years is best shown by the story of Fouchet, still a classic episode in contemporary Dutch foreign policy. The French proposals of 1960–62 for foreign policy cooperation contained clearly unacceptable implications for the supranational character of the EC, but the Atlantic implications caused the most alarm, as became clear from the predominant role which the famous 'préalable anglais' played in torpedoing the Gaullist project. For the entry of Britain was primarily sought in order to strengthen the Atlantic dimension of Europe, and to counterbalance a French–German axis.[7] We shall see below what has happened with this celebrated 'préalable anglais' after a quarter century of European Political Cooperation.

This (super)loyal Atlantic posture was paralleled by a number of principles towards the idea of a possible EC role in the world. Basically, for many years the Dutch continued to reject the idea of an independent political and military European Union. Each proposal for European cooperation in this regard met with strong suspicions and ran up against the policy of NATO's primacy. The EC was chiefly considered as an economic and social entity, open to further enlargement, but with merely a 'civilian' mission in world affairs. The then State Secretary for European Affairs, L. J. Brinkhorst, perceived the EC in the early 1970s as:

being active in the world, but not in the sense of playing the big power game; contributing to worldwide development by means of constructive policies in the fields of trade and foreign aid, assisting in the wise management of national resources, setting an example by its improvement of the quality of life, by a happy compromise between society's demands for freedom and equality, social justice and individual opportunity. . . . Only this Europe will be an additional force for stability and progress in the world, instead of a new factor of uncertainty, disruption, and discord.[8]

Obviously the Dutch still had a long road to go before they found themselves able to accept Article J.4 of the Maastricht Treaty (the CFSP shall 'include all questions related to the security of the Union, including the eventual framing of a common defence policy'), twenty years later.

'Tiersmondism'

The Third World too provided ample opportunity to continue as it were the 'colonial project' (in the sense of helping poor people on their way to development) in a new, wider setting. Dutch development cooperation became big business in the 1970s, with a huge budget (comparatively one of the largest in the world, and in absolute terms not far behind for instance, the total British aid effort), and a large staff (more than one-third of the personnel of the Dutch Foreign Ministry consists of development experts). Strong sympathies for certain progressive Third World regimes or opposition groups were expressed, sometimes in open conflict with other EC states or with the USA. Especially under Jan Pronk, the Socialist Minister for Development Cooperation in the Den Uyl Government (1973–7) – back in the same position in the Lubbers-III Government (1989–94) – Holland frequently adopted a more radical policy than its European partners.[9] Gross aid quadrupled in those years and by 1976 it had already reached the unprecedented level of 1.2 per cent of GNP.[10]

Minister Pronk was, furthermore, the driving force behind a host of 'forced idealistic measures',[11] ranging from verbal support for North Vietnam and Cuba, sympathy for liberation movements and the tightening of sanctions against South Africa, to a solo course in multilateral organizations like UNCTAD. In the aftermath of the oil crisis (1973–4) and the ensuing North–South dialogue, Dutch foreign policy turned increasingly into Third World policy.

By explicitly siding with the Third World and by showing sympathy for certain anti-Western regimes and movements, Minister Pronk almost automatically created frictions with various EC and NATO partners. The Netherlands was often only backed by some Scandinavian countries and many of the ambitious plans had to be shelved. The gap between intentions and realization 'grew perhaps to unbridgeable proportions',[12] while at the same time the Netherlands acquired the reputation of being a 'critical ally' in NATO. A number of proposals for conventional force reductions and steady opposition to NATO's tactical nuclear armaments programme, also contributed to this image.

The Dutch foreign policy style of the 1970s, then, was quite different from the preceding period of Atlantic solidarity and perhaps reflected the still uncertain status of a post-colonial nation. In the meantime EPC had started as a modest way of trying to get the EC member states on one line in certain aspects of international affairs. Since security and defence were kept out as subjects for consultation, while the institutional set-up remained loose and partly informal, The Hague considered the arrangement useful. But on certain points (Middle East, South Africa, role of the European Council) it had difficulties in adapting itself to this new European enterprise in the early years.[13]

ADAPTATION AND NORMALIZATION

The 1980s gradually brought a more stable pattern in Dutch foreign policy. The post-colonial, loss of status syndrome withered away (but not completely) and the Netherlands came to fall more into line with her NATO and EC/EPC partners. Hans van den Broek in particular was an active agent in this process during his long term as Dutch Foreign Minister (1982–92). The process has been marked by a number of features:

1 First, after the domestic deadlock over the installation of cruise missiles had been resolved by Gorbachev's emergence and by the INF Treaty of 1987, The Hague aligned itself quite explicitly with mainstream NATO thinking on such matters as disarmament, out-of-area problems and new doctrines. Van Staden thinks it premature to contend that the Netherlands assumed its former role of loyal ally again, but finds nevertheless that there are no significant differences left between the Netherlands and Western European countries 'as to the general attitudes and commitment to NATO and allied policies'.[14]

2 At the same time, the subject of European security cooperation had definitely lost its earlier forbidding aura. The Dutch openly favoured the development of a European security pillar by the mid-1980s, although within a predominantly Atlantic framework, and using WEU rather than EPC as a basis. In 1987 the Dutch government took an active part in the WEU's coordination of West European naval forces operating in the Gulf, and also in formulating the WEU's Hague Platform on European Security Interests of October 1987.

3 Development cooperation remained an area of high priority (both in budgetary and political terms), but it became more market oriented and followed more closely the ideas of the World Bank, the International Monetary Fund (IMF) or the EC partners. After the hectic Pronk years, a more pragmatic, businesslike approach was gradually established by his successors. They felt that while development aid should be to the benefit of developing countries, it could easily go hand in hand with export

promotion and job creation in the Netherlands itself. The idealist traits of Dutch development policy were toned down. After taking office, Pronk's successor immediately dropped Cuba from the priority list of recipient countries. The total amount of development aid disbursed declined.

By and large, then, Dutch foreign policy assumed a more or less 'European' profile as the 1980s went by. Especially through the frequent consultations of the Twelve (or Ten) in European Political Cooperation, the Netherlands was increasingly compelled to rally behind the common European stance towards various international problems. Although a certain amount of individual leeway remained possible, while from the formal point of view national sovereignty is still largely preserved, in practice Dutch foreign policy gradually had to abandon many of its peculiar traits, due to the nature of intensive European consultations on South Africa, the Middle East, Central America and Eastern Europe. To judge at least from the voting patterns in the UN General Assembly, the Dutch attitude on such issues as apartheid or the Arab–Israeli conflict usually conformed to the EU majority.[15] By the time the 1980s drew to a close, EPC had become the principal 'beacon' for the course of Dutch foreign policy, and as such was perhaps more useful to Dutch policy in NATO than the other way around.[16]

At the same time a number of the Dutch objections to certain institutional developments in EPC also disappeared. The European Council, for instance, became increasingly appreciated as a helpful platform for the successive ambitions of Dutch Prime Ministers (Den Uyl, Van Agt and Lubbers) and was accepted as one of the principal Community organs. The codification of the intergovernmental nature of EPC in the Single European Act was accepted as well, as with the creation of a small EPC Secretariat. But the institutional architecture of European foreign policy still remains a sensitive area for the Dutch (as we shall presently see), and the government has, with some success, always pleaded for a very close involvement of the European Commission with Political Cooperation.

This gradual 'Europeanization' process was not a one-sided affair. Adaptation to both the EPC policies and institutions has been facilitated by the fact that Union membership and Political Cooperation in their turn have created certain new possibilities for the international relations of the Netherlands, be they now clearly subsumed in the larger European enterprise. Participation in fact finding missions, monitoring or peacekeeping operations and, of course, the many tasks of the Presidency, are the more manifest signs in this regard. Holland has on several occasions used EPC as a platform for the promotion of human rights, still one of the few 'special' areas in Dutch foreign policy. The creation of an EPC Working Group on Human Rights in 1986 was a Dutch initiative, as was, a few years later, the compilation of the *Human Rights Reference Handbook*, a kind of internal EPC policy guide issued (by the British Presidency) in 1992.

APPROACHING MAASTRICHT

Before we analyse in more detail the present foreign policy dilemmas of the Netherlands as a member of the European Union, a brief retrospective of the Dutch position in the 1996-IGC on Political Union may be instructive, since it displays in the confines of one turbulent year such interesting parameters of contemporary Dutch foreign policy as: the relative distances to Washington and Paris; the federal or intergovernmental options; domestic influences on European integration; the burdens of the EC Presidency, and Dutch influence in the EU.

Even before the actual negotiations had started, Kohl and Mitterrand submitted a letter to the Italian Presidency (in December 1990, on the eve of 'Rome II'), in which they proposed that WEU be linked to EC–EPC and become subject to the general directives of the European Council. This plan, which after further elaboration was presented to the IGC on Political Union in February 1991, triggered a vehement debate between the 'Atlanticists' within the EC, headed by the UK, the Netherlands, Portugal and Denmark, on the one hand, and the 'Europeans', led by France, backed by Spain, Italy and initially, Germany, on the other.

The controversy did not so much relate to the fact that the Twelve should take more responsibilities in the field of security – on this subject there was and still is a consensus among virtually all member states – but rather to the question of how this enhanced responsibility might be institutionalized. The Franco-German proposal favoured a structure in which the WEU, under the global political supervision of the European Council, was to become a definite instrument of the European Union. Paris felt particularly attracted to this structure since it enhanced the authority of the European Council, in which the President of France, as the only head of state present, holds a relatively prominent position.

This was a reason for the Netherlands, next to the 'Atlantic' argument, to raise, as early as December 1990, objections to the proposal. Foreign Minister van den Broek also invoked help from Washington in order to reinforce the Dutch position in the negotiations, particularly with respect to the Franco-German tandem. In this sense the episode did indeed bring back some memories of 'Fouchet', despite the degree of 'Europeanization' already achieved in Dutch foreign policy.[17]

Another incident was also instructive for the Dutch position. It occurred during the Dutch EC/IGC Presidency in the second half of 1991. The Luxembourg Presidency (with the help of French diplomats) had submitted a complete draft treaty for Political Union at the IGC in April. Even at an early stage, this document had encountered various objections from member states, and when the Netherlands took over the Presidency it was still far from being approved. The Hague deemed it appropriate to come up with an entirely new draft treaty in order to break the deadlock. Instead of the pillared structure proposed by Luxembourg, the Dutch opted for an unified 'tree' structure with an enhanced role for the Commission, the European Parliament, and the Court of Justice in various sectors.

This draft was immediately torpedoed when it was introduced on Monday 30 September 1991 in the ministerial IGC meeting. It was rejected by nearly all the member states; the Netherlands was only backed by Belgium and the European Commission. Even Spain and Germany, although favourable towards certain federal elements in the Dutch blueprint, did not come to the rescue of the Dutch.

What were the underlying reasons behind this defeat? Strictly speaking the Dutch draft did not differ that much from the Luxembourg proposals, but the fact that The Hague presented it as a completely new text of Dutch origin was widely felt to be too pretentious. For a variety of reasons the preceding warnings and signals sent by the various capitals, and for that matter also by the Dutch Permanent Representative to the EC, were not properly understood in The Hague. It is worth analysing this breakdown in communication in more detail since it reveals a number of peculiarities regarding the Dutch role in the EC in general and the Presidency in particular.[18]

Public opinion and European integration

In Dutch public opinion there has existed for many years a broad consensus on the desired federal outline of European integration. This consensus is backed by all the major and medium-sized political parties; only the far left and far right fringe parties do not support this consensus. Furthermore it is backed by trades unions and employers' organizations, and by many other social groups, rallied behind the Dutch European Movement. As a result of this consensus there has never been a real political debate in the Netherlands on the major issues of European integration. What is more, economic integration has always been highly profitable for the Netherlands. Dutch economic growth has been more substantial than it would have been without the EC. There is hardly any social or economic sector in the Netherlands which has suffered adverse effects from European integration. Moreover, until the early 1990s the Netherlands was a net recipient of the EC, in budgetary terms, courtesy of German and British tax payers.

The idea of a more or less federalist European Union therefore encountered no objections, the less so as long as it remained shrouded in a utopian veil. Right on the eve of the IGCs, the Second Chamber called on the government – in a widely supported motion – to preserve the federalist aspects of the prospective treaty revisions. This is why State Secretary Dankert, former president of the European Parliament and himself a convinced 'Europeanist', could seize the opportunity in the summer of 1991 to put forward a federally inspired draft, which implicitly carried the full support of Dutch parliament and society, and was engineered by the experts at the Directorate-General on European Cooperation in the Dutch Ministry of Foreign Affairs (traditionally of federal stock).

Crisis overload

This strategy was facilitated by the fact that Minister van den Broek in his capacity as EC President was almost fully occupied at the time (summer 1991) with the outbreak of civil war on the Balkans and with the permanent crisis in the former Soviet Union, culminating in the aborted coup in Moscow (August) and the Soviet Union's ensuing political disintegration. For a country with hardly any substantial diplomatic expertise *vis-à-vis* Eastern Europe, or significant experience in the field of crisis management, this meant that it was forced to resort to all available means (even having to call on retired senior diplomats) to be able to prepare, for instance, missions of the troika or to provide staff for the Yugoslavia conference (which started in The Hague in September 1991).[19] As a result Minister van den Broek was fully preoccupied with crisis management in the EPC context, and had little time to deal with other aspects of the EC Presidency, including the management of the IGC–EPU.

The personal factors

Finally, a personal factor had also probably come into play. During the Dutch Presidency, Minister van den Broek was time and again outstripped by his German counterpart Genscher, who, by persistently making pleas for the recognition of Croatia and Slovenia, not only thwarted EC policy, but also frustrated the Dutch Presidency. This deeply annoyed van den Broek, who felt (with some justification) that Bonn was undermining EPC rules with respect to prior consultations and the conduct of the Presidency.

This irritation probably contributed to the fact that van den Broek, when he eventually presided over the meeting on the Dutch draft on Black Monday, stubbornly refused to make concessions, although it was technically still easily possible to amend the overambitious draft treaty. Thereupon the Netherlands was forced to resort to the Luxembourg draft.

After a few weeks the gunsmoke had cleared, however, and the Dutch Presidency was able to find a happy end in Maastricht, partly through the intervention of Prime Minister Lubbers, who had tactically remained backstage during the mishap of Black Monday.[20] But the episode taught the Dutch some useful lessons about the limits and possibilities of their influence in contemporary European affairs.

CURRENT DILEMMAS

The end of the Cold War, the disintegration of the Soviet Union, German reunification, and the Treaty of Maastricht all more or less reinforced the process of 'Europeanization'. Although NATO still performs some essential security functions for Europe and takes new tasks, doctrines and memberships into consideration, its global strategic dimension has been obviously diminished since the dissolution of the East–West balance, and the reduced significance of an American counterweight against Soviet military power. With the collapse of their colonial empire the Dutch lost their overseas interests in Asia and the Pacific, but could, as we have seen, still find overseas compensation in the wide North Atlantic waters, and their strategic coastal areas in and around the North Sea. With the collapse of the Soviet empire this particular overseas role has faded away as well, and in a sense Holland is, more than ever before in its history as a national state, thrown back upon the shores of the European continent. The Maastricht Treaty has led to a further adjustment of Dutch policy-making to the imperatives of European unification, including the CFSP. This is not to suggest, however, that with the Treaty on European Union we are more or less approaching the 'end of Dutch foreign policy'. Both in formal and in material respects there is still room for national manoeuvring, and foreign policy-makers in The Hague are kept occupied by a number of dilemmas, partly related to their long overseas past. The principal foreign policy problems for the Netherlands in the 1990s might be grouped under five headings.

Defence and security

As a consequence of NATO's political and military transformation, the Dutch armed forces are being completely reorganized. The reduction of personnel in the 1990s will be in the range of 45 per cent, conscription will be abolished, while equipment and budgets will be adapted accordingly. In 1990 the Dutch armed forces (both military personnel and civilians) amounted to nearly 130,000 persons; in 1998, when the reorganization should be completed, this number will be reduced to about 70,000.[21]

The larger part of the Dutch Army is fully incorporated into a German–Dutch Army corps with an integrated command structure. Plans for a virtual merger between the Royal Dutch Navy and the Belgian Navy are in an advanced state. New flexible units have been created (in particular the Air/Mobile Brigade of about 3,500 troops) for new political and military tasks, both inside and outside Europe. The command structure, fighting doctrines and operational tasks of the Dutch defence forces have been virtually 'denationalized'.

European security is, according to the Dutch government, now primarily a matter of multilateral crisis management, to be conducted through the various international bodies (UN, NATO, OSCE, WEU) with responsibilities in the field of security. The defence of the realm is not completely forgotten in the new Dutch priorities, nor are the core functions of NATO. But a direct military threat from Russia or any other power is no longer considered a distinct possibility and concern for the territorial integrity of the Dutch state takes only second place, at least for the time being.

Despite all these changes, at least one classical dilemma remains: where exactly should Dutch efforts be located on the Euro-Atlantic map? Although we may assume that, as a rule of thumb, Dutch foreign policy is now primarily shaped through the proceedings of the CFSP in general political terms, it is also true that NATO's political consultation machinery and Washington's interest in European affairs remain positively appreciated in The Hague. Furthermore, in strict military–operational terms NATO's infrastructure is still considered indispensable for any serious crisis management operation beyond traditional peacekeeping. The Maastricht perspective on the link between the EU and the WEU is accepted, but as long as the operational capability of the WEU planning cell remains weak, the WEU is not considered to be a key organization in the present Dutch security set-up.

The Dutch attitude to the Eurocorps is even more reluctant, since this 'European Army' has situated itself in principle outside NATO's command structure. Besides, the virtual integration of the Dutch army into the (NATO-tied) German–Dutch Army Corps, made it physically impossible to allocate substantial numbers of troops to the Franco-German led Eurocorps. There are just two or three Dutch officers liaising with the Eurocorps headquarters in Strasbourg, a modest arrangement that suits The Hague very well.

In addition to these Euro-Atlantic concerns, the UN system (in particular) and the OSCE are considered useful in terms of providing for the necessary legitimation of European security activities. The UN Agenda for Peace, with its rich menu of quasi-military options like preventive diplomacy, peace-making, peace forcing, peacekeeping, and peace building, is strongly supported by the Dutch government. By the mid-1990s Dutch troops were involved in six or seven UN operations, ranging from UNAVEM II in Angola, UNTAC in Cambodia, UNOMSA in South Africa, UNAMIH around Haïti, to UNPROFOR I and II in former Yugoslavia.

The Organization for Security and Cooperation in Europe (as the CSCE became known in 1994) is considered similiarly useful as an instrument for political stability in Europe. The Dutch government works hard to give it a higher legal status, and was pleased with the nomination of former foreign minister Max van der Stoel as the first OSCE High Commissioner on Minorities. Together with his German colleague Klaus Kinkel, Foreign Minister Peter Kooijmans initiated a joint plan for improving decision-making of the OSCE in the spring of 1994.

All these activities in the UN or OSCE framework draw a lot of attention in the Dutch mass media, and might easily give the impression of a nation actively involved in world affairs, and fully prepared to take all necessary measures together with her partners in order to restore or preserve peace and stability, including military ones. Appearances can be deceptive, however. Peacekeeping is much cheaper than defence in both budgetary and manpower terms. As noted above, defence expenditure is being strongly reduced, and peacekeeping operations cost only a fraction of the total available budget. Even in 1994, with just 3,300 personnel involved in UN missions, the Dutch Defence Minister, Relus ter Beek, aired his concern that the limits of the Dutch contribution to peacekeeping operations would soon be reached.

Bilateralism revived?

A second set of challenges is formed by the Dutch international position in its bilateral aspect. Dutch foreign policy after the Second World War has always predominantly been conducted through the big multilateral channels of NATO, the EC and the UN. Within and outside those frameworks, Holland (as every other country) has maintained an extensive network of bilateral relations, largely subordinate to the priorities of the various international bodies, but partly independent thereof.

This network of bilateral relationships is being remodelled, due to the big transformations in East and West (but also the South). Some features stand out:

Relations with London, Bonn and Paris

The metamorphosis of NATO has as its logical corollary that Dutch relations with London, Bonn and Paris are also appreciated in a different way. In the 1960s The Hague cherished the 'préalable anglais' because Britain was valued both as a security gangplank to the USA and as a counterweight to Franco-German plans. Today these functions are less obvious. The diminished Atlantic security dimension makes the London–Washington 'special relationship' less essential, and (for example) the joint UK/NL Amphibious Force (created in the 1960s for a task on NATO's northern flank) less crucial. There is a growing feeling among certain Dutch politicians and opinion leaders that the British role in Europe and the European Union on the eve of the twenty-first century is not very constructive, from either an economic/monetary, or a political perspective.[22] Franco-German bilateralism is still viewed with some misgivings (as the Corfu European summit in June 1994 showed), but it is also recognized in The Hague that cooperation between the two countries is an essential prerequisite for European stability at a time when the European Union is threatened by the combined forces of rising unemployment, an adverse public opinion (or serious political crises) in several member states, and the uncertain perspective of a widening membership. We should certainly not draw too many conclusions from this changing picture. The relationship between The Hague and London is still in all respects extremely stable and friendly (while Paris for instance has been viewed in the past with considerable mistrust),[23] even if the general orientation seems to be shifting in an easterly direction.

The swing to Germany

It is not wholly surprising that against this backdrop of reversed alliances, Dutch opinion (at least élite opinion) is increasingly, and openly, in favour of a strong(er) political attachment to Germany. Though the Dutch government is still discreet in this regard for obvious diplomatic reasons (and the subject remains a very sensitive one among certain sections of the broader public), it has requested an opinion from the Advisory Council for Peace and Security on the future prospects of the Dutch–German relationship.[24] All major parties represented in the Second Chamber of Parliament have declared themselves to be in favour of a stronger political orientation towards Germany, and this view is supported by leading intellectuals and journalists.[25] In economic respects the relationship between the two neighbours was already very close, as reflected in the mutual trade figures or the DM–florin connection in the European Monetary System, and so (through NATO) has been security cooperation. The rather open political sympathy for Germany is, however, a new phenomenon, and as such is perhaps symptomatic of the continental–European direction of Dutch foreign policy in recent years. The creation of a joint German–Dutch Brigade (now the Army Corps) in March 1993 (legitimized under Article J.4.5. of the Treaty of Maastricht) was partly meant to find new tasks for the armed forces in the post-Cold War setting, but it is also symbolic of the weakening pull of a long overseas tradition (keeping in mind also what we have just said about the UK/NL Amphibious Force).

Regionalization

The West European unification process has not only bound the member states to stricter common rules and legislation, but has at the same time contributed to the regionalizing – and federalizing – tendencies within some member states. In particular the more prosperous regions in Western Europe (i.e. Catalonia, Northern Italy, Flanders) tend, armed with claims to regional autonomy, to bypass their own national capitals, and to deal directly with both 'Brussels' and other political and economic centres in Europe.

In Belgium, this 'regionalization' process found a natural breeding ground in an already deeply divided country, and has resulted in the creation of three autonomous regions, and three autonomous communities, all with certain foreign relations powers, in addition to those of the federal Belgian government. In this kaleidoscopic diplomatic spectrum, prosperous Flanders has become the main economic and political interlocutor for The Hague, though the Dutch government takes great care to maintain, at least officially, an evenhanded approach with the authorities of the Walloon entity. Again, the new bilateral pattern is not radically different from the previous relationships, but regional political cooperation among the low countries has become more complicated, while the economic and monetary tasks of the Benelux (which celebrated its fiftieth anniversary in 1994) have been or are being taken over by the European Union. Although there are normally Benelux consultations on the eve of a European Council meeting, while the three from time to time adopt common positions in, for instance, the OSCE, the Benelux does not really operate as a political bloc. Even more, the Dutch government is becoming reluctant to present Benelux too much as an entity within the European Union, out of fear that in the next round of EU treaty revisions, the group will be considered as more or less one member state by the others, with all the diminishing returns for each in institutional respects.[26] A pioneering Benelux role in, for instance, the CFSP is now even less likely than before. (The only thing left to be mentioned in this respect is the longstanding Dutch logistic and personnel support for the Luxembourg diplomatic service, in particular during the Luxembourg Presidencies of the EU).[27]

The new states to the East

Another problem is the conduct of bilateral relations with the new states in the former Soviet Union. Holland has not much experience with this 'heartland' of the continent. Relationships with the new Baltic states and the other Republics were opened with some unease in 1991–2, and there is a persistent lack of money and experts to staff embassies. Here more than elsewhere, The Hague uses the multilateral channels of the EU, OSCE or the EBRD, while it strongly supports the attempts to create joint diplomatic missions among the Fifteen.

It is perhaps illuminating for the toughness of diplomatic traditions that even after the opening up of Eastern Europe, the Dutch government does not yet possess a single large- or middle-range diplomatic mission in any East European or former Soviet capital. The Dutch embassy in New Delhi still remains larger than the Dutch embassy in Moscow or Kiev.[28]

Whither the Third World?

The third large issue area of contemporary Dutch foreign policy remains development cooperation. Here fundamental changes abound as well. The concept of 'Third World' as a collective name for the destitute former colonies is no longer very appropriate. In the Middle East, Southeast Asia and Latin America, a number of countries have come to achieve development to such an extent that they match the rich West in several ways. Numerous problems in the Third World, like environmental pollution, the scarcity of raw materials, or soaring debts, are not only inherent to poverty or underdevelopment. Many of these problems are found equally in Eastern or Southern Europe, or they have, like the problem of refugees, a diffuse, worldwide character. Both geographically and ideologically, concepts like 'Third World' or 'North–South' conflict have consequently lost much of their relevance. Moreover, due to the collapse of socialism in Eastern Europe, various 'alternative' development models in, for example, Cuba, China or Tanzania, have also lost their appeal to certain sections of Dutch public and élite opinion. The world is now virtually decolonized. The days of apartheid have gone, and so has a standard object of Dutch moral concern. Minister of Development Cooperation Pronk has more or less admitted these developments in his White Paper *A World of Difference* (1991): 'The year 1990 is a psychological turnabout in post-war history. It marks the end of decolonization and the end of the Cold War'. The end of the East–West conflict, between the First and Second World, also marks the end of the Third World as a distinguished form of political identity for developing countries.[29] In the view of Minister Pronk this implies that the development issue is no longer exclusively related to the Third World.

But the relationships between the Netherlands and its former colonies are not yet completely 'normalized'. Virtually one-third (generally the better educated) of the population of Surinam lives in Holland. This impoverished and very unstable country, which is a bottomless pit for development money and an important link between the Colombian drug cartels and the North American and European consumer markets, causes endless headaches for the Dutch government (as for the American Drugs Enforcement Administration, well represented in the US Embassy in The Hague). The Fifteen are undoubtedly quite happy to leave this particular country as a Dutch 'domaine réservée' in the foreign policy of the European Union. Through the Netherlands Antilles the Dutch are still a player in the Caribbean region, conducting a regular political dialogue with Venezuela and other states in the area.

The relationship with Indonesia is completely different. This country – the fourth largest in the world in population terms – is one of the rising tigers in the very dynamic economic environment of the Association of South East Asian Nations (ASEAN) and the Asia–Pacific region. Though its relationship with the Netherlands became stable as the years went by, it was never exclusive, nor very easy. The Hague in particular had problems with the human rights record of the Suharto governments, while Jakarta complained (for the same reason, among other things) from time to time about the patronizing habit of its former colonizers.

The relationship went sour after a bloody incident in November 1991 in Dili, the capital of East Timor, where units of the Indonesian army killed dozens of unarmed people who were demonstrating for independence. The massacre caused much indignation in The Hague and the Dutch government called for an investigation. Minister Pronk threatened to suspend development aid if Jakarta did not adequately respond to the international protests. At that point the Indonesian government retaliated in kind. In March 1992 it decided no longer to accept any Dutch development assistance (a small part of the total amount of aid it received in any case), and asked the World Bank to form and preside over a new group of donor countries. The influential Intergovernmental Group for Indonesia (IGGI), which had so far met every year in Amsterdam under Dutch chairmanship, was dismantled.

The Dutch nation was stunned. The unexpected Indonesian step was felt as the very last move in the long process of decolonization, and it was precisely meant in that way. Jakarta wanted to signal that in the present world the relationship between a leading regional power in Asia and an ordinary member state of the European Union would no longer be determined by any colonial prerogative. For the policy-makers in The Hague this was surely another painful lesson after half a century of traumatic decolonization already. In combination with the unification tendencies taking place at the same time in Western Europe (and Germany), it underlined once more the Dutch predicament in contemporary world politics.

The politics of rank

Although the manifold multilateral and bilateral concerns of agriculture, peacekeeping, human rights, refugees, interest rates, cabotage, trade in services, and the pollution of the Rhine or the North Sea, undoubtedly form the bulk of contemporary Dutch external relations (sometimes just domestic politics writ large), one sensitive foreign policy issue reemerges time and again: a preoccupation with rank and prestige. The Netherlands is labouring under what sociologists call 'rank disequilibrium', caused by the combination of certain medium-range power characteristics with the resources of what is clearly only a small European country. The frustration of Holland is that it is not large enough to belong, for instance, to the upper layer of the Fifteen, while it does not feel small enough to be heaped on the mounting pile of European 'Kleinstaaten'.

On many economic indicators the Netherlands belongs to the upper 10 per cent of the more than 180 countries which today occupy the world's surface.[30] In terms of GNP, trade, foreign investments or development aid the Netherlands is approaching the fringes of G-7 qualification. The Dutch share in the ECU basket was in 1994 on an equal level with the share of the Pound Sterling. But in other respects Holland is clearly no match for the Big Four, and it was forced to notice after 1986 that Spain had become the largest of the medium-range member states in the European Union (while elsewhere in the world, as we have seen, many younger states have become major economic or political competitors as well). This slightly downward-mobile, medium-range status inconsistency creates diplomatic problems which 'real' small countries (like Luxembourg or Denmark) usually do not have.

The Hague, for instance, is still very much on its guard against possible 'directoires' being formed by the larger EU or NATO states, although, as we have seen, it participates in an extensive network of bilateral consultations, while the idea of 'core groups' becomes much more attractive when Benelux countries are included. The Dutch government is in principle in favour of further enlargement (if the prospective members fulfil the entry conditions), but not if a new wave of smaller members is going to lead to institutional adaptations in favour of the larger member states. The government sticks to the 'disproportionality principle' and was relieved when the Brussels European Council of December 1993 decided not to diminish the position of the Netherlands in the new rotation scheme of the EU Presidency after 1995. In a Benelux memorandum, published on the eve of the Lisbon European Council in June 1992, the Dutch viewpoint on enlargement and institutional reforms is succinctly formulated: 'The basic idea which should be endorsed is that in the Commission, the Council, and the European Parliament the larger countries will have to accept some over-representation of the smaller member states'.[31]

Holland knows that it is definitely outside the G-7, but it is inside the G-10, and it takes great care to keep membership of this latter club restricted. The repeated attempts of Spain to become a member of this economic–financial body were defeated by the Dutch, with the argument that if Spain could become a member, then Austria, Sweden or Norway would also have to be taken in, with the risk of diluting the G-10 to the point of identity with the G-24. But in due course, EMU will probably help to diminish the significance of the G-10. Status concerns also often dominate the discussion on Dutch representation in international organizations. Dutch candidacies for high-level nominations in international organizations, or for the seat of such organizations in The Hague or Amsterdam, are broadly spelled out in the media.

Such matters are not just considered in terms of their functional relevance for certain specific national or other interests, but very much in terms of a perception of declining international rank and prestige.

The organization of foreign policy

This broad variety of Dutch external relations is steered from The Hague by a comparatively large ministry. The size of the ministry and of the foreign service reflects the still substantial international involvement of the Netherlands. Around 1,700 people staff the ministry itself, while nearly 2,000 diplomats occupy more than 85 embassies and other missions abroad. But there are frictions.

First, despite all the newly proclaimed political and economic tasks in the 'new world order', there remains a remarkable lopsidedness between the resources spent, for instance, on Eastern Europe or the former Soviet Republics and the expenditure on the traditional overseas development assistance.[32] The Directorate-General for Development Cooperation in the Foreign Ministry spends much more money than the DG for European Cooperation.

A persistent political problem of the organization of foreign policy is related to the competition between the Foreign Minister and the Prime Minister about the primacy of interdepartmental coordination. In the Dutch constitution the Prime Minister is just *primus inter pares*; the Foreign Minister bears the prime responsibility for the conduct of foreign affairs. Things are different in the European Union. Due to the steadily increased role of the European Council over the years in both Community and CFSP matters, and because of the growing involvement of domestic ministries and subnational authorities with the business of the European Union, the logic of giving the Prime Minister a larger share in the coordination of European politics also became more obvious. Hence there is an inbuilt tension between the two offices, particularly when two strong politicians like Lubbers and Van den Broek are their occupants.

CONCLUSIONS

The basic pattern of post-war Dutch foreign policy has been determined to a considerable extent by the necessity of adapting state and society to a less influential position in international affairs. In a world with rising regional power centres in the former colonial areas, amidst a European Union of fifteen or more member states, and now in the shadow cast by a united Germany, Holland has perhaps more than at any time in the past settled into its true international place, according to its size, economic strength and reputation. Immediately after the Indonesian declaration of independence, half a century ago, some observers feared, as we have seen, that the Netherlands would soon decline to be just 'a farm by the North Sea'. On the eve of the twenty-first century this picture seems not too wide of the mark for a country reliant on its agro-business as one of the mainstays of its economy. But we should not exaggerate. The Second World War and decolonization together triggered a structural decline for the countries of Western Europe, but international security cooperation and economic integration have prevented a free fall. The EC has contributed to unprecedented levels of prosperity, has come to the 'rescue of nation-state' and has also preserved or restored, through her external economic and political relations, something of the international position of Western Europe and its members.

This holds true for EPC and CFSP and their effects on Dutch foreign policy. After a hesitant start in the early 1970s, with the experience of 'Fouchet' still not forgotten, EPC gradually became an integral part of Dutch foreign policy-making. The CFSP forum is not exclusive in this respect, but it has probably become the primary political reference point for the bulk of the Dutch foreign policy decisions, including those on European security. As such the CFSP is an important stepping-stone for Dutch policies in fora like the OSCE or the various UN bodies. NATO is still considered an essential organization for strict military purposes; Washington is sometimes a useful tactical ally against Paris, but political consultation among the EU-15, with all its bilateral or trilateral variants, takes prime place in Dutch foreign policy, in terms of both substance and procedure. Compared with the situation in, say, the 1960s, this undoubtedly marks a certain degree of success for European Political Cooperation.

This point is also reinforced insofar as the many domestic pressure groups in the Netherlands, political parties, trade unions and other segments of public opinion, demand for their causes (of the Palestinians, the ANC, minorities in Central America, or the victims of the Balkan wars), that the Dutch government should first of all take an initiative to rouse its EU partners.

Even if over the years The Hague had to adapt some of its more idiosyncratic viewpoints (on for instance the Arab–Israli conflict or apartheid) to the evolving EC majority, Political Cooperation has also provided some spin-offs, like a place around the table with the big Four or Five, or participation in the Troikas, the highlights of diplomacy during a Presidency. EPC and the CFSP have surely also provided a useful platform for specific Dutch foreign policy interests, in particular the promotion of human rights. This dimension remains a central concern in Dutch foreign policy, irrespective of the geopolitical regions involved. But even on these points it is fully realized in The Hague that a unilateral Dutch foreign policy does not make much sense any more, and that the success or failure of national initiatives is to a large extent determined by the limits and possibilities of a common European foreign policy.

NOTES

1 I have borrowed the term 'continental commitment' from the title of a book by Michael Howard, in which he very aptly described the awkward British position

between overseas and European obligations. See Michael Howard, *The Continental Commitment, The Dilemma of British Defence Policy in the Era of Two World Wars*, Harmondsworth, Penguin Books, 1974.

2 The reader will recall that in the seventeenth and eighteenth centuries the Netherlands themselves were known as the United Provinces.

3 As formulated by Arend Lijphard in his classical work: *The Trauma of Decolonization*, Yale University Press, New Haven, 1966.

4 The argument in this paragraph is partly based upon my chapter in N. C. F. van Sas (ed.), *De kracht van Nederland* [The strength of the Netherlands], Haarlem, H. J. W. Becht, 1991.

5 Ibid., pp.205–6.

6 Lijphart, op.cit., p.105.

7 As I observed in my chapter on the Netherlands in Christopher Hill (ed.), *National Foreign Policies and European Political Cooperation*, London, RIIA/Allen and Unwin, 1983, p.170.

8 As quoted in Hill, op.cit., p.168.

9 Ibid., p.169.

10 Joris J. C. Voorhoeve, *Peace, Profits and Principles, A Study of Dutch Foreign Policy*, The Hague/Boston/London, Martinus Nijhoff, 1979, pp.259, 274.

11 J. J. C. Voorhoeve, 'De slinkende rol van Nederland' [The declining role of the Netherlands], *Internationale Spectator*, vol. 35, 1981, p.72.

12 J. J. C. Voorhoeve, *Peace, Profits and Principles*, op.cit., p.259.

13 For a more extensive survey of Dutch EPC policies in the early 1970s see my contribution to Hill, op.cit.

14 Alfred van Staden, 'The changing role of the Netherlands in the Atlantic Alliance', *West European Politics*, vol. XII, no. 1, 1989, pp.108–9.

15 See P. Luif, *Abstimmungsverhalten der EG Staaten und anderer ausgewählter Staaten in der UN-Generalversammlung*, Laxenburg, Österreichisches Institut für Internationale Politik, 1993, unpublished manuscript. Cf. Elfriede Regelsberger, 'European Political Cooperation', in J. Story (ed.), *The New Europe*, Oxford, Blackwell, 1993, pp.279–80.

16 As may appear from the following statement by the Dutch foreign minister: 'It would be most ideal if the positions adopted in the EPC framework would determine the viewpoints taken by the member states in other fora like NATO, WEU, of the UN Security Council', Rijksbegroting, 1994. Hoofdstuk V Buitenlandse Zaken, 23400 V, Memorie van Toelichting [*Explanatory Memorandum to the 1994 Budget, Ch. V Foreign Affairs*], p.36.

17 Cf. Bob van den Bos, *Can Atlanticism Survive? The Netherlands and the New Role of Security Institutions*, The Hague, Netherlands Institute of International Relations Clingendael, 1992, pp.45–7.

18 Cf. Robert Wester, 'The Netherlands and European political union', in Finn Laursen and Sophie Vanhoonacker (eds), *The Intergovernmental Conference on Political Union, Institutional Reforms, New Policies and International Identity of the European Community*, Maastricht, European Institute of Public Administration, 1992, pp.163–76. For a lucid analysis of the background of 'Black Monday' see: Michiel van Hulten, *The Short Life and Sudden Death of the Dutch Draft Treaty towards European Union*, unpublished mimeo, 1994.

19 The Dutch ambassador in Paris, Henry Wijnaendts, was temporarily withdrawn from his post in order to prepare the Yugoslav Peace Conference in The Hague, and to operate as a special EC envoy. He wrote an interesting book about this heavy test for Europe's foreign policy (and the Dutch Presidency): H. C. Wijnaendts, *l'Engrenage; Chroniques Yougoslaves, Juillet 1991 – Août 1992*, Paris, Ed. Denoël, 1993. See also Alfred Pijpers (ed.), *The European Community at the*

Crossroads: Major Issues and Priorities for the EC Presidency, Dordrecht/Boston/
London, Martinus Nijhoff Publishers/TEPSA, 1992, several parts.

20 Cf. Helen Wallace's assessment of the Dutch Presidency in 1991: 'That the EC
reached the point it did at Maastricht was a very substantial achievement. Hence
this is a great tribute to the abilities of the Dutch in manipulating the IGC text
as they did especially in its later stages.' Helen Wallace, 'A Critical assessment
of the styles, strategies and achievements of the two presidencies', in: Emil J.
Kirchner and Anastasia Tsagkari (eds), *The EC Council Presidency; the Dutch
and Luxembourg Presidencies,* London, UACES, 1993, p.48. For a similar view
see the contribution of Fraser Cameron of the European Commission in the
same volume.

21 See for the relevant figures of manpower and budgetary adaptation: *Priori-
teitennota* [Priorities Whitepaper of the Dutch Defence Ministry – Another World,
another Defence], Tweede Kamer, 1992–1993, 22975.

22 On this Dutch perception of the UK role, see for instance Van den Bos, op.
cit., p.65.

23 Van den Bos writes: 'According to many insiders, including officials at the
Foreign Ministry, there exists both inside and outside the Ministry a "traditional" mistrust of France.' Van den Bos, op.cit. pp.57, 67, 72. A similar
observation is made by Piet Dankert, *Les Pays-Bas et la France: l'Europe s'unit . . .
lentement,* Bergen, Vereniging Volkshogeschool Meridon, 1992, p.8. The new
Dutch Foreign Minister Hans van Mierlo, in office since September 1994, has
taken initiatives to improve the relationship.

24 *Duitsland als Partner* [Germany as partner]. Report of the Advisory Council for
Peace and Security to the Dutch government, The Hague 1994.

25 *NRC Handelsblad* (Rotterdam), 25 November 1993. See also Van den Bos, op.
cit., pp.65, 68, 72. Cf. Dirk Verheyen, 'The Dutch and the Germans: beyond
traumas', in Dirk Verheyen and Christian Soe, *The Germans and Their Neighbors,*
Boulder/San Francisco/Oxford, Westview Press, 1993, pp.59–81.

26 This fear is explicitly stated by the Government in the *Explanatory Memorandum
to the 1994 Budget, Ch. V Foreign Affairs,* Tweede Kamer 1993–1994, 23400, no. 2,
p.13.

27 The Netherlands has embassies in 87 countries, Luxembourg only in 19. Dutch–
Luxembourg diplomatic cooperation dates back to the nineteenth century, and
is legally based on the Treaty Regarding Cooperation in the Field of Diplomatic
Representation of 24 March 1964 between the two countries.

28 The Dutch diplomatic missions are divided into three categories: I. large;
II. middle range; III. others. The missions in the first category are: Bonn,
Jakarta, London, Paris, Washington, Brussels (EU), Brussels (NATO). To the
second category belong: New York (UN), Brussels (bilateral), Madrid, New
Delhi, Paramaribo, Rome, Tokyo, Düsseldorf (Consulate-General), New York
(Consulate-General). See *Explanatory Memorandum to the 1994 Budget, Ch. V
Foreign Affairs,* Tweede Kamer 1993–1994, 23400, no. 3, p.10. Cf. no. 2, p.238.

29 *Een Wereld van Verschil* [A world of difference], Tweede Kamer 1990–1991,
21813, no. 1–2, p.70.

30 As may be calculated from *The Economist Pocket World in Figures, 1994 edition,*
Harmondsworth, Penguin Books, 1993, pp.22 ff.

31 Quoted in L. J. Bal, R. Gans and J. Q. Th. Rood, 'Institutionele hervorming van
de Europese Unie' [Institutional reform of the European Union], *Internationale
Spectator,* vol. 48, 1994, p.112.

32 See on this point in particular: Jan Zielonka, 'The Dutch version of Ostpolitik',
in Alfred Pijpers (ed.) *The European Community at the Crossroads,* op.cit., pp.
205–216.

Chapter 13

Portugal

Pressing for an open Europe[1]

Álvaro de Vasconcelos

Portugal has a vital interest in Europe developing a common foreign policy. It is equally vital to Portugal that the idea of an open Europe is consolidated, meaning that the Union should not become from an economic and human point of view a closed trading bloc with a minimalist view of its own identity, and that it should increasingly seek a central role in world affairs. During the 1991 intergovernmental conference Portugal affirmed that 'the Community's external relations should be geared to the prime objective of building a Europe that is open to the world'.[2] Historical, cultural, and geographical factors have made Portugal a country with deep roots in Europe and strong links to other parts of the world, particularly to the other Portuguese-speaking nations, namely: Angola, Brazil, Cape Verde, Guinea-Bissau, Mozambique, São Tomé e Príncipe. Portugal's traditional ties to other parts of the world have also led to an international effort by Lisbon to grant East Timor, a territory illegally occupied by Indonesia and still technically under Portuguese administration, the right to self-determination. Portugal also continues to have links with the Far East because of its administration of Macao, which is scheduled to return to Chinese sovereignty in 1999.

In my opinion, the less constrained at its geographic periphery, the more active and global the European Union becomes in international issues, the more Portugal will feel that its own particular foreign policy objectives are being met by the Union. Were the European Union to revert to the stage of being a mere market, albeit huge, Portugal would be little more than a poor relation. If the capacity for international political action counts, however, then the existing Lusophone area in Africa and Latin America will also be credited to Portugal's status within the European concert. In Prime Minister Cavaco Silva's words, 'a Europe speaking with a louder voice in the international arena favours the affirmation of Portugal in the world, and especially our traditional external relations with Africa, Latin America and the Maghreb'.[3] In this light, it becomes clear why one of Portugal's concerns as regards the European Union's external action, which has been revealed since the fall of the Berlin Wall, is the need for a balance to be struck between the Union's eastward and southward priorities.[4]

EUROPE AND THE ATLANTIC?

With the exception of the Salazar years, the choice between Europe and the Atlantic has never been an insoluble dilemma for Portugal's foreign policy.[5] For the supporters of the 'ancien régime', membership of the European Community (which, had it been sought, would anyhow have been refused given the anti-democratic nature of the Salazar period) was totally incompatible with the emphasis given to the continuation of the African policy and to relations with Brazil. In those days, the choice to be made was a simple one: Portugal had to opt for the Atlantic as opposed to Europe, since Europe also meant democracy and decolonization.[6] Ironically, this Atlantic option, and leaving aside the politico-diplomatic rhetoric of good relations with Brazil, led to the continuation of an absurd colonial war in Africa and deteriorating relations with the USA,[7] the most important Atlantic power of the time. Salazar had never hidden his suspicions of American intentions, while Lisbon unilaterally continued to stress the ever less meaningful, but traditional, Anglo-Portuguese alliance.

In practical terms, Portugal's Atlanticism in those days meant participation in NATO (Portugal being a founding member) and a relationship with the USA built essentially around the Defence Agreement, in existence since 1951, which allowed the USA access to military facilities in the Azores, especially the Lages airbase. Both participation in NATO and Portuguese–American relations understandably suffered, however, as a consequence of the nearly fifteen years up to 1974 when Portugal concentrated on the sole objective of maintaining its overseas territories amidst unanimous international condemnation.

Between the onset of democratic rule in 1974–5 and Portugal's entry into the European Community on 1 January 1986, the Atlantic option began to signify the development of what the democratic leaders of the day saw as a privileged relationship with the USA and a more active participation in NATO. The new emphasis given to Atlanticism was to a large extent an 'interiorization' of the Cold War, or in other words, a natural consequence of the struggle which the main democratic parties waged against the Soviet-backed Communist Party in the period 1974–5.[8] The bilateral defence agreement with the USA was extended in 1983 for another seven years, amidst a wealth of statements stressing the vital importance of such a relationship for Portugal. During the consultations on the first review of the agreement in the post-Cold War era (which resulted in a revised agreement signed in 1993) Lisbon made an effort to extend Luso-American co-operation beyond its traditional domain into other fields such as economics and technology, and sought increased cooperation in foreign policy.[9]

Closer cooperation between Lisbon and Washington led to the creation of a troika along with the now Russian Federation in 1990 during the Angolan peace process to monitor events in this troubled African state. This troika, which from late 1992 onwards began working closely with the UN, is still in operation.[10]

The other traditional elements of Portuguese Atlanticism, Lusophone Africa and Brazil, were for a variety of reasons relegated to second place during the early years of the post-1974 democratic regime. The appearance of Marxist-inspired regimes in the former Portuguese overseas territories following decolonization greatly strained relations between them and the ruling political parties in Portugal in the second half of the 1970s, and the relations between Portugal and the new independent countries suffered accordingly.

However, by the early 1980s normal state-to-state relations began to emerge. In the early days of independence, the adoption of Portuguese as the official language by nationalist leaders of Lusophone Africa was designed to provide a unifying factor to countries made up of a variety of nations and whose borders, arbitrarily drawn at the Berlin conference, often cut across national groups, which were thus split between different states. The present-day leaders of Lusophone Africa, while stressing the import- ance of the Portuguese heritage, are increasingly aware of the need to value traditional cultures and languages.[11] As far as Brazil is concerned, in spite of all the rhetoric surrounding a Luso-Brazilian community, relations with Brazil, by far the largest Portuguese-speaking country, have remained until quite recently confined to cultural affairs. It should be highlighted, how- ever, that Brazil values its European and Portuguese cultural roots and even managed not to condemn publicly Portugal's colonial policy (singling itself out among otherwise almost unanimous condemnation) in the UN.[12]

The strongly pro-NATO, Atlanticist position held by the leaders of the country's main political parties in the period before European membership was not in itself anti-European. The then European Community and NATO were seen as complementary aspects of a world to which Portugal wanted to belong. From the onset of the democratic transition in Portugal, it was clear that Community membership was an overriding top priority in Portuguese foreign policy. As then Prime Minister Mário Soares used to say, Community membership was a national project which would endow Portugal with a new destiny. Eight years later, having become President of the Republic in the meantime, he would conclude that: 'Community membership has continued to be an invaluable contribution to bolster Portugal's position in the contemporary world, its measure of intervention in world affairs thereby becoming, in proportion, superior to its dimension as a nation.'[13]

Two rival camps emerged during the pre-accession debate in Portugal. On the one hand, there were those both on the traditional left and the traditional right who feared that membership would cause Portugal to lose freedom of external action and gradually drift away from the Lusophone world, thus putting at stake its very survival as an independent entity in the Iberian Peninsula; on the other hand, there were those who strongly believed that membership of the Community in no way prejudiced the country's 'Atlantic vocation'[14] and proposed a Euro-Atlantic foreign policy.[15] The latter has remained the most basic premise behind foreign policy since the end of the 1970s and the consolidation of democratic rule.

Integration in Europe had an important and logical effect: it brought Portugal and Spain closer together than they had ever been for centuries. For the first time since the Second World War, Portugal and Spain began to share the same fundamental options in foreign and security policy – NATO (since Spain's accession in 1982) and the European Community. Also for the first time bilateral relations were now placed within a multilateral framework. It should be noted in this regard that Portugal and Spain also share parallel interests outside Europe, particularly in Latin America and the Maghreb, in relation to which there has been a greater co-ordination of positions during the annual Iberian summits between the leaders of the two countries.[16]

FOREIGN POLICY PRIORITIES AND EUROPE

In analysing the main foreign policy priorities and how they relate to Europe, it becomes clear that Portugal seeks in relation to Portuguese-speaking Africa and South Africa to prolong, through Europe, a national foreign policy objective (the 'national' prevails over the 'European' in this area), while with regard to Latin America the objectives are to value or give substance to national objectives through the Community factor. The Mediterranean and to a lesser extent Central and Eastern Europe have become a part of Portuguese foreign policy as a consequence of European integration. East Timor, on the other hand, is a theme that Portugal has brought into European Political Cooperation, with particular emphasis on the human rights dimension.

The Lusophone world

Membership of the Community and participation in EPC have actually proved a factor in strengthening Portugal's relations with the Lusophone world, as the pro-Europeans had anticipated during the pre-accession debate. The decision of the five Lusophone countries in Africa (Angola, Mozambique, Cape Verde, Guinea-Bissau and São Tomé e Príncipe) to join the Lomé system further substantiated the notion that by joining Europe Portugal would not sever its ties with Africa.

Portugal's interests in relation to Africa within EPC are all too exclusively focused, as some contend, on Lusophone countries and to a lesser extent on South Africa. This is a common trait of the African policy of all other former colonial states, namely Britain and France, who tend to focus on the Francophone and Anglophone areas respectively. Diplomatic efforts by Portugal within the Community led to the treatment of the Lusophone Five as a regional entity on the basis of cultural affinities, this being the sole regional grouping that is not defined from a geographical viewpoint (i.e. whose borders are not contiguous). All five countries have engaged, after 1989, in transition processes, with a widely differing degree of success. Since then the theme of democratic transition in Africa has become prominent in Portugal's initiatives within EPC, and as a result communiqués have been issued to welcome the 'sense of civic responsibility' in the aftermath of each election.

Portugal has, since 1986, adopted in EPC a distinctive position in relation to South Africa, considering economic sanctions ineffective and opposing new sanctions. It has to be said that some 50–70,000 Portuguese living in South Africa could head for home in the event of a worsening crisis and that developments in South Africa have direct implications in Angola and Mozambique. In the first of the yearly reports produced by the Foreign Ministry since accession to the Community, it was stated that Portugal's 'determination' had contributed to 'check the escalation of punitive sanctions of an economic nature against South Africa'. The government felt sanctions were especially damaging to the less well off, having particularly in mind the considerable migrant miners' community from Mozambique.[17] Portuguese positions were not far from those of Britain or Germany, who shunned the more radical stances of France, Denmark, the Netherlands and Ireland. Since the very beginning, Portugal lent its support to F. W. de Klerk's reforms. In 1990, on the occasion of the Dublin informal ministerial meeting, Portugal along with Britain stood for support and encouragement for the reform and political dialogue initiated by President de Klerk, and Lisbon persistently proposed, throughout the rest of that same year, that the EC sanctions imposed in 1985 and 1986 be eased.[18]

Insofar as the peace and transition processes in its own former colonies are concerned, Portugal's action is mainly national, and the European framework is seen as a means to gather political support for its own stances or to muster economic support for the necessary reconstruction of those countries. In the Angolan process, Portugal has led the troika of international mediators, which includes the USA and the USSR (later, Russia) in the negotiations that brought about the Bicesse peace accords signed on 31 May 1991. During the negotiations, João de Deus Pinheiro, Foreign Minister at the time, spoke in favour of a 'miniature European Marshall Plan' to be implemented immediately after the Angolan election. It was on Portugal's initiative that the Twelve greeted the holding of the Angolan election in October 1992. And when Unita, upon losing the election, cried fraud and went back to the battlefield, Portugal tried to find support within the Community to force Unita to abide by the election results, declared 'free and fair' by the UN. Portugal intends to look for economic support among its European partners to help the stabilization process and assist in rebuilding the country as soon as a UN-brokered accord is reached.[19]

Similarly in 1993, when the government of Guinea-Bissau threatened to join the Francophone area if Portugal refused to refrain from pressing for free pluralistic elections, Portugal tried to lead the Belgian presidency into adopting firmer stances on human rights and democratic values, thereby trying to neutralize a possibly less consistent French approach.

The contribution which the international dimension of the two Iberian countries could make to Europe's position in the world, especially in relation to Euro-Latin American relations, was recognized by the Twelve even before the membership of Spain and Portugal came about. Although both countries became part of EPC with observer's status, upon signing the treaty of accession in July 1985, they had already been involved in EPC initiatives, albeit on an informal basis, when it came to issues like South America (e.g. the San José I meeting in 1984). Moreover, a joint declaration of intent relative to EC relations with Latin America was appended to the treaties of accession of the two Iberian states, pointing out that 'on the occasion of the accession of Spain and Portugal', the Community has the 'intention of developing and improving the economic and commercial relations and co-operation with the aforementioned countries [of Latin America]'.[20]

Portugal's European dimension has been increasingly valued by Latin American countries as a means of forging closer relations with the European Union. Brazilian sociologist Hélio Jaguaribe defined the role played by Portugal in the following manner:

> As an EC member state and as a participant in the Luso-Brazilian cultural universe, Portugal will open a door for Brazil and its Latin American partners when it comes to the European Community. Portugal can also in the same manner help the Community understand that it is very much in the Union's enlightened interest to adopt a more favourable relationship with Brazil and Latin America.[21]

Portugal's membership of the EC has profoundly changed its relationship with Brazil, both politically (institutionalization of Luso-Brazilian summit meetings) and even economically. Brazil has not only become a large investor in Portugal, but Portugal has also become a popular destination for Brazilian migrants. Brazil's interest in Lisbon's position as a bridge with the European Union led it to follow closely Portugal's preparation of its EC presidency, through the sending of various missions.

The 1992 Portuguese Presidency of the EC led in fact to a deepening of the EC–Brazil relationship. A third-generation agreement was signed, overcoming the opposition of member states like Britain, in June 1992, which diversified areas of cooperation, namely by encouraging cooperation in technology, the environment and telecommunications. The Portuguese Presidency also privileged group-to-group relations with Latin America through support for subregional integration processes already underway in Central America and the Southern Cone (i.e. Mercosur: Brazil, Argentina, Uruguay and Paraguay), starting a series of informal meetings between the Twelve and the Mercosur foreign ministers (the first took place in Guimarães, on 1 May 1992) with a view to putting such consultations on a regular and institutionalized basis. Moreover an interinstitutional agreement was signed on 29 May 1992 between the European Commission and the Mercosur Council. The purpose was to develop technical cooperation and to transfer integration know-how, by supporting setting up Mercosur institutions and the common market.[22]

Meetings between the Twelve and the Rio Group[23] which continue to be held regularly are typical of Political Cooperation in the sense that it remains essentially declaratory and causes some measure of frustration on the Latin American side. More often than not, only Portugal, Spain and the country holding the EU presidency are represented by senior ministers in meetings with their Latin American counterparts. The meetings between the Twelve and the Mercosur Four are significant in the sense that while emphasizing the relationship with a regional integration process, one with which, furthermore, the Twelve have established a varied agenda, the dialogue is both more substantial and still encompasses the political dimension. The Twelve have in fact been eager to respond to the integration process of Mercosur. Portugal and Spain have been particularly active in cooperation with the German Presidency in this regard, and the Essen Council in December 1994 agreed that there should be 'an early opening of negotiations with the Mercosur states on an inter-regional framework agreement'.

Spain and Portugal became the champions of a privileged relationship between the Community and Latin America. Both countries believe that it is against the EU's best interests to shut itself away from a part of the world closely linked through history, culture, and language to Europe, and which furthermore is now almost entirely made up of democracies, albeit fragile, and which contains a collection of market economies with strong financial and business sectors (a non-negligible 'comparative advantage'). Moreover, in these last few years there has been a marked improvement in the general economic situation throughout the region. The priority status which the Mercosur subregional process is being accorded by the Twelve clearly favours Portugal's position in European foreign policy towards the region.

The Mediterranean: 'Europeanization' of Portuguese foreign policy

Unless one goes back to the fifteenth century, the Mediterranean can be seen as one particular area where Portuguese involvement is a direct consequence of EU membership. The notable exception is relations with Morocco, not only because it is close by but also given the context of transatlantic and Iberian relations.

Until 1986, Portugal clearly thought that its foreign policy priorities were concentrated in the Atlantic and that involvement in the western Mediterranean would cause excessive overlapping with Spanish priorities, while showing an interest in the Middle East would somewhat limit its bargaining power towards the USA, since Portugal would no longer be in a position to argue that their use of the Lages base in the Azores was exclusively an American interest: the same logic applied when it was suggested that Portugal could contribute to the multinational force sent to Lebanon in 1982.[24]

At the time when, in 1983, French President François Mitterrand made the proposal in Marrakesh for a conference involving France, Italy, Spain, Algeria, Tunisia and Morocco, Portugal was invited merely as an observer, and this was considered convenient by Lisbon. As a consequence of European integration, however, the Mediterranean, especially North Africa, became a part of Portugal's foreign policy agenda. Portugal's interest in the region has actually grown, both within EPC and at the southern European and the bilateral level, on foreign policy and defence aspects alike. This is made easier by the fact that the western Mediterranean is an area virtually free of domestic constraints: neither the Maghreb, nor Islam are domestic political factors due to the conspicuous absence, at least for the time being, of a resident emigrant population originating in the Maghreb.

Portuguese foreign policy has increasingly tended towards 'Mediterranization' as a result of the common perceptions Portugal shares with other Southern European countries,[25] that is the shared concerns over possible developments in the neighbouring Maghreb region. The Maghreb is also seen as an area which is important in terms of European foreign and security policy where Portugal is poised to have a role (i.e. as a window of opportunity in terms of its own status in Europe).

Later, when President Mitterrand relaunched the Mediterranean cooperation initiative in 1988, Portugal fully participated and was one of the original signatories of the Rome declaration which launched the Five-plus-Five cooperation process.[26] Favouring a subregional approach, Portugal was sceptical towards the Spanish–Italian proposal of a conference on security and cooperation in the Mediterranean, following the CSCE model, involving the European countries, the USA, Russia and the Islamic countries from Mauritania to the Persian Gulf. During its EC Presidency, Portugal would have liked to see the Five-plus-Five dialogue develop into a Twelve-plus-Five dialogue. Efforts made in this direction came to no avail, however, since the whole initiative was more or less paralyzed due both to sanctions against Libya and to the Algerian crisis. It is unclear whether, like President

Mário Soares, the government would have preferred a condemnation of the Algerian authorities at least to be implied in the wording of EC positions towards Algeria, after the election process was interrupted in December 1991. But as a result of differing positions among the Twelve the fact is that the January 1992 statement and the declaration on Algeria were exceptionally mild. The European Parliament's veto on the financial protocol with Morocco led Portugal and the other southern Europeans (notably Spain) to seek an alternative solution, which was found in the Declaration of the European Council in Lisbon on Euro-Maghreb relations. This points to the 'gradual creation, in time, of a free trade area'.[27]

Together with its Southern European partners, this time including Greece, Portugal took part in the Forum for Dialogue and Cooperation in the Mediterranean, launched in Alexandria, largely on Egypt's initiative, in July 1994. Algeria, Morocco and Turkey were also involved, with the idea to improve the political capacity for dialogue in the region. Three expert working groups were set up to deal specifically with cultural, political and economic and social issues.

Nonetheless, Portugal faces a foreign policy dilemma when it comes to the Mediterranean: because many of the products exported by the southern Mediterranean countries are similar if not identical to those exported by Portugal (especially textiles), Lisbon finds it hard to repeat the type of active diplomacy it has carried out in the political sphere in relation to strengthening Euro-Maghreb economic relations, which would mean calling for a no barrier, free trade policy. Portugal shares the hesitations of the Southern European countries when it comes to opening up trade with the Maghreb, and would also like to see financial instruments made more freely available instead. Although the free trade area arrangements currently being discussed between the EU and Morocco (the idea being to bring in Tunisia and in time perhaps Algeria) originated in a Spanish proposal, the Southern European countries, including Spain, want to leave agricultural produce out altogether.

East Timor and human rights: a new item on the EPC agenda

Portugal's accession has introduced on to the EPC agenda the question of East Timor, the former Portuguese colony militarily occupied by Indonesia in 1975. Portugal did not accept the occupation and subsequent annexation, nor did the UN, which in the resolutions passed in December 1975 condemned Indonesia and supported Portugal's pledge to the right of the East Timorese to self-determination, freedom and independence.[28]

Between 1975 and 1982 successive resolutions were adopted by the General Assembly on East Timor with fewer and fewer favourable votes (72 to 10 in 1975, 50 to 46 in 1982), and all the Twelve, with the exception of Greece and Ireland, systematically abstained. Portugal's support thus came mainly from countries aligned with the USSR, which was naturally a cause of some embarrassment.

Accession to the European Community in fact coincided with a changing of the guard both in the presidency and the premiership (Mário Soares having been elected to replace General Eanes who had served two terms, while Cavaco Silva was also elected with an impressive electoral support). This was seen as a fresh opportunity for Portugal to break its isolation in the western camp in relation to East Timor.

Portugal has therefore persistently sought support among its EC partners for its condemnation of the annexation and of the persistent violation of human rights by Jakarta. But the EC member states have reacted cautiously to Portuguese proposals, avoiding in particular the issue of self-determination, mainly because of the place of Indonesia, one of the most important Islamic countries, in the context of EC–ASEAN relations. However, they have slowly begun to address the question of East Timor; in September 1988 the EC Presidency (held by Germany) made the first reference to the issue, notably expressing the desirability of an 'acceptable international settlement' of the question of East Timor, although falling short of an explicit reference to human rights, in its statement before the forty-third plenary session of the General Assembly of the UN. Because of Portugal's persistence, the Twelve gradually reached a consensus in emphasizing the defence of human rights in East Timor, which subsequently became a part of the declarations issued by the EC Presidency,[29] while also supporting the contacts between Portugal and Indonesia under the auspices of the Secretary General of the UN.

The turning point came with the serious incidents in East Timor on 12 November 1991, when the Indonesian army opened fire on a peaceful group of demonstrators in Dili which resulted in some 200 people being killed[30] and made headlines in the Western media. The Twelve strongly condemned the Indonesian army's violent action as an outright violation of the most basic human rights. Having dropped its original intention of pushing for self-determination for the East Timorese, Portugal was able subsequently to follow up on the East Timor dossier during its Presidency, strongly emphasizing the human rights dimension. However, the draft resolution submitted by Portugal on behalf of the Twelve to the Commission on Human Rights in Geneva, on 29 January 1992, demanding the respect for human rights in East Timor, was watered down owing to US pressure into a statement of the chair of this UN body, mentioning the Dili killings and urging Indonesia to take action on the matter. In March 1993, a resolution was again presented to the Commission where the Twelve voiced their 'grave concern' over 'continuing and serious human rights violations' in this territory.[31] And this time the resolution was passed. The same was not true however, in 1994, when yet again the wording became vaguer to accommodate Indonesia into the broad consensus required for a chairman's statement to be made. Strong economic interests on the part of a number of member states (Germany and to a lesser extent Britain) conflict with Portugal's principled positions, supported by countries less interested in the region together with Ireland, for whom self-determination is a sensitive issue, and the Netherlands, which fell out with Jakarta over aid and human rights. These interests are particularly evident during the meetings between the Twelve and ASEAN. The statements issued after these meetings, however, now explicitly mention the issue of human rights, to the Asians' dislike, although falling short of the explicit reference to East Timor which Portugal would like.[32]

Since the third generation EC–ASEAN agreement is up for negotiation, Portugal has made granting the respective mandate to the Commission conditional on Indonesia's pledge to respect human rights in East Timor. Initially dependent almost exclusively on Portugal's initiative the question has been brought up by other member states, notably Ireland. In July 1994, after serious incidents in a church in Dili, the Twelve issued a statement stressing 'the need for observance of Human Rights, particularly as regards freedom of worship' in East Timor.

Accommodating principles and interests is not always an easy task, as this particular case seems to prove. Portugal is trying to single out the human rights issue and pushing for it to be dealt with as a matter of principle, while other member states tend to regard it as one among others that should be taken into account in the broader set of economic and strategic issues in the region. The fact remains that member states have finally proven their solidarity in this issue, so that East Timor is now a part of the EPC agenda and one that is taken into account in the Presidency's decisions, in the UN General Assembly and the Commission on Human Rights, and in EC–ASEAN relations.

With Timor, a new emphasis has also been added to the human rights and democracy issue in Portuguese foreign policy as a whole. This issue is equally relevant in the difficult question of returning Macao to full Chinese sovereignty in 1999, two years after Hong Kong. Notwithstanding the particular obstacles which the process may encounter, the question of a coherent human rights policy is obviously a point to be borne in mind. In brief, Portugal considers human rights a horizontal issue, in the sense that it decisively cuts across its own and the European Union's cooperation efforts (i.e. one that Portugal is resolved to deal with both bilaterally and in its actions as an EU member).[33]

Portuguese foreign policy both towards Lusophone Africa and East Timor is strongly influenced by domestic factors (the only other comparable case in this regard being bilateral relations with Spain). Lusophone Africa, Angola in particular, is present in Portuguese politics as a divisive issue, and most Portuguese will have not only an opinion but a strong position of love or hate for the two rival movements, the MPLA and Unita.

This alone would suffice to explain the restraint which the government has shown with regard to Unita's violation of the peace accord that had led to the 1992 election. While it did condemn Unita for going back to war, the harsher words were left to the UN Security Council and EPC statements, which the government certainly supported but could not publicly endorse without paying an internal political price. The Portuguese public stands for a stronger condemnation of Indonesia and a tougher fight for self-determination for East Timor. Widespread criticism against the 1992 consensus on the issue at the UN Commission on Human Rights seems to confirm this. Naturally, therefore, public pressure is an obstacle to greater diplomatic flexibility in the contacts with Indonesia.

PORTUGAL AND THE DEVELOPMENT OF A COMMON FOREIGN AND SECURITY POLICY

East–South equilibrium

German unification and the great changes in Central Europe were initially viewed in Portugal with a degree of apprehension. It was feared that a marginalization of the South (Southern Europe, at first, and then the non-European outer circles) would undoubtedly follow. Shortly after the mesmerizing event in Berlin, Mário Soares stated that: 'We will be affected by this, although less so than Latin America or Africa. I am well aware that EC resources are limited and that today Eastern European countries will be their priority destination, but to penalise the Latin Americans or the Africans would be an act of sheer madness.'[34]

Hence Portugal was concerned that a correct balance be struck between the East and the South; this preoccupation dominated the Portuguese Presidency and was apparent in the first drafts of the report on priority areas for the development of CFSP. In the third draft, presented to the informal meeting of foreign ministers in Guimarães, possible regions and countries for joint actions were extensively enumerated: Central Europe; the Maghreb and the Middle East; North America; Latin America and the Caribbean; Africa; Asia and the Pacific.

This document was criticized both for under-prioritizing and for insufficiently dealing with security issues.[35] In the final document on CFSP approved by the Lisbon European Council, on 26–7 June 1992, the geographical overstretch was not retained, and the idea put forward by various delegations in Guimarães for a common position towards developing countries was not adopted. Those more specifically Portuguese priorities such as Africa and Latin America would be given much less attention by the European Council, which allocated the two of them no more than a single paragraph,[36] and that only in the context of North–South relations, against six pages devoted to relations with Africa and Latin America in earlier versions. Geographical proximity and important political, economic or security interests prevailed, and thus the Maghreb and the Middle East were placed on an equal footing with Central and Eastern Europe (this was favourably viewed in Portugal as going in the direction of an East–South equilibrium). The dilemma faced by Lisbon in this regard is not to forget, while championing the cause of the South, the importance of stability in Central and Eastern Europe for the development of the Union and thus the imperative need for Portugal to support those fledgling democracies and the resolution of conflicts such as that underway in the former Yugoslavia. This has become clear to the Portuguese government since 1991, as Foreign Minister Durão Barroso's words illustrate. Asked whether Portugal's interests were more clearly at stake in Africa or in Bosnia, he did not waver: 'Portugal's priority interests lie, beyond a shadow of a doubt, in Europe and in the European Union.'[37] Although this says nothing about Bosnia, it does signify that were the European process to collapse, Portugal would be one of those with more to lose.[38] At the same time, it is true that Portugal has gradually become more concerned with Central and Eastern Europe and cast aside its original reticence over the accession of the Visegrad states.

Joint Actions

Portugal has generally stood for the promotion of Joint Actions. But it has also warned that too many of them could have a trivializing effect while at the same time creating expectations that cannot be fulfilled,[39] particularly because of their financial and budgetary implications. The case-by-case budget approach is not commended in Lisbon, and Portugal thinks that funds for Joint Actions should come from a special budget. The fact that the first Joint Action was the mere monitoring of Russian elections was seen as proving the point about risking a loss of credibility.

Promoting regional stability is one of the horizontal concerns of CFSP to which Joint Actions, in Lisbon's view, should conform. This accounts for its support for the Pact for Stability, which Lisbon considers the most relevant of the first five Joint Actions agreed. The inclusion of Africa as a possible area for joint action in addition to those already agreed at the June 1992 Lisbon Council was accepted, and Portugal thinks support for the consolidation of South African democracy to be a meaningful action. Portugal's proposal on 20 May 1994 for a Joint Action in Mozambique involving monitoring the country's first ever free elections, helping with the huge refugee and homeless problem, assisting with the reintegration of demobilized personnel, and supporting the rebuilding of this devastated country was certainly more controversial. First, because it goes against Portugal's argument for selectiveness, and second because it breaks with the notion, still held in many quarters, that former colonies should be a *chasse gardée* for national initiatives. Traditionally, Mozambique has been a source of Luso-British friction, and the proposal, which was set, moreover, in a regional perspective, met with Britain's immovable opposition. As a result, there was indeed no Joint Action, although the Twelve decided in July that they would provide electoral technical assistance, funded from the Community Cooperation budget.

The development of a European defence identity

For countries such as Britain, the Netherlands, Portugal and Italy, the relationship with the USA is perceived not only as a crucial factor in maintaining both an inter-European equilibrium and security on the continent, but also as another means of bolstering the country's position within the context of European Union. This explains Portugal's attachment to the Atlantic Alliance and its generally cautious attitude towards a European defence identity.

During the Intergovernmental Conference's discussion over the development of a common defence policy, Portugal allied with the Atlanticist group, arguing that the Atlantic Alliance remained the fundamental pillar of European defence and that any step towards a European defence identity should in no way affect the transatlantic relationship. Portugal opposed the creation of a European defence identity within the European Union, and aligned with those who argued for WEU being kept as an autonomous organization, that would perform a bridging role between NATO and the European Union.[40]

The creation of a Franco-German Eurocorps was generally met with widespread criticism throughout the political spectrum as well as from within the military establishment. The Eurocorps was viewed in Portugal as no more than a French initiative to establish a rival organization to NATO that would lead to 'transatlantic decoupling'. The criticism levelled by the Bush administration at attempts to create a European defence identity was well received in Portugal.

France's decision to move closer to NATO and the explicit support which the new Clinton administration has given to the idea of a European defence identity, as was evident in the January 1994 NATO summit, has also led to a narrowing of the gap between the pro-European line, which Portugal has generally adopted since the signing of the Maastricht Treaty, and its position on a European defence policy. In the light of this, Portugal's Defence Minister recently commented that Portugal may shortly be sending an observer to Eurocorps, and it has decided to participate in the Air–Naval Mediterranean Force, formed already by Italy, France and Spain, as well as allowing the Marines to participate in the WEU's Anglo-Dutch amphibious brigade.[41]

It should be noted, however, that this small measure of involvement represents a departure from traditional Portuguese positions, that is, to avoid direct participation in armed conflict in Europe altogether. The Gulf War may have provided the last example of the traditional pattern of Portuguese involvement, even if its foreign and security policy was already tending towards 'Europeanization' at the time. While expressing 'solidarity with our allies' the Prime Minister indicated right from the start of the Gulf crisis that 'Portugal will not be directly engaged in the armed conflict'.[42] Solidarity took the form of granting the USA full overflight rights and unrestricted use of the Azores base, and making medical and hospital care and personnel and transportation facilities available. Under the framework of WEU coordination, a support ship was made available to the British naval forces, and transport aircraft flew several missions carrying both relief medical aid and military material to Turkey.[43] In any case, solidarity with NATO and the European Union/WEU, as events determine, remains a strong precondition for any Portuguese military involvement in the European strategic environment (i.e. Central and Eastern Europe and the Mediterranean).

Despite the new awareness of the importance of the political dimension inherent in European integration, Portugal has not escaped the general post-Cold War tendency to a relapse into the 'nationalization' of defence policy. While after the end of the colonial wars the Soviet threat made it impossible even to think about choosing between Europe and the South in security terms, the debate over what option to take has now resurfaced.

The Portuguese Eurosceptics restate the traditional argument that Portugal's peripheral position in Europe protects the country from involvement in the continent's regional conflicts, and therefore that Portugal will be best served by strengthening its presence in Africa, whether through bilateral or multilateral UN actions. Portugal already has a communications battalion in the UN operation in Mozambique, and was instrumental in the failed attempt at setting up a new, unified Angolan army, while it has taken steps to intensify military cooperation as a whole with the Lusophone African Five.

The military efforts made by Portugal, like those of France or the UK, both of which are also involved in Angola and Mozambique, are clearly outside the European domain, and consist either of a bilateral initiative or an action within the context of the UN. It seems desirable that the military efforts of member states when it comes to UN operations, whether outside Europe or not, should become progressively 'Europeanized', in order to prevent the renationalization of foreign policies which post-Cold War events have persuaded certain member states active outside Europe to undertake.

For the Euro-Atlanticists, Portugal's borders no longer stop at the national frontiers and the African effort which they consider important is not as decisive, as participation in the European Union and fulfilling the obligations which stem from membership. For this group the borders of

Germany and Italy (i.e. the outer borders of the Union) are also Portugal's security frontiers. The underlying rationale behind this argument is that such a position prevents a few key states achieving a quasi-hegemony in the European Union, including defence.

The current Portuguese concepts of defence, approved in 1993, are a compromise formula between two main schools and, not surprisingly, they display a number of ambiguities. For its part and for the time being, CFSP is certainly not free from ambiguity, but is rather built around it. Whether or not the ambiguity in Portuguese thinking will be resolved depends primarily on a clarification of the European Union's own stances, hopefully resulting from a further deepening of European integration, where it is most needed – in the realm of political union.

The institutional dimension

Portugal belongs to the group of countries that in the 1991 IGCS stood for the need to maintain the intergovernmental character of the foreign policy pillar of the Union. On the basis of its positive experience within EPC,[44] the Portuguese government feels that purely extending the mechanisms of Community decision-making to encompass foreign policy would not sufficiently safeguard the specifics of Portugal's international experience and its traditional ties.[45] The idea of a voting strength ultimately based on the criteria of size enjoys little sympathy in Portugal. The opposition of many to qualified majority voting is also explained by concerns relating to the need for CFSP to integrate fully the specific and varied contributions of member states in foreign policy.

Portugal values Europe's ability to forge close relations with various areas of the globe, by pooling the privileged cultural and historic links of its members. This is one of Europe's particular strengths. The Union must be capable of balancing integration to the East and Centre with a greater opening to, and spirit of cooperation with, the South – not only because of the need to achieve greater projection in world affairs, but also due to the need to balance its own internal equilibrium. A Europe centred on the East alone would marginalize countries which have important relations with areas of the world outside of continental Europe. Even the Franco-German axis would come under pressure if relations with the South were ostensively neglected.

From a Portuguese perspective the institutional reform scheduled for 1996, which aims at conferring upon the Union greater capabilities in terms of both foreign and defence policy, should not lead to the creation of a directorate or the end of Union presidencies by smaller states. The appearance of a directorate would be tantamount to an abandonment of the European project. It would mean going backwards to a League of Nations phase or even to a balance of power system. Furthermore, it is impossible to assess the specific contribution that each country can make to the Union's foreign policy based merely on the size of its population. How can one weigh the value of historical and cultural ties? A similar argument can be made in terms of the Presidency, which has at times brought other nations closer to the Union. This was the case of South America during both the Portuguese and the Spanish Presidency of the Community.

Portugal has a vital interest at stake in a political and open Europe which takes into consideration the specific contribution which each member country can make. In a European Union that is little more than a civilian power, giving priority to the economic instruments of external relations, Portugal remains little more than a poor relation; yet in a Europe capable of taking on its full international role, with a strong political output, Portugal's heritage makes it a more relevant partner.

NOTES

1 This chapter draws widely on the author's contribution to IEP's project Spain and Portugal in EPC.

2 Memorandum from the Portuguese delegation, 'A União Política na perspectiva da Conferência Intergovernamental' [Political union with a view to the Inter-governmental Conference], Lisbon, Ministério dos Negócios Estrangeiros [Ministry of Foreign Affairs], 30 November 1990, in Finn Laursen and Sophie Vanhoonacker (eds), *The Intergovernmental Conference on Political Union*, Maastricht, EIPA/IEAP, 1992, pp.304–12.

3 Aníbal Cavaco Silva, *Afirmar Portugal no Mundo – Discursos Proferidos durante a Vigência do XII Governo Constitucional*, Lisbon, INCM, February 1993, p.157.

4 This concern was particularly apparent during Portugal's membership of the troika and subsequently during its first EC Presidency, which began in January 1992. The need to strike a balance between an opening to the East and the needs of the South was indeed laid out in the programme of the Portuguese Presidency. Cf. statement of Foreign Minister João de Deus Pinheiro, quoted in *Diário de Notícias*, 17 January 1992.

5 See José Calvet de Magalhães, *Breve História Diplomática Portuguesa*, Lisbon, Europa-América, 1991.

6 The attitude of the Portuguese government towards Europe prior to 1974 is thoroughly described and analysed in José Calvet de Magalhães, 'Portugal na Europa: O Caminho Certo', *Estratégia – Revista de Estudos Internacionais*, no. 10–11, Winter 1993–4.

7 On the history of Portuguese–US relations, and on presentday economic and security relations, see José Calvet de Magalhães, Álvaro de Vasconcelos and Joaquim Ramos Silva, *Portugal: An Atlantic Paradox*, Lisbon, IEEI, 1990.

8 For the Cold War era, see Álvaro de Vasconcelos, 'Portuguese defence policy: internal politics and defence commitments' in John Chipman, (ed.), *Nato's Southern Allies: Internal and External Challenges*, London, Routledge, 1989, pp.86–139.

9 Álvaro de Vasconcelos, 'A Ideia de um Tratado Luso-Americano', *Público*, 14 April 1993.

10 For a discussion of the Angolan process and the UN involvement, see Moisés

Venâncio, *The United Nations, Peace and Transition: Lessons from Angola*, Lisbon, IEEI, Lumiar Papers, no. 3, September 1994.

11 Diogo Pires Aurélio, 'A Questão Nacional em Angola e Moçambique', *Estratégia – Revista de Estudos Internacionais*, no. 7, Spring 1990.

12 Only once did Brazil actually vote against Portugal in the UN: on 31 July 1963, when Security Council Resolution 5380 was passed, in which Portugal was invited to recognize the right to self-determination of its overseas territories forthwith. Eight Security Council members voted for the resolution and three abstained (France, Britain and the USA).

13 Mário Soares, *Intervenções 8*, Lisbon, INCM, April 1994, p.162.

14 Jaime Gama, Foreign Minister in 1983–5, summarized this point of view, stressing: 'the role Portugal may come to play, both as a factor of expansion of the European area towards Africa and Latin America and in bringing Community logic, institutions and decisions closer to those Latin American and African regions. . . . As a member of the Community, Portugal will contribute to a greater interest, in both directions, in relations between Europe and Africa.' *Política Externa Portugesa 1983–1985*, Lisbon, Ministério dos Negócios Estrangeiros, 1985, p.197.

15 For a discussion of this 'natural and basic premise' of Portuguese foreign policy, see José Calvet de Magalhães, 'Portugal e o Euro-Atlantismo', *Estratégia – Revista de Estudos Internacionais*, no. 1, Spring 1986, pp.21–34.

16 In the summit meeting held in Palma de Majorca, although bilaterals were dominant in the meeting's agenda, it is interesting to note that Portugal and Spain decided to coordinate actions towards the Maghreb. *Público*, 18 December 1993.

17 *Portugal nas Comunidades Europeias – Primeiro Ano*, Lisbon, Ministério dos Negócios Estrangeiros, 1987, p.200.

18 *Portugal nas Comunidades Europeias – Quinto Ano*, Lisbon, Ministério dos Negócios Estrangeiros, 1990 p.392–3.

19 Yet another outburst of heavy fighting after the Lusaka accord had been completed, after eighteen-month long negotiations mediated by the UN, delayed the signature of the agreement from 15 to 20 November. Even then, neither President dos Santos nor Jonas Savimbi appeared to sign in person.

20 The impact of Portuguese and Spanish membership on the European Union's relations with Latin America is analysed by Angel Viñas, 'Portugal y España en la Unión Europea ante los desafíos del Sur', *Estratégia – Revista de Estudos Internacionais*, no. 12, Spring 1995.

21 Hélio Jaguaribe, 'Portugal e o Brasil perante a Integração Europeia', *Estratégia – Revista de Estudos Internacionais*, no. 6, Spring 1989.

22 Celso Lafer, 'Acordo Mercosur/CE' in *A inserção internacional do Brasil*, Brasília: Ministério das Relações Exteriores, 1993, p.26.

23 Formed by the members of LAIA (Argentina, Bolivia, Brazil, Chile, Colombia, Ecuador, Mexico, Paraguay, Peru and Uruguay), plus, with an observer status, a Central American country and the country holding the presidency of the Caribbean Community.

24 Álvaro Vasconcelos, 'Portuguese defence policy: internal politics and defence commitments', in John Chipman (ed.), *Nato's Southern Allies: Internal and External Challenges*.

25 See Álvaro de Vasconcelos, 'The shaping of a subregional identity' in Roberto Aliboni (ed.), *Southern European Security in the 1990s*, London and New York, Pinter, 1992, pp.15–27.

26 Declaration on cooperation in the Western Mediterranean, signed in Rome on 10 October 1990, by Portugal, Spain, France, Italy (later joined by Malta) and

the five members of the Arab Maghreb Union: Algeria, Libya, Mauritania, Morocco and Tunisia.

27 Lisbon European Council, 26–27 June 1992, *Conclusions of the Presidency*, Appendix Four, SN 3321/1/92, p.48.

28 General Assembly resolution 3485, 12 December 1975, adopted by 72 votes to 10, with 43 abstentions; and Security Council resolution 384, of 22 December 1985, adopted unanimously.

29 It is interesting to compare the reference made to East Timor in the 43rd Session of the UN General Assembly in 1988 with the speech of the EC Presidency in 1994:

> Concerning the question of East Timor, the Twelve reiterate their support for the contacts between Portugal and Indonesia under the auspices of the Secretary-General of the United Nations. They express the hope that it will soon be possible to achieve progress, thus paving the way to a just, comprehensive and internationally accepted settlement of the question, with full respect of the interests of the people of East Timor.

The speech of the EC Presidency in the 49th session in 1994 states:

> The European Union continues to support a dialogue without preconditions between Portugal and Indonesia under the auspices of the United Nations Secretary-General. In that context, it took due note of the fourth round of meetings held by the UN Secretary-General with the foreign ministers of Portugal and Indonesia on 6 May 1994. The Union encourages all efforts aiming at a just, comprehensive and internationally acceptable settlement to the question on East Timor with full respect for the legitimate interests and aspirations of the East Timorese people, in conformity with the principles embodied in the charter of the United Nations. The European Union remains deeply concerned at reports of continuing human rights violations in East Timor. In its statement on 18 July, the Union expressed its concern about the most recent incidents in Dili which have again heightened tension in the territory. The respect for human rights is a vital prerequisite for a lasting solution to the question of East Timor. In this context the European Union calls upon the Indonesian government to comply fully with the relevant decision adopted by the Commission on Human Rights.

30 Indonesia admitted to some fifty killings.

31 This was abundantly reported in the Portuguese press. See for instance, 'CE Quer Timor aberto à ONU', *Diário de Notícias*, 3 March 1993.

32 *Le Monde*, 1–2 November 1992.

33 Statement on the Portuguese Presidency of the European Union, issued by the Prime Minister's office in 19 December 1991, p.10.

34 Mário Soares, *Intervenções 4*, Lisbon, INCM, April 1990, p.591.

35 *Europe*, no. 5722, 4–5 May 1992, p.5.

36 Lisbon European Council, *Conclusions of the Presidency*, Appendix One, SN 33221/1/92, p.33.

37 Foreign Minister Durão Barroso, interviewed by *Público*, 9 January 1994.

38 Idem.

39 Idem.

40 Aníbal Cavaco Silva, *Afirmar Portugal no Mundo – Discursos Proferidos durante a Vigência do XII Governo Constitucional*, Lisbon, INCM, February 1993, p.129.

41 'Portugal Quer Reforçar Posição na UEO', *Público*, 25 March 1994.

42 Press statement released by the PM's Office, 1 March 1991, p.4.

43   For a detailed description and assessment of Portuguese participation in the Gulf crisis, see Álvaro Vasconcelos, 'Portugal, the Gulf crisis and the WEU', in Nicole Gnesotto and John Roper (eds), *Western Europe and the Gulf*, Paris, Institute for Security Studies of WEU, 1992, pp.109–25.

44   See João de Matos Proença, 'A Cooperação Política Europeia', *Estratégia – Revista de Estudos Internacionais*, nos. 10–11, Winter 1993–4; Álvaro Vasconcelos, 'Portugal and European political cooperation', *The International Spectator*, vol. XXVI, no. 2, April–June 1991.

45   See Manuel Fernandes Pereira, 'A Evolução da Posição Portuguesa na Negociação sobre a PESC', in *Política Internacional*, vol. 1, no. 6, Spring 1993, p.31.

Conclusions

The European rescue of national foreign policy?[1]

David Allen

The period of EU foreign policy cooperation surveyed in this volume has been marked by two key turning-points. By Christmas of 1990 the Cold War system in Europe had clearly come to an end with the agreed withdrawal of the Soviet Union from Eastern and Central Europe, the collapse of communism and the peaceful reunification of Germany. The short-term perception that the global order, within which the European system was located, would in future be determined by a form of bipolar cooperation between two market-oriented, democratic superpowers was confounded at the end of 1991 when the Soviet Union ceased to exist, leaving the USA as the predominant, if not hegemonial, power in the international system. The second turning-point was related to the first and involved the negotiation and eventual ratification of the Maastricht Treaty on European Union (TEU). At the end of 1993, when the TEU came into effect, the system of European Political Cooperation that had existed since 1970, formally came to an end and was replaced by the Common Foreign and Security Policy (CFSP – the so-called second pillar of the European Union).

CONTINUITY IN AN ERA OF CHANGE

Inevitably, many of the chapters in this book are dominated by the reactions of the member states of the European Union to, and participation in, these two significant events, and by subsequent and possible future developments in EU foreign policy cooperation in what has become known as the 'new Europe'. In fact, of course, the individual chapters, in their examination of developments in the 1980s, also serve to illustrate a considerable continuity of behaviour from the Cold War to the post-Cold War period and from EPC to the CFSP. Throughout the 1980s the question of security cooperation within the EPC framework was increasingly on the agenda. There was a growing concern about the 'consistency' of the EC's external political and economic activities, which was inextricably intertwined with an ongoing debate about the role of foreign policy cooperation in the evolution of the European Union. There were signs of a growing tension between the interests and behaviour of the larger and smaller member states and there were clear indications of a changing relationship between the West European states and both superpowers well before the dramatic systemic changes at the end of the decade.

However, the preceding chapters also suggest that during the 1980s and up until the end of the Cold War system, the member states had reached a new plateau of cooperation in the foreign policy sphere, in which the gradual convergence of their national foreign policies had led to the development of a growing West European identity in the international system, of a different order to that which had emerged in the 1970s. In mid-decade they had managed to consolidate many of their achievements in Title III of the Single European Act, in which EPC was given a treaty base for the first time, in which the role of the Commission (and the European Parliament) in EPC was given formal legal recognition and in which provision was made for the establishment of a small EPC secretariat, based permanently in Brussels and designed to assist the rotating Presidency in the management of EPC business as well as in its coordination with the external economic activities of the European Community.

Furthermore our volume records the successful incorporation during the 1980s, despite a sticky start for Greece, of three new member states into the EPC process. The Twelve, no less than the Nine and then the Ten appeared in the 1980s to have further consolidated a system of foreign policy cooperation which sought to preserve the treasured principle of sovereignty in an area central to the independent life of the member states, while at the same time enabling them, as all the chapters record, to benefit from the advantages of mutual consultation, support and coordinated diplomatic action. In participating in a system which enabled them to preserve, and in some cases extend, national foreign policies and national diplomatic services while enjoying the collective economic and political advantages of Community membership, the member states, both large and small, appeared to have created a happy situation whereby they were able, in terms of sovereignty and integration, both to 'have their cake and eat it'.

The problem arose from the fact that their decision to distinguish between the political, economic and security aspects of their collective external behaviour and between intergovernmental and supranational methods of policy-making, while continuing to maintain individual national stances on most of these issues (except of course those, like trade and some aspects of development aid where the treaties gave the Community exclusive competence), meant that they presented a confusing and often incoherent face to the outside world. There is little evidence in any of the preceding chapters, other than, as one might expect, in that which deals with the European Commission, that this external incoherence, which many associated with an inability to convert potential into actual leadership and influence in the international system, was much of a cause for concern for any of the member states. There is, thus, no evidence that any of the member states of the then Community saw any real net advantage to be gained from further subsuming their separate identities into a collective whole. They were not dissatisfied generally with the actual output of EPC which was seen by most as an important addition to, but not a replacement for, a national foreign policy competence based on a national determination of interest. Indeed EPC can be seen, in Milward's terms, as the means by which member states made their positions less rather than more vulnerable.

Apart from the Commission, which had no constituency of its own, having been appointed by the member states (although the European Parliament could dismiss it!), there is little evidence that the European identity that began to emerge in the 1980s was based on any particularly strong notion of an identifiable European interest. Instead what emerged was a series of declarations and actions which represented a balance of nationally defined interests – albeit a balance which on occasions represented the median rather than a lowest common denominator position. Where member states had strong individual interests which were either of little concern to the other members or were irreconcilable with the collective interest, then our contributors demonstrate that EPC presented no real barriers. There were, however, those states like the Benelux, Spain and West Germany, who saw enhanced foreign policy cooperation as a significant contribution to the general development of the European integration to which they were committed. To the extent that they argued for a reduction in intergovern-mentalism and the incorporation of EPC into the Rome Treaty procedures, including the use of majority voting, as well as for a greater involvement of the Commission and the European Parliament (and perhaps ideally even the European Court) they were anxious to enhance and develop integra-tion along 'federal' lines as much as they were motivated by concerns about the efficiency or the output of the EPC process. Ironically it was the states, like Britain and France, that were most anxious to preserve the separate intergovernmental status of EPC, which found themselves arguing for and conceding reforms, such as those contained within the London Report or the Single European Act, so as to improve the actual performance of the collective foreign policy procedures. The principles behind the overall development of the European experiment and the practical development of foreign policy cooperation have been difficult to disentangle ever since the Fouchet proposals of the early 1960s (which while ostensibly focusing on foreign policy were in fact designed to undermine supranationality and the growing influence of the European Commission) and our contributors demonstrate that the 1980s were no exception to this general rule.

In retrospect many would say that the West Europeans within the European Community were able successfully to operate the system of EPC in the manner suggested above, because of the nature of the Cold War system.[2] This meant that the ultimate responsibility for the orderly management of European international relations lay with the two superpowers, regardless of whether they were in combative or cooperative mode. Indeed at the time American observers, most especially Henry Kissinger (both in and out of office), tended to lay the charge that EPC was a complex, ineffective and rather luxurious system that reflected the 'free-riding' nature of the collective West European role in the international system.

DRIFTING APART?

It is worth looking in more detail at the impact of the end of the Cold War system on the individual and collective foreign policy activities of the EU member states. On the one hand many realists have argued that the end of the Cold War system would probably also lead to the end of the institutions, including the EC and EPC, which were associated with it. They see the cooperation that underpinned the institutions created during the Cold War as essentially transitory and anticipate that, freed from their mutual security concerns by the disappearance of the Soviet Union, the larger member states of the EU will revert to the unilateral pursuit of national interests determined by calculations of relative power. Others, the liberal institutionalists, for instance, would argue that institutions do not just reflect the short-term power calculations and balances of otherwise competing sovereign states but are indicative of, and an autonomous influence on, a system of international relations in which some of the participating states find continuous advantage in a formalized process of cooperation such as the EU and EPC.[3] For those who reject the pessimism of the realist view, and that would have to include most of the contributors to this volume, the change in the structure of the international system, marked by the end of the Cold War, presents significant opportunities, as well as challenges, for the system of foreign policy cooperation that has developed in Western Europe.

While the Warsaw Pact and Comecon confirmed the realist predictions by disappearing almost overnight, and while NATO's *raison d'être* is clearly fundamentally challenged by the structural changes in the system, many believed that the European Community's hour had come with the end of the Cold War. To begin with there were hopes that the end of the superpower confrontation would lead to a lifting of constraints on the evolution of the Community as an international actor and that in the new system the EC would be able to both 'widen' and 'deepen'. The end of the Cold War challenged the neutrality of states like Sweden, Austria and Finland which had been seen as an insuperable barrier to them entering the Community and thus participating in EPC. Similarly the end of communism and moves towards both democracy and a market economy meant that the states of Eastern and Central Europe might now also be eligible for membership of the EU and thus of EPC. The changing nature of the security structure in Europe meant that, in the foreign policy sphere, collective considerations of the defence, as well as the political and economic, aspects of security became both a possibility and a probable necessity for the member states of the European Community, a development reflected in all the chapters of this book.

Although our contributors can be predominately classified as 'institutionalists', in that they mostly reflect the member states' optimism about the continuing relevance and practicality of the European Community and EPC, their analyses also suggest that the unbridled optimism that characterized the immediate post-Cold War period may have been relevant only in the short term. While it is clear that none of the present member states consider the EU and its foreign policy aspirations to be an irrelevance in the new environment, they are all anxious to maintain the cooperation that has been achieved and that some are keen to advance it further, whether intergovernmentally or supranationally, it is also clear that there has been a certain amount of drifting apart from one another in their national foreign policies. Some of the 'glue' that bound the member states together during the Cold War and which meant that they were always inclined to seek a compromise of their positions when faced with the hostility of the Soviet Union or even the rivalry of the USA, has been diminished by the end of the superpower confrontation. In short, when the major powers and, to a much lesser extent, the smaller powers of the EU consider their national positions in the new European system they increasingly find themselves viewing the situation differently.

It is not clear at this point of time, nor will it be in the immediate future, whether this drifting apart represents a steady and unidirectional divergence of perceptions and actions or whether the EU member states are merely enjoying more freedom to move both away from and back to one another. To use the monetary analogy it is as if the individual states have gone from a system of relatively fixed exchange rates (foreign policy relationships) to one where they are now floating freely. The question remains as to whether we will continue to see fluctuating divergence within certain limits (the foreign policy equivalent of the monetary snake) or whether, in the foreign policy sector, some of the differences are likely to become permanent and entrenched. Thus while Spain clearly has a stated interest in the advancement of Western European Union at the expense of NATO, Denmark would appear to be in the opposite situation with a clear preference for the maintenance of the NATO security structures and the minimization of WEU activity. Similarly, after sharing much the same views about developments in Yugoslavia during the Cold War, Britain, France, Germany and Italy, and, of course, Greece, found themselves taking up strikingly different positions both at the inception of the conflict in the former Yugoslavia and subsequently. The scars inflicted may last for some time.

More significantly, it is clear that Britain, France and Germany have fundamentally differing views (with the smaller states equally but less significantly divided) about the desirability of enlargement of the EU to the East and the deepening of the Union as it is presently constituted as well as about the relationship between widening and deepening. This is inherently a matter of foreign policy. The British seem to believe (most vociferously during Mrs Thatcher's premiership) that any enlargement is attractive because it will lead to a weakening of the Union's supranational elements and federal ambitions. The British calculation has always been a quantitative one, based on the erroneous assumption (to date at any rate) that the achievements of the Community – the 'acquis communautaire' – could not be stretched to include new members without being watered down On the other hand it would also seem to be the British belief that the achievements of EPC/CFSP – the 'acquis politique' – which are valued by Britain – are infinitely stretchable to include as many states as wish to participate.

The French have always shared the British view of the relationship between widening and deepening but have tended to come to the opposite conclusion about the attractiveness of further enlargement to Eastern and Central Europe. This, however brings the French into conflict with Germany for the Germans have never accepted the notion that wider means weaker and have instead tended to perceive the question of enlargement towards the East as both essential and as a welcome stimulus towards deepening the present Union.

THE INSTITUTIONAL DIMENSION

Many of the chapters here focus attention on the institutional aspects of the relationship between the member states within EPC and the CFSP. In particular the role of the Presidency of the Council features strongly in the perceptions of the smaller states and much concern has been voiced by states like Denmark, Luxembourg and Ireland about suggestions that, in an enlarged Union, the role of the rotating Presidency should be reconsidered. It is clear that the smaller states are anxious to dispel the idea that they are not able to cope with the burden of the Presidency and to continue enjoying the prominence in international politics that goes with it. Indeed it is probably fair to say that, with the singular exception of the first Greek Presidency, it is difficult to find examples of either new members or small states who have been embarrassed or proved embarrassing when their turn came to take over the Presidency. The fact that Greece assumed the Presidency so soon after accession, combined with a certain apprehension about the policies it might wish to pursue, can be said to have had a major impact on the rapid development of the troika system. The ability of the preceding and succeeding Presidency states to ensure that ongoing business is not overlooked and that representational and negotiating roles are not neglected or abused provides a useful safeguard within the rotating system. Indeed during the last Greek Presidency the German representatives were able to use their troika role to ensure that consultations relating to the sensitive issues of both Turkey and the FYROM were maintained.

It is clear too that the smaller states see the rotating Presidency as affording them the chance to keep the major powers at bay, as well as allowing them to ensure that their own interests are given some prominence on the EPC/CFSP agenda. There is a clear concern expressed by some of the smaller states, that obviously wish to maintain their separate identity in the international system, about any proposals that might either hand the running of the CFSP over to a *directoire* of the major states or, as was spectacularly demonstrated by the events leading up to the first Danish referendum on Maastricht, to the European Commission. For all the present member states, with the possible exception of the newly federated Belgium, participation in the CFSP is valued for the stimulus that it gives to the continued assertion of national individuality in international politics rather than as a step towards the submerging of those separate identities into some sort of European identity. The continued opportunity that the present Presidency arrangements offer to order the CFSP agenda and to represent the Union as a whole for six months is clearly as important to the member states as any arguments about the need for efficiency and continuity in a Union of expanding numbers.

Therefore it does not seem likely that, during the next IGC, proposals such as those so disastrously advanced by the Dutch in 1991 to integrate the intergovernmental CFSP pillar into the EC policy-making and implementing structure are going to receive much support from anything like a majority of the member states. They might, however, be interested in developing more fully the role of the expanded Secretariat, now fully integrated into the Council Secretariat. Several of the smaller states have clearly benefited since 1987 from assistance in running their Presidency both from the troika arrangements and from the EPC Secretariat (now the expanded CFSP Secretariat) in Brussels.

The exception to this enthusiasm for the continued separate intergovernmental basis for the CFSP is, of course, the Commission which now appears to have shifted its ground on the whole question of consistency between CFSP and EC matters. In the 1980s, as Nuttall's chapter makes clear, the Commission was most keen to protect its unique competencies within the EC structure from the intrusion of the member states, in particular the larger ones and most especially Britain and France. More recently the Commission seems to have detected advantage from a blurring of competencies and policy-making processes. Nevertheless it has to be said that as an independent actor in the CFSP process, the Commission has maintained its reputation for reticence when it comes to operationalizing its formal right of attendance at all EPC/CFSP meetings (since the Single

European Act) or its new right of shared initiative within the CFSP (since the Treaty on European Union.) While Nuttall records one or two instances of the Commission successfully injecting its own perceptions into EPC deliberations in the 1980s one is nevertheless left wondering why the Commission is so anxious to extend its authority further in the CFSP when it apparently has so little of actual substance to contribute to the development of foreign policy positions and actions. As so often in the past there is a danger that in seeking to extend its formal legal competence for the sake of furthering integration as it sees it, the Commission is in danger of demonstrating its actual incompetence to carry out such duties. It is certainly less of an actor than it has the potential to be.

Another area where the member states seem anxious to preserve their ability to act individually as well as collectively in the international system concerns the issue of representation. It is ironic that while the larger states, with the singular exception of Germany, have all experienced financial problems in maintaining the size of their diplomatic services and extensive level of their national representation, many of the smaller states in the Union have justified an expansion of resources for national diplomatic services by citing the need to participate effectively in the CFSP. Of course there remains a large gap between the reach of the British, French, Italian and German diplomatic services and the rest and there is a sense in which they are all challenged by the extensive and rapidly growing external representations of the Commission. There is also a sense in which all the member states are united in their desire to restrain the challenge of a quasi-European foreign office and diplomatic service built upon DG1A and the staff of the Commission's external representations. The smaller member states will continue to benefit from their CFSP-related contacts in the complex of working groups, and via COREUs, and they clearly value being able to exploit the information and expertise generated by the diplomatic services of the larger states.

For their part it may well be that in the future, in order to resist the growing challenge from the Commission, the larger member states may have to consider either the pooling of diplomatic resources or even a division of labour in certain parts of the world. Both Britain and France are, for instance, clearly struggling at present in their efforts to maintain comprehensive national representations in all the states of the former Soviet Union. Although the natural inclination of all the larger states would appear to be to preserve as much as possible of their individual foreign policy machines, they may well decide in the future that they can learn something from the ways in which the smaller states have gained from the CFSP process. It remains the case that all national diplomatic services would prefer to pool a certain amount of their resources and therefore preserve a large part of both their effectiveness and their individuality rather than consider the creation of a full-blown European diplomatic service, particularly one based in Brussels and most particularly one that might evolve out of the European Commission.

Nevertheless it is clear that the continuous enlargement in which the EU is engaged does raise a serious question about the balance between the large and small states in a system that retains an insistence on consensus. Even if one accepts the arguments of participants that, in practice, the 'club atmosphere' (which in any case may be harder to preserve as membership becomes more diverse) means that consensus usually forms around the median position, there remains a danger that the larger states will become frustrated by the ability of the smaller states to prevent the achievement of consensus. The most spectacular recent example of this, which informs much of the debate about the need to reform the CFSP to prepare for future enlargement, concerns the refusal of the Greek government to permit the other member states collectively (they have all done it individually) to recognize the FYROM. Many would argue that it is this frustration that has led to Britain, France and Germany participating in the Contact Group (with the USA and Russia) in an, admittedly unsuccessful, bid to find a resolution of the situation in the former Yugoslavia. Realists would predict that we are likely to see more of this ad hoc behaviour, and others would agree – if the search for consensus within the CFSP proves to be frustrated by its procedures, and ultimately by one member state.

However, it should also be made clear that there is not very much evidence in the chapters dealing with the larger states of any great frustration about the way that the CFSP operates on most issues. Britain, France and Germany are not states that have clear national positions which they are prevented from implementing by consensual procedures of the CFSP. Some of the potential frustrations are, of course, forestalled by the anxiety of many smaller states and new members to participate constructively in the CFSP and to make the necessary national adjustments to enable this to occur. Greece's position on the FYROM can be seen as an act of rebellion against the consensus, but it can also be seen as a perfectly reasonable defence of the sort of individual vital interest that the CFSP system was designed to protect.

What is clear is that the choice for the EU member states is no longer between the multilateral action of the Fifteen on the one hand and unilateral action on the other. No state in the Union seems anxious to attempt to go it alone in contemporary international politics, least of all the newly unified and potentially much more powerful Germany. To the extent that individual states feel that their special interests are likely to be neglected within the CFSP then they are most likely to seek similar minded allies from within the Union – hence the establishment recently of subgroups concentrating on developments within the Baltic area, within Central Europe and in relation to North Africa. Even where an EU state feels that it is at odds with the objectives of other member states, then the natural reflex would seem to be to search for some EU partners – the unilateral pursuit of all but the most limited of objectives would not seem to be an option that the member states of the Union are any longer prepared to consider. The nuclear weapons of Britain and France are a giant exception to this rule, but here too isolation may prove increasingly uncomfortable.

DEMOCRACY, MONEY AND THE CENTRALIZING DILEMMA

One area that remains underdeveloped at both the national and European level is that of the democratic control of the collective foreign policy activities of the EU member states. While the European Parliament has now quite considerable powers over the external relations of the European Community (considerably greater in fact than those enjoyed by a number of national parliaments in relation to the external activities of the member states) it has not made much headway in relation to the CFSP other than in those areas where the decisions taken are subsequently implemented using the resources of the European Community. As in other areas of integrative activity the individual member states are divided in their views about extending the powers of the European Parliament, with Germany and Spain in the forefront of those who would like to see more obvious democratic control of foreign policy at the European level, while Britain and Denmark, and to a lesser extent France, argue that national parliaments are the most appropriate institutions for scrutinizing intergovernmental cooperation, given that it is designed to preserve notions of national sovereignty.

The ability of the European Parliament to exert influence on the CFSP is critically dependent on the attitude of the Presidency country. While a Presidency such as that of Spain or the Netherlands is usually anxious to keep the Parliament informed about CFSP developments, others such as France and Britain have proved more reluctant. Nevertheless, it should be pointed out that when the British, during their Presidency, offered to brief members of the European Parliament on EPC matters provided they were prepared to come to London, the MEPs refused on the principled grounds that it was up to the Presidency to come to the European Parliament. Despite the existence of clear foreign policy expertise within the Europe Parliament, the member states' governments seem anxious to preserve as much executive control as they can and, to the extent that they are prepared to submit to democratic scrutiny, with one or two exceptions they show a clear, and some would say deeply hypocritical, preference for preserving the rights of their national parliaments in this area.

One area where the European Parliament may find itself able to get a handle on CFSP activities is via financing, for the member states have not been so successful in maintaining a clear distinction between European Community activities, which are financed from the Community budget and therefore subjected to the scrutiny and control powers of the European Parliament, and the activities of the CFSP. If the CFSP was truly intergovernmental and separate from the European Community then one might argue that it should be financed by the member states themselves – as was EPC. The TEU is not that helpful on this matter for it makes a distinction between the 'administrative' and 'operational' costs of implementing the CFSP. Administrative costs are automatically charged to the Community budget but the Council is given the choice as to how operational costs are to be charged. It can decide unanimously to charge them to the Community budget or it can choose to finance them directly from the member states. The Council has not been very successful in organizing finance through the member states, partly because of wrangles about how the bills should be divided up (a GNP scale is usually used) and partly because of the reluctance of the member states to pay up. For example, six months after it was agreed to split the cost of administering the Bosnian city of Mostar in 1994 between the Community budget and the member states, only Ireland, Greece and Denmark had paid up their contributions. As a result the Council decided that for 1995 all the costs of administering Mostar would be charged to the Community budget. These are collective action problems of the kind all too familiar to the UN.

The member states, for some of whom fundamental principles of intergovernmentalism are involved, would appear to be caught on the horns of a dilemma. Anxious to preserve their independence and to give both the European Parliament and the Commission as little control of their CFSP activities as possible, the member states have a principled interest in paying for the CFSP themselves. However most diplomatic services have a natural resistance to multilateral calls on their often tightly restricted budgets and so have a pragmatic interest in 'losing' such expenditure in the overall Community budget. For some states the dilemma is less painful than for others. While Belgium is quite happy to see the CFSP financed from the Community budget with all the attendant controls that this entails, states like Britain and France would prefer to see national financing as the general rule. In practice, they often find it judicious to ignore the questions of principle in order to, as they see it, save a few posts in their national diplomatic services. The problem therefore is that while the CFSP is meant to be intergovernmental and under the exclusive control of the sovereign member states, in practice they have not been able to get their act together and have had effectively to concede that the CFSP will be predominately financed from the Community budget – to the extent that it will produce significant Joint Actions requiring substantial resources.

For most of the 1980s the member states of the EU had little real difficulty in determining the foreign policy issues that they would pursue collectively and those that they would pursue unilaterally, albeit increasingly with EPC/CFSP cover, or with at least the tacit approval of the other member states. It was accepted that Britain and France, as nuclear powers and permanent members of the UN Security Council had a special role to play in the world, while the system was also informal and flexible enough to cope with occasional idiosyncratic behaviour by its members. Within a general Cold War dominated consensus covering the nature of East–West relations, dealings with the developing world and the importance of the non-military resolution of disputes, individual governments were able to bring their particular interests to bear on the EPC process. This was particularly the case with enlargement where new members were often seen as potential 'bridges' between the Community and various parts of the outside world. In the period covered by this book both Portugal and Spain have worked hard to get their particular interests in Africa and South America placed higher on the EPC agenda than they were previously. Spain has succeeded in getting Spanish objectives accepted as Community objectives and thus partially financed by Community funds. More recently the arrival of Sweden and Finland has been seen as a possible bridge to the Baltic states while Austria would seem to be providing the same service for Hungary that Denmark has (now with help from Sweden) provided for Norway.

THE DOMESTIC PUSH AND PULL

One of the major themes of this book has been the growing role of domestic factors in foreign policy deliberations at the national level. It is a truism that all aspects of European integration both intergovernmental and supra-national have been built from the top down. The state of affairs that exists today represents the culmination of a series of deals between relatively strong European governments which were confident that they could carry along their domestic populations. The fact that economic cooperation has been developed primarily within the supranational arrangements set up by the Rome Treaty and that foreign policy cooperation has been primarily intergovernmental fundamentally reflects the preferences of national governments and their assessments of the balance of gains and losses that were likely to arise from seeking the advantages of cooperation while preserving as much national autonomy as possible. It has become apparent in recent times and especially since the end of the Cold War that the nature of the state in Western Europe (and indeed elsewhere in the international system) has changed to the extent that domestic forces have come to take a much greater interest and play a much greater role in the external activities of governments. This has given rise to a significant reduction of their foreign policy flexibility and challenges the élite consensus on which the European Union in all its guises was built. The more that domestic forces shape foreign policy then the more national idiosyncrasies and interests will be highlighted, often in a way which challenges consensus at the European level. European integration in general and the EPC/CFSP procedures in particular, worked in the way that they did because governments were given a pretty free hand by their electorates in their dealings with the governments of other states. All this would appear to have changed in recent years and the EU national governments can no longer rely on the domestic acceptance of deals done with their EU partners. Thus while the twelve EC governments eventually reached an agreement with which they were satisfied at Maastricht, their problems began when they tried to ratify those agreements back home. Similarly, while the Swiss government had little difficulty in both applying for and successfully negotiating membership of the EEA it could not persuade a majority of its electorate that this was in the Swiss national interest – much the same occurred when the Norwegian government negotiated membership of the EU and then failed to obtain a supportive vote in a national referendum.

It is argued here, and it has been demonstrated in the country studies, that this sea change in the nature of European states is likely to inhibit significantly the development of the CFSP because it will tend to highlight national differences, resist further inroads into national sovereignty and require national governments regularly to demonstrate how collective policies and positions provide specific advantages (and minimal costs!) to the participating states. It will therefore be that much harder to build a collective foreign policy by coordinating national policies, if they are increasingly domestically oriented and developed by politicians who are forced to have a keen idea of the short-term electoral implications of any stance which they might choose to adopt.

A further complication is added by the fragmenting tendencies within European states. Although enthusiasts of 'multi-level governance' make much of the integrative possibilities of a growing European regionalism it is clear that this tendency can only confuse the management of a collective European foreign policy. Apart from increasing the temptation for EU states to meddle in each other's internal affairs (see the references to the Netherlands's increasingly complex relations with Flanders and Wallonia) and thus potentially damage the 'zone of peace' that characterizes relations between EU states, the CFSP depends heavily on the central governments of the member states being in a position both to negotiate and to deliver policy positions. If Bonn is to be challenged by the Länder, or Madrid by Catalonia, or Rome by northern Italy, or indeed London by Scotland, then the task of foreign policy coordination will become that much more complex.

In essence we are suggesting that the states of the EU are becoming weaker in that their executives have less freedom of action and are becoming more distinctively different from one another as a result of responding to differing domestic rather than similar international stimuli.

POLICY ISSUES

One consequence of enlargement, however, is that it is becoming much harder to identify the priority of the EU's foreign policy interests, especially now that the agenda of the CFSP is potentially much freer and larger in the new European environment. One potential conflict of interest informs almost all the chapters in this book and that revolves around the concern that a number of states are expressing about the German and British support for a concentration of attention on the situation in Eastern and Central Europe, and the assumption that the Union's best interests will be served by facilitating the soonest possible admission of those states to the Union itself. While France fears any weakening of the ties that bind a Union (and Germany), states like Spain, Portugal, Greece and, to a lesser extent, Ireland have good cause to fear the financial costs of an enlargement to the East. It is generally accepted that neither the CAP nor the Structural Funds can be offered to the Eastern applicants on the same terms that the present members currently enjoy and therefore an eastern enlargement means a probable change in the current arrangements which will leave them worse off than at present. These states therefore have a considerable financial incentive to push the case for a renewed foreign policy focus on the Mediterranean area. Furthermore, Spain, Portugal and Greece are joined by Italy and France in voicing similar security concerns about the Mediterranean area, and in particular North Africa, to those that are expressed by Germany and her allies about Eastern Europe. There are therefore a number of cross-cutting elements which suggest that in the future the member states are likely to be seriously divided on the issue of foreign policy priorities now that the discipline imposed by the Cold War has evaporated.

In terms of the argument abut North Africa and Eastern Europe the issue is further confused by the fact that, while multilateral solutions are sought for both security dilemmas, those most concerned about North Africa cannot hold out, as those concerned with Eastern Europe can, the prospect of eventual membership of the EU. With regard to both areas of interest there is another potential divide between those states like Britain, which are primarily interested in using the CFSP to develop notions of stability and who believe that the best thing that the Community can offer is access to its markets, and those like Spain and France who would like to see restricted access but offers of financial aid given to North Africa. Both contrast with Germany which is keen to share the burden of aid giving, which it supports, with the other EU members.

Things do not look much clearer on the security front. As the contributions indicate, the states are uncertain and divided about the exact nature of the threat to security in Western Europe and they are similarly divided between those who have a preference for working with a reformed NATO (and thus guaranteeing continued American involvement) and those who would prefer to operate within the Western European Union. The basic conflict that is inherent in the ambiguous references to WEU in the Maastricht Treaty – on the one hand referring to it as the 'defence arm of the Union' and on the other as the 'European arm of NATO' has been greatly modified by changes in the American position (so that the Clinton administration now seems ready to accept that WEU and NATO need not be seen as in potential conflict with one another), but it remains the case that security questions are as likely to divide the EU member states as to unite them.[4] While many of the chapters in this volume agonize about the future role of WEU and its relationship to the EU and the USA, there are surprisingly few references to what might be described as the new items on the security agenda. Thus the question of mass immigration or of environmental degradation or even the extent to which European states should involve themselves in military activity away from Europe receive little consideration (with the exception of the many references to the internal divisions over the Gulf War) even though they are likely to bring to the fore differing national perceptions and priorities. At the level of generality, there is a consensus that effective security can only be achieved together; on particular problems, unity starts to splinter.

CFSP: A LOSS OF MOMENTUM

Where does this leave our consideration of the nature of the actors in the CFSP process? They would all appear to share a common interest in maintaining the core elements of the European Union which means protecting the single market and possibly the common policies from external or internal subversion (although Britain's attitude towards the CAP and certain of the budgetary arrangements remains a notable exception to this general observation). The member states share a general interest in the preservation and promotion of democracy and market economies although they do not necessarily agree on how this is best to be achieved. They share an interest in preserving the zone of peace that they have created and in extending it, possibly by enlargement but also by encouraging other regional groupings to follow the West European example.

While the Twelve were prepared to express considerable solidarity in the face of enlargement to fifteen, requiring that the new members accept both the 'acquis communautaire' and the 'acquis politique' in its entirety, there are now growing signs of significant divisions between emerging subgroups of states of the Union. We have already mentioned the potential conflict between those who would concentrate on Eastern Europe and those who favour the Mediterranean as a primary focus. Most of the other states, and particularly Italy, have expressed concern about discussions between Germany and France around the notion of a 'core Europe', particularly to the extent that the core might be regarded as exclusive rather than merely the fast track of a multi-speed Europe. Britain and France remain, for the time being, states with an enormous extra European presence by dint of their possession of nuclear weapons and their permanent membership of the UN Security Council. They are, however, threatened by the new status of a reunified Germany and by the new possibilities of rank improvement that are open to Germany, Italy and Spain because of the changes in the nature of power and influence in the international system. While concern with relative rank and influence clearly affects all the member states, large and small alike, they also demonstrate remarkably little enthusiasm for chancing their arm and going it alone in the new and apparently less restrictive international system.

All the states have a stake in the continuance of the CFSP but few demonstrate any real enthusiasm for advancing the arrangements much beyond what exists already. Some of course would like to see the CFSP brought into the EC part of the TEU but even the Benelux states and Germany would draw the line at introducing majority voting on military matters, and few states seem prepared to consider establishing the sort of central institutions that would enable the CFSP to make a fundamental integrative leap forwards. In truth it is hard to imagine a genuine common foreign policy without a common diplomatic service and a means of identifying and operationalizing a notion of the European interest. National foreign policies are usually identified by their pursuit of the national interest. The national interest is, at one level, that set of interests identified by the elected government. It is difficult therefore, to separate the notion of a foreign policy from the idea of a state with a set of interests identified by a government. Because it is clear that no European government, again with the possible exceptions of Belgium and Luxembourg, is, as yet, prepared to commit suicide by agreeing to the establishment of a government, as opposed to governance, at the European level, it is hard to see how the CFSP can develop beyond the ceiling that it has already reached. The realists are probably wrong when they pessimistically anticipate the collapse of all the institutionalized arrangements that characterized collective foreign policy cooperation between European states during the Cold War, but it is excessively optimistic to believe that the current level of institutionalization, which allows for the parallel pursuit of national foreign policies, can develop much further. It may even be optimistic to believe that an enlarged Union of more heterogeneous states, governed by élites whose margin of manoeuvre is increasingly restricted by domestic forces and which are no longer bound so closely together by the 'glue' of Cold War systemic imperatives, can preserve the degree of foreign policy cooperation and collective action that existed prior to 1989. There is little in this volume to suggest that the demise of the European state as a foreign policy actor is imminent. On the contrary the balance of experience of EPC and the CFSP for both large and small states alike would seem to suggest that they have created the means for preserving (and in some cases advancing) a degree of autonomy in the contemporary international system. *

NOTES

1 See Alan S. Milward, with the assistance of George Brennan and Federico Romero, *The European Rescue of the Nation-State*, London, Routledge, 1992. This conclusion takes as its working hypothesis an adaptation of Milward's thesis that European integration is the way in which the nation-state has adapted and survived in post-war Europe.
2 For the most influential expression of this view, see John J. Mearsheimer, 'Back to the future: instability in Europe after the Cold War', *International Security*, vol. 15, no. 1, pp.5–56 (and comments by Hoffmann and Keohane, vol. 15, no. 2, Fall 1990, pp.191–9.
3 Indeed some go further, to talk of an Atlanticist or even a global 'pluralistic security community'. See Richard Ned Lebow, 'The long peace, the end of the Cold War, and the failure of realism', *International Organization*, vol. 48, no. 2, Spring 1994, pp.268–73.
4 Not least because individual member states themselves waver on their commitment to a new security order. See Amand Menon's analysis of belated French moves back towards NATO in 'From independence to cooperation: France, NATO and European security', *International Affairs*, vol. 71, no. 1, January 1995, pp.19–34.

Index